P9-AQC-271

Essays on Comparative Institutions

Essays
on Comparative
Institutions

S. N. EISENSTADT

The Hebrew University
Jerusalem, Israel

John Wiley & Sons, Inc., New York · London · Sydney

Library of Congress Catalog Card Number: 65-21442
Printed in the United States of America

Preface

THE ESSAYS collected here have as their central focus the analysis of the processes of institutionalization and the comparative study of institutions. Needless to say they do not attempt to deal with all the major institutional spheres. They only bring together the analyses on which I have been working for the last fifteen years.

These analyses encompass studies of age-groups and youth culture, bureaucratic structures and processes of bureaucratization, problems of social mobility, and processes of communication and reference-group behavior.

These essays deal with two different aspects of the study of institutions—with what may be called fully structured and organized institutions, like age-groups and bureaucratic organizations, on the one hand, and with behavioral processes and related personal attitudes, on the other. In more recent developments of sociological and anthropological analyses, these two orientations tended to go in separate ways. Whereas to some extent such separation is natural and explained by the nature of the different problems addressed by such studies, it is a major contention of these essays that it is important to attempt to bring these two approaches together and that the study of the processes of institutionalization may provide a good focus for such bringing together.

These analytical orientations are spelled out in the first chapter, written especially for this book. Although the formulations contained in this chapter are necessarily tentative and preliminary—and certainly do not give definitive answers to many of the problems raised—they attempt to spell out some of the major problems in the analysis of processes of institutionalization.

This point of view is also presented in the different essays collected in this book. Because these essays range over a period of about fifteen years, they necessarily represent different levels of awareness of these various analytical problems. Even though many differences in emphasis, clarity, and the formulation of the concrete problems exist, the various essays collected here all share the confrontation between the structural and the behavioral and attitudinal aspects of institutions, of processes of institutionalization. This similarity is due perhaps in no small degree to the fact that the field studies were undertaken in Israel, a society whose institutional contours were only beginning to be shaped and crystallized and in which the existence of a given institutional structure could not be taken for granted. Yet at the time when most of these essays were written, the confrontation between the structural and the behavioral aspects of institutions was not always fully articulated. Hence, the results of more recent researches have been added to each section in order to present and articulate this confrontation in a fuller way.

My concern with the problems of comparative institutional analyses has many roots. It developed as the result of the combined training in sociology and history that I received at the Hebrew University. The impetus provided by this training was greatly reinforced by my stay at the London School of Economics (in 1947 and 1948), where the tradition of concern with comparative institutions was carried on by Morris Ginsberg and T. H. Marshal, while, in anthropology, R. Firth, L. Mair, A. Richards, and the late S. F. Nadel, in London, E. E. Evans-Pritchard, M. Fortes, and Max Gluckman, at Oxford, were dealing with various aspects of institutional analysis within the framework of anthropological studies and tradition.

At that period Edward Shils was teaching at the London School of Economics, and through him and through our continuous association since then I was able to come into direct personal contact with the American sociological tradition and with the renewed interest in the classical tradition of Durkheim and Weber, in general, and with comparative studies, in particular. Later I had many opportunities to meet and associate with Talcott Parsons, to whose works and many discussions much of my interest and work in this field is indebted.

This interest was again reinforced while I was reorganizing the curriculum of the Sociology Department of the Hebrew University in the late forties and early fifties. Here again I had the great privilege and pleasure of the guidance and help of Morris Ginsberg, who came to Jerusalem, and I would like to record here my debt to him. Other opportunities to follow up this interest came when I was invited to serve as a Visiting Professor at the University of Oslo in the autumn of 1958, where I concentrated my lectures and seminars on the problems of comparative institutions, and when, at the University of Chicago, I gave a seminar on comparative bureaucratic institutions, together with P. M. Blau and Elihu Katz. Since then I have been dealing with these problems with greater intensity, both in Jerusalem—where I greatly enjoyed and benefited from discussions with my colleagues J. Ben-David, J. Katz, and Y. Talmon in Sociology, and J. Prawer in History, and with generations of students—and in 1962 and 1963, when I served as Carnegie Professor at M.I.T. and joined Professors Parsons and Bellah in the seminar on "Social Evolution" in the Department of Social Relations at Harvard.

I would like to thank here the following organizations which granted permission for me to reprint essays: The Royal Anthropological Institute of Great Britain and Ireland for the article previously appearing in *Man*; the University of Chicago for permission to republish the essays appearing in *Current Anthropology*; the International African Institute for the article published in *Africa*; Bailliere, Tindall and Cox and the Institute for the Study of the Treatment of Delinquency for the article published in the *British Journal of Delinquency*; the International Sociological Association for the essays published in *Current Sociology* and *Transactions of the Second World Congress of Sociology*; Cornell University for permission to reprint the essay which appeared in the *Administrative Science Quarterly*; Tavistock Publications for the article from *Human Relations*; *The Public Opinion Quarterly*; and the American Sociological Association for the material reprinted from the *American Sociological Review*.

I would like to thank heartily my colleague Professor Elihu Katz for his permission to publish our joint essay on "Some Sociological Observations on the Response of Israeli Organizations to New Immigrants." I would also like to thank Professor Morris Janowitz for his help in the publication of these essays and his very helpful advice during their preparation, Mr. William Gum, Social Science Editor at John Wiley and Sons, for his interest in their publication, Mrs. Patricia Gurevitch for her help in the preparation of the essays for print and in the editing of the new material, and Mrs. R. Shaco for her help in reading the proofs.

June, 1965   S. N. EISENSTADT

Contents

SECTION I

Theoretical Orientations

THREE ESSAYS which attempt to deal with major theoretical or analytical problems of study of institutions are presented in this section.

The first essay (Chapter 1), "The Study of Processes of Institutionalization, Institutional Change, and Comparative Institutions," is entirely new and spells out, as has already been indicated, my present approach to the studies of institutionalization, institutional change, and comparative studies of institutions.

The second essay (Chapter 2), that on "The Relations between Sociological Theory and Anthropological Research," deals with one aspect of this broad field—namely that of the extent of coalescence between different institutions in different societies. Written in 1948, it contains a strong "structural" bias, and there is little emphasis on the behavioral aspects of processes of institutionalization.

The third essay (Chapter 3), "Anthropological Studies of Complex Societies," attempts to evaluate the contribution of one school or the major type of approach of social anthropology (especially the English "school") to the study of institutions. This evaluation is attempted through analysis of the problems encountered by anthropologists in their efforts to apply the specific model or models which evolved in their "natural" setting of primitive societies to the study of more "complex" ones.

In this essay I attempt to show that the use of this model made very specific contributions to the understanding of complex societies, but that these contributions were limited by the very strength of the model. In order to overcome these limitations it was necessary to contrapose this model with other models that were developed within other social sciences. The analysis of several of these implications spells out in greater detail some of the problems raised in the introductory essay, especially the problem of different types of mechanisms of institutional exchange which are predominant in different societies or institutional spheres. According to the special tradition of *Current Anthropology*, where this essay was first published, it was sent to several scholars, whose comments were published together with it. Many of these comments have pointed out very important problems from the point of view of this analysis.

Chapter I

The Study of Processes
of Institutionalization,
Institutional Change,
and Comparative Institutions

PART I   The Study of Processes of Institutionalization

Introduction—Historical Background

The comparative study of social institutions has been, together with study of processes of change, among the most important foci of classical sociological and anthropological thought and theory, although the relative emphasis on each of these aspects varied among the "Founding Fathers." The eighteenth century figures—Montesquieu, Ferguson, and the Scottish philosophers—were more interested in comparative studies than in the analysis of social change. Marx and, to some extent perhaps, Toqueville were much more interested in analysis of processes of change of Western societies, although they (especially Marx) never entirely neglected the comparative "angle" (1). The great figures of evolutionary thought, such as Comte, Spencer, and Hobhouse (2), tried to present a synthesis of these two aspects by showing what seemed to them to be the universal trend of development of human society through a comparative analysis of customs and

The research reported in this paper has been sponsored by the Air Force Office of Scientific Research, OAR, through the European Office, Aerospace Research, United States Air Force. The author is indebted to Elihu Katz, Ozer Schild, and Yonina Talmon for comments on earlier versions of the paper.

institutions. This synthesis was not accepted, and its rejection brought also the disavowal of the evolutionary perspective.

Insofar as the study of comparative institutions in the classical period went beyond general evolutionary orientations, it was mostly based on the "correlational" method, best exemplified in the classical work of Hobhouse, Wheeler, and Ginsberg (3). In this work, various types of institutions—kinship arrangements, ecological patterns, modes of subsistence, or types of political organization—were correlated with each other bringing together a great wealth of material, a wealth which only very recently was again taken up in comparative studies. In this way, many of the more naive evolutionary assumptions were subjected to a critical analysis, while at the same time confirming the existence of some general trend of development in the direction of growing societal complexity.

The French "school" did not develop the important comparative indications contained in Durkheim and Mauss' work (4) beyond the studies of Davy and Moret on the development of "organic" political and juridical institutions.

Of the great "postevolutionist" founding fathers, only Max Weber expressly addressed himself to a new, more complex, and sophisticated analysis of comparative structures and processes of change. Instead of postulating a general and universal trend of development for all societies and using comparative analysis to illustrate this general trend, he used it in order to illuminate a certain particular trend which predominated in one society or group of societies. By analyzing such a trend, some light was then thrown on similar or opposite trends in other societies or conditions (5).

Weber's most famous analysis of this kind was that of the economic orientations of the great world religions which he used as a background for the analysis of the specific religious constellations in Europe—the rise of the Protestant Ethic—which, according to him, led to the development of Capitalism. But his work abounds in many other examples of comparative analyses, be they types of charismatic authority and routinization of charisma or the trend to bureaucratization within modern societies. As is well known, his comparative studies are also based on the elucidation of basic categories of types of social action, thus indicating the importance of combining basic conceptual and comparative-institutional analyses.

As a result of developments which took place in the social sciences in general and in sociology and anthropology in particular from the second to the fourth decade of this century, interest in this broad comparative field and in change-oriented studies has become rather peripheral. Only in the last decade or two has interest in the systematic study of comparative institutions and of the conditions of their development and change regained some of its centrality in the social sciences.

True enough, some basic insights about these problems, derived from the classical schools, had become incorporated into the body of sociological and anthropological thought, and they were no longer recognized as constituting specific problems. Thus the universal existence of basic institutions—economic, political, religious (cultural), educational, and of corresponding natural groups in any society—and the existence of varieties of such institutions in different societies have become a basic assumption of any sociological or anthropological work, a part of the fundamental definition of society. But the specific concern with the study of processes of institutionalization in general and with the comparative study of institutions in particular had become greatly weakened and neglected.

In the meantime, other major concerns and foci of sociological and anthropological thinking and research developed. In sociology there took place a great expansion of research techniques, on the one hand, and of socio-demographic studies, studies of social determinants of behavior and attitude of individuals, and studies of small groups, on the other hand (6).

The major development and advance in the analytical sphere proper, namely, the analysis of societies as *systems* of social interaction, activities, or groups, had been neglected by the evolutionary sociologists. The most important development here has been that of the so-called "functional" school in social anthropology, connected with the names of Malinowski and Radcliffe-Brown (7), and somewhat later the development of the "theory of action" of the so-called "structural-functional" approach in sociology, most closely identified with the names of T. Parsons, E. Shils, R. Merton, and many of their associates and students (8).

The functional school in anthropology arose to no small extent as a reaction against the evolutionary and "diffusion" schools and has focused, both from methodological and analytical points of view, on the studies of single societies. Radcliffe-Brown, Malinowski, and the first generation of their students emphasized the importance of intensive field study of one single society or aspect thereof, as well as the analytical study of the working of society as a system of interconnected parts. The basic components of this system were the major institutional fields, such as economic or political activities or the "basic" natural groups (i.e., family groups), and their concrete interrelations constituted one of the basic concerns of most of the specific analytical field studies. Yet both their existence in all societies and their variability between different societies were usually accepted as given and did not constitute, until recently, a major problem of inquiry. It was mainly the ways in which such institutions were interrelated in a given concrete society or at most in a given type of society (e.g., in those characterized by the predominance of the unilineal descent groups) that was analyzed in these studies. The extent of their inter-relationship—a crucial problem for the testing of the functional approach—was rarely explored.

Similarly, in the initial phases of the development of the structural-functional school, comparative analysis did not constitute one of the important aspects of its analytical endeavors. Here, also, the existence of some basic institutions and their variability in different societies was taken for granted. At the same time, however, there developed within this school an important analytical shift in the approach to the comparative study of institutions. This shift was effected through the perception of institutionalization of behavior and norms as a process with potentially different results, and not always as fully given in the structure of a society.

All these developments constituted a very important background and stimulus for the renewal of interest in comparative studies and added greatly to the analytical tools with which such analysis could be attempted, once the interest was aroused.

The first important impetus to this new systematic comparative analysis of institutions developed in social anthropology. The major landmarks in England were the publication of *African Political Systems*, followed by *African Systems of Kinship and Marriage*, and then extended into many other directions (9). In these works, the comparative analysis was undertaken by the intensive examination of several case studies in light of some guiding hypotheses. In the United States, the major turning points from this point of view were the publication of Murdock's *Social Structure* (10) and the upsurge of cross-cultural research most closely related to the "Culture and Personality" "school" (11). Here, the more general and more fully-formalized hypotheses were usually tested, through statistical methods, over a wide sample of societies.

At the same time, a growing interest in this field developed within sociology proper. The convergence of a broader, institutional approach in political science and history and the development of area studies have, in their turn, also contributed greatly to the renewal of interest in comparative studies.

The New Starting Points for Institutional Analysis—the Concepts of Systemic "Needs" and Preconditions

This new interest in comparative studies enables one to reformulate some of the basic problems of institutional analysis in terms of recent sociological theory.

Of course, this new approach had to overcome the most obvious pitfalls of the older schools, especially evolutionary, in dealing with problems of comparative social structure and of social and institutional change. These older models mainly broke down on two stumbling blocks. The first was the assumption—even if only implicit—of more or less general unilinearity in the development of human societies, and of a rather general universality of the major stages of development of societies. The second stumbling block of most of these older theories was the lack of specification of the systemic characteristics of the "entities" (i.e., societies or institutions) that constituted, as it were, the major units of evolution, as well as the mechanisms and processes of change through which the transition from one type or stage of society to another was effected. Most of the classical evolutionary schools did not specify what characteristics of societies or institutions explain the existence within them of both boundary-maintaining mechanisms and of specific tendencies to change. They tended, rather, to point out general causes of change (economic, technological, spiritual) or some general trends inherent in the development of societies (i.e., the trend to complexity). Very often they tended to confuse such general tendencies with the causes of change or to assume that these general tendencies provide detailed explanations of concrete instances or descriptions of the concrete mechanisms of change. Similarly, they often tended to explain the existence of any specific institutional type or form—be it a form of marriage or political authority—in terms of its appropriateness to a given level of complexity or development of a society.

The new approach in comparative studies had to overcome some of these pitfalls as well as be able to explain the variability of institutional complexes in terms of the new analytic tools of sociological theory in general and of analysis of change in particular. Indeed, the first comparative analyses undertaken mostly by anthropologists, although still to some extent couched in terms of the correlational method, i.e., correlating the existence of one economic institutional type with another (such as demographic or political), looked on these correlations as mutual conditions. They assumed or proposed that the structure of one institutional field created some resources or activities which were "needed" for the functioning of the other institutions or of the "social system" as such.

This new approach did not take the existence of any institution in general and of its specific contours in any concrete setting in particular for granted but explained them in terms of some "needs" of other institutional spheres or of more general needs of society or social system. Both the universality of an institution and its variabilities in different societies were often explained in terms of such systemic needs or properties.

These broad assumptions created many new problems, and these problems constitute the starting points for a possible approach to general institutional analysis and particular comparative analysis—i.e., the analysis of what may be called "institution-building," the processes of institutionalization in any society, on the one hand, and the problems of comparisons between the institutions of different societies, on the other.

The analysis of a few recent studies may throw some light on these questions and help to elucidate the analytical problems. These studies are chosen largely at random as possible illustrations of some of the major subjects of comparative institutional analysis, especially of the extent to which the crystallization of various institutional patterns can be explained in terms of societal and personal needs and of the inter-relations between them.

Analysis of Universal Institutional Norms—"Marriage and the Family"

We may perhaps begin with Levy and Fallers' discussion (12) about the universality of the nuclear family. This analysis starts as a critique of Parsons' (13) attempt to prove the necessity of the univer-sal existence of the nuclear family in terms of the basic needs of any social system to socialize its members in a variety of roles, especially sex roles. They start from the premise that some basic societal needs exist, in this case the need for socialization of the young, and they admit that the very nature of these needs necessarily imposes certain limitations on the structure of the institutions which are able to "ful-fill" them. In other words, any institution or group which will have to respond to (or take care of) such needs must have some minimal "core characteristics"—in this case it will have to be a "kinship-structured" unit. But, according to their view, these minimal core characteristics can exist within many different types of broader structural forms, such as the classical nuclear family or various types of broader family groups, and need not be limited to any *single* form of kinship or family units.

Whatever the merits of their specific arguments, they contain some important implications from the point of view of the comparative study of institutions. The recognition of the fact that there does exist a multiplicity of forms of kinship units which may fulfill the need for socialization necessarily poses the problem of the specific conditions under which one and not another type of family structure develops, functions, and fulfills the general need of socialization, of the ways in which the general need of socialization becomes structured under different social conditions, and the mechanisms through which it be-comes linked to specific structural, institutional forms of the family.

Some answers to this problem are implicit in Homans and Schnei-der's *Marriage, Authority and Final Causes* (14). Their main concern in this work is to offer a critique of Levi-Strauss' explanation of the prevalence of certain types of marriage norms, such as the so-called matrilineal cross-cousin marriage, through the analysis of "final causes." In other words, they criticize the attempt to explain the existence of these norms by the functions they perform for the society, i.e., by their performance of certain societal needs (in this case by being optimal for the maintenance of social solidarity). One (although not the only) of their main arguments against the final cause explanation is the lack of specification of the mechanisms through which these final or "efficient" causes operate within a society. They attempt to provide a more detailed analysis on the basis of efficient causes through the specification of the ways through which one of the basic prerequisites of the society—in this case the need for social arrangements for marriage—may be articulated and crystallized in specific norms through the activities of individuals. They propose that this articulation is effected through the impact of certain structural characteristics of the family (in the case of patrilinearity or matrilinearity) on the motives or orientation of action of potential brides and bridegrooms who are placed within it and who have to undertake the act of marriage. According to Homans and Schneider, prospective brides and bridegrooms, by virtue of these sentiments, tend to develop a predisposition to marry certain types of their relatives (cousins).

This analysis has several implications. On the concrete level it postulates that the fulfillment of the general societal need for institutionalization of mating and regulating jural rights in procreation is activated (at least in the societies studied by them) through the needs of certain (in this case universal) categories of people within the social structure and through their willingness to provide various resources at their disposal in order to satisfy these assumed needs. On a more general level it has even broader implications. Starting from a critique of explanation of crystallization of institutional arrangements in terms of the general needs of a society, they have attempted to provide an alternative analysis through the specification of attitudes, sentiments, and needs of individuals. These are not, however, "random" individuals. They are placed in very definite structural positions, and their specific needs and predispositions to undertake institutional tasks and norms are engendered through the "pressures" exerted by them in these structural positions.

But this analysis contains several weak points, such as the assumption of the direct relation or exchangeability between certain attitudes and sentiments (in this case those derived from the patrilineal complex) and specific types of jural or normative specification of rights and activities of individuals (15). Another weakness, closely connected with the former, is the lack of specification of the relations between these attitudes and the general, institutional types of resources, like property or manpower, which are presumably mobilized through the "sentiments" of these people. The people who provide some of these resources are not only the brides and bridegrooms but also the respective families of orientation for whom the brides and bridegrooms constitute an investment of various initial resources. Hence we have a case not only of direct but also of indirect exchange. But the exact relations between the sentiments of the potential brides and bridegrooms and the interests and commodities at the disposal of these groups and of their representatives are not specified. The continuity of society is presumably maintained through the activities and relations between these people and groups, and this means that the connection between the sentiments and activities of these varied categories of people and the "needs" of society are not fully explored or even posed.

But whatever its shortcomings, the analysis does provide an important contribution to an approach to comparative analysis. It implies that differentially structured needs—attitudes of people placed in definite structural positions in a society—may activate different activities and resources, and that the exchange of such resources through various mechanisms of exchange constitutes the crux of the crystallization of various types of institutional norms and frameworks. However, this important insight has to be further explored and explicated. We may attempt to do so by analyzing some of the problems and shortcomings of our own analysis of age-groups (16).

Analysis of Universal Grouping in a Society—Age-Groups

The central hypothesis of this study has been that in "universalistic" social systems organized or semiorganized age-groups tend to arise under specific social conditions, i.e., "in those societies whose main integrative principles are different from the particularistic principles governing family and kinship relations." The tendency to crystallize certain types of organization based on age is also explained through the way in which certain universal societal and psychological needs become structured or organized in such societies.

These needs are, first, the general societal need or structural prerequisite of a society for the socialization of the young and of their development into adults and, second, the need of growing individuals to attain personal identity and social status within their society. It is these general needs which seem to serve as the background for the development of more specific motivations which activate people to undertake membership in different age-groups. Under such conditions there develops, according to this hypothesis, a double tendency or propensity—the propensity of the adolescent to join youth and age-groups and the propensity of the society to organize such groups.

These hypotheses and specifications did not, however, deal with all the aspects of the problem. They did indicate the nature of the people, that is the adolescents, whose needs for attainment of personal identity and social status were structured under these conditions so as to predispose them to join or become members of age-groups. Here, as in the former case of marriage norms, these people or positions constitute a universal category within the society, and hence the general societal need for socialization is naturally manifest in their own need for attainment of social maturity. But, on the other hand, these hypotheses, and the analyses brought in for their support, did not indicate systematically enough the kind of roles and positions whose occupants are especially sensitive to the needs of the adolescents and the nature of the resources through which the various organizations capable of gratifying such needs could be organized. In general it was not explored whether any direct or indirect exchange took place between adolescents and their families and various representatives of the broader institutional structure, and what its nature was.

Similarly it was assumed that in most cases (with rare exceptions) there would exist some leader or leaders willing and able to respond to such needs and to organize the youth groups. The possibility that such leaders might not exist was not raised at all. Similarly the *exact* ways in which different types of leaders or representatives of the broader institutional structure with different resources at their disposal tended to organize different types of age-groups were not adequately analyzed. The differences in the structure of age-groups were related to broad structural characteristics of the societies, such as the extent of specialization or of achievement orientation that prevailed within them, but the exact mechanisms through which these characteristics facilitated the organization of different types of age-groups by different leaders was not satisfactorily specified. Hence, the exact mechanisms through which these different resources were "exchanged" were not fully explained. Because of this, the processes of change and possible extinction of any given form of age-groups were also not adequately treated.

Thus we can discern several additional problems in the comparative study of institutions. In the area of marriage, for example, various norms regulate the relations between structurally equivalent groups that in principle encompass all the members of a society. Here, however, we find a different situation. While the age-group organization may in principle encompass all members of a certain universal category in society, in order to become crystallized they must be organized through the activities of people occupying specified positions of elites or leaders which differ structurally from those of the adolescent.

Hence, the relation between individual predispositions and societal needs becomes of necessity much more complicated and even problematic, and the people or parties whose activities "represent" society have to be specified and analyzed further. Similarly, the relations between resources offered by the adolescents and the various societal goals of such elites must also be analyzed and specified. Because of all these reasons, we find here a much more variegated complex of indirect exchanges that needs to be explored systematically.

Analysis of Specific Groups—Development of Bureaucratic Organizations

Several additional problems of institutional analysis connected with variation of indirect exchanges can be derived from a brief analysis of some recent works on bureaucracy that starting from Weber's classical model (17) have developed and changed some of its basic assumptions. Weber's model of bureaucracy refers both to the basic characteristics of bureaucracy and to some of the conditions under which these characteristics tend to develop. Several recent works, especially those of Udy, Stinchcombe, and Harrison (18), have pointed out that the various elements which constituted Weber's "ideal type" of bureaucracy do not necessarily *always* go together. There seems to be a structural basic core—similar to that of Levy and Fallers for the family (although on a different level of abstraction)—which is common to all goal-oriented organizations tending to the attainment of specific goals or, in his words "rational administrations."

This core is composed, according to Stinchcombe, of

1. Differentiation of the work role from home life (and other deep interpersonal commitments).

2. The organization of work statuses into some sort of career, in which future rights and duties depend on present performance according to specified standards.

3. A stable allocation of work to persons formally identified as able and willing to work and subject to discipline by understood work standards and payment by the administration only when such workers are "productive."

4. A stable legitimate way of communicating at least the goals to be reached by subordinates and of seeing that these goals are accomplished (19).

Beyond this structural core many possibilities of variations exist in the additional characteristics of different organizations directed to the implementation of specific goals. The specific characteristics of a bureaucracy, such as the hierarchical arrangement of authority, large-scale organization, and "computative" criteria of decision making (20), constitute only one such possibility.

This necessarily raises several questions with regard to the conditions that give rise to the development and institutionalization of organizations. Weber's analysis postulated that most important among such conditions are a relatively great scope of societal and economic differentiation and of market economy, availability of relatively mobile manpower, and legal frameworks which assure the stability of contracts.

Here several problems arise. First, there is the general problem that these conditions seem to be related to *all* types of such organizations and do not specify the constellations of these conditions which are related to different types of specificity-oriented organization. But beyond this general problem more specific ones emerge about the relations of these conditions to each other and the development of the various types of rational or goal-oriented organizations.

Some of these conditions, such as the development of social differentiation, indicate the ways in which certain types of needs develop and become structured among certain groups and strata within the society. The specification of these conditions postulates that under certain societal conditions there may develop among certain parts of a society needs which cannot be satisfied through the existing (usually traditional) groups, organizations, and institutions and that, by inference, these people or groups are willing and able to pay something for the satisfaction of these needs. Weber was dealing here mainly with institutional commodities, such as money, labor, or political support and commitment, although among them certain psychological attitudes, like *motivation* to work in certain types of organization, may be also of great importance.

Other conditions, such as the existence, within the society at large or within those sectors thereof, of mobile labor or of certain legal norms, specify types of resources and frameworks without which it would be impossible to maintain the types of organization which may help in the satisfaction of such varied needs.

There can also be discerned another type of condition—namely the extent to which there exist people, entrepreneurs, who are able and willing to invest some of their own resources (such as capital, time, initiative in the establishment and maintenance of organizations) for the satisfaction of varied needs and wants of other people. Most of the discussions about bureaucracy have assumed first—as in the case of the organization of age-groups—that this type of entrepreneur will always emerge. However, even less than in the case of age-groups, this cannot be taken for granted, and we must ask first whether and under what conditions they may emerge at all; second, where are such organizations placed in the social structure; third, what different types of such entrepreneurs, using different resources, may arise, and how may their different placement in the social structure affect the characteristics of the groups they organize.

Finally, there is the problem of how different types of entrepreneurs, acting under different social conditions, responding to various needs, and using diverse kinds of resources, tend to organize different types of specificity-oriented organization. Here, of course, the problem of various types of indirect exchange between different social groups or categories of people becomes very important.

Some Problems of Institutional Analysis in Terms of Needs and Exchange

The analysis of developments in the study of bureaucracy has raised additional analytical problems that stem from the multiplicity of institutional and organizational forms and from the heterogeneity of such institutional form in a society. These new problems are rooted in the fact that here we do not necessarily deal with universal societal needs or with needs of universal categories of people but with more specific and limited needs of *certain* groups and strata within the society. It is because of this that the identification of different types of entrepreneurs who are able and willing to articulate the various goals through which such needs may be taken care of becomes complicated and important.

But, for these reasons, the chain of indirect exchange becomes much more variegated and extended. The successful implementation of such goals is dependent not only on the availability of certain resources among the people whose needs these goals may gratify but also on the availability of other types of resources among other groups in the society, and it is only insofar as some viable arrangements which bind all these groups are crystallized in some system of exchange that these new organizations can persist. A similar analytical paradigm could be applied to any other institutional or organizational form—be it a different form of economic enterprise, religious organization, or political dominance, many of which can be found in Weber's own work.

The preceding analyses point out several difficulties or weaknesses which can be discerned in most of the aforementioned approaches to the comparative study of institutions. The first weak point, common to most comparative analyses, is the assumption of the uniformity or homogeneity of any given institution within a society. Whereas an assumption like this may be excusable to some extent with regard to

marriage laws and norms (although even here the differences between prescribed and actual marriage behavior are of great interest
[21]), it is much less so with regard to such organizations as age-
groups and especially to different types of bureaucratic organizations.

Second, the explanation of any given institutional form by reference to the needs of individuals and of society by now necessitates the
clear distinction between the needs of individuals and those of society.
But most of the existing analyses do not always specify (1) the ways
through which various specific needs of different groups are articulated within a society, (2) the ways through which presumed societal
needs are articulated in concrete activities, whether special types of activities or aspects of all activities of individuals in special structural
position, and especially (3) the ways and mechanisms through which
the two types of needs become linked.

Moreover, most analyses tend to assume that such needs must be
fulfilled and fail to investigate the degrees to which they are indeed
satisfied and the conditions which facilitate or impede the satisfaction
of such different degrees of needs.

Finally, most of these analyses do not specify the ways in which
such needs and their relations to various structural arrangements may
change. They usually assume that the same conditions which explain
the initial development or crystallization of a given institutional pattern necessarily explain its continuity also. Hence most of these analyses do not deal, except by implication, with processes of change of
institutions and especially with the ways in which a given institutional
arrangement may become defunct.

The Analysis of "Partial Institutions"—The Culture and Personality Approach

We have dealt only with basic institutions, economic, political, cultural, and religious, which constitute a component part of any society,
a part of the definition of society. No society can be envisaged without
some crystallization of these institutional spheres, although not only
their specific contents but also the degree of their relative "efficiency"
may vary greatly between societies. Each of these institutional spheres
also entails the setting up of norms regulating mutual obligations in-

cumbent on different positions as well as, usually, the establishment of some organizational frameworks.

However, side by side with these types of institutions, the study of which has taken up the greater part of the relevant literature, there also develop within any society a great variety of other types of institutions—some of them cultural symbols, others what may be called "partial" institutions. These are distinguished from basic institutions in that they do not (except when fully embedded in such basic institutions) entail the setting up of norms of mutual obligation between categories of people, but tend more to emphasize ritual or patterns of behavior and/or orientation toward various culture symbols (22). Various ritual ceremonies, bodies of customs, bodies of folkloristic tradition, or styles of art may be examples of partial institutions. All of these may vary in the extent of their universality, that is, the extent to which they can be found within a wide range of societies, the extent to which they are spread within a given society, and the extent to which they are institutionalized from within.

The study of such partial institutions has been very much in the forefront of parts of classical anthropological and ethnological studies, but only recently has the interest in at least some of these problems been revived. One starting point for renewed attention to these problems is the various "Culture and Personality" studies (23). Another which deals more with cultural symbols is the revival of interest in studies of ritual, myth, and folklore (24). An analysis of the assumption of some of the newer studies of partial institutions may throw additional light on the problems of institutional analysis in general and comparative analysis in particular.

The major assumptions underlying the Culture and Personality studies of varied institutions are that such institutions provide solutions to specific constellations of needs, drives, or conflicts between them, among the members of a society. These needs or drives are construed either as subconscious drives or as more conscious ones. The exigencies of fulfillment of these needs or drives in society, the possible conflicts among them and between them, and various basic sociocultural norms in the society constitute the basic starting points of most Culture and Personality studies.

These conflicts are seen as developing from the encounter between some basic psychological needs of individuals and the institutional setting of the society, especially as it is mediated through the process of socialization.

Various partial institutions—initiation rites or patterns of sorcery —are then explained in terms of their gratification of such various needs or of their resolution of these psychological conflicts which develop among the members of the society. Thus, the summary of one of the best known, recent studies in this field, Whiting, Kluckhohn, and Anthony's analysis of male initiation rites, illuminates this point.

The cross-cultural evidence indicates that: (1) A close relationship is established between mother and son during infancy as a consequence of either (a) their sleeping together for at least a year to the exclusion of the father or (b) the mother being prohibited from sexual intercourse for at least a year after the birth of her child or (c) both of these together have measurable consequences which are manifested in cultural adjustments at adolescence.

(2) The cultural adjustments to the presence of the above factors are made when the boy approaches or reaches sexual maturity. These adjustments are either (a) a ceremony of initiation into manhood involving at least one and generally several of the following factors: painful hazing by the adult males of the society, tests of endurance and manliness, seclusion from women, and genital operations, or (b) a change of residence which involves separation of the boy from his mother and sisters and may also include some formal means for establishing male authority such as receiving instructions from and being required to be respectful to the mother's brother or the members of the men's house.

(3) If both the factors specified in (1) are present, the consequences at adolescence tend to be more elaborate and severe than if only one is present.

(4) The cultural adjustments specified in (2) also occur in societies where the father does not have the right to discipline his son, whether or not the conditions specified in (1) are present. (25)

Whatever the merits of any specific hypotheses developed in these studies, their basic assumptions pose several problems. One is the lack of full explication of the different possibilities or alternative solutions to the problems or needs generated through a given process of socialization and of the conditions under which any single solution tends to develop. (Similarly, a given pattern of socialization or child rearing is very often assumed in these studies to be the natural outcome of certain environmental factors; the possibility of different responses to such factors is not explored.) Second, there is inadequate recognition of the possibility of *nonsolution* of certain of these problems. A good example of the possibility of the nonfulfillment of certain "latent" needs is the almost total disappearance of initiation rites in most parts of modern societies, despite the alleged existence of some need for such rites among wide parts of the population (26). Here even more than in the case of basic institutions, the necessity of the gratification or solution of some such need becomes even more problematic and instead of being taken for granted has to be viewed as a problem of research.

Third is encountered the problem of the identification and availability of societal positions, the occupants of which help to crystallize the various solutions to such needs or drives. This is, of course, closely connected with the problem of relations between gratification of various personal needs or drives and of societal needs or the needs of the social system. In most Culture and Personality studies, the general supposition exists that the stability of a society is greatly dependent on the extent to which its institutions and customs are able to gratify such needs and hence that the existence of appropriate customs has an important survival value for the society. But beyond this there is little specification or explication of the ways in which the crystallization of such customs or partial institutions are related to the social division of labor or to the working of different groups or categories of people in the society (27).

Problems in the Analysis of Folklore

A similar range of problems can be discerned in some of the recent studies of folklore which have developed distinct analytical orientations. Many of these studies start from the existence of some universal cultural framework, data, or "store" of human culture which can be found in principle in all or most cultures or societies. These data, images, or symbols are, at least implicitly, often assumed to correspond to some universal human or social needs, to some universal basic, almost unconscious categories of human thought, or to the basic data and problems of human existence, such as problems of life and death, good luck or misfortune, to the problems of establishing private and collective identity, or to some of the vicissitudes and uncertainties given in the very nature of orderly social life. These data constitute the main beginnings for the crystallization of different concrete symbols, myths, legends, and folktales (28).

But, unlike the basic institutional frameworks in which the limits of structural variability are to some extent set by the functional needs of organization and by the interrelatedness of such different institutional fields, the case here is more complicated. The general "store" of human culture and perception of the vicissitudes of human existence from which these cultural artifacts take off is much more variegated. The potentialities of change and of crystallization of different concrete forms are here much greater. Similarly, there exists a broader variety of levels of crystallization, of normative sanctioning, and of diffusion of various cultural items among different groups in the society. There exists a great and constant fluidity in the crystallization of diverse types of images, symbols, and tales taken up by different groups in the society (29).

While it is possible to attempt the full explication of the relation and possible homology of the structure (morphology) of myths (legends or tales) and the social structure in relatively closed, primitive societies, this becomes much more difficult in "complex" or "advanced" societies. Although a purely structural, formal, morphological study of the structure of some myths prevalent in those complex societies, or of their major ideologies or of various literary works, can certainly be attempted, a full analysis of the different symbolic universes existing in such societies, of their diffusion within the society, and of their relation to the basic aspects of the social structure becomes much more difficult (30). Instead of assuming, as to some extent is done even if implicitly in many anthropological works, the existence of a close correspondence between the symbolic representations of a people and their social organization, one must pose the very possibility of and the degrees of such correspondence as a problem for research (31).

Here, perhaps even more than in some of the partial institutions studied by the Culture and Personality school, the identification of

the social positions in which occupants take the initiative in crystallizing and articulating these varied types of cultural symbols and
creation becomes even more complicated. Similarly, the nature of the
exchange which tends to develop in such situations is not immediately
visible.

As in the case of partial institutions, we do not study here the basic
institutional or organizational framework within which some structural positions of power almost always exist. It is much more difficult
to envisage and specify such positions exactly, the occupants of which
tend to crystallize these myths in symbols. As these cultural artifacts
are not very "homogeneous" or fully crystallized and may often be in
a constant state of flux among different groups of population, it is, in
principle, easier to postulate the crystallization of such institutions not
only or mainly through the activities of people placed in structurally
specific positions of norm setting or leadership, but also through processes of imitation of the first lucky finder of a given solution or
through diffusion of such solution into different groups of a society.

But even so, the explication of the ways and mechanisms through
which different solutions are taken up by various groups becomes
sanctioned in different degrees and should not be taken for granted,
but should, rather, constitute a problem for research.

*Institutionalization as Processes of Exchange—Interpersonal
Exchange—Homans' Analysis*

The preceding analysis of some problems in comparative institutional analysis has indicated that it might be profitable to approach
institution-building or institutionalization as a process of crystallization of different norms and frameworks which takes place through a
series of exchanges between people placed in different structural positions in the society and which, in turn, regulates some crucial aspects
of such exchanges. This analysis has also pointed out some of the com-
plexities and difficulties in the application of this approach, especially
in the specification of the different ways in which the *indirect* exchange which seems to constitute a crucial aspect of this process of institutional exchange is regulated.

This brings our analysis close to two recent attempts, one by Homans (32) and another by Levi-Strauss (33), to explain the nature of crystallization of different institutions as a result of a series of exchanges between different people or groups of society. A critical examination of these two approaches may greatly facilitate the elucidation of some of the more general problems of the study of the processes of institutionalization as outlined above.

Homans' attempt at institutional analysis is part of, or a derivation of, his more general attempt to explain social behavior in terms of exchange. This general approach is perhaps best summarized in his following statement:

The current job of theory in small-group research is to make the connection between experimental and real-life studies, to consolidate the propositions that empirically hold good in the two fields, and to show how these propositions might be derived from a still more general set. One way of doing this job would be to revive and make more rigorous the oldest of theories of social behavior—social behavior as exchange.

Some of the statements of such theory might be the following. Social behavior is an exchange of goods, material goods but also non-material ones, such as the symbol of approval or prestige. Persons that take much from others are under pressure to give much to them. This process of influence tends to work out at equilibrium to a balance in the exchanges. For a person engaged in exchange, what he gives may be a cost to him, just as what he gets may be a reward, and his behavior changes less as profit, that is, reward less cost, tends to a maximum. Not only does he seek a maximum for himself, but he tries to see to it that no one in his group makes more profit than he does. The cost and the value of what he gives and of what he gets vary with the quantity of what he gives and gets. It is surprising how familiar these propositions are; it is surprising, too, how propositions about the dynamics of exchange can begin to generate the static thing we call "group structure" and, in so doing, generate also some of the propositions about group structure that students of real-life groups have stated.

In our unguarded moments we sociologists find words like "reward" and "cost" slipping into what we say. Human nature will break in upon even our most elaborate theories. But we seldom let it have its ways with us and systematically follow up what these words imply. Of all our many "approaches" to social behavior, the one that sees it as an economy is the most neglected, and yet it is the one we use every moment of our lives—except when we write sociology (34).

As is well known, Homans' analysis deals almost exclusively with exchanges of personal attitudes, sentiments, and activities within relatively restricted, face-to-face, informal settings, such as work groups which exist within wider institutional and organizational frameworks, the existence of which are, for the purpose of this analysis, usually taken for granted by him. But beyond contributing to the study of such interpersonal relations Homans claims also that the type of exchange found in such interpersonal relations can serve both as a prototype of and as the starting point for the crystallization of broad institutional settings and norms. The major differences between the "preinstitutional" exchange (that is, informal, interpersonal) and the fully institutionalized one seem to be, according to him, that adherence to institutional norms is based on the assurance of secondary as well as primary rewards (through such media as money or political power) and on the investment, by the leaders or norm setters, of different resources such as money, manpower, time, effort, which they are able to use as capital for providing both short- and long-term rewards for their followers (35).

Thus in Homans' analysis it is clear that the commodities exchanged in interpersonal and institutional settings differ from one another. The major commodities which are exchanged in interpersonal relations are mainly personal, "informal," attitudes or activities, be they help in some tasks, such as execution of work tasks set up by the more formalized settings, personal esteem, or power with regard to these relations. The major commodities of exchange in the broader institutional social setting are mainly money, institutionalized "prestige," and formalized status. But according to Homans a close similarity or homology between these two types of commodities *qua* means of exchange exists.

This assumed similarity between exchange in the informal, personal, and the broader institutional settings has to be closely examined from the point of view of our concern here. The claim of similarity or homology between the processes of exchange of interpersonal relations and the processes of institutionalization necessarily rests on several assumptions. First, it rests on the assumption that the commodities exchanged in both types of situations and the norms which regulate such exchanges are analytically similar (i.e., in the points which are crucial for the process of exchange), except that they are more fixed and based on "capital" in the broad institutional fields of societies. Second, the claim of similarity is based on the assumption that these different types of commodities are, in a way, interchangeable, that is, that the interpersonal attitudes crystallize into the various kinds of institutional commodities, even if the two never merge entirely.

However, a closer examination of these two assumptions will show us that some very crucial differences exist both between the commodities exchanged in interpersonal and institutional settings and the norms which regulate these exchanges. Two such differences are of special importance. One is that institutionalized commodities have, even within a primitive society in which exchange is relatively restricted and fixed, a much wider scope of generality, of applicability to wider sets of situations, and are relatively interchangeable between different groups and situations in the society. At the same time a second difference is that most of this exchange is *indirect*—it is not of a "barter" character in limited face-to-face relations; it takes place between people who are not in direct contact, and it involves the use of generalized media of exchange to an extent which is inconceivable in an informal group. True enough, such media of exchange become, from the psychological point of view, *direct* rewards of reinforcements for the persons concerned. But from the organizational view they have an autonomy of their own (as evident for instance in the specific rule of different markets—merit for money or labor), and their becoming a primary reward only reinforces this autonomy.

Third, and closely connected with the former, is the fact that the flow of these media and of the respective commodities is regulated by sets of formalized norms which regulate in a relatively continuous way the rates of exchange between different commodities and uphold the legitimacy of the generalized media of exchange. Last, the *variety* of the commodities exchanged within any wider institutional setting, such as economy, polity, and between such settings is necessarily much greater than in the interpersonal relations.

Cultural and Institutional Exchange—A Discussion of the
Works of Levi-Strauss and Leach

Here we come close to Levi-Strauss and Leach's formulations. The
following quotation from one of Levi-Strauss' latest works dealing
with a comparison between totemic and case societies illustrates his approach.

By way of conclusion I should like to emphasize four points. First,
totemism which has been formalized in what may be called the "language
of primitiveness" can equally well be formalized in that "language of castes"
which were thought to be the very opposite of primitiveness.

Secondly, in its social undertakings, mankind keeps maneuvering within
narrow limits. Social types are not isolated creations, wholly independent
of each other, and each one an original entity, but rather the result of an
endless play of combination and recombination, for ever seeking to solve
the same problems by manipulating the same fundamental elements. This
game always consists in a give-and-take, and what is given or taken must
always belong either to the realm of nature (natural products) or to the
realm of culture (goods and services), the exchange of women being the
only formula that makes it possible to overcome this duality. Thus exchange
of women not only ensures a horizontal mediation between groups of men,
it also ensures a mediation, which we might call vertical, between nature
and culture.

Thirdly, as we have seen, the tremendous differences existing between
totemic groups and caste systems, in spite of their logical inverted similarity,
may be ascribed to the fact that castes are right and totemic systems are
wrong, when they believe that they provide real services to their fellow
groups. This should convince us that the "truth-value" is an unavoidable
dimension of structural method. No common analysis of religion can be
given by a believer and a non-believer, and from this point of view, the
type of approach known as "religious phenomenology" should be dismissed.

Lastly, by analyzing a specific example, I have attempted to validate a
methodological approach which I have been trying to follow in France
and which Dr. Leach is following in England. According to this approach
societies are not made up of the flotsam and jetsam of history, but of

variables; thus widely different institutions can be reduced to transformations of the same basic figure, and the whole of human history may be looked upon merely as a set of attempts to organize differently the same means, but always to answer the same questions . . . (36).

A similar formulation can be found in some of the works of Leach.

When two local descent groups A and B are in relation the "things" which can be exchanged to express this relationship can be roughly categorized as follows:

I. Tangibles
   (a) "women" and "men"
   (b) labour of men or women
   (c) consumer goods and money
   (d) capital goods
   (e) ritual objects of no intrinsic value
II. Intangibles
   (f) "rights" of a territorial and political nature
   (g) relative "status" or "prestige"

The last item cannot be defined except in terms of the cultural situation; it is simply "that kind of reputation which gains a man the admiration of his fellows," it may be derived from murder in one society, philanthropy in a second, saintliness in a third.

In every relationship between individuals and between groups, items in the above list are exchanged. It is in the nature of most such "exchanges" that, as regards the tangible items a, b, c, d, e, there is always an imbalance on one side or the other. The exchange account is balanced by the intangible items f and g (37).

Perhaps the most interesting point in the analysis of Levi-Strauss and Leach is the recognition of the specific, distinct nature of the commodities which are exchanged in the institutional frameworks of society. They stress that these commodities are not (only or mainly) personal relations or sentiments but are specific general commodities given in the very nature of human institutional and cultural order and therefore exchangeable and to some extent interchangeable. Hence, as stated in a recent review:

Reducing marriage to communication of women between individuals or groups, which may or may not be accompanied by counterpresentations of other valuables, creates a general theory from which can be generated a number of more specific models (38).

In this their analysis comes close to some of the most important recent systematic sociological thought, as developed mainly by Parsons, which attempts to specify systemic variety of the different types of institutional "commodities" which "pass," as it were, within and between the major institutional spheres of a society (39).

But at the same time Levi-Strauss and Leach's analyses do not, at least in hitherto published works, fully recognize the consequences of the great diversity of these various institutional commodities. "Commodities," "services," and "products of nature" are not fixed or given. They are a creation of human culture, and their values are mainly symbolic. Within each of these realms there exists not only the possibility of variability of permutations within a fixed universe but also the continuous possibility of the creation or invention of new contents, orientations, and symbols (40). Even if such changes and innovations can be derived from fixed, given, immanent characteristics of different cultural and symbolic fields—something which in itself is at most only an assumption yet to be tested—their *specific* crystallizations in concrete societies have to deal with varied systemic exigencies and problems of each symbolic and institutional sphere, with their concrete interrelations in the given context, and in their relations to their environment.

More significantly they do not seem to distinguish, between on the one hand, those symbols which denote the basic desiderata and exigencies of human existence, define the contents and limits of individual and collective identity and thus set the frameworks and limits to the flow of different commodities in institutional exchange, and on the other hand those norms which regulate this flow. Moreover, the "principles" or "laws" of exchange which govern the flow of different institutional commodities, whether women, commodities, or different types of services, tend to vary greatly, and it appears wrong to assume, as Levi-Strauss seems to do in at least some of his works, that they are necessarily identical or homologous. They may differ greatly between the cultural-symbolic sphere and the institutional spheres on the one hand, and among different institutional spheres on the other (41).

Parsons and Smelser's analysis of the systemic interrelations ("inputs" or "outputs") between different institutional spheres and the designation of the different types of institutional commodities which are exchanged in this way provides a crucial first indication for an analysis of such variety of systems of institutional exchange, even if it does not until now deal explicitly with the problem of the variability of the laws and rates of exchange in different institutional and societal settings and of their setting up and institutionalization (42).

Two Major Aspects of Institutional Exchange— "Equivalent" Exchange and Norm Setting and Goal Articulation

This variability and possibility of change and innovation in the crystallization of such diverse institutional commodities emphasizes the importance of setting up varied types of norms of exchange and principles of legitimation of these norms and of their setters.

In more general terms, this variability means that in the analysis of societal exchange—the exchange of institutionalized (and possibly also of interpersonal) commodities—two aspects must be distinguished. One is the direct or indirect exchange of various commodities between individuals, groups, or categories of people (be they kinship groups or territorial, economic, or political units) who are structurally equivalent, whether they are equal or arranged in some hierarchical order (43). Second is the exchange between those individuals who are able to articulate varied collective goals and crystallize valid norms and those groups or strata who are willing to "pay" something (i.e., other types of norms or goals)—but not an equivalent commodity—for the crystallization and upholding of such norms. They are willing to provide such payments presumably because the norms answer their need for some general stability or more specific needs and problems.

Hence the capacity to create and crystallize such norms, to articulate various goals, to establish organizational frameworks, and to mobilize the resources necessary for all these purposes (such as the readiness to invest in the appropriate activities) is a basic aspect or constituent of the flow of exchange in any society (44).

It is, of course, obvious that this capacity to set norms and organize various institutional frameworks is closely related to control over basic institutional positions and resources such as power, wealth, or symbols. But the mere control of such resources is not sufficient to assure the effective institutionalization of such norms and the successful articulation of varied societal goals. The differential capacity for such norm setting and for the articulation of goals is not always confined to various hierarchically superior positions or to positions of representation of various given structural units, and it may often cut across them. Thus the patterns of social, institutional exchange are organized in any society not only according to principles of reciprocity and hierarchy between structurally equivalent groups and positions, but also according to the differential capacity to set norms and articulate varied social goals.

The activities of people in crucial positions from which norms are set and the crystallization of such positions and norms are not, of course, entirely random. They are set by the structural (i.e., institutional) placement of their positions and by the limits set by needs and systemic properties of their own and of other institutional spheres. They are set by the basic "structural core" of each institutional sphere or subsphere. These limits are not, however, fully fixed at any concrete situation, and the process of institutionalization is to a great extent a process of innovation of various appropriate institutional norms and of setting up, beyond such structural cores, new types of structural frameworks.

Role Crystallization

The importance of the "innovative" aspect of crystallization of institutional frameworks can perhaps best be seen in the analysis of crystallization of roles (45). For a very long period of time roles have been designated as the basic units of social behavior of individuals, and it has been one of the major contributions of the structural-functional schools to emphasize the great importance and the dynamic quality of roles as perhaps the most important "meeting" point between individual behavior and societal functions. But this idea of role has usually been treated as a unified concept, representing a function-ally indivisible unit. However, recent analysis indicates that roles are composed of several components, such as their "goals," their norms, and relations to other roles. Although certain components do in fact tend to go together, they may also vary independently and should be studied from this viewpoint. The variations are not, of course, infinite, but each of these components is often subject to independent influ-ences and may thus constitute a focus of change, affecting the role as a whole in different ways and to varying degrees. Hence, the concept of role should not be taken as "given"—as a pattern of behavior (or of a normative definition of behavior) which is given and fixed in the in-stitutional structure of society and to which the individual must adjust himself through the process of socialization and through interaction with other people. Rather, the very formation of any specific role, the articulation of its goals, and the crystallization of its components is an outcome of various social forces or mechanisms which create—out of the potential of many contents, demands, and institutional and per-sonal needs existing in the given society—the actual specific crystal-lizations of the different components of role. The components of any role might consequently be profitably studied according to the degrees of institutionalization in each role and/or according to whether all or only some of them become institutionalized to any given extent.

Similarly, the crystallization of different roles may, in its turn, influence the development of the institutional structure of a society. The processes of creation and crystallization of different roles takes place continuously in all societies—even the most stable ones. Even if, in some cases, the basic definition of a role is more or less constant over long periods of time, the relative emphasis on its components will vary according to different situations and forces which impinge on it. Thus, instead of taking the role-map of a given society as if it were completely fixed and given, it has to be perceived as being con-tinuously recrystallized.

Roles can be seen as the focal point of the institutionalization of rules of exchange around specific socially-articulated goals, and the fact that they have to be analyzed in terms of continuous crystalliza-tion indicates that the same applies to the analysis of institutional norms and frameworks.

Major Aspects, Levels, and Mechanisms of
Institutional Exchange

The preceding analysis points out that, instead of speaking of institutions to be compared as given, constant, self-contained entities, it might be more profitable to talk about the *process of institutionalization* and look on it as a process of continuous crystallization of different types of norms and frameworks regulating the processes of exchange. But such crystallization is not, of course, random or purely accidental. Such processes always take off from several, fixed, starting points given in the nature of the major institutional spheres and their core-structural characteristics and in the nature of the cultural universe. Hence the study of processes of crystallization of different types of institutional complexes as systems of exchange has to start, first, from the analysis of these general potentialities, the general types of resources of the major institutional and cultural spheres, and from an analysis of the possibilities, as well as the limits, of their variability. The crystallization of concrete institutional forms includes the development—from the general potentialities of each institutional sphere and the predispositions of the holders of strategic positions within it—of new types of major institutional commodities and the crystallization of varied norms and rates of exchange. The crystallization of such norms of exchange includes, in any institutional system, several basic aspects (46).

The first such aspect is the definition of the basic goals of human existence and endeavor to the realization of which the varied human activities in society may be oriented and the definition of those goals which are explained as nonexchangeable. In every society there develop certain types of symbolic expression which deal with the indication of the primordial attribute of human existence, the goals of human existence, and with the designation of any society or part thereof as a proper place for the undertaking of human endeavor and interchange. These symbols define the basic precontractual norms of society, define certain situations and commodities which are not exchangeable ones, reinforce the basic norms of reciprocity and exchange within the society, define the norms which regulate such exchange, as well as point out some possible—realistic or imaginary—forms of escape from the outcomes of such norms and rules (47).

These varied symbolic expressions are articulated both in fully institutionalized and formalized settings and in a much more variegated and diffused way—which has yet to be systematically investigated—in various myths ("folk-tales") and other "partial" institutions.

The setting up and transmission of such symbols and orientations on the normative and cognitive levels alike constitutes also a crucial part of the process of socialization and communication in any society (48).

A very important and crucial element of this primary aspect of any exchange is the definition of certain goals and situations as nonexchangeable. The most important illustrations of such nonexchangeable commodities are the symbols and situations of basic cultural, societal, and personal identity, such as those of personal honor and virtue of the limits, nature, and belongingness to different collectivities. In every society these constitute what may be called the basic, primordial core of personal relations and of orientations to the broader social order, and they are usually perceived as prior to any concrete exchange and as in themselves not exchangeable (49).

The second major aspect of institutional exchange is the setting up of initial bargaining positions of different individuals or groups within the society.

Third is the setting up and organizing of different generalized media of exchange such as money or generalized political support. These norms and media necessarily vary in the different institutional spheres. Each of the different institutional spheres or types of commodities usually involves a different type of exchange orders such as market orders in the economic sphere or the interrelationship of power, support, and bargaining in the political sphere.

Fourth is the setting up of various frameworks, organizations, and norms which serve as channels of exchange and which aim at assuring the relatively smooth functioning of the processes of exchange and at the upholding of the norms of exchange by those participating in it. Legal institutions, systems of communication, economic or political markets, administrative organizations and frameworks serve as best examples of such mechanisms.

Last is the *treble* process of legitimation—legitimation of the basic norm of exchange, of the media and channels of exchange, and of the concrete rates of exchange.

This process of continuous crystallization of institutional norms and settings of exchange takes place, in every society, on several different planes or levels. One is the exchange between structurally equivalent (whether equal or unequal, reciprocal or hierarchical) units bound together by bond of "mechanical" solidarity in those institutional spheres, like kinship, where the exchange between the basic units is mostly of identical commodities and in those cases—like in marriage arrangements—which encompass universal categories of people in society and where the gratification of their needs is closely interlinked with the very existence of the society. Second, it is effected between individuals and groups in different structural positions which are already bound by ties of "organic solidarity" (i.e., by interdependence growing out of the complex division of labor). Third, cutting across these two former types, an exchange is effected between the holders of differential positions in terms of norm setting and articulation of goals. Last, it is effected on the level of setting up of the basic, often diffuse, primordial symbols of human existence, of reciprocity, and of precontractual norms.

Each of these different levels of exchange tends to depend more—although probably not entirely—on different mechanisms. Thus the first type seems to rely mainly on direct, barter-like directions between various individuals and groups, on the relative lack of distinction between different institutional orders, on the embedding of all of them in the structure of complete groups, and on the overlapping of membership between the major groups. The second level of exchange depends more on various impersonal exchange mechanisms, like economic or political markets. The last two are more dependent on the maintenance of special communicative and hierarchical situations, a close relation between the different orders of exchange, and the more basic, primordial symbols of human existence and of the societal order.

These varied mechanisms are perhaps most closely interwoven in so-called primitive societies, and it is no accident that many anthropological studies do not distinguish between them and tend to assume that the first types of such mechanisms, together perhaps with the last, are the most prevalent for social control (50).

But it is doubtful whether this is the case, even in these societies. In more intricate groups, the complexity of the different levels and mechanisms of exchange is even more varied and should, of course, constitute an important focus of comparative research. The crystallization of some such viable orders of exchange poses some of the basic problems and challenges of institutionalization, innovation and crystallization of norms, articulations of goals, and mobilization of resources.

But society cannot take for granted that, even if the potential (the various potential needs) for such crystallization of norm setting and goal articulation exists, crystallization will indeed take place and that people will be found who are able or willing to invest in arriving at them and in setting up norms and organizational frameworks. If such positions do not become crystallized or filled, there may easily develop a disintegration of any given social system or the institutionalization of a system at a very low level of efficiency. But assuming the existence of some minimal availability of such positions and people, it is the variability in availability and orientations in any given situation which constitutes the major problem of comparative studies.

Individual Attitudes and Institutional Crystallization— Communication, Mobility, and Role Formation

Here again, we touch on the problem of the relations between individual attitudes and behavior and the crystallization of institutional norms and frameworks. A very important problem in institutional analysis is constituted by the conditions under which personal attitudes and sentiments become "translated" into institutional commodities, or the conditions under which they constitute important resources for the crystallization of institutional norms and frameworks.

As yet, it is not at all clear in what way various personal sentiments and activities, limited to different, but still true for similar, informal settings, become exchanged or crystallized into the more fully institutionalized commodities and norms. Most studies of social determinants of behavior and attitudes have rarely attempted to analyze how these attitudes and behavior affect the process of setting up new norms and organizational settings. Merei's study of institutionalization of leadership in children's groups is one of the exceptional works which attempts to analyze the relations between individual attitudes and the crystallization of institutional (or group) norms and frameworks (51).

Although such studies are relatively few, and they certainly do not support the direct relation between attitudes and sentiments on the one hand and the undertaking of jural injunctions and the crystallization of institutional norms on the other, it would be wrong to assume —as Levi-Strauss seems to do (52)—that such sentiments and attitudes are necessarily "secondary" for the understanding of processes of institutionalization. Some indications of the importance of attitudes in processes of institutionalization can perhaps be found in several recent studies.

Some writings in the field of social psychology indicate that an individual's performance of various roles and tasks—and his upholding of norms—may vary greatly according to his evaluation of their contribution to his own values and goals (53). Some of these studies tend to indicate that initial patterns of socialization and child rearing, while certainly not linked in a necessary way to any one concrete institutional form or organization, may predispose the members of a society to covet certain types of commodities, to define certain situations or goals as unexchangeable, and to be ready to enter into exchange which is regulated by certain types of norms of exchange.

Needless to say these very values and goals are acquired by individuals in the process of their socialization in society. The extent to which this process creates new needs and orientations or only develops in certain directions some inherent capabilities is, from the point of view of the present analysis, immaterial. In any case, the acquisition or development of such capabilities includes the crystallization of certain basic orientations to the nature of the world of human existence and the social order and to the various rules of social exchange. But it does not necessarily ensure the individual acceptance of the specific institutional goals or of the specific institutional order existing with it. On the contrary, the development of these capabilities may well first of all inculcate attitudes of critical evaluation of such order in terms of the individual's orientation—including the orientation to a certain type of societal order. It is the individual's evaluation of the contribution of a given group, of institutional settings or tasks to his own goals, and of his conceptions of social order that seem to be of crucial importance in influencing his adherence to institutional norms and performance of the appropriate institutional and group norms and tasks.

The lack of identification or satisfaction of individuals with an organizational setting does not in itself necessarily lead to immediate disorganization or to the "disappearance" of the appropriate norms. This process tends rather to operate somewhat more indirectly: it may influence the accessibility of various resources which are available to some, as contrasted to other, groups; it may greatly influence the predispositions to enter into some types of exchange rather than others and, hence, also influence the chances of competing leaders and norm setters. Hence the processes through which individuals are sensitized to the symbol norms and goals of various groups in society and the ways in which they internalize and maintain various norms and criteria of evaluation may be of crucial importance for the interlinking of their attitudes and sentiments with the setting up and maintaining of institutional norms and frameworks.

Within this context, several areas of study may be of special interest. One area is studies of communication and reference-groups' behavior, that is, of the processes through which such norms are "transmitted" to individuals and through which individuals orient themselves to certain groups in society (54). The second is studies of mobility that investigate the relation between individual motivation and aspiration, and the choice of different institutional positions and norms (55).

Last, and of great importance in this context, is the study of the crystallization of societal roles (56) and especially of individuals participating in such crystallization. Most studies in this field have dealt with the individual's adaptation to a given role and with his ability (or inability) to perform it. In fact, the picture found in or implied by literature often painted the individual as progressing through some basic age, sex, and fundamental institutional—economic, occupational, political, and religious—roles. It seems, however, that such a conception is oversimplified. The individual's progress in diversified roles necessarily brings him into situations which are, or at least may be, organized in different ways from the point of view of his ability to fulfill his own goals. That is to say, the individual is faced, in different situations, with social forces which impinge upon him in varying ways and degrees. The performance of roles by individuals should not be viewed as a static assumption (or nonassumption) of certain attributes and as a realization of certain types of fixed expectations and norms set by society. It should rather be conceived as a much more differentiated process in which the individual's aspirations and perceptions interplay in a variety of situations, emphasizing in each different aspects of normatively regulated behavior. Indeed, it is this "encounter" between individuals and the supposedly given roles that often creates the possibility of role innovation—of change in the constellation of different components of roles and of subroles.

Within the context of these problems may also be studied the extent to which social structure is a statistical outcome of aggregate individual choices, a problem recently taken up in anthropological literature (57).

Some Unsolved Problems—Final and Efficient Causes

The postulation of such processes of exchange as a starting point for institutional analysis does not in itself fully explain the causes of the development of any given institutional complex. Nor does it fully explain why any specific institutional complex developed out of competition with other solutions which were possible at a given juncture, or why *any* institutional complex became crystallized at such juncture at all, or why norms and organizations were successfully crystallized by the appropriate individuals in such a way as to ensure some fulfillment of societal needs or some societal survival or adaptation. The full analysis or explanation of the exact ways and mechanisms through which societal adaptation or the fulfillment of societal needs is linked to patterns of personal and institutional behavior of individual members of society—in other words, the adequate analysis of the relation between final and efficient causes as explanations of institutional analysis —still poses many problems. This is true, both on the level of the development of some general, universal, institutional pattern like the incest taboo, or on the level of more specific patterns.

Several researches have indicated, in a rather hypothetical way, some processes or mechanisms which may be of crucial importance from this point of view. One very broad type of mechanism, which is perhaps most difficult to specify and which certainly merits much more detailed, systematic study, is something akin to the "natural selection" process. The other is a more conscious recognition, by holders of various social positions, of the use of certain arrangements for societal adaption (58). All these are as yet, however, very preliminary indications which necessitate much additional study. But the approach outlined above may prove useful as a step in dealing with these problems. This approach views the formalization of institutions and the "comparative" study of institutions as a study of the varied conditions and ways in which different types of roles, norms, and institutional frameworks of exchange tend to crystallize.

This approach points out, first, that, insofar as we attempt to analyze such exchange in terms of needs of individuals and of social systems, it is necessary to emphasize that such needs are not "universal" and unchanging but become differentially structured in different societies or parts of societies. Moreover, such needs are not randomly or equally distributed among the members of a given society but crystallize in different ways among people occupying different structural positions, and it is especially necessary to specify those positions in which the occupants may develop special sensitivity to so-called "societal needs."

Second, this approach emphasizes that most of the exchange which takes place in an institutional setting is indirect exchange, in which generalized media of exchange play a crucial role, and that the more direct interpersonal exchange in which individual attitudes and sentiments constitute the most important commodities is not necessarily homologous to the indirect and institutional one. At the same time, however, these attitudes and sentiments may constitute very important conditions for crystallizing and maintaining frameworks of institutional exchange.

Third, this approach emphasizes that, although in each institutional sphere certain basic structural characteristics and types of commodities, and certain minimal requisites of its effective function operate, the crystallization of any concrete institutional system, of any concrete norms and frameworks of exchange is variable, within broad limits, and depends on the concrete constellation of the position, power, and creeds of the various groups and individuals in any given situation.

Last, however, we emphasize that the mere development within any society of certain needs does not in itself ensure the crystallization of such an institution and the maintenance of effective exchange between its component parts. In the crystallization of such frameworks a crucial part is played by those people who evince a differential capacity to set up norms and articulate goals, but the availability of such people, or their concrete orientation and activities, is not always ensured or determined by the development of the varying needs among different groups in a society. It seems to us that such a formulation or model has several advantages over the former more static types of models in the comparative studies of institutions, and it can be helpful both for the study of processes of institutional change and for pointing out some of the possible approaches to comparisons between institutions.

PART II   Analysis of Institutional Change and of Comparative Study of Institutions

Institutionalization and Change

The preceding analysis assumes that the institutionalization of any institutional system in itself creates potentialities and directions for change (59). The institutionalization of any social system means that certain norms, sanctions, and organizations which regulate the access to different positions and establish certain norms of exchange are set up and that policies through which these norms can be upheld and applied to a relatively large and complex variety of social situations are implemented. These things are done by people who are placed, or attempt to become placed, in structurally strategic positions and who aspire to certain important goals. Such norms regulate the provision of various resources from other parts of the society to these power positions, to the new organizations, to some of the relations among the different groups in the society, and to the obligations of the occupants of these positions toward various groups in the society.

While the occupants of these positions obviously attempt to set up norms in accordance with their own values, goals, and interests, they also create or define certain norms shared by a number of groups. Very often they legitimize these norms by values that are purportedly shared to some extent by a large part of the society and symbolized by themselves. Hence, such values tend to be binding on the occupants of these positions.

But whatever the success of such attempts to establish and legitimize common norms in terms of common values and symbols, these norms are probably never fully accepted by the entire society. Most groups within any society or collectivity tend to exhibit some autonomy in terms of their attitudes toward these norms and in terms of their willingness or ability to provide the resources demanded by the given institutionalized system. While for very long periods of time a great majority of the members of a given society or parts thereof may be identified to some degree with the values and norms of the given system and may be willing to provide it with the resources it needs, other tendencies also develop. Some groups may be greatly opposed to the very premises of the institutionalization of a given system, may share its values only to a very small extent, and may accept these norms only as the least among evils and as binding on them in a very limited sense.

Others may share these values and accept the norms to a greater degree but may look on themselves as the more truthful repositories of these same values, may oppose the concrete levels at which the norms are institutionalized by the elite in power, and may attempt to interpret them in different ways, that is, attempt to establish other bargaining positions and varying norms of exchange. Others may develop new interpretations of existing values and strive for a change in the very bases of the institutional order. Hence any institutional system is never fully homogeneous—fully accepted or accepted to the same degree by all those participating in it—and these different orientations may become foci of conflict and of potential institutional change.

Even more important, from the point of view of our analysis, is that, whatever the initial attitudes of any given group to the basic premises of the institutional system, these may greatly change after the initial institutionalization of the system. Any institutionalization necessarily entails efforts to maintain the boundaries of the system, through continuous attempts to mobilize resources from different groups and individuals and to maintain the legitimacy of its values, symbols, and norms. But continuous implementation of these policies may affect the positions of different groups in the society and give rise to continuous shifts in the balance of power among them and in their orientations to the existing institutional system and its values and to the norms of exchange which it sets up.

Moreover, the institutionalization of any system usually creates new collectivities and organizations, such as the bureaucratic organizations in centralized empires. These organizations necessarily develop needs, interests, and orientations of their own which may impinge on various other groups and institutional spheres and change their attitudes toward the premises of the system. Similarly, changes in the balance of forces within the system also facilitate the development and maturation of certain inherent tendencies in the structure and the orientation of key groups and elites, as, for example, in the tendencies of some religious groups to develop and establish wider universalistic orientations and membership units which may then expand beyond the basic premises of the given institutional system.

These processes may be intensified by the systematic relations between any given institutional framework or sphere and other frameworks within the society. Whatever the degree of integration of the total society, some such relations between different institutional spheres, for example, the political and the economic or the political and the kinship systems, are inherent in any on-going society. But as has been often pointed out, the basic or predominant orientations and norms regulating the flow of exchange in each of these institutions tends, as seen above, to differ to some extent.

The occupants of major positions within these different institutional spheres may attempt to maintain their autonomy and may tend to make contradictory demands on different groups for provision of the necessary resources. Each may look for support from different groups in the society, thus exacerbating potential conflicts among the various groups, changing their relative strengths, and possibly undermining the premises of any institutional system. These contradictions, conflicts, and shifts in the balance of power may give rise to the depletion of resources needed to maintain any given system, or they may result in the crystallization of new foci of resources and orientations, which in turn may seek to create a new institutional system.

These contradictions and conflicts and the events leading to different processes of change are also closely linked to the relations between any given institutional system and its "external" environment. Each institutional system is especially sensitive, in terms of dependence on resources and maintenance of its own boundaries, to certain aspects of its relations to its environment.

Thus the very nature of the crystallization of institutional systems creates the possibility that "antisystems," groups with negative (passive or active) orientations toward the premises of the system, will develop within them. While the nature and strength of such antisystems may vary in different institutional systems (i.e., religious, political) and in different societies and while these systems may often remain latent for very long periods of time, they may also constitute important foci of change under propitious conditions.

Some of these antisystems can be viewed as temporary "reversals" by various lower groups of the dominant values of the given system and as attempts to uphold, at least on certain occasions, a different value scheme (60). Others may have wider and more continuous organizational tendencies. Both can, under certain conditions, serve as starting points for processes of institutional change.

The existence of such contradictions or conflicts among the different institutional spheres and among different groups does not, of course, preclude the possibility that the system will maintain its boundaries more or less continuously, through a hierarchy of norms and an accommodation or partial insulation of different subsystems, and that a definite order and stable relations among the system's parts will persist. But the possibility of conflict and potential change is always present, rooted in the various process of crystallization and maintenance of institutional systems, and the direction and occurrence of change depend heavily on the nature of this process (61). Just as the predilection for change is necessarily built into any institutional system, so the direction and scope of change are not random but depend on the nature of the system generating the change, on its values, norms, and organizations, on the various internal forces operating within it, and on the external forces to which it is especially sensitive because of its systemic properties. These various forces naturally differ between different institutional spheres and between different societies, but the very sensitivity of these forces and the tendency to change are inherent in all of them.

Approaches to Comparative Analyses of Institutionalization

Most of the preceding discussion has been limited to the analysis of processes of institutionalization and of crystallization of various institutional norms and frameworks. It has not dealt, as yet, except by implication, with problems of *comparative* analysis, that is, with the problem of the extent and the ways to which it is possible and profitable to *compare* the institutional frameworks of different societies, and not only to compare the general characteristic *processes* of crystallization of institutions but also to compare the types of institutional norms and frameworks that exist and become crystallized in different societies.

In the history of the social sciences, many attempts to construct such types have been made. In most of these attempts, one can discern two major starting points for such comparisons. One is the construction of types of institutions according to the levels of "complexity" of any given institutional setting. In more recent analytic terms this approach can be reformulated according to the extent of differentiation and "specialization" of different institutional spheres.*

Another basic approach to comparative typology—found especially

---

* Thus, for instance, a comparative analysis of political institutions may start with the classification of different types of political systems according to (a) the development, to some extent, of special political roles and organization, or, in other words, the development of a distinct political-institutional sphere, (b) the development of a specific political group or ruling class, and (c) the extent of complexity of the political struggle and the process and scope of political activity in the society. By this is meant, first, the areas of social life and the social groups affected by the activities of central political organs and dependent on those activities for the maintenance of their own solidarity and organization and, second, the extent of participation by these groups in political activities. Similar attempts at classification can, of course, be attempted with regard to all other institutional spheres (62).

in the works of Max Weber and in many of the anthropological works on kinship—is based not so much on the extent of differentiation of specialization of various institutional spheres, but rather on the different types of major value orientations or integrative (and exchange) mechanisms which regulate one or several institutional spheres. Thus most of the "traditional" anthropological studies dealing with kinship attempt to specify the focal points of the jural and normative specifications of different kinship and descent organizations, be they matrilineal or patrilineal, organized in unilineal or bilineal descent groups, and so forth.

Similarly, Levi-Strauss and Leach's approach to comparative structural analysis implies that different societies—and their concrete analysis has, until now, been mostly limited to primitive and caste societies—can be analyzed in terms of the combination between the different integrative or regulative principles which, according to their view, are inherent in the nature of the major institutional system, be it kinship, language, politics, or economics (63).

Weber's numerous comparative analyses have placed great emphasis on the types of integrative orientations and mechanisms that tend to develop in different institutional spheres at various stages of their development. Thus, to give only a few examples, his analyses in the sociology of religion have emphasized the major type of different value orientations which may develop at any given stage of religious differentiation and which may serve as a starting point for the formation of new religious orientations and organizations (64). Similarly his analysis of the major forms of legitimation has emphasized a similar aspect in the political field. But in the analysis of the economic and political spheres, he stressed mostly the various types of integrative mechanisms and organizations—whether they were bureaucracy, party organization, or various types of market systems which might arise at any given stage of economic or political development. In most of these studies there is greater emphasis on various integrative principles or orientations and organizations than on a comparative analysis of different mechanisms of exchange and regulation, a subject which is still very much before us.

In recent times perhaps the most important example of the comparative approach can be found in Parsons' seminal paper on the different types of systems of stratification in modern societies (65).

Here, as is well known, he attempts to analyze the system of stratification of various (especially modern) societies in terms of their respective value orientations and in terms of the institutional derivation of such orientations.

These two major approaches to the construction of types of societies are closely connected with the two major aspects of our model of processes of institutionalization. The first criterion, that of differentiation or specialization, indicates the extent and nature of the development of the basic characteristics, of different institutional and cultural spheres, of the extent to which their respective positions become differentiated from one another and their resources released from mutual ascriptive bonds. The greater such differentiations, the more complex the various regulative and integrative problems, and the greater the readiness of different groups or categories of people within the societies to invest some of these resources in diverse types of exchange—whether in exchange with different types of major institutional resources or in exchange for organizational and norm-setting leadership. The second criterion, that of variegated integrative orientations and criteria, is closely related to the different types of norms of exchange and to the major types of mechanisms of regulation and exchange which tend to develop in societies.

The Feasibility of Comparative Analysis

Needless to say, the exact specification of such types depends greatly on the particular interests of the student. Such specification may include broad types of institutional frameworks (the major types of political, economic, or religious systems) or the analysis of special organizational features or any specific type of institution or what we have called partial institutions (66).

But the basic problem in comparative studies is not whether it is possible to construct such types according to any relevant criteria but whether it is at all worthwhile to do so. The major test of worthiness is not only the extent to which such types with common characteristics can be discerned among various societies—something which may be, to no small extent, a matter of definition. The more important test of the worthiness of such analysis is, first, whether common features delineate characteristics which are important for the understanding of the working of these types—as special, institutionalized systems, with boundary-maintenance and systemic problems of their own which differ from those of other systems. Second, such a test is greatly dependent on the degree to which it is possible to discern both the societal conditions common to different societies under which each type of institutional system develops and becomes crystallized and the conditions of their change and transformation.

Some skepticism has recently been voiced about the extent to which such comparison is of any value beyond the range of societies with close cultural and geographical ties (67). Another criticism is that most of the hitherto analyzed studies give us only "empirical generalizations," and not laws that predict relations between such general concepts as "reciprocity," "solidarity," and the like (68). But, with regard to all these questions, the proof of the pudding is, of course, in the eating—it is only through attempts at the construction of such types, at different levels of abstraction, that the limits of the usefulness of the comparative approach and the possibility of subsuming these types under general laws can be discerned.

Several recent works at different levels of analysis—those on overall types of institutional systems (political, economic, religious) or on various partial institutions or various partial types of organization—seem to indicate that the possibility of such comparative analysis implicit in both Weber's and Durkheim's works is certainly feasible, even though it is, as yet, far from being achieved (69).

The Analysis of Covariability of Institutional Spheres

These varied researches of different types of institutional systems throw some light on a few of the most important problems of institutional analysis in general and comparative analysis in particular. One such problem is that of the extent of independent variation of different institutional spheres when coalescing in the same society (70). The other is the problem of direction of institutional and societal change.

On a concrete level, the major question in the first problem is whether, for instance, any special type of economic institution always goes together with a particular type of political-religious institution, and vice versa, or whether there exists a great or perhaps limitless variablity in the possibility of such correlations. Although no attempt at a full-scale comparison of such variability, even for any single broad type of society, has been attempted since the work of Hobhouse, Wheeler, and Ginsberg, the available evidence indicates that there does not exist a clear determination between different institutional and symbolic systems, but only certain mutual limitation. Thus, for instance a relatively great variety of political systems can coexist with a certain type of kinship economic organization. The unilineal descent groups can exist, it seems, together with centralized primitive kingdom or with patrimonial and conquest societies. Similarly, an economic system characterized by the prevalence of "barter," nonmonetary, markets can be found in centralized primitive monarchies and in certain patrimonial as well as feudal political systems.

On the other hand, this variety is not limitless. Thus it is very difficult to conceive of the coexistence of a unilineal descent group with a modern industrial setting or with a universalistic, centralized, bureaucratic, political system. It is also difficult to envisage the coexistence of, let us say, a patrimonial political system with a high level of economic market order.

How then can both of these variabilities and limitations be explained, and what are their implications for institutional analysis? The variability of each institutional system can be explained, to some extent, by the institution's specific orientation as manifest in the activities of the occupants of its most important positions, in its specific, structural, core problems and exigencies. The mutual limitation of variability in the interrelationship between different institutional spheres which can exist in any society is explained by the fact that each institutional sphere is dependent on others for various resources for its own effective functioning, that is, for the maintenance of its specific structural forms, activities, and rate-norms of exchange.

While the general types of such resources ("inputs" and "outputs") are necessarily the same in all societies, the specific types of resources of any *specific* institutional sphere vary greatly according to their own characteristics and problems. For instance, although all political systems are necessarily influenced by external exigencies and pressure, the special sensitivity of the centralized bureaucratic empires

(71) to such exigencies and pressures and to international economic fluctuations was shown to be rooted, first, in the great emphasis of their rulers on military and expansionist goals and, second, in the reliance of these rulers on various resources, the availability of which was dependent on international economic situations. The dangers of excessive taxation and inflation in these political systems were again rooted in the high expense of the implementation of the rulers' goals and in the great importance of various flexible resources for the implementation of these goals and for the general political position of the rulers of these empires.

Similarly, such resources can be provided by varied types of arrangements in other institutional spheres but not by all such types. Thus, taking again the centralized empires, we see that their rulers were in need of both "traditional" and more complex, differentiated political support and were dependent on both types. The rulers' traditional dependence on other parts of the social structure was manifest in their need to uphold their traditional legitimation and the traditional, unconditional political attitudes and identifications of many groups. On the other hand, the rulers' tendency toward political independence and autonomy made them dependent on types of resources which were not available through various ascriptive-traditional commitments and relations. The rulers were, as shown above, in need of more flexible support and resources which were not embedded in ascriptive-traditional groups, which were not committed for more or less fixed goals, and which could be used by them for the implementation of their varied goals according to their own political consideration (72).

The extent of the relative autonomy of each institutional sphere in relation to others probably does vary between different institutions and between situations. It is probable that the symbolic sphere usually exhibits a larger extent of autonomy than others. All of these problems have yet to be investigated in greater detail. Yet the existence of such variability does not mean that it is of no importance or consequence for the working or stabilizing of any society or of one of the "component" institutional systems.

As seen above, one of the major causes for changes in any institutional system is rooted in the differences in and possible conflicts between the orientations and activities of the institutional systems which coalesce in any situation. Hence, the degree of stability or instability of any given system necessarily varies according to the nature of the institutional arrangements of its "sister" systems and the ways in which their interrelations in any concrete setting influence overall adaptability to their environments.

To give a few examples, again from the centralized empires, various invasions, rebellions, and the famous "dynastic cycles" in China have not undermined the basic institutional structure of the Chinese Empire for a very long period of time (from the Han to the Ching). This fact can be understood if one remembers the Empire's geopolitical position, which made it to some extent relatively immune from the heavy impact of external forces, and the fact that the relative weakness of the aristocracy and the predominance of the gentry tended to enhance the position of the centralized rulers, and that the Confucian literati and bureaucracy, who constituted the backbone of the social and political structure and intervened between the central government and the major social strata, provided an indispensible framework of continuity and unity of the Empire. When we compare this Empire with the geopolitical exposure of the Byzantine Empire, with its strong sensitivity to invasions and international developments, its continuous struggle between the aristocracy and the free peasantry, or with the great importance of the autonomous religious and cultural groups in the Roman or Arabic Empires, we may understand the Chinese Empire's greater vulnerability to external pressures and their rulers' lack of ability to cope with the internal forces which developed within (73).

Comparative Analysis of Institutional Change: The Problems of Reappraisal of Evolutionary Perspectives in Institutional Analysis

These considerations, especially as they apply to the analysis of overall broad types of the major social institutions, bring the preceding analysis within the scope of the second problem mentioned above (i.e., the problem of the comparative study of social change). This second problem is closely related to the possibility of a reappraisal of the evolutionary perspective in comparative studies (74).

The main problem here is the extent to which such changes may be envisaged as crystallizing into developmental "stages"—a key concept in classical evolutionary thought. In the older evolutionary school, such stages were construed mostly in terms of "specialization" and "complexity." In recent works these stages are, to a large extent, replaced by the concept of "differentiation." This replacement is not merely semantic; it reflects an important theoretical advance in the study of society—an advance that greatly facilitates critical re-evaluation of the evolutionary perspective in the social sciences.

Differentiation is, like complexity or specialization, first of all a classificatory concept. It describes the ways through which the main social functions or the major institutional spheres of society become dissociated from one another, attached to specialized collectivities and roles, and organized into relatively specific and autonomous symbolic and organizational frameworks within the confines of the same institutionalized system. In broad evolutionary terms, such continuous differentiation has usually been conceived as a continuous development from the "ideal" type of the primitive society or band in which all the major roles are allocated on an ascriptive basis, and in which the division of labor is based primarily on family and kinship units (75). Development proceeds through various stages of specialization and differentiation.

The more differentiated and specialized institutional spheres become more interdependent and potentially complementary in their functioning within the same overall institutionalized system. But this very complementarity creates more difficult and complex problems of integration. The growing autonomy of each sphere of social activity and the concomitant growth of interdependence and mutual interpenetration among spheres pose more difficult problems for the "structural representatives" of each sphere, in crystallizing their own tendencies and potentialities and in regulating its normative and organizational relations with other spheres. And at every "advanced" level or stage of differentiation, the increased autonomy of each sphere creates more complex problems of integrating these specialized activities into one systemic framework. Continuous regulation of these more specialized units and of the flow of "free-floating" resources among them necessitates the institutionalization of certain symbolic, normative, and organizational patterns—written language, generalized legal systems, and various types of complex social organization—which evince, at each more complex level of differentiation, a greater scope of generalization. These patterns also necessitate the establishment and maintenance of more complex and variegated mechanisms of exchange.

How do the preceding considerations affect the possibility of reappraising the evolutionary perspective in sociological theory? Such a reappraisal is contingent on the explication of three major problems. First, the occurrence of changes that facilitate growing differentiation must be explained. Second, the conditions that ensure institutionalization of more differentiated systems must be understood, and, third, the possibility that parallel systems might develop within different societies should be evaluated. We are as yet far from any definitive answers to these questions, but we can at least point out some of the most important problems.

The passage of a given society from one stage of differentiation to another is contingent on the development within it of certain processes of change which create a degree of differentiation that cannot be contained within the pre-existing system. Growing differentiation and the consequent structural breakthroughs may take place through secular trend of differentiation, through the impact of one or a series of abrupt changes, or through both. These tendencies may be activated by the occupants of strategic roles within the major institutional spheres as they attempt to broaden the scope and develop the potentialities of their respective spheres. The extent to which these changes are institutionalized, and the concrete form they take in any given society necessarily depend on the basic institutional contours and premises of the pre-existing system, on its initial level of differentiation, and on the major conflicts and propensities for change within the system.

But the successful, orderly institutionalization of a new, more differentiated, social system is not a necessary outcome of every instance of social change or of increased social differentiation within a society. Moreover, the concrete contours of such institutionalization may greatly vary among different societies at similar or parallel stages of differentiation.

The growth of systemic sensitivity to a broader and more variegated environment, to new problems and exigencies, does not necessarily imply the development of the ability to deal with these problems, nor does it indicate the ways in which these problems may be solved. At any given level of differentiation, an institutional sphere may or may not achieve an adequate degree of integration, and the potentialities unfolded through the process of differentiation may be "wasted" (i.e., fail to become crystallized into an institutional structure).

The Variability of Responses to Structural Differentiation —And Their Causes

At any level of development, response to the problems created by the process of differentiation may take one of several forms. The most extreme outcome is failure to develop any adequate institutional solution to new problems arising from growing differentiation. Aside from biological extinction, the consequences may be total or partial disintegration of the system, a semiparasitic existence at the margin of another society, or total submersion within another society. A less extreme type of response tends to lead to "regression" (i.e., to the institutionalization of less differentiated systems, less complicated and flexible patterns of exchange [76]). Many such regressive developments are only partial in the sense that within some parts of the new institutional structure some nuclei of more differentiated and creative orientations may survive or even develop. Sometimes, but certainly not always, these nuclei "store" entrepreneurial ability for possible— but not inevitable—future developments.

Another possibility, which perhaps overlaps with the last one but is not always identical with it, is the development of a social system in which the processes of differentiation and change go on relatively continuously in one part or sphere of a society without yet becoming fully integrated into a stable, wider framework. In such situations, a continuous process of unbalanced change may develop, resulting either in a breakdown of the existing institutional framework or in a relatively low level of integration (77).

A fourth, and perhaps the most diversified, type of response to growing differentiation consists of some structural solution which is, on the whole, congruent with the relevant problems of differentiation at a given stage. But within this broad type a wide variety of concrete institutional arrangements, of different concrete norms and rates of exchange, is possible. Such solutions usually have varied structural results and repercussions. Each denotes a different structure crystallized according to its own criteria and diverse modes of interpenetration of the major social spheres.

To illustrate this point again by examples from the great centralized empires (78), we see that, although the initial stages of socioeconomic differentiation were relatively similar in Byzantium, in the later (abbasid) Caliphate, and in post-Han China, each of these societies developed characteristics over all institutional structures. The Byzantine Empire became a highly militarized, politically oriented system, whereas, in the Caliphate, a theocratic structure developed, based on continuous attempts to institutionalize a new type of universalistic politico-religious community. China developed a centralized system based, at the center, on the power of the Emperor and the bureaucracy and, at the local level, on the relative predominance of the gentry. The selective channels of the examination and the recruitment of the literati were the major mechanisms integrating the local and central levels.

The great range of institutional and integrative contours of different societies arriving at similar levels or stages of differentiation may be due to several varying, yet interconnected, reasons. First, societies arrive at the same level of differentiation through different historical paths and through a variety of concrete structural forms, and, hence, subsequent structural forms may vary greatly. One aspect of the variety among these antecedents of any stage is of special interest. Within many relatively undifferentiated societies exist enclaves of much more differentiated and specialized activities, especially in the economic and cultural spheres. Cities function in many societies not only as administrative or cultural centers but very often as distinct entities, to some extent separated from the rest of society and evincing a much higher degree of differentiation and specialization in the cultural or economic field. Similarly, monasteries and monastic orders, sects and academies, and very often special ethnic and religious minorities and special religious-tribal federations may, to some extent, be detached from the wider society and evince, at least in certain spheres, a higher degree of differentation. In modern times, various political, religious, and intellectual sects and elites may constitute important enclaves of differentiated activities. Such enclaves may be very important sources of innovation within a society. Their presence or absence in any "antecedent" stage may greatly influence the scope and nature of the different integrative solutions that may be institutionalized at a later stage of differentiation.

Third, the variability of institutional contours at the same level of differentiation also stems from differences among the elites which become predominant in any case. Elites may develop either in different institutional spheres or in the same sphere but with different ideologies and orientations of action. Some of them may be more influential than others in establishing the detailed contours of the new institutional system.

Elites and Differentiation in Processes of Institutional Change

These considerations indicate that we must discard the assumption underlying, even if only implicitly, many studies of comparative institutions in general and of modernization in particular—that the conditions giving rise to structural differentiation and to "structural sensitivity" to a greater range of problems, also create the capacity to solve these problems or to determine the nature of such solutions.

The crucial problem is the presence or absence, in one or several institutional spheres, of an active group of special "entrepreneurs," an elite, able to offer solutions to the new range of problems. Among modern sociologists, Weber came closest to recognizing this problem when he stressed that the creation of new institutional structures depends heavily on the "push" given by various "charismatic" groups or personalities, and that the routinization of charisma is critical for the crystallization and continuation of new institutional structure. The development of such charismatic personalities or groups constitutes perhaps the closest social analogy to "mutation." The degree of these personalities' ability to forge a viable way may be an important factor in the process of survival, or "selection," of different social systems.

As yet we know little about the specific conditions, as distinct from the more general trend to structural differentiation, that facilitate the rise of new elites and that influence the nature of their basic orientations, on the one hand, and the relations of the elites with broader strata, on the other. Available indications are, however, that factors beyond the general trend to differentiation are important. For example, various special enclaves, such as sects, monasteries, sectarian intellectual groups, or scientific communities, play an important role in the formation of such elites. And a number of recent studies have indicated the importance of certain familial, ideological, and educational orientations and institutions (79).

Within this context the whole problem of the extent to which institutional patterns are crystallized not through "independent invention" within a society but through diffusion from other societies should be re-examined. Cases of diffusion might be partially due to the successful "importation," by entrepreneurial groups on the margins of a given society, of acceptable solutions to latent problems or needs within that society.

Thus, at any given level of differentiation, the crystallization of different institutional orders is shaped by the interaction between the broader structural features of the major institutional spheres and the development of elites or entrepreneurs in some of the institutional spheres of that society, in some of its enclaves, or even in other societies with which that society is in some way connected.

The variability in the concrete components of such interaction helps to explain the great—but not limitless—variety of structural and integrative forms that may be institutionalized at any given level of differentiation. It indicates also that while different societies may arrive at broadly similar stages of evolution in terms of the differentiation of the major institutional and symbolic spheres, the concrete institutional contours developed at each step, as well as the possible outcomes of such institutionalization in terms of further development, breakdown, regression, or stagnation, may greatly differ among them.

The study of the interaction between processes of differentiation and the formation and activities of different elites may help to explain systematically the possibilities of institutionalization of integrative principles of different institutional settings, norms and rates of exchange, and concrete structures at a given level of societal differentiation. It also constitutes a useful way of combining the analysis of the general characteristics of processes of institutionalization, as setting up of different frameworks and norms of exchange with comparative analysis of different types of institutions and of processes of institutional change.

NOTES

1. For a general discussion of these developments see, for instance, Howard Becker and Harry Elmer Barnes, with the assistance of Emile Benoit-Smullyan and others, *Social Thought from Lore to Science*, second edition, Washington: Harren Press, 1952.

2. For one of the best expositions of the limitations of the classical approach by one of the most prominent contemporary sociologists steeped in this very approach, see Morris Ginsberg, *On the Diversity of Morals*, London: William Heinemann Ltd., 1956, Chapters 11 and 12.

3. Leonard T. Hobhouse, G. C. Wheeler, and Morris Ginsberg, *The Material Culture and Social Institutions of the Simpler Peoples: An Essay in Correlation*, London: London School of Economics, 1915.

4. Emile Durkheim, *Les Règles de la méthode sociologique*, second edition, Paris: Presses universitaires de France, 1957. Marcel Mauss, *The Gift: Forms and Functions of Exchange in Archaic Societies*, translated by Ian Cunnison, London: Cohen and West, 1954. Marcel Mauss, *Sociologie et anthropologie*, Paris: Presses universitaires de France, 1950. Marcel Mauss, "Etude de morphologie societe," *L'Année sociologique*, Vol. IX, 1906. Robert Hertz, *Mélanges de sociologie et folklore*, Paris: F. Alcan, 1928. Alexandre Moret and Georges Davy, *From Tribe to Empire: Social Organization among Primitives and in the Ancient East*, London: K. Paul, Trench, Trubner and Co., 1926. Georges Davy, *La Foi jurée*, Paris: F. Alcan, 1922. Robert N. Bellah, "Durkheim and History," *American Sociological Review*, Vol. XXIV, August 1959, pp. 447–461; Vol. XXV, June 1960, p. 406.

5. Max Weber, *The Protestant Ethic and the Spirit of Capitalism*, translated by Talcott Parsons, London: G. Allen and Unwin, 1950. Max Weber, *Gesammelte Aufsätze zur Religions Soziologie*, Tubingen: J. C. B. Mohr, 1920, 3 Vols. Max Weber, *Wirtschaft und Gesellschaft*, Tubingen: J. C. B. Mohr, 1922. Reinhard Bendix, *Max Weber: An Intellectual Portrait*, Garden City, N.Y.: Doubleday, 1960.

6. For one of the best analyses of developments in American Sociology,

see Edward A. Shils, *The Present State of American Sociology*, Glencoe, Ill.: The Free Press, 1948. For other surveys of developments, especially in the period between the wars, see the various chapters on sociology in different countries in Georges Gurvitch and Wilbert E. Moore (editors), *Twentieth Century Sociology*, New York: The Philosophical Library, 1945.

7. A. R. Radcliffe-Brown, *The Andaman Islanders*, Glencoe, Ill.: The Free Press, 1958. A. R. Radcliffe-Brown, *Structure and Function in Primitive Societies*, London: Cohen and West, 1952. B. Malinowski, *Argonauts of Western Pacific*, London: Routledge and Sons, 1922. B. Malinowski, "Culture," *Encyclopedia of the Social Sciences*, New York: Macmillan, 1931, pp. 621–645. For a critical survey of developments in social anthropology, see E. E. Evans-Pritchard, *Social Anthropology*, London: Cohen and West, 1951.

8. Talcott Parsons, *The Social System*, Glencoe, Ill.: The Free Press, 1951. Talcott Parsons and Edward A. Shils (editors), *Towards a General Theory of Action*, Cambridge, Mass.: Harvard University Press, 1951. Robert Merton, *Social Theory and Social Structure*, Glencoe, Ill.: The Free Press, 1957. Kingsley Davis, *Human Society*, New York: Macmillan, 1950. Marion J. Levy, Jr., *The Structure of Society*, Princeton: Princeton University Press, 1952 (mimeographed).

9. M. Fortes and E. E. Evans-Pritchard (editors), *African Political Systems*, London: Oxford University Press, 1950. A. R. Radcliffe-Brown and D. Forde (editors), *African Systems of Kinship and Marriage*, London: Oxford University Press, 1950.

10. George P. Murdock, *Social Structure*, New York: Macmillan, 1949.

11. For general surveys of the Culture and Personality school, see J. M. Whiting, "The Cross Cultural Method," in G. Lindzey (editor), *Handbook of Social Psychology*, Reading, Mass.: Addison-Wesley, 1954, Vol. I, pp. 523–532, and Melford E. Spiro, "An Overview and a Suggested Reorientation," in Francis L. K. Hsu (editor), *Psychological and Anthropological Approaches to Culture and Personality*, Homewood, Ill.: Dorsey Press, 1961, pp. 459–493.

12. Marion J. Levy, Jr. and Lloyd A. Fallers, "The Family: Some Comparative Considerations," *American Anthropologist*, Vol. LXI, August 1959, pp. 547–551.

13. Talcott Parsons, "The Incest Taboo in Relation to Social Structure and the Socialization of the Child," *British Journal of Sociology*, Vol. V, 1954, pp. 101–117.

14. George C. Homans and David M. Schneider, *Marriage, Authority and Final Causes: A Study of Unilateral Cross-Cousin Marriage*, Glencoe, Ill..: The Free Press, 1955, reprinted in George C. Homans, *Sentiments and Activities: Essays in Social Science*, New York: The Free Press of Glencoe, 1962, and reviewed by Robert H. Lowie in *American Anthropologist*, Vol. LVIII, 1956, p. 1144, and by Rodney Needham, *American Journal of Sociology*, Vol. LXII, 1956, pp. 107–108.

15. The most extreme criticism of this work can be found in Rodney Needham, *Structure and Sentiment: A Test Case in Social Anthropology*, Chicago: University of Chicago Press, 1962. A more balanced and favorable evaluation can be found in J. Berting and H. Philippsen, "Solidarity, Stratification, and Sentiments," *Bijdragen tot de Taal, Land-en Volkenkunde*, Deel 116, 1960, pp. 55–81.

16. S. N. Eisenstadt, "African Age Groups," *Africa*, 1954 (Chapter 4 in this book). S. N. Eisenstadt, *From Generation to Generation*, Glencoe, Ill.: The Free Press, 1956.

17. Weber, *Wirtschaft und Gesellschaft*, *op. cit.*, especially pp. 126 ff., 158–165, and 758–778. For a more recent exposition, see Peter M. Blau, *Bureaucracy in Modern Society*, New York: Random House, 1956, pp. 28–34.

18. Arthur L. Stinchombe, "Bureaucratic and Craft Administration of Production: A Comparative Study," *Administrative Science Quarterly*, Vol. IV, 1959, pp. 168–187. Stanley H. Udy, Jr., " 'Bureaucracy' and 'Rationality' in Weber's Organization Theory," *American Sociological Review*, Vol. XXIV, No. 6, 1959, pp. 791–795. Paul M. Harrison, *Authority and Power in the Free Church Tradition*, Princeton: Princeton University Press, 1959. S. N. Eisenstadt, "Bureaucracy and Bureaucratization," *Current Sociology*, Vol. 7, No. 2, 1958 (included in Chapter 7 of this book).

19. Stinchombe, *loc. cit.*

20. These terms are adopted from James D. Thompson and A. Thuden, "Strategies, Structures, and Processes of Organizational Decision," in James D. Thompson et al. (editors), *Comparative Studies in Administration*, Pittsburgh: University of Pittsburgh Press, 1959, pp. 195–217.

21. See, for instance, the review of Needham, *Structure and Sentiment*, *loc. cit.*, by F. G. Lounsbury in *American Anthropologist*, Vol. LXIV, 1962, pp. 1302–1310, and Berting and Philippsen, *loc. cit.*

22. Levi-Strauss gives a similar distinction in *Anthropologie sociale*,

Annuaire du Collège de France, 1960, Paris: Collège de France, 1961, p. 199.

23. See Whiting, *loc. cit.,* Hsu, *loc. cit.,* and also Anthony F. Wallace, *Culture and Personality,* New York: Random House, 1962.

24. These new tendencies in folklore studies are summarized in two recent articles: Richard M. Dorson, "Current Folklore Themes," *Current Anthropology,* Vol. IV, No. 1, February 1963, pp. 93–113, and J. L. Fischer, "The Sociopsychological Analysis of Folktales," *Current Anthropology,* Vol. IV, No. 3, June 1963, pp. 235–295. Among the more recent analytical works on folklore, see: Melville J. and Frances S. Herskovitz, *Dahomean Narrative: A Cross-Cultural Analysis,* Evanston, Ill.: Northwestern University Press, 1958; C. Levi-Strauss, "The Structural Study of Myth," *Journal of American Folklore,* Vol. LXVIII, October 1955, pp. 428–444. C. Levi-Strauss, *"La Geste" d'asdival, annuaire, 1958–9,* Ecole partique des hautes études, section des sciences religieuses, pp. 2–43, Paris: Presses universitaires de France, 1958. Lucien Sebag, "La Geste de kasewat," *L'Homme,* T. III, No. 2, 1963, pp. 22–77.

25. John M. Whiting, Richard Kluckhohn, and Albert Anthony, "The Functions of Male Initiation Ceremonies at Puberty," in Eleanor E. Maccoby, Theodore M. Newcomb, and Eugene L. Hartley (editors), *Readings in Social Psychology,* third edition, New York: Henry Holt and Co., 1958, pp. 359–371.

26. Bruno Bettelheim, *Symbolic Wounds: Puberty Rites and the Envious Male,* Glencoe, Ill.: The Free Press, 1954. S. N. Eisenstadt, "Archetypal Patterns of Youth," in *Daedalus,* Vol. IX, No. 1, 1962, and in Eric H. Erikson (editor), *Youth: Change and Challenge,* New York: Basic Books, 1963.

27. See Frank W. Young, "The Functions of Male Initiation Ceremonies: A Cross-Cultural Test of an Alternative Hypothesis," "Comment" by John M. Whiting and "Rejoiner" by Young, *American Journal of Sociology,* Vol. LXVII, No. 4, January 1962, pp. 379–396.

28. Dorson, *loc. cit.* Also see Roger Caillois, *Man, Play, and Games,* translated from French by Meyer Barash, New York: The Free Press of Glencoe, 1961, where human play is analyzed into its basic component parts and illustrations are given of their crystallizations in different societies. See also Roger Caillois, *Quatre essais de sociologie contemporaine,* Paris: Oliver Perrin Editeur, 1951.

29. One of the most interesting analyses of these problems can be found

in some of the literature on the language of children by Iona and Peter Opie, *The Lore and Language of School Children,* London: Oxford University Press, 1961. Also see Peter Opie, "The Tentacles of Tradition," *New Society,* Vol. 2, No. 50, September 12, 1963, pp. 9–12, for a more general discussion of the changeability and variability by different forms of folklore and myths. See also Edmund Leach, "Anthropological Aspects of Language: Animal Categories and Verbal Abuse," in Eric H. Lenmemberg (editor), *New Direction in the Study of Language,* Cambridge, Mass.: Technology Press, 1964, pp. 23–63; Leach, "Beasts and Triangles," *New Society,* No. 12, October 4, 1962, pp. 21–23; Leach, "Barbar's Civilisation Analyzed," *New Society,* No. 12, December 20, 1962, pp. 16–17.

30. For one of the best attempts at such morphological analysis of myths in more complex societies, see C. Levi-Strauss, "L'Analyse morphologique des contes Russes," *International Journal of Slavic Linguistics and Politics,* Vol. III, 1960, pp. 122–149. In some of the older works of the French "schools," a few of the problems of such variability and changeability were taken up. See, for instance, S. Czarnowski, "Warunki Spojeczne Zmiany Znaczenia Symbolow Literackich," in *Dziela,* T. I, Warszwa: Polska Akademia Nauk, 1956, pp. 197–213; *Ibid.,* T. III; Caillois, *Man, Play, and Games, loc. cit.,* and C. Levi-Strauss, "Where Does Father Christmas Come From?" *New Society,* No. 64, December 19, 1963, pp. 6–9.

31. This point is stressed by Needham:

"Symbolic classifications vary, not only, as is obvious, with the general complexity of culture of which they are part, but—in the field which traditionally and in this context especially occupies us—with the type of descent system. Very roughly, we may say that in cognatic societies the relation of symbolic to social order may be insignificant or minimal, while in lineal descent systems the relation may commonly be discerned in a range of particulars, or in certain institutions, but not usually in any comprehensive manner. But in one type of lineal descent system, viz., that based on prescriptive alliance, there is a remarkable concordance of structure between symbolic forms and the social organization: they are aspects of one conceptual order."

See Rodney Needham, "A Structural Analysis of Aimol Society," *Bijdragen, op. cit.,* p. 105.

32. See George C. Homans, "Social Behavior as Exchange," in Homans, *Sentiments and Activities, loc. cit.,* and George C. Homans, *Social Behavior, Its Elementary Forms,* New York: Harcourt, Brace and World, 1961.

33. C. Levi-Strauss, *Anthropologie structurale*, Paris: Plon, 1958.
C. Levi-Strauss, *La Pensee sauvage*, Paris: Plon, 1962.

34. Homans, *Social Behavior*, *op. cit.*, pp. 292–293.

35. *Ibid.*, Chapter 13.

36. C. Levi-Strauss, "The Bear and the Barber," *The Journal of the Royal Anthropological Institute of Great Britain and Ireland*, Vol. 93, Part I, January–June 1963.

37. Edmund R. Leach, *Rethinking Anthropology*, London: University of London, The Athlone Press, 1961, pp. 101–103.

38. See p. 216 of W. Davenport, "Social Organization," in Bernard J. Siegel (editor), *Biennial Review of Anthropology, 1963*, Stanford: Stanford University Press, 1963, pp. 178–276.

39. See especially Talcott Parsons and Neil J. Smelser, *Economy and Society: A Study in the Integration of Economics and Social Theory*, London: Routledge and Kegan Paul, 1956.

40. P. Ricoeur, "Structure et hermeneutique," *Esprit*, 31ᵉ Année, No. 322, November 1963, pp. 596–626, and C. Levi-Strauss, "Reponses a quelques questions," *ibid.*, pp. 628–683. And also Raphael Pividal, "Signification et position de l'oeuvre de Levi-Strauss," *Annales*, 19 Année, No. 6, November–December 1964, pp. 1087–1100.

41. Similar criticisms have been made from different points of view about the applications of linguistic models to the study of society. David F. Aberle, "The Influence of Linguistics on Early Culture and Personality Theory," in Gertrude E. Dole and Robert L. Carneiro (editors), *Essays in the Science of Culture, in Honor of Leslie A. White*, New York: Thomas Y. Crowell and Co., 1960, pp. 1–30. Andre G. Haudricourt and Georges Granai, "Linguistique et sociologie," *Cahiers internationaux de sociologie*, No. XIX, 1955, pp. 114–129. A similar analytical point is made by D. M. Schneider in his review of Leach's *Rethinking Anthropology*, in *American Anthropologist*, Vol. LXIV, 1962, pp. 833–843, when he points out that Leach, in his emphasis on the "exchange" functions of institutional alliance, forgets to stress the basic function of marriage in regulating procreative sexual relations.

42. Parsons and Smelser, *loc. cit.*

43. Levi-Strauss has stressed the "duality" and "complementarity" of "reciprocity" and "hierarchy" as two basic modes of social regulation, see C. Levi-Strauss, "Reciprocity and Hierarchy," *American Anthropologist*,

Vol. XLVI, 1944, pp. 266–268, and in a fuller way, *Anthropologie structurale*, Paris: Plon, 1958, p. 342 ff.

44. The capacity to articulate collective goals as a distinct aspect of groups is stressed in John W. Thibaut and Harold H. Kelley, *The Social Psychology of Groups*, New York: John Wiley and Sons, 1959, especially Chapter 14. For an interesting case study on the "emergent" quality of articulation of group goals in relation to individual needs, see Charles K. Warriner, "Public Opinion and Collective Action: Formation of a Waterhead District," *Administrative Science Quarterly*, Vol. 6, 1961–1962, pp. 332–359.

45. S. N. Eisenstadt, Dov Weintraub, and Nina Toren, *Analysis of Processes of Role-Change: A Proposed Conceptual Framework*, final research report, Jerusalem: Department of Sociology, The Hebrew University, 1963, Technical Note No. 7, Contract No. AFGI (052)–480 (mimeographed).

46. The following is a brief statement of an approach now being worked out in greater detail by the author and E. Schild.

47. Caillois, *Man, Play, and Games, loc. cit.* Many studies of so-called "escapist" functions of some types of mass communications should be reviewed in this framework. See S. N. Eisenstadt, "Studies in Reference Group Behaviour: I. Reference Norms and the Social Structure," *Human Relations*, Vol. VII, No. 2, May 1954, pp. 191–216 (reprinted as Chapter 12 in this book). See also, Hugh Daziel Duncan, *Communication and Social Order*, Totowa, N.J.: The Bedminster Press, 1962.

48. In this context the work of Jean Piaget may be of special significance, especially insofar as it deals with the interrelation of the development of different types of "mental" structures and emphasizes the relation to the "moral" (precontractual) and more instrumental orientations and cognitive structures.

49. See Edward Shils, "Primordial, Personal, Sacred and Civil Ties," *British Journal of Sociology*, Vol. VIII, No. 2, June 1957, pp. 130–146, and Shils, "Centre and Periphery" in *The Logic of Personal Knowledge*, Essays presented to Michael Polanyi, London: Routledge and Kegan Paul, 1961, pp. 47–131.

50. See S. N. Eisenstadt, "Anthropological Studies of Complex Societies," *Current Anthropology*, Vol. II, No. 3, 1961 (reprinted as Chapter 3 in this book).

51. Frenc Merei, "Groups Leadership and Institutionalization," *Human Relations,* Vol. II, No. 1, January 1949, pp. 23–39.

52. C. Levi-Strauss, *Totemism,* Boston: Beacon Press, 1963, p. 103 ff.

53. Thibaut and Kelley, *loc. cit.* James G. March and Herbert A. Simon (with the collaboration of Harold Guetzkow), *Organizations,* New York: John Wiley and Sons, 1958.

54. Merton, *op. cit.,* especially Chapters VIII and IX, and Chapter 17 in this book.

55. See Chapter 10 in this book.

56. Eisenstadt, Weintraub, and Toren, *loc. cit.*

57. On this problem, see Edmund R. Leach, *Pul Elya: A Village in Ceylon,* Cambridge: Cambridge University Press, 1961. Edmund R. Leach, "The Sinhalese of the Dry Zone of Northern Ceylon," in George P. Murdock (editor), *Social Structure in Southeast Asia,* Chicago: Quadrangle Press, 1960, especially pp. 125–126. George P. Murdock, "Cognative Form of Social Organization," *ibid.,* especially pp. 12–15. Also see Meyer Fortes, "Introduction," in Meyer Fortes (editor), *Marriage in Tribal Societies,* Cambridge Papers in Social Anthropology, Cambridge: Cambridge University Press, 1962, pp. 1–13, where an attempt is made to explain institutional (marriage) behavior in terms akin to "game theory." Fortes' analysis seems to me to be more fruitful than those of Leach and Murdock because it takes more fully into account that individual choices, which indeed influence the crystallization of social structure, are in themselves not entirely limited by the structural positions of the "chooser" and by the specific structural or institutional problems they confront in a given situation. See also Fortes' earlier analysis in "Time and Social Structure: An Ashanti Case-Study," in Meyer Fortes (editor), *Social Structure,* studies presented to A. R. Radcliffe-Brown, Oxford: Clarendon Press, 1949, pp. 55–85; Alan Howard, "Land, Activity, Systems and Decision Making Models in Rotuman," *Ethnology,* Vol. II, No. 4, October 1963, pp. 407–441.

58. See, for instance, David F. Aberle, Urie Bronfenbrenner, Ackhard H. Hess, Daniel R. Miller, David M. Schneider, and James N. Spulber, "The Incest Taboo and the Mating Patterns of Animals," *American Anthropologist,* Vol. LXV, April 1963, pp. 253–265. See also Allan D. Coult, "Unconscious Inference and Cultural Origins," *American Anthropologist,* Vol. LXV, February 1963, pp. 32–36. For a good illustration of some assumptions about the "causes" or explanations of institutions which

are implicit in many works, see the very interesting essay by Pierre Claspres "Exchange et pouvoir: philosophie de chefferie indienne," *L'Homme*, T. II, 1964, pp. 51–66. In this essay, which constitutes an application of Levi-Strauss' method, the existence of basic structural characteristics of a given social order is taken for granted and used as an explanation for the concrete institutional setting, instead of being seen as a problem itself. For a more cautious approach, similar in some ways to the one proposed here, see George K. Zollschan and Robert Perucci, "Social Stability and Social Process: An Initial Presentation of Relevant Categories," in George K. Zollschan and Walter Hirsch (editors), *Explorations in Social Change,* Boston: Houghton Mifflin Co., 1964, pp. 99–125.

59. This is adapted from the conclusions of S. N. Eisenstadt, "Institutionalization and Change," *American Sociological Review*, Vol. 29, No. 2, April 1964.

60. W. F. Wertheim, "La Société et les conflits entre systèmes de valeurs," *Cahiers internationaux de sociologie*, Vol. XXVIII, January–June 1960, pp. 33–46.

61. Some parallel indications can be found in Thomas F. O'Dea, "Sociological Dilemmas, Five Paradoxes of Institutionalization," in Edward A. Tiryakian (editor), *Sociological Theory, Values, and Socio-Cultural Change, Essays in Honor of Pitirim A. Sorokin*, New York: The Free Press of Glencoe, 1963, pp. 71–91. See also Neil J. Smelser, *Theory of Collective Behavior*, New York: The Free Press of Glencoe, 1963, especially Chapters II and III; Alvin W. Gouldner, "Reciprocity and Autonomy in Functional Theory," in Llewellyn Gross (editor), *Symposium on Sociological Theory*, Evanston, Ill.: Row, Peterson, 1959, pp. 241–271; Gideon Sjoberg, "Contradictory Functional Requirements and Social Systems," *The Journal of Conflict Resolution*, Vol. IV, June 1960, pp. 198–258.

62. See, in greater detail, S. N. Eisenstadt, *The Political Systems of Empires*, New York: The Free Press of Glencoe, 1963, Chapter I.

63. Levi-Strauss, *Anthropologie structurale, op. cit.*, pp. 317–351, and Marc Gaboriau, "Anthropologie structurale et histoire," *Esprit, op. cit.*, pp. 579–594.

It might be worthwhile to give here a quotation from Leach, *Rethinking Anthropology, op. cit.*, pp. 103–104.

" . . . Finally there emerges from this discussion an important principle of method. If anthropologists are to arrive at any valid principles of social organization, the general method must be comparative. But the original comparative method, exemplified in its most overwhelming form by the work of Frazer, rested on the comparison of cultural traits. Under the impact of functionalism, which insisted upon the analysis of whole cultural systems, this type of comparative method fell into disrepute simply because it appeared to be an impossibility—the body of data that would be involved in an adequate comparison was altogether too vast.

Since 1930, however, Radcliffe-Brown and his followers have had some success in applying a different kind of comparison, namely, that of whole political systems. In a comparative method of this latter kind cultural features are to a large extent ignored, and the 'things' which are compared are really simplified models of the societies under discussion, as observed from a particular point of view. In practice 'the particular point of view' has been that of kinship, and despite the very great value of works such as *Social Organization of Australian Tribes, Social Anthropology of North American Tribes, African Political Systems* the generalizations that emerge are liable to be distorted on this account.

My own argument, in which to a great extent I follow Levi-Strauss, is that the comparison of models rather than of 'whole cultures' is a necessary and valid method—indeed I would go much further in such abstraction than has usually been the case with the followers of Radcliffe-Brown. But at the same time I would insist that the comparison must always take into account the whole range of institutional dimensions with which the anthropologist normally has to deal and must start from a concrete reality—a local group of people—rather than from an abstract reality—such as the concept of lineage or the notion of kinship system."

64. Max Weber, *The Sociology of Religion,* translated by Ephraim Fischoff, Boston: Beacon Press, 1963, especially Chapters IV, X, and XI.

65. Talcott Parsons, "A Revised Analytical Approach to the Theory of Social Stratification," in Reinhard Bendix and Seymour M. Lipset (editors), *Class, Status, and Power: A Reader in Social Stratification,* Glencoe, Ill.: The Free Press, 1953, pp. 92–129.

66. Reinhard Bendix, "Concepts and Generalizations in Comparative Sociological Studies," *American Sociological Review,* Vol. 28, No. 4, August 1963, pp. 532–539.

67. Evans-Pritchard, *Social Anthropology, op. cit.,* especially Chapter V, and in greater detail E. E. Evans-Pritchard, *The Comparative Method in Social Anthropology,* Hobhouse Memorial Lecture, London: Athlone Press, 1963. Most of Evans-Pritchard's criticisms are directed against

the "simple" naive correlational method (i.e., the correlation of simple cultural traits or items) and do not deal fully with the comparative analysis of different institutional spheres or subsystems.

68. See Rodney Needham, "Introduction," in Emile Durkheim and Marcel Mauss, *Primitive Classification*, London: Cohen and West, 1963, pp. XLI ff.

69. Some pertinent reviews of relevant material can be found in Clifford C. Geertz, "Studies in Peasant Life," in Siegel, *Biennial Review of Anthropology, 1961*, Stanford: Stanford University Press, 1962, pp. 1–42; A. Kimball Romney, "Social Organization," *ibid.*, pp. 215–250; W. Davenport, "Social Organization," in Siegel, *Biennial Review of Anthropology, 1963*, Stanford: Stanford University Press, pp. 178–228.

70. On this problem see also S. F. Nadel, *The Foundations of Social Anthropology*, London: Cohen and West, 1951, Chapter IX, pp. 222–256.

71. S. N. Eisenstadt, *The Political Systems of Empires*, loc. cit. S. N. Eisenstadt, "Processes of Change and Institutionalization of the Political Systems of Centralized Empires," in George K. Zollschan and Walter Hirsch (editors), *Explorations in Social Change*, Boston: Houghton Mifflin Co., 1964, pp. 432–452.

72. *Ibid.*

73. *Ibid.*

74. In greater detail see S. N. Eisenstadt, "Social Change, Differentiation and Evolution," *American Sociological Review*, Vol. 29, No. 3, June 1964.

75. For a recent discussion of primitive societies from an evolutionary point of view, see Elman R. Service, *Primitive Social Organization: An Evolutionary Perspective*, New York: Random House, 1962.

76. Alexander A. Gerschenkorn, *Economic Backwardness in Historical Perspective: A Book of Essays*, Cambridge, Mass.: The Belknap Press of Harvard University, 1962, Chapter VIII. S. N. Eisenstadt, "Breakdowns of Modernization," *Economic Development and Cultural Change*, Vol. XII, No. 4, July 1964, pp. 365–367.

77. S. N. Eisenstadt, *Essays on the Sociological Aspects of Political and Economic Development*, The Hague: Mouton and Co., 1960.

78. Eisenstadt, *The Political Systems of Empires*, loc. cit.

79. David C. McClelland, *The Achieving Society*, Princeton, N.J.: Van Nostrand, 1961. David C. McClelland, "National Character and Economic Growth in Turkey and Iran," in Lucian W. Pye (editor),

Communication and Political Development, Princeton, N.J.: Princeton University Press, 1963, pp. 152–182. Everett E. Hagen, *On the Theory of Social Change: How Economic Growth Begins,* Homewood, Ill.: The Dorsey Press, 1962, especially Chapter X. Clifford Geertz, "Social Change and Economic Modernization in Two Indonesian Towns" in Hagen, *ibid.,* pp. 385–421.

Chapter 2

The Relations between Sociological Theory and Anthropological Research

I

In the first part of this paper I shall consider the place of "ultimate values" in systematic sociological theory and in the second the bearing of these considerations on anthropological research. It should be emphasized from the beginning that in my view there is no theoretical distinction between sociology and social anthropology.

The problem of values in systematic sociological theory has been most adequately analyzed by T. Parsons, and what follows is mainly based on his analysis (1). Ultimate values constitute an inherent analytical element of the "structure of social action," the analysis of which starts with the ends-means schema. The structure of social action is composed of institutional roles which determine the activities of the members of a social system as oriented toward various ends and toward one another. These roles define the specific ends which

Reprinted from *Man*, No. 161, November 1949. This essay, which has special reference to the problem of values, was given as a talk at the Graduate Seminar of Anthropology at the London School of Economics. It is intended as a cursory review of some of the problems and not as a detailed examination of the literature mentioned, nor is this literature representative of anthropological research in general. The author is indebted to Professor R. Firth and the members of the seminar for many interesting criticisms and valuable suggestions.

individuals pursue and the appropriate means by which these ends may be achieved. Ultimate values enter into this schema as ends of actions, either as "empirical" or as "transcendental" ends. Theoretical consideration of empirical facts has shown that the various ends existing in a social system are not random but usually constitute interconnected systems. Different social systems have different value systems. The ultimate values have, however, also a specific bearing on the structure and systems of means, of which the three principal means— the technological, the economic, and the political—may be connected in various ways with the ends. This connection may be graded from "intrinsically rational" to "symbolic" (either religious or magical). Various characteristics of the ultimate values may be of great signifi- cance in determining the nature of this connection or the relationship between ends and means. Many transcendental ends—existing in all social systems—entail, by definition, symbolic activities, whereas many empirical ends necessitate the pursuit of rational activities. "Valuational attitudes" also constitute inherent elements in the social orientation of the members of a system toward one another, espe- cially when the social relationships are seen—in a way—as ends in themselves, without being oriented toward any specific end. This is true of those relations in which the communal (*gemeinschaftliche*) as opposed to the "societal" (*gesellschaftliche*) element prevails.

This short analysis indicates the main modes in which ultimate ends bear on the structure of social actions, of which they are a basic element. What has been said so far indicates a phenomenological analysis based, as in the work of Parsons, on the development of social theory in its relation to social research. It means that these elements, values, and valuational attitudes exist in every social system; conse- quently, the basic nature of social systems is defined so as to include these elements. The most important problem for us, however, is the implications of this analysis for sociological research. Any such impli- cation can be based only on the assumption that the valuational ele- ment is an independent variable, amenable to empirical investigation of its relations to other elements of the social system, and this assump- tion has been proved correct by many leading writers on sociology— Pareto, Durkheim, Weber, Mannheim, etc. It would perhaps be worth while to indicate some of the most important theoretical prob- lems arising from these assumptions so that we may better understand the relation between the present state of anthropological research and the central theoretical problems of systematic sociology, i.e., those problems which are logically deducible from the phenomenological analysis of the different variables (analytical elements) inherent in a system of social action.

II

The most general problem is that of the stability of social systems, a problem which under different guises dominated sociological thought from the beginning (2). This problem may be stated in the following way: Under what conditions does a social system perpetuate itself (i.e., do the individuals participating in it continue to perform the roles inherent in this system)? By "conditions" I mean the appropriate combination of the various elements of the system, both those mentioned above and the "psychological" elements of individual gratification and participation. If we assume that values constitute an independent variable, we may reformulate the problem from a somewhat different aspect in this way: What are the specific properties of a system of values which are necessary for the stability of the social system of which the given system of values forms a part? This statement of the problem emphasizes the importance of analysis of "systems" of values. I do not mean by this, however, logically coherent systems of beliefs and propositions, but essentially a systematic juxtaposition of various basic aspects of values bearing on social action. It is well known that there are many relatively stable systems of values which are not logically coherent. What, then, are the necessary gratifications to the individuals as actors in the social ends-means schema, without which no system can endure, and what are the relations of various aspects of value systems to these gratifications? Such aspects as promises of future gratifications and increasing deference, the relations of these promises to various empirical actions, the ensurance of security, and the various definitions of security, etc.—all these may prove to be essential for the solution of our problems. I wish to emphasize the great importance, in this context, of the word "relation," because it indicates the basic connection between the systems of values and the structure of social action. These relations may be stated here in the most general terms, as follows: A system of values which legitimizes transcendentally a social situation which is deprivational for some members of the system cannot be stable unless it contains also some values, connected (situationally) with the former, the pursuit of which defines some concrete situations as gratifying (e.g., providing social and emotional security and promises of more distant gratification) to the same members. Or: Any system of values which can be realized only by a long chain of intermediary means actions must, to be stable, define the various social situations in which these means are pursued as a continuous series from the point of view of the "social perspective" (to use Kurt Lewin's terminology) of the participating actors. If these hypotheses should prove correct, we could analyze various concrete systems of values as approximating in different degrees to these conditions.

This is, of course, a very inadequate formulation; to be adequate it should have been stated in terms of *all* the elements of the system of action. This indicates that the complete solution of this problem would involve the analysis of all the possible aspects of values which bear upon various elements of social action (and vice versa). It is superfluous to say that such a complete analysis does not exist today; it is doubtful whether it will ever be achieved, and its achievement would mean, in a way, the logical and empirical closure of systematic sociology. We may, however, strive after this unattainable goal.

This brings us to the second problem, or rather set of problems. It may be stated as the degrees of existential compatibility between different concrete systems of values and various "systems" of other elements of social structure. In this category would be included such problems as: Which systems of values are compatible with a subsistence economy, a feudal system, etc.? Or, conversely: Which political (economical, etc.) systems are compatible with a given system of values? Compatibility is, of course, a matter of degree and the various social tensions or situations of *anomie*, resulting from different degrees of incompatibility, would constitute a part of the research. In fact the totally stable system is an ideal construct.

This set of problems is of a lower degree of abstraction than the former; this does not mean, however, that the two are not connected. If we assume sociology to be a unitary scientific discipline and not a loosely connected set of descriptions and problems, then it is obvious that the problems of the lower degree of abstraction should be derived from and included among those of a higher degree. In other words, if we formulate a hypothesis that a specific system of values is compatible (or incompatible) with a specific economic or political system, this hypothesis will be scientifically valid only if we can demonstrate that the relations between these two concrete systems are indices of the general conditions of the stability (or instability) of social systems. This may be obvious, but it entails various very important consequences for research, especially in the problems of descriptive classification, which we shall discuss briefly later on.

The last set of problems concerns the conditions under which various systems of values change and new systems emerge. These problems should, of course, also be included under the universal propositions of systematic sociology. In this way only can we approach something similar to causal generalizations.

III

I now discuss briefly the relation of anthropological research in its present state to these problems of theoretical sociology.

One of the most important contributions of anthropology was toward the elucidation of the basic, phenomenological analysis. In the works of Radcliffe-Brown and Malinowski the problems of ultimate transcendental ends and symbolic means and their relations to social action were most thoroughly analyzed, and the present stage of elaboration of the basic system of social action is greatly indebted to them. Almost all works of their disciples are based on this analysis and demonstrate it in particular concrete settings. A further very important contribution of recent anthropological research lies in the second set of problems, i.e., the relative compatibility of various systems of elements of social action. Most of the so-called "comparative studies" come in here. Among these I would especially mention Malinowski and Firth's studies of primitive economics, Evans-Pritchard's studies of witchcraft and magic, such volumes as *African Political Systems*, Nadel's *Black Byzantium*, Mead and Kardiner's studies in comparative psychology, and many others of which the above mentioned are the prototypes. Most anthropological literature contains very valuable material for such comparative studies, although of different range, specificity, and abstraction. I think that most of these researches compare very favorably with most of the specifically "sociological" researches, because their systematic treatment is based on the basic categories and elements of social action. The main problem which they pose before us is their relation to the first sets of problems —the general conditions of stability of social systems. Although anthropological materials provide a mine for the elucidation of these problems, until lately, they were scarcely utilized in this way (3).

This unclarified relation to the basic problem of social theory is most clearly seen in the various classificatory and descriptive terms used in anthropological literature. It is difficult to understand the relations between many of these terms. They are usually relevant to the specific problem investigated. This is, of course, entirely legitimate and inherent in the nature of scientific work. The difficulty is that the problems themselves are often theoretically unrelated, i.e., are not derived from central problems of sociological theory and are not included under universal propositions. We can always try to find this relation, but only in a roundabout way, and then we always meet the stumbling-block of discrete systems of terminology. In other words, we lack universal indices.

This lack is especially felt in the classification of ultimate values. While solid foundations do not exist in the field of social (political, economic, kinship, etc.) organization, the theoretical classification of various aspects of systems of values bearing on social action is still in its very beginning. I think that most of these beginnings hardly approach the last important development of systematic theory in this field, namely Max Weber's system of religious sociology. Anthropological material abounds in data on cults, magical observances, ethical principles, etc. These data are not always classified in coherent systems related to systems of other elements of social action and derived from central problems. There is often some confusion between descriptive and theoretical problems. Though we have many accurate and detailed descriptions of religions of conquerors, it would be difficult to find adequate comparative material for the solution of such a problem as: What are the aspects of systems of value of conquerors which are necessary for their fusion in one comparatively stable social system with the conquered? The pooling of the necessary materials, from anthropological and historic sources, would at least necessitate a great deal of retranslating of terms. Lately, however, many important advances have been made (4) which at least indicate the possibility of a more unified sociological systematic research.

As for the third range of problems—namely the changes in systems of values, etc.—anthropological literature, especially that on acculturation and culture change, abounds of course in relevant data. The theoretical situation is, however, similar to that discussed above. Once more we lack interrelated sets of problems derivable from universal propositions. The present world range of sociological and anthropological researches does make possible a very wide and comprehensive scheme of comparative research, oriented toward the solution of such problems. Some of these problems may be thus formulated: What aspects of religious and ethical systems have special attraction for people undergoing processes of economic detribalization and being drawn into fields of capitalistic colonial enterprise? Under what conditions do secular values and communal symbols emerge and maintain themselves? What are the characteristics of communal value attitudes emerging under given conditions of culture contact (the given conditions should include the respective ends and means and the degree of possibility of their realization in the given situation)? The more general problem may be stated in this way: What aspects of values as ultimate ends and as symbols of communal attitudes are more likely to emerge in various situations of *anomie* concurrent to processes of culture contact?

Many of the culture-contact studies provide us with relevant material, well organized in the basic categories of social action. The next step should be their explicit inclusion under general problems and propositions.

One could find many reasons for this relative incongruence of anthropological researches in the academic history of anthropology. One does, however, sometimes meet a more important justification: It is said that the main task of the anthropologist is to find and describe new data. I think this argument is already outworn, although it emphasizes the technical difficulty of a balance between the presentation of new material and theoretical formulations. From the theoretical point of view the argument is not valid. Even the most innocent piece of description is imbued with classifications implying conceptual schemes. It is much better to make these schemes explicit and to submit them to a rigorous scientific discipline.

What has been said should not be interpreted as shunning small problems and aspiring to a rash and quick solution of universal problems by magical devices. I have tried only to point some possibilities for a more unified and systematic approach in research.

NOTES

1. Talcott Parsons, "The Place of Ultimate Values in Social Theory," *International Journal of Ethics*, Vol. XLV, 1935. *The Structure of Social Action*, New York: McGraw-Hill, 1937. "The Role of Ideas in Social Action," *American Sociological Review*, Vol. III, 1940.

2. It has in fact been shown that sociological inquiry arose under the stimulus of the instability of modern society.

3. Very important beginnings in this field are Kluckhohn and Hallowell's works on the problems of anxiety and magic, etc.

4. A very important redirection is contained in E. E. Evans-Pritchard's, *Witchcraft, Oracles and Magic among the Azande*, Oxford: The Clarendon Press, 1937. See on this Max Gluckman, "The Logic of African Science and Witchcraft," in *Rhodes-Livingstone Institute Journal*, Vol. I, June 1944. See also the very important number of *Africa* on Witchcraft, Vol. VIII, No. 4, October 1935.

Chapter 3

Anthropological Studies of Complex Societies

I

The purpose of this paper is to analyze some of the problems arising out of the application of the methods and approaches developed in social anthropology to the study of more complex societies—whether "historical" or modern societies or parts thereof. We hope to show both the contributions and limitations of some of the concepts and tools of social anthropology in the study of more complex societies. We shall not deal here with general anthropological approaches to such studies (Mandelbaum 1956), nor with such general concepts as "culture" or such general problem areas as "culture and personality," which have developed mainly in anthropology. Nor shall we be concerned with studies of tribal or peasant communities by anthropologists or other scientists who have employed concepts and techniques common to many behavioral sciences.

We shall, rather, concern ourselves mainly with the potential contributions to the study of complex societies that have been made by

Reprinted from *Current Anthropology*, Vol. 2, No. 3, June 1961. I am indebted to Dr. J. Ben-David, Prof. M. Gluckman, Prof. D. G. Mandelbaum, Dr. J. Talmon-Garber, and Dr. A. Weingrod for reading the draft of this paper and commenting on it in great detail. The work on this paper has been facilitated by a free grant-in-aid from the Behavioral Sciences Division of the Ford Foundation.

one specific branch of anthropology, namely, social anthropology as it
has been developed in England (for a general survey see Evans-
Pritchard 1951; Beattie 1956) and to a smaller extent in U.S. and
France (Eggan 1950, 1957; Levi-Strauss 1959). These social-
anthropological studies have developed a distinct theoretical model
which deals with a certain order of problems or of social phenomena.
The development of this model, and of specific rigorous techniques of
field work, accounts for the great impact of social-anthropological studies on our general understanding of the working of human societies.
Out of the application of this model to the study of complex societies,
several problems have emerged which may be of great interest from
the point of view of general anthropological and sociological theory.

What, then, is this model, and to what kinds of problems is it applied (1)?

Its most distinctive characteristic is that it combines the description
and analysis of social behavior, group structure, and institutional settings into one set of interrelated concepts and analytical tools.

On the purely descriptive level, social anthropologists usually deal
with observed patterns of social behavior of individuals in different
social situations and in different groups, and with statements by individuals of norms which would be appropriate to such different situations (Beattie 1959, and, in more detail, Emmett 1958). However,
this description of social behavior is, at the same time, a study and
analysis of the structure of groups and societies.

This type of analysis is achieved through the great emphasis on social behavior as related to various norms which are said to be operative in the social structure. Most of the social-anthropological descriptions of social behavior are studies of the ways in which major norms
found in these societies are upheld by individuals, of the interrelations
between these different norms, and of the ways in which these norms
influence and regulate the relations between different groups in
society.

Thus we find in these studies, for instance, a great emphasis on the
institutional norms directing and restricting individual behavior in
the major fields of social life—marriage and family life, economic, political or ritual organizations. Second, and in close connection, we find
an analysis of the consequences of upholding such norms for social

and intergroup relations within a given society—e.g., how the marriage of a man from group A to a woman from group B affects relations between these groups. Different institutions and the social activities of individuals are analyzed, not only within their own spheres, but also as links between several groups in the society, and as contributing to the continuity of these groups and of the society in general. Thus, for instance, the rules that govern economic or political activities are explained in terms of the "needs" of these groups and of the society as a whole. (For a very pertinent formulation see Fortes 1953, and Gluckman 1956.) Thus, various norms and the patterns of behavior which uphold them are seen mostly as institutional directives upholding the interrelations among different groups in the society and the continuity of the society as a whole. In this way, most anthropological studies combine in one basic model the analysis of social behavior, institutional norms, groups, and societies. They explain patterns of social behavior through analysis of group structure, institutions, and "total" societies.

Neither this model nor the various studies which have been guided by it have usually dealt with the problems of the kinds of interrelationships between such different variables as social behavior or group and institutional structure—i.e., which variables are dominant or influential in general or in various typical situations. Rather, it has been assumed that all these variables are always very closely interrelated through their contributions to one another, and to the society as a whole through what are usually called their "functions." (For a partial exception, see Worsley 1956.)

II

This model necessarily raises the question of the mechanisms through which the interrelationships among these variables are maintained. Few examinations of the functional analysis in anthropology (the very type of analysis which stresses interrelationships among different parts of society or culture) have dealt explicitly with this problem (for a partial exception, see Beattie 1959). However, social anthropological studies contain certain postulates, analyses, and descriptions of such mechanisms, and these analyses constitute one of the basic contributions of social anthropology to the study of human society and social processes.

1. The first such mechanism is the interaction of the *same* persons or groups in different situations, an interaction which makes their mutual commitments in one situation or group greatly influence their behavior in others. In the societies studied by anthropologists, the existence of such close relations between the same people in different groups and situations constitutes a very important mechanism regulating social behavior, on the one hand, and intergroup relations on the other (see Barnes 1959). Gluckman has advanced his analysis by showing how close interrelations among the same people in different situations create conflicts between them, and how those conflicts, which seem disruptive, in reality help enhance the solidarity and functioning of the groups and the society through the crosscutting of interests among the same people participating in these varying situations (Gluckman 1956).

2. The second mechanism is the specific type of relation between what may be called "culture" (or rather, values) and ritual symbols, on the one hand, and social relations, on the other hand. Values and symbols are analyzed by social anthropologists on two levels. An analysis of these various beliefs and cultural symbols as systems in their own right has recently developed (Forde 1954; Evans-Pritchard 1956). More common, however, is the analysis of values and symbols in relation to various fields of social activity—family, kinship, or political activities. Whereas anthropologists have usually recognized the autonomy and distinctiveness of the sphere of values, they have also emphasized the direct relevance of primordial or sacred symbols and rituals for most types of social activities in the societies they study, and the interlocking of these activities in a way which assures that they are given "meaning" in terms of these symbols and values.

3. The third mechanism, stressed by most of these studies, is the continuous interrelation in these societies of different types of social activities in most groups and situations. Ritual, jural, contractual, and political activities—clearly distinguishable from one another (Evans-Pritchard 1954)—are seen as interwoven in most of the situations and groups of these societies, so that each activity directly depends on, articulates with, and is upheld in terms of, the others. Epstein (1954)

has put this point thus: "Most of the major social functions are fulfilled by the same small groups."

These three mechanisms are found to regulate the direct interrelation of social behavior to group and institutional structure, in most parts of the societies studied by social anthropologists. Analytically, the most important aspect of these mechanisms is that they are embedded in the very structure of the major social situations and major groups in the society and are not organized in special distinct ways or orders. Perhaps this characteristic explains why the social-anthropological model did not explicate the interrrelationship of its different variables and could use as analytical tools concepts *describing* the structure of various groups.

III

These assumptions guided the work of social anthropologists for at least the first two decades, even though there were frequent differences of emphasis among individual anthropologists and among the many trends which developed within social anthropology.

It is beyond the province of this paper to analyze or even summarize all the contributions of social anthropologists, or to discuss the many specific hypotheses they have developed in the application of this model to the different societies which they study. But it would be worthwhile to indicate briefly some major trends or emphases which have developed in social anthropology—without attempting to provide a full list. All of them have stemmed, in a way, from the basic common assumption of their model, but each has emphasized different aspects of it.

1. There are numerous well-known studies—which need not be enumerated here—that emphasize the analysis of "total" tribal societies and very often are identical with analysis of wide ecological communities (e.g., Evans-Pritchard 1940; Krige 1943).

2. There are studies which are also concerned with total societies but tend to concentrate on the analysis of these societies from the point of view of one major institutional sphere—marriage and kinship, political structure, or stratification (e.g., Fortes 1945, 1949*b*; Kuper 1947).

3. An interesting offshoot of the second trend are the general studies of certain institutional groups, which are basic constitutents of any human society, and some of their basic characteristics. The studies of the domestic group, edited by Goody (1958) and brilliantly summarized by Fortes (1958), are the best recent examples of this development. We find here an attempt to analyze what may be called the natural life histories and life cycles of its basic constituents—parents, children, and kin.

4. Studies of a great variety of customs and institutional arrangements in terms of their relation to various aspects of social structure and to the functioning of the major natural groups of the society as well as of the society as a whole constitute the fourth trend. Examples of this approach include the analysis of joking relations and of the "mother's brother" (Radcliffe-Brown 1952; Goody 1959), and the studies of witchcraft, blood-brotherhood (Evans-Pritchard 1933; Eisenstadt 1956), magical hair (Leach 1958), and many other types of institutional devices or customs. These studies have often taught us to look beyond the manifest content of these usages and have sharpened our understanding of the "meaning" of various customs and types of social and human interaction, such as commensuality or even sexual relations, in terms of primordial images and sacred symbols.

5. There are various comparative studies and analyses which have developed within the fold of social anthropological studies, the best examples of which are *African Political Systems* (Fortes and Evans-Pritchard 1940), *African Systems of Kinship and Marriage* (Radcliffe-Brown and Forde 1950), *African Worlds* (Forde 1954), and *Tribes Without Rulers* (Middleton and Tait 1958).

The societies studied by social anthropologists evinced great variation in the exact structure of different natural groups and institutions —territorial, kinship, and age groups, and various types of associations or political groupings. But in spite of these variations, anthropologists found that the close interrelationship between individual behavior, group structure, and institutional norms was always maintained by the mechanisms outlined above. It is true that anthropologists and sociologists are now beginning to doubt whether all of the social organization of these societies can be explained in such terms. Recently, it has been claimed that the absence of historical records in such societies and the two or three years that most anthropologists spent in the field "blinded" them to possibilities of change, of differentiation and variability of individual behavior, and of development of new group structures. It has also been claimed that the theoretical nature of their starting point may have biased anthropologists to emphasize those situations in which behavior was regulated by the mechanisms postulated by their model. Some of the most recent developments in social anthropology itself—for instance, Turner's (1957) study of Ndembu village life—illustrate certain of these short-comings. (Additional criticism can be found in Fortes 1949*a*, Gellner 1958, and Gluckman 1959*b* give a fuller analysis.) Without doubt, however, this model contributed to the analysis of the functioning of at least some aspects of the societies studied.

IV

Armed with these basic concepts and approaches, social anthropologists began to study other types of societies, both historical and contemporary (modern), applying their approach and the assumptions implicit in their model to understanding the working of these societies. These studies can, in principle, be divided into several distinct types or categories, broadly similar to those outlined above for more characteristic anthropological studies.

The first category comprises studies of ecological communities— mostly of peasant villages and other units that are similar to, but not identical with, those in tribal societies. The most important of these studies are Arensberg and Kimball (1948) on the Irish peasant, Frankenberg (1956) on football and politics in a Welsh village under the impact of industrialization, Pitt-Rivers (1954) on the structure of an Andalusian village and its place in Spanish society, Barnes' (1954) study of a Norwegian parish, Srinivas' (1952) work on the Coorgs of India, and some of the Indian village studies (e.g., Marriott 1955).

The second category comprises studies of one main type of "natural" or institutional group in complex societies, usually examined in relation to the wider institutional setting. Naturally enough, the most frequently studied institutional unit is the family and kinship unit, but studies of such institutional settings as economic and political structure can also be found. Within this category may be distinguished three main types of studies, which overlap to some extent. The first type of study, which deals with the internal structure of such groups, includes, Freedman's (1957) work on Chinese marriage in Singapore, and the studies of family and kinship structure in modern society by Young and Willmott (1957), Firth (editor) (1956), and Bott (1957).

The second type comprises studies which emphasize the interrelationships between these groups and the wider institutional settings of their societies. The best examples are Firth's (1946) study of Malay peasant economy, Freedman's (1958) work on the Chinese lineage organization, Miller's (1954) "Caste and Territory in Malabar," Mayer's (1960) *Caste and Kinship in Central India,* Bailey's (1957) study of the interrelation between modern economy and caste in an Indian village, and Gullick's work on Malayan political structure (1958). These studies aim at understanding the operation of groups with which anthropologists were traditionally concerned—the peasant village, the lineage, the caste, or kinship unit—in more complex (but not yet modern) societies; to what extent they maintain their corporate identity; what functions such groups perform for their members in relation to the wider society; how the more general political or economic forces impinge on these units, as well as how these units are integrated within this wider institutional structure.

There are other studies which concentrate on the analysis of a specific form of "natural group" or institution within a complex society and attempt to explain its relation to various aspects of the broader social structure. Smith's (1956) study of the Negro family in British Guiana, which attempts to explain the general social conditions that facilitate the development and maintenance of the matrifocal system of domestic relations and household grouping in the Caribbean, is the most important work of this type.

It is worthwhile to note an interesting convergence of the social anthropological studies discussed here with the somewhat different anthropological tradition represented by Redfield's studies (1955, 1956) of the "Great" and "Little" Tradition and the mechanisms of transmission from the former to the latter. These studies were most explicitly focused on an analysis of the mechanisms connecting such "closed" units as village, family, or caste with the more central institutional system of relatively complex societies.

The third category comprises studies which attempt to analyze the "total" structure of relatively complex, but not modern, societies. The outstanding examples are Nadel's (1942) study of the Nupe and Leach's (1954) *Political Systems of Highland Burma*. Although Leach's work, as its title indicates, deals mainly with political institutions, it is really concerned with the analysis of the concept of "total" society so often used by social anthropologists.

A special category of anthropological studies of "complex" situations, which cuts across the classification used above, includes those dealing with tribal groups or subunits in situations of change under the impact of modern conditions. Examples are Gluckman's (1958) "Analysis of a Social Situation in Modern Zululand," Epstein's work (1958) on urban politics in Africa, Little's (1955) study of voluntary associations, Mitchell's (1956) description of the development of a particular dance among urbanized Africans, and Watson's (1958) study of the impact of a money economy on two African tribes. Stemming from earlier research on "detribalization," these studies have gradually focused on understanding the impact of processes of modernization on tribal structure and the reorganization of this structure in the new situations. They have also concentrated on the ways in which new types of groupings, such as urban association trade unions, tend to crystallize in these new settings.

In addition to these, we may also mention various studies in other fields—especially industrial sociology (Burns 1955; Bradney 1957 *a, b;* Gluckman 1956)—which deal with the nature of the personal and intergroup relations operative in modern industrial settings. These were influenced by some of the approaches to social anthropology, even if they do not apply the social-anthropological "model" in the same consistent way as those cited above.

V

The ultimate aim of these studies is to show how social behavior in complex societies is also determined by the groups and institutions in which individuals participate, and how such behavior contributes to the functioning of different groups in the society and of the society as a whole. But the facts which they have to explain, and the problems they have to analyze, differ somewhat from those which are usually dealt with in anthropological studies. It is true that most of these studies deal with types of groups or institutional units which are, to some extent, similar to those studied in tribal societies, yet these units are not as self-contained or closely overlapping as in the latter. In the complex societies, the units interlock into wider settings in ways different from those of primitive societies. It is this interlocking that creates many problems for the understanding of patterns of social behavior and their relation to group and institutional structure in these societies.

Thus Barnes, in his study of the Norwegian parish (1954), faced not only the problem of explaining the ways in which the members of the parish are interrelated, or in which different committees in the parish work, and how they are related to the kinship, working, and class structure *within* the parish. He had also to deal, first, with the problem and the possibility that members of the same general social category will be able to choose different roles and participate in different associations, second, with the development of new groups and types of activities under the direct impact of outside forces, and, third, with the relations of all these groups to whatever may be called the overall Norwegian society.

Pitt-Rivers (1954) was dealing not only with the internal structure of his Andalusian village but also with the problem of *differential* impact of the central forces on the activities of different individuals, belonging perhaps to similar groups in the village.

In addition to investigating internal village politics, the importance of football and various ceremonies in the framework of these politics, and their impact on the unity of the village, Frankenberg (1956) is also concerned, even if indirectly, with the impact of wider forces, such as those of industrialization, on the internal cohesion and continuity of the village.

In his study of Chinese lineage organization, Freedman (1958) is interested not only in the internal structure of the lineages, but also in the ways these interacted with the overall political structure and with the imperial bureaucracy; how they were able to adjust themselves to this bureaucratic, nonkinship organization, and what functions they performed within that wider context.

In his work on Chinese marriage and kinship in Singapore (1957),

Freedman is dealing not only with the internal structure of the major kinship and marriage groups as relatively "closed" units, but also with the problem of the breaking up of these corporate units and of the influence of the "anonymity" of Singapore city life on marriage and kinship behavior, on these units, and on family and kinship relations.

Nadel (1942) was the most explicit in focusing his interest on the overall working of a complex society without concentrating exclusively on any small subunit. Throughout his study of the Nupe, he was interested in describing and analyzing how different local groups and different types of ordered social activities—economic, ritual, educational, and political—are related to the working of the overall Nupe society, and how they create the specific Nupe identity.

Little (1955), Epstein (1958), Banton (1957), Mitchell (1956), and Watson (1958) deal not only with the processes of change and disintegration of tribal units, but also with the ways in which these groups are transformed in a new setting—how entirely new groupings are formed; how conflicts that do not necessarily contribute to the equilibrium of the encompassing society may develop between various types of groups, and how these groups compete for the allegiance of the same persons, or influence their behavior in contradictory ways. Thus, they also had to explain the ways in which the people they studied were drawn into social frameworks and influenced by social forces of processes transcending the major natural ecological groups (e.g., wider occupational, economic, or political forces), and how the behavior of people in these groups, and their choices of roles, is related not only to their immediate group allegiances, but also to wider social forces, some of which did not originate within the "old setting."

VI

Thus, the problems which were either implicit or explicit in the data presented by social-anthropological studies of complex societies are of a somewhat different order from those involved in the study of tribal societies.

The main difference could be found in the fact that patterns of social behavior in these complex societies were influenced and regulated by many forces and factors which were not embedded in the structure of the major social groups or their interrelations (e.g., they were not regulated by the interrelations between domestic, kinship, and local groups), and which were not necessarily borne out by people interlocked in the same situations and groups.

This difference has, necessarily, posed problems of the nature of the mechanisms regulating the relations between various types of social behavior, group structure, and the wider institutional structure of a society. How, then, did the social anthropologists approach these problems, and what were their contributions toward their solution?

It is here that the most important contributions of these studies can be found. These contributions were primarily made through the discovery of several distinct ways in which the regulative mechanisms found in tribal societies operate in more complex societies as well, and the discovery that in the latter societies such mechanisms are not necessarily always embedded in concrete groups.

These studies discovered and analyzed various areas of life in complex societies in which very close interrelations exist between people participating in different situations and groups, and these interrelations regulate their social behavior in different groups. The importance of this type of mechanism in corporate groups and institutional fields within complex societies is best exemplified by Freedman's *Lineage Organization in South-eastern China* (1958) and Miller's work on caste in Malabar (1954). Young and Willmott's (1957), Firth's (editor) (1956), and Bott's (1957) studies of family and kinship in London, although more limited in scope, also show the importance of these close personal interrelationships in the structure of at least some corporate groups and institutional settings of modern societies. Such close relations were also often found to be operative in many informal social relations not organized in corporate groups or institutional frameworks.

Barnes (1959), in his review of Frankenberg, has aptly summarized the importance of this mechanism in some ecological units of modern societies:

In Pentrediwaith the same core of individuals interact with one another in many different situations, and their behavior in one context is influenced by their commitments in many others. This is true of almost all communities in the primitive world, and it is a necessary condition for using the slow and indirect field techniques specific to social anthropology (cf. my [i.e. Barnes'] "Class and Committees in a Norwegian Island Parish," *Human Relations*, Vol. VII, 1954: 44). The ethnographer, with his traditional distrust of direct questions and questionnaires, and his desire to do more than test a bald hypothesis or establish a correlation, is particularly well qualified to observe these lengthy and devious sequences of social action and to analyze them in sociological terms. As social anthropologists we have long held, either as an article of faith or a matter of academic political expediency, that we have valuable contributions to make in the study of advanced societies, but it has not always been clear, either to us or to our colleagues in other disciplines, precisely what these special contributions are. At one time the answer might have been "community studies." But some of these, although informative, appear not to differ greatly from the studies carried out by geographers and other social scientists with background and objectives different from those of social anthropologists; other studies under this rubric are merely social surveys of populations which may or may not form a community. Frankenberg's pioneering study of Pentrediwaith shows that one useful contribution which social anthropology can make to the investigation of advanced societies is the observation and analysis of politics round the village pump.

The anthropological studies cited here have also found that direct relations between primordial symbols and values and various social relations are operative in several areas of complex societies. Such direct relations have been found, first, as Young and Willmott's (1957) studies have especially shown, in the field of family and kinship relations. Second, anthropologists have found such relations to be very important in an individual's attitude toward his community or society. Third, they have also been found to be operative in more diffuse social areas and relations. (For a more general evaluation of the place of primordial images in social organization see Shils 1957.)

Thus, various studies (Burns 1955; Bradney 1957 *a, b;* Lupton and Cunnison 1957) have shown that in many areas of life in complex modern societies there develop, between persons participating in some common formal frameworks, different types of relations, which are regulated either by their intrrelations in other situations or by such primordial images and symbols as "manhood," "human trust," and "age," or sharing of common "fate," "neighborhood," or "goodness." Such relations and symbols have been found to cut across hierarchical relations—or any other formal relations and groups—and also to influence patterns of friendship and diffuse personal relations. Such relations may often be more forceful than the formal role definitions and may greatly influence the performance of these formal roles. Similarly, some of these studies indicate that different usages—such as commensuality, certain types of friendship, name-giving, gift-giving, plays, and matches—in many of the complex and even modern societies, are often imbued with various primordial meanings and values (Gluckman 1959a). These studies, for instance, deal with the ways in which many conflicts develop between the European industrial forces and the more traditional tribal forces, and how some continuous— although not necessarily stable—interrelations develop between these opposing forces.

While some results of these studies may seem identical with those of various researchers on "primary groups," in fact they often go beyond the latter, or at least complement them. Most research on primary groups has pointed out mainly the importance, within formal organizations, of so-called solidary and face-to-face relationships. Social-anthropological studies, however, have gone—potentially at least —beyond these findings. They show how these formal frameworks not only are imbued with solidary relations, but are also greatly influenced by the same individual's *personal* commitment in other settings and situations and are invested with certain primordial meanings which are prior to the formal role definition as well as to the various solidary relations, and may even, to some extent, regulate them.

Several of those studies attempt to apply some of the more general principles of social organization, and especially of the interlocking of potentially conflicting forces in one "total field," to more complex situations or societies. Thus, several studies of "colonial" situations in Africa, or of certain aspects of industrial structure (Gluckman 1956, 1958), have sharpened our awareness of how conflicting forces may sometimes become interrelated in a single "total field," and of how different concrete patterns of behavior in such a field can be explained in terms of the relative strength of these conflicting forces within their common framework, and of the functioning of this framework.

Significantly, of all the regulative mechanisms found in the social-anthropological model, only one—that of the coexistence of different types (jural, political, economic, ritual, etc.) of social activities in the same groups or situation—was not found to be of great importance in the complex societies.

VII

The studies which have shown how various mechanisms operate in complex societies have also contributed, explicitly or implicitly, to the analysis of two other aspects of these societies.

First, the delineation of the areas and relations in complex societies in which the types of relations postulated by the model of social anthropology still persist points more sharply to those structural points at which these cease to operate and are replaced by more general and differentiated mechanisms of ordering social activities—even if, as we shall see, specific anthropological concepts do not help very much in the analysis of these mechanisms.

To give only one example, we may quote Freedman on some of the problems of Chinese marriage in Singapore (1957):

Marriage in Singapore no longer represents a link between two corporate groups, and Chinese in the Colony, while preferring to seek their brides within their own dialect-groups (and often within narrower divisions of these groups), treat a new marriage as a matter concerning only the bridal couple and their fellow household-members. Members of clan associations may be invited to wedding celebrations but they have little direct interest in the marriage formed. The structure of Singapore Chinese society makes for the individualization of marriage. This process is also sanctioned by modernist ideas which derive their potency from their connection with twentieth century nationalism.

In the disruption of marriage the inadequacy of Chinese mechanisms to control domestic disputes is very apparent. Since there are no clearly defined larger kinship units, no local units in urban life, and no formal structure of authority in the rural settlements, marital quarrels tend frequently to find their way to persons and bodies standing outside the limits of Chinese society itself. It is at this point that "government," in the shape of the magistrates' courts and the Department of Social Welfare, intervenes decisively in Chinese life. Divorce among Chinese in the Colony is essentially a matter of mutual agreement between the spouses. However, just as in the formation of marriage the anonymity of Singapore life allows uncertainties in the status of men and women as husbands and wives, so in the disruption of marriage there are sometimes ambiguities which arise when wives leave their husbands (or are abandoned by them) and "follow," as the Chinese say, "other men."

Among studies, of a somewhat different anthropological tradition, that bear on this problem, we should again mention Redfield's (1955, 1956) work on peasant societies. He has described the differentiation of the different orders of social relations in the more complex societies, but at the same time has given us a feeling for the interrelation of these different orders—even if he did not explain this analytically.

Second, these studies can contribute much to the development of comparative studies. This can best be seen in Smith's work on the West Indian Negro family (1956). Smith attempts to give an exact specification of those broader mechanisms of societal differentiation which impinge on and influence the structure and functioning of family organization. Thus, he argues that the husband's role in the matrifocal family is strongly correlated with the role of men in the economic system and in the system of social stratification in Guianese society. This specification, when fully worked out, may serve as a starting point for further comparative work on the family, and for parallel attempts in other fields (Eisenstadt 1957). Similarly, Watson's (1958) analysis of the impact of a money economy on tribal society contains very interesting hypotheses about the influence of different structural variables (e.g., patrilineal and matrilineal descent, patrilocality and matrilocality) on the process of adaptation of modern forces within this tribal framework, and in terms of the maintenance of this framework.

Finally, these studies, especially those related to problems of change, have necessarily called attention to certain problems of the processes of transition from relatively homogeneous societies to more differentiated social orders, and have pointed out some of the problems and patterns of behavior and structure which develop in such a process.

VIII

The significance of all these contributions goes beyond their specific analyses of the areas enumerated. Their main significance for sociological analysis lies in their enlarging our understanding of the complexity and variety of the social mechanisms which regulate social behavior and organize the division of labor and the interrelations between different groups in so-called complex societies. Sociological and anthropological analysis has often tended to classify societies into "types" in terms of some such major mechanisms. Mechanical and organic solidarity, *Gemeinschaft* and *Gesellschaft*, "sacred" and "secular" societies, "folk societies," and often the very terms "primitive" and "complex" societies have been used to denote these types. And although it has become almost a commonplace of sociological and anthropological literature that "pure types" of such societies do not exist, sociological and anthropological analysis seldom attempts to delve too deeply into the implications of this assertion for the analysis of concrete ways of social organization. It is here that the social-anthropological studies of complex societies have made their most distinct contribution to sociological theory. They have clearly indicated how regulative mechanisms, belonging as it were to one type of society, operate in some parts of other types of societies and constitute basic components of social organizations. Moreover, they have shown that in the complex societies these regulative mechanisms do not operate in closed, watertight compartments, but instead very often interpenetrate with other mechanisms, permeate the same areas of social life as similar mechanisms, and are not necessarily always embedded in the structure of the major groups of a society. In this way, these studies have contributed to the reassessment of the sociological image of modern societies. They have shown, at least by implication, that modern society is not a "mechanized" one, in which atomized individuals live in separation, ruled only by impersonal forces. Rather, various closely interwoven personal and group relations, on the one hand, and relations permeated with symbolic and primordial meanings, on the other hand, constitute basic components of even the most differentiated type of society.

Of special significance from this point of view is the implication of these works for the analysis of the place of primordial symbols and ritual values in the organization of a society. The importance of "ritual" or religious activities in primitive societies has often been explained mainly in terms of little social differentiation, and of the intensity and closeness of social interaction. But anthropological studies of complex societies (as well as several other studies) indicate that the significance of primordial images and of rates of interaction and social differentiation may vary independently, that symbolical primordial images and values cannot be reduced to such rates of interaction, and that they constitute an independent realm which is autonomous and of great importance in any society, even if the ways in which they operate differ from society to society.

IX

The important contributions of social-anthropological studies of complex societies do not, however, necessarily imply that such studies have solved all the problems which were implicit—and also, very often, explicit—in their materials.

While these studies pointed out some of those areas in the social structure of complex societies in which certain regulative mechanisms most predominant in primitive societies were operative, they were less successful in analyzing areas of social structure—which are still of predominant importance in most of these complex societies—within which such mechanisms do not operate.

As we have seen earlier, their data show the existence, in these societies, of many aspects of social behavior which could not be explained solely in terms of place in a given group or institution, or in terms of contribution to the functioning of these groups in the total society. These data have also indicated that in most complex societies, the different types of social activities—ritual, economic, contractual, political, etc.—are not closely interwoven and interrelated in the same situations or groups. In complex societies, each of these types of activities often tends to crystallize into specific institutional frameworks or orders of its own. Therefore it was more difficult to point out the ultimate ritual or primordial sanctions of many contractual types of behavior.

In more concrete terms, these studies and the concepts employed in them did not explain how behavior was regulated in situations in which individuals could choose between different roles and groups, and in which different and contradictory institutional forces and groups (e.g., tribal and family loyalties, and modern political or occupational groupings) impinge on the individuals participating in them, and may often have made different—even contradictory—demands.

The concepts could not explain the ways in which many patterns of individual behavior and activity (e.g., in leisure time activities, in work place, and in family groups) were not entirely bound to concrete groups or embedded in them, but were widely dispersed among different and seemingly unconnected situations.

They did not explain how new patterns of behavior, groups, and situations (e.g., modern working situation, trade organization, political affiliation) were continuously emerging, crystallizing, and impinging on different individuals and making different, often conflicting, demands.

They did not explain the ways in which different types of social activities—contractual, juridical, political, ritual, etc.—are organized in different "orders" within a society, and how all these orders impinge on and regulate various situations, groups, and patterns of behavior within the society.

They did not explain how—if at all—many conflicts between different groups in these societies (e.g., political and economic conflicts between Europeans and Africans cutting across any such society) were regulated, or how they could be said simply or outrightly to contribute to the continuous integration of an ongoing society. This also seems to apply to the analysis of the function of any one group within the "total" society. These studies have shown that, in the more complex societies, it was more difficult to delineate the exact function of each such group within the "total" social structure, or the exact functions which any such groups performed in relation to the basic institutional spheres (e.g., economic or political) of the society. Hence, it seems that the whole concept and reality of the "total" society is here much more problematic than in the study of primitive societies, and that this "total" society is no longer a relatively well-circumscribed group with clear ecological, personal, and cultural boundaries (2).

Thus, most anthropological analyses of complex societies were unable to analyze fully the problems of a complex division of labor in society. The only partial exception is, again, Nadel's work on the Nupe (1942). His descriptions of the political, ritual, and economic life of different groups within the Nupe State are intended not only to present an internal analysis of these groups, but also to show how different types of activities (e.g., economic, political, ritual) are organized in the various orders of mechanisms which affect the "whole" of Nupe society. Nadel clearly distinguishes purely economic, semi-market activities or ecological arrangements from such organizations as age-groups and various ritual-symbolical activities (e.g., the Ganni ritual, Nadel 1949), which serve as mechanisms for the transmission of sacred common symbols to different subgroups in the society. While he shows how even economic or political activities and mechanisms are directed and influenced by "cultural" or ritual values, he recognizes that these are not always embedded in the structure of the different groups, but rather work through different, more complicated, mechanisms. He points out some of the ways in which they seem to operate, even though he also does not fully analyze how each of these social orders and mechanisms is organized, or how they operate together in a relatively complex society.

X

The difficulties met by social anthropologists in explaining all the problems of the division of labor in complex societies can most clearly be seen, perhaps, through an analysis of the concepts they employed and coined for the study of the complex societies, once they found that their traditional techniques and concepts did not suffice to deal with all the problems inherent in the material. The most important concepts evolved for these purposes are "network," developed by Barnes (1954) (and also used by Bott 1957), "social field," initially developed by Fortes and by Gluckman and his students (1958), and "social organization," as developed by Firth (1951).

The term *network* is used by Barnes (1954, p. 43) in the following way to describe the complexity of the social relation to be found in Bremnes:

Each person is, as it were, in touch with a number of other people some of whom are directly in touch with each other and some of whom are not. Similarly each person has a number of friends, and these friends have their own friends; some of any one person's friends know each other, others do not. I find it convenient to talk of a social field of this kind as a network. The image I have is of a set of points some of which are joined by lines. The points of the image are people, or sometimes groups, and the lines indicate which people interact with each other. We can of course think of the whole of social life as generating a network of this kind. For our present purposes, however, I want to consider, roughly speaking, that part of the total network that is left behind when we remove the groupings and chains of interaction which belong strictly to the territory and industrial systems.

The concept denoted by the terms *social field* (which was also used, although in a different way, by K. Lewin and in sociometry) and *social situation* has been developed by Fortes (1949*b*) and then used by Barnes (1954), Gluckman (1958), and Epstein (1958) to deal with the new type of total society which they found, and with the interrelations between its parts. Barnes (1954, pp. 42–44) uses this concept.

Thus in terms of this analysis we can isolate three regions or fields in the social systems of Bremnes. Firstly there is the territorially-based social field, with a large number of enduring administrative units, arranged hierarchically, one with another. . . .

The second social field is that generated by the industrial system. Here we have a large number of interdependent, yet formally autonomous units such as fishing vessels, marketing cooperatives, and herring-oil factories, connected with each other functionally rather than hierarchically, yet each organized internally in a hierarchy of command. . . .

The third social field has no units or boundaries; it has no coordinating organization. It is made up of the ties of friendship and acquaintance which everyone growing up in Bremnes society partly inherits and largely builds up for himself. Some of the ties are between kinsmen. A few of them are between people who are not equals, as between a man and a former employer with whom he has kept contact. Most of the ties are, however, between persons who accord approximately equal status to one another, and it is these ties which, I think, may be said to constitute the class of system of Bremnes. The elements of this social field are not fixed, for new ties are continually being formed and old links are broken or put into indefinite cold storage.

A somewhat different definition is given by Epstein (1958, p. 234).

"The Copperbelt," then, has to be seen as a single field of social relations which is composed of different sets of relations, each of which forms a distinct sub-system. Fundamental to this social system is the dominant cleavage between Europeans and Africans, and this cleavage influences behavior and institutional growth within each part of the social field. At the same time, each sub-system enjoys a certain measure of autonomy; they do not react in the same way and at the same time towards the external stimuli making for social change.

The term *social organization* has been used by Firth (1954) to denote the difference between the "formal" or normative social structure and the patterns of individual behavior which develop within that structure.

These concepts, and especially that of social network, are very useful in that, first, they describe some of the more complex interrelationships which tend to develop between the more closed "homogeneous" groups and the wider social setting, and, second, they may make us sensitive to the complex nature of the forces which operate within any single unit of behavior or group within these groups and societies. But, with the partial exception of "network," they do not help greatly in the systematic analysis of the great variety of problems of social division of labor, which are explicit or implicit in the material presented in social-anthropological studies of complex societies.

Thus, while the concept of social field (or fields) and subsystem *does* tell us that we have to look for some general divisions of society and their interrelations (economic, political, etc.), it does not help us to find explanations of the principles of such interrelationship, or of the ways in which different groups and social situations are interrelated with respect to these divisions. It does not help in the systematic analysis of the ways in which these divisions impinge in different ways on different individuals, or explain why some individuals are drawn more than others into a given field. Nor do the uses of this concept explain the ways in which possible conflicts between such fields develop and are, or are not, resolved.

Similarly, while the concept of social organization does indicate clearly the existence of the problem of differences between individual behavior and institutional structure, it does not, as yet at least, show us what are the major components of this social organization, how they vary, and in what ways they may affect different aspects of social structure.

It is perhaps only the concept of network that to some extent provides a potentially new analytical tool. It clearly describes or points out the existence of some differential interrelation between different people who are not organized in corporate groups, and it may help in the analysis of the relation of different persons, acting in such a network, to different types of social roles and institutional frameworks. In this way, the concept of network does at least point out one way—beyond embedding in the structure of concrete groups—in which the various regulative mechanisms can be organized. However, although Bott has analyzed the relations between certain types of networks and division of labor (1957), this concept has not yet been used to explain how different people are drawn into different networks, or how such networks develop. Moreover, the concept is still limited to that type of social relation in which some of the close interrelationship exists between the same people in different situations.

Thus it may be said that, although these concepts describe important aspects of social organization and structure in these societies, most of them (with the partial exception of network) do not help in an analysis of the systematic variations of behavior in those types of situations in which close interrelations between individual behavior, group structure, and institutional order do not exist (3). These concepts could not be applied to the analysis of different mechanisms of regulating social behavior, or of social division of labor, which were not embedded in the structure of concrete groups, or to the problems inherent in the coexistence and development of different orders of social relations in the same society.

From this point of view it is interesting to note two facts:

1. Insofar as anthropologists deal with these different institutional

orders, they tend to employ the usual sociological nomenclature, usually without attempting any critical appraisal of it.

2. It is very significant, from this point of view, that most of these anthropological studies (with the partial exception of Epstein's) have not made *systematic* use of the concept of "role"—nor have they critically appraised it. The importance of this concept, from the point of view of our analysis, is that it is the basic sociological concept (even if one of the first to coin it was an anthropologist, Linton) which attempts to link together individual behavior and its social function, not only on the level of concrete groups. Its aim is to show how the behavior of individuals in different positions in the society is influenced, not only by membership in concrete groups, but also by various broader institutional settings and forces, each of which attempts to define certain aspects of a social position; to make (very often new) demands on its incumbents; and to employ different sanctions to ensure their acceptance of such demands.

The limitations of these analyses are perhaps most evident when they deal with the problems of change. Social-anthropological studies dealing with this problem do not usually explain how new frameworks of social organization—new "social fields"—have emerged out of the older ones, or how the new institutional order and norms that develop have become crystallized (4). Nor do they systematically explain the forces which influence different individuals to choose between alternatives in the new situation. Rather, most of these studies take the existence of some of these new frameworks for granted. Starting off from this premise, they tend to investigate the different groupings that exist within them.

It is very interesting to compare, from this point of view, Watson's analysis of the impact of money economy on the Mambwe with other studies of change, for instance that by Epstein. Watson's main topic focused on the continuous functioning of the tribal groups, and how money economy did *not* destroy tribal cohesion. Hence, his analysis is much more akin to the usual anthropological studies and gives a much more "complete" picture of a still relatively undifferentiated society than does Epstein's analysis of more complex situations, which necessarily focused on individual behavior and the structure of groups in a given situation, taking the development of the situation more or less for granted.

XI

We see, thus, that social-anthropological studies have made a distinct contribution to the analysis and understanding of complex societies and have provided new perspectives for such analyses. On the
other hand, they were not very successful in analyzing *all* the different aspects of social organization in these societies, and especially
those problems of the complex division of labor which were related to
the coexistence of different types or orders of social activities, or to the
simultaneous operation of different types of regulative mechanisms
within a given society.

Although the most significant general contribution of these studies
was their showing systematically that within any "type" of social structure there operate varied, different types of regulative mechanisms,
they did not go on to analyze the general theoretical implication of this
finding: *how* these different types of regulative mechanisms operate
in the same society, and what are the relations between them. It was
exactly at this point that their analysis stopped, and they have concentrated mainly on the operation of one (broad) type of such mechanisms within complex and modern societies.

However, a further exploration of this implication, and of the general problems arising from the anthropological study of complex societies, may contribute much to general sociological theory, and may
also help reassess the analysis of tribal societies. Several studies of
simple societies, such as Turner's (1957), as well as some of Leach's
queries about the anthropological definition of social structure (Leach
1954; Gellner 1958)—not to mention Levi-Strauss' analyses of
different orders of social life (1953, 1959)—have pointed out that, in
at least some areas of social life in primitive societies, there operate
types of regulative mechanisms that are more varied than has been
postulated by the social-anthropological model, and that in these societies even these mechanisms are not always embedded in concrete
groups—even if the degree of differentiation between them is less
than in the more complex societies.

The further exploration of the insights gained through analysis of
the limitations encountered in applying the model of social anthropol-

ogy to complex societies may stimulate such reassessments of simple societies by looking for areas in their social structure where more differentiated regulative mechanisms of social behavior operate side by side with those mechanisms which are embedded in the structure of concrete groups. In this way, as well as through sharper confrontations between the continuously developing anthropological and sociological studies of complex societies, the full implications of these studies for sociological theory and analysis may be brought out.

NOTES

1. We shall not deal below with the historical development of this model and with the various trends within it, but shall concentrate mainly on its basic and salient features (Evans-Pritchard 1951; Beattie 1956).

2. It is significant to note that some doubts about the validity of the concept of "social structure" or total society were pointed out by Leach (1954) in his study of the Burmese highlands.

3. The criticism leveled against the Warner "school's" application of social anthropology stressed this point in a pertinent way (Goldschmidt 1950).

4. A possible partial exception to this is Worsley's (1957) study of cargo cults. But, significantly, this study uses specific anthropological concepts to a smaller degree.

REFERENCES

Arensberg, C. M., and S. T. Kimball, 1948, *Family and Community in Ireland,* Cambridge, Mass.: Harvard University Press.

Bailey, F. G., 1957, *Caste and the Economic Frontier,* Manchester: Manchester University Press.

Banton, M., 1957, *West African City: A Study of Tribal Life in Freetown,* London: Oxford University Press (for the International African Institute).

Barnes, J. A., 1954, "Class and Committees in a Norwegian Parish Island," *Human Relations,* 7: 39–58.

———, 1959, "Politics without Parties," *Man,* 59: 13–15.

Beattie, J. H. M., 1956, "Social Anthropology," *The New Outline of Modern Knowledge* (editor A. Pryce-Jones), New York: Simon and Schuster, pp. 252–278.

———, 1959, "Understanding and Explanation in Social Anthropology," *British Journal of Sociology*, 10: 45–60.

Bott, E., 1957, *Family and Social Network*, London: Tavistock Publications.

Bradney, P., 1957*a*, "The Joking Relationship in Industry," *Human Relations*, 10: 179–187.

———, 1957*b*, "Quasi-familial Relationships in Industry," *Human Relations*, 10: 271–279.

Burns, T., 1955, "The Reference of Conduct in Small Groups: Cliques and Cabals in Occupational Milieux," *Human Relations*, 8: 345–486.

Eggan, F., 1950, *Social Organization of Western Pueblos*, Chicago: University of Chicago Press.

———, 1957, "Foreword," *A Natural Science of Society*, by A. R. Radcliffe-Brown, Glencoe, Ill.: The Free Press.

Eisenstadt, S. N., 1956, "Ritualized Personal Relationships," *Man*, 96: 1–5.

———, 1957, review of *The Negro Family in British Guiana*, by R. T. Smith, *British Journal of Sociology*, 8: 283–284.

Emmett, D., 1958, *Function, Purpose and Powers*, London: Macmillan.

Epstein, A. L., 1954, *Juridical Techniques and the Judicial Process* (The Rhodes-Livingstone Papers, No. 23), Manchester: Manchester University Press.

———, 1958, *Politics in an Urban African Community*, Manchester: Manchester University Press (for the Rhodes-Livingstone Institute).

Evans-Pritchard, E. E., 1933, "Zande Blood Brothership," *Africa*, 6: 369–401.

———, 1940, *The Nuer*, Oxford: Clarendon Press.

———, 1951, *Social Anthropology*, London: Cohen and West.

———, 1954 (editor), *Institutions of Primitive Society*, Oxford: Basil Blackwell.

———, 1956, *Nuer Religion*, Oxford: Clarendon Press.

Fallers, Lloyd A., 1956, *Bantu Bureaucracy: A Study of Integration and Conflict in the Political Institutions of an East African People*, Cambridge: Heffer (for East African Institute of Social Research).

Firth, R., 1946, *Malay Fishermen: Their Peasant Economy*, London: Kegan Paul, Trench, Trubner and Co.

————, 1951, *Elements of Social Organization*, London: Watts.

————, 1954, "Social Organization and Social Change," *Journal of the Royal Anthropological Institute*, 84: 1–20.

———— (editor), 1956, *Two Studies of Kinship in London*, London School of Economics Monographs on Social Anthropology, No. 15, London: Athlone Press.

Forde, C. D. (editor), 1954, *African Worlds*, Oxford: Oxford University Press.

Fortes, M., 1945, *The Dynamics of Clanship among the Tallensi*, London: Oxford University Press (for the International African Institute).

————, 1949*a*, "Time and Social Structure," in *Social Structure* (editor M. Fortes) 54–84, Oxford: Clarendon Press.

————, 1949*b*, *The Web of Kinship among the Tallensi*, London: Oxford University Press (for the International African Institute).

————, 1953, "The Structure of Unilineal Descent Groups," *American Anthropologist*, 55: 17–41.

————, 1958, "Introduction," in *The Developmental Cycle in Domestic Groups* (editor J. R. Goody), Cambridge: Cambridge University Press.

Fortes, M., and E. E. Evans-Pritchard (editors), 1940, *African Political Systems*, London: Oxford University Press (for the International Institute of African Languages and Cultures).

Frankenberg, R., 1956, *Village on the Border*, London: Cohen and West.

Freedman, M., 1957, *Chinese Family and Marriage in Singapore*, London: H. M. Stationery Off.

————, 1958, *Lineage Organization in Southeastern China*. London School of Economics Monographs on Social Anthropology, No. 18, London: Athlone Press.

Gellner, E., 1958, "Time and Theory in Social Anthropology," *Mind*, 67: 152–203.

Gluckman, Max, 1956, *Custom and Conflict in Africa*, Oxford: Basil Blackwell.

————, 1958, *Analysis of a Social Situation in Modern Zululand* (The Rhodes-Livingstone Papers, No. 28), Manchester: Manchester University Press.

————, 1959*a*, "Football Players and the Crowd," *The Listener*, February 1959.

————, 1959*b*, *The Use of Ethnographic Data in Social Anthropological*

Analysis of Great Britain, International Sociological Association (mim.).

Goldschmidt, W., 1950, "Social Class in America—A Critical Review, *American Anthropologist,* 52: 483–498.

Goody, J. (editor), 1958, *The Developmental Cycle in Domestic Groups,* Cambridge: Cambridge University Press.

——, 1959, "The Mother's Brother and the Sister's Son in West Africa," *Journal of the Royal Anthropological Institute,* 89: 59–88.

Gullick, J. M., 1958, *Indigenous Political Systems in Western Malaya,* London School of Economics Monographs on Social Anthropology, No. 17, London: Athlone Press.

Krige, E. J., and D. Krige, 1943, *The Realm of a Rain-Queen,* London: Oxford University Press.

Kuper, H., 1947, *An African Aristocracy,* London: Oxford University Press (for the International African Institute).

Leach, E. R., 1954, *Political Systems of Highland Burma,* London: G. Bell.

——, 1958, "Magical hair," *Journal of Royal Anthropological Institute,* 88: 147–156.

Levi-Strauss, C., 1953, "Social Structure," in *Anthropology Today* (editor A. L. Kroeber), 524–554, Chicago: University of Chicago Press.

——, 1959, *Anthropologie structurale,* Paris: Plon.

Linton, R., 1940, *Acculturation in Seven American Indian Tribes,* New York: Appleton-Century.

Little, K., 1955, "Structural Change in the Sierra Leone Protectorate," *Africa,* 25: 217–253.

Lupton, T., and S. Cunnison, 1957, *The Problem of Social Context in the Analysis of Workshop Behaviour* (mim.), paper presented at a meeting of the Association of Social Anthropologists.

Mandelbaum, D. G., 1956, "The Study of Complex Civilizations," in *Current Anthropology* (editor W. H. Thomas), 203–226, Chicago: University of Chicago Press.

Marriott, M. (editor), 1955, *Village India,* Chicago: University of Chicago Press.

Mayer, A., 1960, *Caste and Kinship in Central India,* London: Routledge and Kegan Paul.

Middleton, J., and D. Tait (editors), 1958, *Tribes without Rulers,* London: Routledge and Kegan Paul.

Miller, E. J., 1954, Caste and Territory in Malabar, *American Anthropologist*, 56: 410–420.

Mitchell, J. C., 1956, *The Kalela Dance* (The Rhodes-Livingstone Papers, No. 27), Manchester: Manchester University Press.

Nadel, S. F., 1942, *A Black Byzantium*, London: Oxford University Press (for the International Institute of African Languages and Cultures).

――――, 1949, "The Ganni Ritual of Nupe: A Study in Social Symbiosis," *Africa*, 19: 177–186.

Pitt-Rivers, J. A., 1954, *The People of the Sierra*, London: Weidenfeld and Nicolson.

Radcliffe-Brown, A. R., 1952, *Structure and Function in Primitive Society: Essays and Addresses*, London: Cohen and West.

Radcliffe-Brown, A. R. and D. Forde (editors), 1950, *African Systems of Kinship and Marriage*, London: Oxford University Press.

Redfield, R., 1955, "Societies and Cultures as Natural Systems," *Journal of the Royal Anthropological Institute*, 85: 19–32.

――――, 1956, *Peasant Society and Culture*, Chicago: University of Chicago Press.

Shils, E., 1957, "Primordial, Personal, Sacred and Civil Ties," *British Journal of Sociology*, 8: 130–146.

Smith, R. T., 1956, *The Negro Family in British Guiana*, London: Routledge and Kegan Paul.

Southall, A. W., 1954, *Alur Society*, Cambridge: University of Cambridge Press.

Srinvas, M. N., 1952, *Religion and Society among the Coorgs of South India*, Oxford: Clarendon Press.

Turner, V. W., 1957, *Schism and Continuity in an African Society*, Manchester: Manchester University Press.

Watson, W., 1958, *Tribal Cohesion in a Money Economy*, Manchester: Manchester University Press.

Worsley, P. M., 1956, "The Kinship System of the Tallensi: A Revaluation," *Journal of the Royal Anthropological Institute*, 86: 37–75.

――――, 1957, *The Trumpet Shall Sound*, London: McGibbon and Kee.

Young, M., and P. Willmott, 1957, *Family and Kinship in East London*, London: Routledge and Kegan Paul.

SECTION II

Age-Groups and Youth Culture

IN THIS SECTION three essays have been collected. The first, on "African Age-Groups," attempts to present a series of structural hypotheses about the social conditions which give rise to the existence of organized age-groups in different tribal societies in Africa.* This essay (Chapter 4) presents probably the most purely structural analysis in the whole collection, and some of its resultant analytical shortcomings have been analyzed briefly in Chapter 1 of this book.

Some of the implications of these shortcomings are spelled out in a fuller way in the second essay (Chapter 5) of this section, "Delinquent Group Formation among Immigrant Youth," which deals with the development of delinquent youth groups among immigrant groups in Israel. The central problem of this essay is based on the recognition of the fact that both "conformist" and "delinquent" youth cultures or groups may develop under similar broad structural conditions. Hence it is necessary to go beyond such broad structural conditions and to specify the additional conditions which give rise to different types of youth cultures and youth organizations and to different degrees of structuralization of such grouping, norms, and attitudes related to them. Here different behavioral and attitudinal aspects become of greater importance.

* These hypotheses were tested out on a wider scale in the author's book *From Generation to Generation*, Glencoe, Ill.: The Free Press, 1956.

The last essay (Chapter 6) in this section, most of which is based on new materials, approaches this problem in a somewhat fuller way. The analysis presented starts from some of the basic structural assumptions which were spelled out in the preceding essays and then attempts to go beyond them by analyzing the continuously changing patterns of youth culture in modern societies. It emphasizes the heterogeneity, variety, and changeability in the development of these youth cultures and in this way also emphasizes the importance of different behavioral and attitudinal processes in the crystallization of such groups and institutional settings.

Chapter 4

African Age-Groups: A Comparative Study

The purpose of this study is to present a comparative analysis of men's age-group (or age-set) systems in Africa and to determine: (a) some of the main structural differences between the various age-set systems, and (b) the conditions (or the types of societies) in which the different systems arise and the functions they fulfill. For reasons of space the material is presented summarily, no full description or complete inventory of age-sets being included. The societies on which the analysis has been chiefly based are the following:

ACEPHALOUS SEGMENTARY TRIBES. The Nuer (17, 18), the Topotha, Latuka, and other Nilotic tribes (68, 13), the Lango (38), the Turkana and other tribes of the Karamajong cluster (36, 37), the Bantu Kavirondo (81), the Gusii (60, 61), the Dorobo (42, 44), the Nandi (40, 43), the Kipsigis (69, 72), the Suk (Pokot) (70), the Meru (52, 39), the Murle (55), the Kamba (56, 51), the Kikuyu (46, 14, 16, 72), the Galla (82, 15, 72), the Pokomo (71), the Masai (63, 32, 53), the Tiv (11, 2, 1), the Nuba group (66), and, for comparative purposes, the Tallensi (29, 30, 31).

AUTONOMOUS VILLAGE SOCIETIES WITH SPECIALIZED ASSOCIATIONS. The Yakö (23, 24, 25, 26), the Southern Ibo and Ibibio

Reprinted from *Africa*, 1954. I am indebted to Professor Daryll Forde for assistance in analyzing and presenting the material, as well as to Professors E. E. Evans-Pritchard, M. Fortes, M. Gluckman, S. F. Nadel, I. Schapera, and Dr. J. Peristiany for valuable discussions of the problems.

groups (62, 35, 79, 80, 28, 45), some Yoruba tribes (22, 27, 8, 4, 5), and, for comparative purposes, other Yoruba groups, the Kpelle (83) and Mende (57, 59).

CENTRALIZED CHIEFDOMS. The Swazi (6, 49), Zulu (33, 47, 10, 58), the Tswana group (76, 77, 78), the Nyakyusa (84), and, for comparative purposes, the Ashanti (12), the Pondo (41), the Bemba (74, 75), the Lozi (34), and the Nupe (65, 66, 67), the Lovedu (48), and Khosa (54).

We shall deal here, however, with only one major type of age grouping which is the most important and the one most commonly found in African societies. The analysis of another type, exemplified among the Tiv and the Nyakyusa, appears in a later publication (see Eisenstadt, *From Generation to Generation*, Chapter V).

The Hypothesis

In attempting to formulate a hypothesis applicable to the conditions of emergence and the functions of male age-sets, some of their basic common characteristics must first be analyzed.

The most common characteristics of age-groups of the type considered here are the following: *

1. The age system is organized in a series of sets conceived as unitary for the whole society (tribe, village, chiefdom, or some local subdivision thereof). Entry into the system, through the formation of a new set, is based on the ascriptive criterion of chronological age and is incumbent on every member of the community who reaches that stage.

2. The system is organized in a series of groups of coevals from the whole tribe, or of parallel groups from different territorial sectors, which cut across groupings based on kinship or residence, such as fam-

---

* The following list of the main characteristics of age-groups of this type applies to all the societies with the partial exception of the Nupe. This exception will be explained in the later part of the paper. This list has some common features with that of J. H. Driberg, "Age Grades," *Encyclopedia Britannica*, 14th edition, but differs from it in some points which seem to be essential to our analysis.

ily and descent units. Passage of an individual from one status or grade to another is effected by a status change of his set as a whole and is both compulsory and automatic.

3. Formation of a new age-set is closely associated, although not necessarily identical—as there is usually a special collective ceremony at the formation of a new set—with puberty rites or tribal initiation into manhood and constitutes a basic prerequisite for the attainment of full (adult) social status.

4. The age-set system tends to stratify the population according to seniority, and the individual's position within the system constitutes an important index of social status and, to some extent, regulates his behavior toward all other members of the society (whether seniors, equals, or juniors).

5. The relations between age mates, and also in certain contexts between members of different age-sets (within the age-set hierarchy), are not those of specific contractual commitments which are entered on voluntarily and which cease with the fulfillment of the commitment. They are of a much more diffuse type, involving general and permanent obligations of cooperation, solidarity, mutual help, and so forth —closely resembling, in this respect, the family and kinship union.* (In some cases, indeed, as among the Nuer, kinship terminology and prohibitions are extended to age-groups.)

6. Despite this similarity, the age-group system is structurally differentiated from the family and kinship (or descent) groups in several ways: (a) as its criteria of membership are universalistic in that they apply to males of the community as a whole, it cuts across the boundaries of these groups breaking into their memberships; (b) the spheres of activities of age-sets and kin groups are always distinct, sometimes even opposed (as in those instances when the "warrior" group members are not allowed to marry, and when those occupied with raising a family seceded from active participation in the age-set system) (39); (c) admission to the age-group always involves some separation from the family and independence of its authority; (d) the family is a group which involves the interaction of members of different ages, the activities of which thus emphasize the relative age differences of members, whereas age-groups emphasize the common age of members.

* This terminology follows that of A. R. Radcliffe-Brown, 1950.

7. Whenever age-groups function corporately, various roles and tasks important for the maintenance of the social system as a whole are allocated to them.

The universal existence of age grading in human societies can be understood in terms of the biological exigencies of socialization and the necessity for the transmission of social behavior and values from generation to generation. The strong emphasis on age differences and the relations of authority and respect which they entail within the family as the first and basic socializing unit constitute a universal institutional device for the transmission of patterns of behavior from generation to generation. The interacting of members of different ages in the same situation and group, yet with different degrees of authority, also facilitates this transmission, through both direct learning and general, diffuse identification with the members of senior age (first the parents).* Kinship relations, which constitute an extension of the age-herterogeneous relations of the family (37), may be understood, from this point of view, as broader and more inclusive channels for the transmission of patterns of behavior and the continuity of the society.

A system of age-sets, that is, of groups of persons classified by age, fulfills functions which are not dissimilar from those of family and kinship and descent groups. Age-sets are, however, structured according to criteria differing from those of family and descent groups, hence, our main hypothesis: That age-set systems arise and function in those societies in which the basic allocation of roles is not overwhelmingly determined by membership in kinship groups, and where some important integrative functions remain to be fulfilled beyond these groups. In such societies, therefore, the descent group is not the exclusive or predominant group to which political, economic, and so forth, functions and offices are allocated, nor is it the main repository and bearer of the ritual values of the society. There exist, consequently, many important social relations and positions within the society, such as leadership in war and the organization of public activi-

* This formulation, presented here in a very summary way, is based on a wider and more elaborate analysis, which is published as part of a general analysis of age-groups and youth movements in *From Generation to Generation.*

ties, the regulation and allocation of which are based on membership of the society as a whole, apart from kinship affiliation to particular groups.

Accordingly age-sets arise to fulfill some of the educational and integrative tasks which are beyond the scope of the family and descent groups. They extend the individual's relations beyond the range of the latter, place him in definite relations, potentially at least, with all other members of the society, and regulate these relations according to an overall universalistic criterion of age.

There are two main and interdependent reasons why age-set systems fulfill these functions: (a) the age criterion is, apart from membership in family and kin groups, the only one which applies to all (male) members of a society and which can be used for the allocation of universal roles; (b) age relations (both age-heterogeneous and age-homogeneous) are, within a society, the main universal relations (once more, apart from family and kinship relations) which are not bound within specific contractual bonds. They can thus serve as a basis for the overall regulation of behavior and for the development of mutual identification between the members and identification of the members with the society and its values.

Validation of the Hypothesis

In seeking to validate this hypothesis we shall consider separately segmentary noncentralized tribes, "autonomous" villages without central political authority (like the Yakö, Southern Ibo and Ibibio groups), and the centralized chiefdoms. As a first step, specific indices will be derived from the initial hypothesis which would apply to each of these types of social organization.

SEGMENTARY NONCENTRALIZED TRIBES. The main criteria for distinguishing between kinship-regulated and other patterns of social organization are the following: (a) the extent to which lineages and clan groups are organized in corporate units within and between which the political activities of the people are coordinated; (b) the extent to which the clan, subclan, or lineage is a territorial unit;

(c) the extent to which there exists institutional machinery for the adjustment of interclan or interlineage quarrels and how far it is incorporated within the kin units; (d) the extent to which the most important ritual, political, and prestige-bearing offices are vested in members of lineages and kin units; (e) the extent to which social relations not confined to these corporate groups are, within the limits of the tribe, regulated by kinship criteria.

The best recorded African example of a segmentary system, in which descent units monopolize the social organization, in which the main social positions are allocated to these units or their representatives, and in which the most important social relations are regulated according to kinship criteria and obligations, is the Tallensi. Among these people no age-groups exist at all, and the life of the individual is entirely encompassed by descent-group and kinship relations.

Among the other segmentary tribes enumerated above there exists no such complete coordination between the political and ritual structure and the various descent units, and among all of them we find corporate age-groups. They can, however, be differentiated according to the extent to which such coordination exists. From this point of view the Turkana, Bantu Kavirondo, Gusii, and after them the Nuer, the Dorobo, and, to some extent, other Nilotic tribes (information about which is not so full) lie at one end of the scale, while the Nandi, Kipsigis, Pokot, Murle, Masai, Kamba, Kikuyu, and Meru are placed at the other (although, of course, there are small differences within these two groups).

Among the Bantu Kavirondo, the Gusii, and Turkana (and probably other tribes of the Karamajong cluster), coordination between the clans and the territorial, political, and ritual institutions is still strong. Even among them, however, and especially among the Bantu Kavirondo, not all intratribal relations are regulated through descent groups and according to kinship principles, for certain important relations and positions are based on criteria of individual achievement (wealth and prowess). Among the Nuer there exists a definite relation between lineage, locality, and authority, although this applies mainly to the dominant lineages and less to the nonaristocratic, while on the whole there is a greater territorial dispersal of members of lineages than among the Tallensi. Although the lineage exists among the Nuer as a corporate unit, no fixed juridical or ritual offices are vested in it and not all interaction between members of the tribe is mediated through the corporate activity of the lineage or complementary kinship relations.

The picture among the Nandi group, the Masai, and so forth, is very different. There usually are no strong corporate lineages; the clans and subclans do not constitute territorial units and they do not coordinate political relations. Interaction of the various subunits of these tribes is regulated mostly on a purely territorial basis. The various offices—political, military, and ritual—are vested in sectors of this territorial system and not in the kinship units. While the literature on the Pokomo, Kikuyu, Meru, Kamba, Galla, and Murle is not as adequate as for the Nandi-Masai groups, the lack of coordination between territorial organization and clanship, the absence or relative weakness of corporate lineages with political functions, and the unimportance of these groups in connection with ritual offices is always stressed.

These differences among the various segmentary tribes are closely correlated with the development of their age-groups. In most general terms this correlation may be stated as follows: The extent of the corporate organization of age-groups and of an age system, the size of the age span over which the age-groups are effective, the extent of the regulation of behavior by age-groups, and the importance of the tasks allocated to them are negatively correlated with the degree to which there is coordination between kin groups and territorial, political, and ritual structures. Among the Nuer, Bantu Kavirondo, Dorobo, Turkana, and so forth, the age-groups do not constitute fully corporate entities and only affect the general attitudes and behavior of their members in relation to each other in emphasizing equality among age mates and respect for seniority.

The reverse is true of the Nandi group, the Masai, Murle, and, to some extent, also of the Kikuyu-Kamba-Meru group. There the age-groups constitute corporate units which, in addition to the general patterning of behavior and attitudes, also perform specific tasks—military, political, juridical—that are of great importance from the point of view of the integration of the social system. They usually form an interlocking hierarchical age system, each position within which is attained in turn by each age-group upon reaching the appropriate stage.*

AUTONOMOUS VILLAGE COMMUNITIES. Autonomous village communities, among which authority is, to a very large extent, vested in special agencies (9)—village councils, titled associations, and so forth —are exemplified by the Yakö, the Southern Ibo and Ibibio, some Yoruba tribes, and probably also other African peasant tribes (50). Among these the degree of coordination between territorial, political, and ritual organization on the one hand and kinship units on the other is slighter than among the aforementioned segmentary tribes. Among the Yakö, the most adequately described of all these people, the village is divided into several wards which form the basic administrative units of the society. Within these wards several generally unrelated patriclans live together, whereas related patriclans may be found distributed over different wards. Ward offices are not vested in particular kin groups, although a group may seek to gain and retain control of such an office, but are achieved on the basis of wealth, age, and various other specific attainments. The organization of village-wide activities in various specialized associations is even less closely related to any kinship or family unit, as membership in the associations is usually achieved by individual effort. The same appears to be true, in broad outline, of the less fully analyzed Southern Ibo and Ibibio communities. Although, as among the Yakö, we find lineages of relatively small depth acting as corporate groups, their importance is not great in defining either the territorial units of society (especially village clusters) or the wider interaction of the members of the society. Within these villages there exists also some economic specialization, which is accompanied by the organization of specific economic activities in groupings that cut across family and kinship units.

Within all these villages we find age-groups that perform various

---

* A similar contrast can be seen between the Moro and the Tira of the Nuba group. Among the Tira, who have a very formalized age-group system (for the ages of 15–26), the various clans are dispersed among several hill communities. Among the Moro, who have only a more fluid, nonformalized recognition of age-groups, the different hill communities are more self-sufficient than among the Tira, and between the clans which constitute each community there exists what Nadel calls a "symbiotic" relationship.

subsidiary tasks within the village, such as economic help, clearing of the bush, maintaining the water supply. They are also important in the lives of their members, through participation in various cere-monies and rituals. They are directed by the officials of the village and of the various associations. They begin formally with initiation into manhood and extend to middle adult age, when their importance wanes. They also participate in various collective rituals.*

CENTRALIZED CHIEFDOMS. The Zulu, Swazi, and Tswana type of chiefdom must be distinguished, for comparative purposes, from that found among the Pondo, Bemba, Khosa, Ashanti, Lozi, and Basuto. Within all these chiefdoms the political sphere extends beyond that of lineage and kinship relations, and political positions and relations ac-quire a certain amount of distinctness and autonomy. But the re-stricted scope of the corporate descent group does not necessarily mean that membership in it is not a basic condition of membership in the whole society. Political relations, although distinct in their organi-zation from descent groups, may yet depend on representation from these groups. The two main types differ, accordingly, insofar as the descent group is the basic unit of social and political life in the one and not in the other. The following more specific indices can be worked out for the purpose of differentiating between them.

1. The extent to which status in the chiefdom is attained through direct allegiance to the supreme chief, or, conversely, the extent to which it is mediated by various subunits based on kinship and descent and is conditioned by membership in these subunits.

2. The extent to which the administrative hierarchy, whose apex is the paramount chief, is or may be in direct touch with all members of the tribe, or, conversely, the extent to which it is necessarily mediated by various hereditary chiefs.

3. The extent to which political and status positions (and especially membership in the chief's council) are vested in representatives or

* The best material for comparison with this type of society can be found in those African societies where there exist titled, or secret, association, member-ship and leadership in which are allocated mostly according to hereditary criteria. Such instances can be found among the Mende, some other tribes of the Liberian hinterland, and some of the Yoruba tribes.

heads of clans, lineages, holders of hereditary local offices, or the extent to which the chief may freely fill these positions and appoint the members of his council and various officers of state without respect to their descent positions.

4. The extent to which the chief is the main legitimate expression and embodiment of the ultimate ritual values of the tribe, or the extent to which these values may also be expressed in rituals enacted within other corporate groups.

If we compare the two groups in terms of these indices, the broad differences are striking, even if in some details (such as the composition of the chief's council) the differences may be only a matter of degree. Among the Swazi, Zulu, and Tswana groups there exists a nonkinship organization of the political life of the chiefdom, while among Ashanti, Bemba, and Pondo most of the political, ritual, and status positions are vested in lineages, clans, or local descent groups. Among the first group we find highly organized age-groups (regiments), while among the second no such groups are found.

It is important to note that those functions—mainly military—which are fulfilled in the first group of tribes by the universal age regiments, are organized in the second on a territorial-kinship basis; various contingents are organized according to loyalty and owe loyalty to their local kin chief.

The existence of the somewhat special type of age-group in the Nupe chiefdom is also clearly related to a nonfamilial, nonkinship division of labor and to a stress on universalistic integrative criteria. On the one hand, Nupe society is stratified into classes based on conquest, and its political organization is semifeudal, headed by a hereditary class of conquerors supported by a class of civil and military officials. A parallel organization can be found in the economic field, in the organization of semihereditary guilds, and so forth. On the other hand, there are opportunities for social mobility and personal achievement which mitigate this "particularistic" organization. The class of civil and military officials is recruited mostly from the conquered people, while a very important stratum in the society is formed by the Moslem *mallams* (teachers), a profession which is open to everybody and enjoys high prestige. What is of special importance here is the fact that this mobility and achievement orientation is universalistic; it is open to everyone and is not organized on a hereditary basis, and it is based on universal participation in the common, ultimate values of the society.

Accordingly, we find age-groups among the Nupe, but of a special kind. The age-groups, in which people of the age span 10–30 participate, exist in every village and urban quarter, but they do not have a unified organization throughout the country. Each system is confined to its own locality, although the organization of each is alike. They are also corporate groups, with a developed internal hierarchy, although they do not perform any central integrative tasks. Their main activities are confined to the ritual sphere, to leisure time, and so on, and their main function is to serve as "schools of citizenship," emphasizing the common values of the society.

Functions of Age-Groups

The data and analysis presented above confirm our hypothesis within the limits of the available African material. The hypothesis was based on various assumptions concerning the functions of age differentiation in the process of socialization and on the maintenance of the stability and continuity of the social system. The most important activities of age-groups can now be reviewed in relation to these functions.

All age-groups develop from informal groups of children. At the admission ceremony these various small groups, coming from different places and sectors of the society, are unified into one set (or subset), fully formalized and institutionalized. This formalization of the larger group entails various crucial changes in the life of the individual and in his social position and relations: first, it confers on him full social status and membership in the tribe, transforming him from a child to an adult, capable of legitimate heterosexual relations.

Second, it frees him to some extent from the discipline of the family and kinship unit and imposes on him, through participation in the group, the more advanced, autonomous adult self-discipline of equals. At the same time participation in the age-group constitutes an important educational experience, through which both the technical knowledge and the symbolical lore of the tribe are imparted to the new members.

Third, the formalization of an age-group provides its members with a new focus of identification with the society, a new frame of reference through which they relate themselves to the total society and identify themselves with its values and symbols.

Fourth, the individual member becomes related, in a new and specific role, to all other members of the society. These relations extend and transform the basic relations initially existing within the family unit—the relations of respect and subordination to parents and of equality with siblings. The personal, particularistic relations of the family and kinship unit are replaced by impersonal, universalistic relations with any member of the society.

Finally, the setting up of formalized age-groups provides institutionalized agencies for the allocation of important tasks and roles in the society at large. The age-groups constitute segments into which the population is divided so as to ensure the performance of certain basic public roles. This allocation is usually so structured as to minimize potential conflicts and competition between the generations and assure harmonious cooperation between them. This is reflected in the symbolic expressions of hostility found in most ceremonies at the handing over of government from one age-group to another.

In all these ways age-groups provide integrative mechanisms which contribute to the continuity and stability of societies which are not organized solely on the basis of descent groups and overall kinship relations. In societies where the allocation of roles is based on kinship, these functions are, on the contrary, performed within the framework of descent groups and kinship relations.

Structural Differences in Different Types of Age-Groups

Hitherto we have discussed age-groups in general, paying little attention to important structural differences between the various types; the difference between a corporate and a noncorporate organization has alone been considered. There are, however, many other important structural differences, and we must consider the extent to which these can be explained within the framework of our hypothesis and related to the different functions which the groups fulfill within their respective societies.* These main differences can be enumerated.

The first difference is the length of the age span covered by the age-group system. In all societies this begins formally or is articulated at initiation (although in the cyclical systems of the Nandi, etc., the individual in a sense belongs to the system from birth), but beyond that the length of the age span varies. In several societies—the Nuer, Bantu Kavirondo, Dorobo, other Nilo-Hamitic tribes, Nandi, Kipsigis, Pokot, Masai, Kamba, Meru, Kikuyu, Galla, and so forth—it covers the whole subsequent life. Among the Turkana, Gusii (and probably other tribes of the Karamajong cluster), its importance wanes in old age, although formally it still persists. It seems also that among the Swazi, Zulu, Tswana, and so on the importance of age regiments diminishes with advancing age. Among the Yakö the importance of the age-sets diminishes generally after middle age, and among most of the Southern Ibo and Ibibio groups and some of the Yoruba tribes they cease to function altogether at middle age, and sometimes even earlier. Among the various Nuba groups the system terminates at approximately 30 years of age, and this tends to be the case among the Nupe.

A second difference is the extent to which the age-groups regulate behavior between all members of the society, or, conversely, the extent to which they emphasize mainly the internal relations of their members. While this may constitute only a difference of degree, the variation in emphasis is clear. Among the Yakö, Southern Ibo and Ibibio, and Nupe the emphasis on internal relations is strong; among the Swazi, Zulu, and Tswana the same is true, although to a smaller degree, whereas the Nuba group constitutes an intermediate type. But in all the other tribes there is stress on an overall regulation of behavior among men through the age-group system.

Third is the extent of the autonomy of the age-group hierarchy (or age system). This autonomy may be estimated from the extent to

* It will not be possible to account for all the known structural differences. On some of them the material is too scanty for any analysis and on others no full explanation can as yet be proposed. An attempt is made, however, to explain some of the main differences.

which the age-groups are directed by persons or agencies outside their own organization, such as village councils, associations, chiefs, or, conversely, the extent to which they are directed only by their own representatives who are officials of the age-group or system. According to these criteria a lack of autonomy exists among the Yakö, Southern Ibo and Ibibio groups, and the Swazi, Zulu, and Tswana, while in all other tribes there is a much stronger emphasis on autonomy.

Finally, there are differences in types of activities and tasks. In this respect the main difference is the extent to which the age-groups perform centrally integrative tasks—government, judiciary, military (as among the Nandi group, Galla, Kamba, Kikuyu, Meru, Pokomo)— or more subsidiary tasks, such as economic help, public works, some police duties, or even merely educational and recreational activities.

It will be seen that there is a definite connection between these various characteristics. Limitation of age span, emphasis on internal relations, lack of autonomy, and performance of subsidiary tasks usually tend to go together. The only important exceptions are the systems of the Nuer, Gusii, and Bantu Kavirondo, among which the groups are not corporate and do not perform "central" integrative tasks, but are nevertheless autonomous and do in some measure regulate behavior between all members of the society and extend throughout the whole life span from initiation. How are these correspondences and differences between the various types to be explained?

Specialization and Structure of Age-Groups

The key to the explanation of the structural differences between age-groups is to be found in the extent to which specialization based on achievement prevails within the various societies. In our basic hypothesis it was postulated that, in societies where the organization transcends kinship and descent ties, age-groups arise because they are the other main type of group to which universal, common roles can be allocated and in which all the members of the tribe can establish universalistic and noncontractual relations. But such common roles are not the only or even the main foci of integration. In some societies many of the integrative tasks are performed in specialized associations recruited on criteria of achievement. Since these criteria are incompatible with the ascriptive nature of age-groups, the preponderance of specialized activities and associations necessarily limits the scope for age-grouping. We may therefore restate our hypothesis in this way: The extent, scope, and articulation of the activities of age-groups, as defined above, are inversely correlated with the degree of achievement-oriented specialization within a universalistic society. Our material bears out this hypothesis. Among the Nandi group, the Kamba, Kikuyu, Meru, Masai, and so forth, the degree of achievement-oriented specialization is minimal, and most of the basic roles—military, juridical—are ascribed to every member of the tribe at different points of his age span, that is, to members of different age grades. There are no specialized political, military, etc., agencies, and the age-groups are very strongly developed and articulated. Among the Yakö, Ibo, Ibibio, and so on, and, in a somewhat different manner, in the Nuba group, we find formal age-groups with the least articulation. This corresponds to the high degree of achievement specialization which is manifest in the various associations which perform the main integrative functions in the society.

A detailed analysis of the material (which for reasons of space cannot be documented here) shows the following relations between various structural differences among age groups and the degree of specialization in social roles:

First, the length of the age span covered by the groups is inversely related to the span of life in which achievement-oriented, specialized activities prevail. Second, the extent of the regulation of overall behavior of the members of society by age-groups is inversely related to the existence of specialized regulative agencies in the society. Third, the degree of the autonomy of age-groups and their performance of primarily integrative activities is also inversely related to the existence of specialized political agencies and seats of authority. In addition it should be noted that in those societies in which age-groups constitute the dominant framework for the allocation of common roles and are the most important indicators of an individual's status, the structural opposition between active participation in the age-group system and family life is strongest. Such opposition is much less articulate in the more specialized societies.

These correlations are also applicable to the other societies in our sample. Among the Zulu, Swazi, and Tswana the principal specializa-

tions are in the political sphere and the main possibilities for individual achievement are to be found in the allocation of political positions
in the service of the chief. We find a corresponding variation in the
structure of the age-groups. As there is a special locus of authority—
the chief—the autonomy of the age-groups is relatively small and the
age regiments do not constitute a self-regulating organization. They
are directed by the chief and their activities are clearly subordinate to
the centers of political power. The extent to which they regulate the
overall behavior of their members and determine their status is more
limited than among the Nandi, for example, but, because of the restricted opportunities for individual achievement in these societies,
their scope is greater than among the Yakö and Ibo.

The Nupe situation is exactly the opposite. Here we find that, owing to the more rigid stratification, the age-groups do not perform any
integrative tasks. They are mainly "prepatory," serving, as Nadel has
phrased it, mainly as "schools for citizenship." There is thus no pressure toward their total subordination to the bearers of authority, and
they can therefore maintain a relatively strong autonomy in their segregated sphere. But this sphere is distinct from those institutionalized
sectors of the society which determine the individual's status in society. This segregation is emphasized in their limited age span and in
the almost total emphasis on internal relations.

The specific cluster of characteristics that exists, among the Nuer,
Bantu Kavirondo, Gusii, Turkana, and so forth, can be similarly explained. Insofar as there exists any specialization in these tribes, it is
still organized within family and descent units (lineages, clans), and
the sphere of universalistic nonkinship relations is correspondingly
limited. But since within this sphere there exists almost no specialization based on individual achievement, age-grouping is developed
there.

The limitation of the articulation of age-groups and of the scope of
their activities within more highly specialized societies does not deny
them important functions within the social system. But these functions are largely of a special character, and the following are the most
important.

First, the age-groups serve as important educational institutions
through which the common values of the society are inculcated in the
members before they set out to engage in competitive and contractual

relations. Thus they serve as important "reservoirs" of solidarity and identification with the society. This function is clearly manifested in the important part they play in integrative ceremonials of their respective societies. Second, insofar as relations between age mates are maintained in later life, when the corporate activities of age-groups diminish, they serve as important structural points for the reactivation of this solidarity. Third, in all these societies (with the partial exception of the urban sector of the Nupe) they still serve as agencies to which certain nonpolitical tasks, important for the functioning of the society, are allocated. Finally, the age-groups also serve as selective agencies, in which future leaders in different spheres of activities are prepared.

REFERENCES

1. Abraham, R. C., *The Tiv People,* London: Crown Agents for the Colonies, 1933.

2. East, R. M. (editor), *Akiga's Story,* London: Oxford University Press, for the International African Institute, 1937.

3. Ashton, H., *The Basuto,* London: Oxford University Press, for the International African Institute, 1952.

4. Bascom, W. R., "The Principle of Seniority in the Social Structure of the Yoruba," *American Anthropologist,* Vol. XLIV, 1942.

5. ———, "The Sociological Role of the Yoruba Cult-Group," *American Anthropologist,* Vol. XLVI, 1944 (Memoirs 63).

6. Bremer, H., "The Development of the Military Organization in Swaziland," *Africa,* Vol. X, 1937.

7. Bernardi, B., "The Age-System of the Nilo-Hamitic People: A Critical Evaluation," *Africa,* Vol. XXII, 1952.

8. Bridel, H., *Notes on Yoruba Age-Grades* (unpublished).

9. Brown, P., "Patterns of Authority in West Africa," *Africa,* Vol. XXI, 1951.

10. Bryant, A. T., *The Zulu People as They Were before the White Man Came,* Pietermaritzburg: Shuter and Shooter, 1949.

11. Bohanan, L., *A Comparative Study of Social Differentiation in Primitive Society,* Doctor of Philosophy Thesis, Oxford, 1951 (unpublished).

12. Busia, K. A., *The Position of the Chief in the Modern Political*

System of Ashanti, London: Oxford University Press, for the International African Institute, 1951.

13. Butt, A., *The Nilotes of the Anglo-Egyptian Sudan and Uganda* (Ethnographic Survey of Africa—East Central Africa), London: International African Institute, 1952.

14. Cagnolo, C., *The Akikuyu: Their Customs, Traditions and Folklore,* Nyeri: Mission Printing School, 1933.

15. Cerulli, E., *Studi Etiopici: I. La Lingua e la Storia di Harar,* Roma: Instituto per l'Oriente, 1936.

16. Dundas, K. R., "The Kikuyu Rika (Age-Sets)," *Man,* Vol. VIII, 1908.

17. Evans-Pritchard, E. E., "The Nuer, Tribe and Clan," *Sudan Notes,* Vols. XVI, XVII, XVIII, 1933–1935.

18. ———, "The Nuer, the Age-Sets," *Sudan Notes,* Vol. XIX, 1936.

19. ———, *The Nuer,* Oxford: Clarendon Press, 1940.

20. ———, "The Political Structure of the Nandi-Speaking Peoples of Kenya," *Africa,* Vol. XIII, 1940.

21. ———, *Kinship and Marriage among the Nuer,* Oxford: Clarendon Press, 1951.

22. Fadipe, N. A., *The Sociology of the Yoruba,* Doctor of Philosophy Thesis, London, 1939 (unpublished).

23. Forde, D., "Kinship in Umor," *American Anthropologist,* Vol. XLI, 1939*a.*

24. ———, "Government in Umor," *Africa,* Vol. XII, 1939*b.*

25. ———, *Marriage and Family among the Yakö of South-Eastern Nigeria,* London: London School of Economics, Monographs on Social Anthropology 5, 1941.

26. ———, "Ward Organization among the Yakö," *Africa,* Vol. XX, 1950.

27. ———, *The Yoruba Speaking Peoples of South-Western Nigeria* (Ethnographic Survey of Africa—Western Africa), London: International African Institute, 1950.

28. Forde, D., and G. I. Jones, *The Ibo and Ibibio-speaking Peoples of South-Eastern Nigeria* (Ethnographic Survey of Africa—Western Africa), London: International African Institute, 1950.

29. Fortes, M., "Social and Psychological Aspects of Education in Taleland," *Africa,* Vol. XI, 1938.

30. ———, *The Dynamics of Clanship among the Tallensi,* London:

Oxford University Press, for the International African Institute, 1945.

31. ———, *The Web of Kinship among the Tallensi*, London: Oxford University Press, for the International African Institute, 1949.

32. Fox, D. S., "Further Notes on the Masai of Kenya Colony," *Journal of the Royal Anthropological Institute of Great Britain and Ireland*, Vol. LX, 1930.

33. Gluckman, M., "The Kingdom of the Zulu in South Africa," in M. Fortes and E. E. Evans-Pritchard (editors), *African Political Systems*, London: Oxford University Press, for the International African Institute, 1940.

34. ———, "The Lozi," in E. Colson and M. Gluckman (editors), *Seven Tribes of British Central Africa*, London: Oxford University Press, on behalf of the Rhodes-Livingstone Institute, 1951.

35. Green, M. M., *The Village Affairs*, London: Sidgwick and Jackson, 1947.

36. Gulliver, P. H., *A Preliminary Survey of the Turkana*, Cape Town: University of Cape Town, Communications from the School of African Studies, 26, 1951.

37. ———, "The Kamarajong Cluster," *Africa*, Vol. XXII, 1952.

38. Hayley, T. T. S., *The Anatomy of Lango Religion and Groups*, Cambridge: Cambridge University Press, 1947.

39. Holding, E. M., "Some Preliminary Notes on Meru Age Grades," *Man*, Vol. XLII, 1942.

40. Hollis, A. C., *The Nandi, Their Language and Their Folklore*, Oxford: Clarendon Press, 1909.

41. Hunter, M., *Reaction to Conquest, Effects of Contact with Europeans on the Pondo of South Africa*, London: Oxford University Press, 1936.

42. Huntingford, G. W. B., "The Social Organization of the Dorobo," *African Studies*, Vol. 1, 1942.

43. ———, *The Political System of the Nandi*, Bachelor of Science Thesis, Oxford, 1949 (unpublished).

44. ———, "The Social Institutions of the Dorobo," *Anthropos*, Vol. XLVI, 1951.

45. Jeffreys, M. D. W., "Age-Groups among the Ika and Kindred People," *African Studies*, Vol. IX, 1950.

46. Kenyatta, J., *Facing Mount Kenya: The Life of the Gikuyu*, London: Secker and Warburg, 1938.

47. Krige, E. J., *The Social System of the Zulus,* Pietermaritzburg: Shuter and Shooter, 1936.

48. Krige, E. J., and J. D. Krige, *The Realm of the Rain Queen: A Study of the Pattern of Lovedu Society,* London: Oxford University Press, 1943.

49. Kuper, H., *An African Aristocracy: Rank among the Swazi,* London: Oxford University, for the International African Institute, 1947.

50. Labouret, H., *Paysans d'Afrique Occidentale,* Paris: Gallimard, 1941.

51. Larby, N., *The Kamba,* Nairobi: Ndia Kuu Press, 1944.

52. Laughton, W. H., *The Meru,* Nairobi: Ndia Kuu Press, 1944.

53. Leakey, L. S. B., "Some Notes on the Masai of Kenya Colony," *Journal of the Royal Anthropological Institute of Great Britain and Ireland,* Vol. LX, 1930.

54. Lestrade, G. P., "Some Notes on the Political Organization of the Bechwana," *South African Journal of Science,* Vol. XXV, 1928.

55. Lewis, B. A., *The Murle Political System,* Bachelor of Science Thesis, Oxford, 1950 (unpublished).

56. Lindblom, K. G., *The Akamba in British East Africa,* Upsala: Appelberg, 1920.

57. Little, K., *The Mende of Sierra Leone,* London: Routledge and Kegan Paul, 1951.

58. Mahlobo, G. W., and E. Krige, "Transition from Childhood to Adulthood among the Zulus," *Bantu Studies,* Vol. VIII, 1934.

59. McCulloch, M., *The Peoples of Sierra Leone Protectorate* (Ethnographic Survey of Africa—Western Africa), London: International African Institute, 1950.

60. Mayer, P., *The Lineage Principle in Gusii Society,* London: International African Institute, Memorandum 24, 1949.

61. ———, "The Joking of Pals in Gusii Age-Sets," *African Studies,* Vol. X, 1951.

62. Meek, C. K., *Law and Authority in a Nigerian Tribe: A Study in Indirect Rule,* London: Oxford University Press, 1937.

63. Merker, M., *Die Masai,* Berlin: Dietrich Reimer, 1910.

64. Murdock, G. P., *Social Structure,* New York: Macmillan, 1949.

65. Nadel, S. F., *A Black Byzantium,* London: Oxford University Press, for the International African Institute, 1942.

66. ———, *The Nupe,* London: Oxford University Press, 1947.

67. ———, "The Gani Ritual of Nupe: A Study of Social Symbiosis," *Africa*, Vol. XIX, 1949.

68. Nalder, L. F. (editor), *A Tribal Survey of Mongalla Province*, London: Oxford University Press, for the International African Institute, 1937.

69. Peristiany, J. G., *The Social Institutions of the Kipsigis*, London: Routledge, 1939.

70. ———, "The Age-Set System of the Pastoral Pokot," *Africa*, Vol. XXI, 1951.

71. Prins, A. H. J., *The Coastal Tribes of the North-Eastern Bantu* (Pokomo, Nyika, Teita) (Ethnographic Survey of Africa—East Central Africa), London: International African Institute, 1952.

72. ———, *East African Age-Class Systems: An Inquiry into the Social Order of Galla, Kipsigis and Kikuyu*, Groningen: J. B. Walters, 1953.

73. Radcliffe-Brown, A. R., "Introduction," in A. R. Radcliffe-Brown and D. Forde, *African Systems of Kinship and Marriage*, London: Oxford University Press, for the International African Institute, 1950.

74. Richards, A. I., "The Political System of the Bemba Tribe of North-Eastern Rhodesia," in M. Fortes and E. E. Evans-Pritchard (editors), *African Political Systems*, London: Oxford University Press, for the International African Institute, 1940.

75. ———, "The Bemba," in E. Colson and M. Gluckman (editors), *Seven Tribes of British Central Africa*, London: Oxford University Press, on behalf of the Rhodes-Livingstone Institute, 1951.

76. Schapera, I., *A Handbook of Tswana Law and Custom*, London: Oxford University Press, for the International African Institute, 1938.

77. ———, "The Political Organization of the Ngwato of Bechuanaland Protectorate," in M. Fortes and E. E. Evans-Pritchard (editors), *African Political Systems*, London: Oxford University Press, for the International African Institute, 1940.

78. ———, *The Political Annals of a Tswana Tribe*, Cape Town: University of Cape Town, Communications from the School of African Studies, 18, 1947.

79. Talbot, P. A., *The People of Southern Nigeria*, London: Oxford University Press, 1926, 4 volumes.

80. ———, *The Tribes of the Niger Delta*, The Sheldon Press, London: Macmillan, 1932.

81. Wagner, G., "The Political Organization of the Bantu of Kavirondo," in M. Fortes and E. E. Evans-Pritchard (editors), *African Political Systems*, London: Oxford University Press, for the International African Institute, 1940.

82. Werner, A., "The Galla of the East Africa Protectorate," *Journal of African Society*, Vol. XIII, 1914.

83. Westermann, D., *Die Kpelle, ein Negerstamm in Nigeria*, Gottingen: Vandenhoeck and Ruprecht, 1921.

84. Wilson, M., *Good Company: A Study of Nyakyusa Age Villages*, London: Oxford University Press, for the International African Institute, 1951.

Chapter 5

*Delinquent Group Formation among
Immigrant Youth*

I

The purpose of this chapter is to analyze some sociological aspects of
the incidence of juvenile delinquency and especially of delinquent
(youth) group formation among immigrants. Most of the material is
based on statistical data and research carried out in Israel,* but comparative studies from other countries, particularly the United States,
have also been used. The chapter is concerned mainly with the influence, on family life and adolescence, of the social processes connected with migration. It does not touch on either biological or psychological aspects of the etiology and typology of delinquents. This
should not be interpreted as claiming any monopoly for sociological
interpretation. On the contrary, it is hoped that the limits and inherent inadequacies of the purely sociological approach will be clearly
emphasized.

Reprinted from *The British Journal of Delinquency*, Vol. 2, July 1951.

---

* Most of the investigations on which this paper is based have been carried out
at the Sociological Research Seminar of the Hebrew University, Jerusalem, unless
otherwise specified. All the references to interviews are from the files of the
Seminar. The sample on which this paper is based is derived from three different
research projects mentioned in Note (3), and totals about 300 families and
450–500 adolescents (aged 13 to 19).

The high incidence of juvenile delinquency among immigrant families, especially in the second generation, has long been stressed in the literature of the subject (especially in America) (1). This incidence has been usually ascribed to different "causes," most of which are in line with the current sociological explanations of juvenile delinquency. The following main factors have been emphasized: (a) broken homes, existing among those immigrants who could not adapt themselves to conditions in the new country, (b) bad economic conditions, usually connected with (a), (c) conflict of cultural elements, norms, habits, consequent on living in two different worlds, and (d) conflict between parents and children, due mainly to (c). Although these explanations do, of course, account in varying degrees for the different manifestations of juvenile delinquency, they seem to us rather inadequate. They have unduly emphasized those aspects of modern migratory movements which are related to social disorganization, conflict, and so forth, and correspondingly the relation between immigration and juvenile delinquency became an obvious, too obvious, one. This undue emphasis does not always enable us to see the problems of juvenile delinquency in proper perspective and does not take into account the full context of social forces bearing on them.

Our investigations suggest that a somewhat fuller understanding of the problem could be arrived at if two more general, sociological characteristics of the processes of adaptation and absorption of new immigrants were taken into account. These characteristics are, first, diminution of the family's effective capacity to satisfy an organized hierarchy of needs and aspirations of its members, and especially of children and adolescents, and, second, limitation of the social sphere and functions of the family, leading to the emergence of specific "youth groups" and "youth culture."

The first characteristic, the process of adaptation to a new country, necessarily transforms both the internal structure of the family and the whole field of social participation of its members. In the first phases of adaptation, a shrinkage in the field of effective social participation of the immigrants usually takes place. Large amounts of energy have to be expended in various activities connected with economic problems and in making fresh orientations in the new country, the usual result of which is that the old family roles cannot be fully sustained. This feeling of the inadequacy of their new family set-up has been spontaneously expressed by about 80 per cent of the new immigrants observed by us and is generally recognized in the literature on immigrants. Such a situation quite frequently gives rise to undue emphasis on some basic needs—food, shelter, sexual relations—and apathy in relation to other, broader social "needs" and problems. It has sometimes even been found that the family ceases almost entirely to function as a social unit. In most cases, however, it is only gradually that the new immigrant extends his participation to broader fields of the new social structure. This process involves many points of tension as the new immigrant must learn not only new "techniques" of behavior, but must rearrange his whole hierarchy of needs and activities, and redefine his conception of himself, his social status, and so forth. This process, which is in any case difficult, is rendered still more difficult by the various dislocations connected with immigration (2). The lack of integration of needs, and so on, may affect, in various degrees, the ability of the family to orient the children and adolescents toward their future social roles and to give them the wider social perspective and values that are essential.

The second characteristic is that along with this transitory process we find in most modern industrial immigration countries a more basic one which has more permanent, structural results. In almost all these countries, the immigrants' adaptation involves a diminution and limitation of the social functions performed by the family. This is due in a large extent to the fact that the immigrants come from "familial" communities (usually peasant or artisan) and find themselves in more individualistic societies, based on a high degree of economic specialization and "universal" citizenship. The family does not constitute, in the countries of absorption, the basic unit of the social division of labor, and many social roles have to be performed by the individual independently of his role and status within the family. The limitation of the sphere of the family and the undermining of the "traditional"-familial scale of values always gives rise in varying degrees to "peer groups" formed at different age-levels by children and adolescents.*
These groups, which emerge in almost any industrial, urbanized so-

* The correlation between a nonfamilial division of labor and the emergence of specific youth groups has been verified by us in a small "cross-cultural" survey of a sample of about fifty societies. The results of the investigation are published in *From Generation to Generation.*

ciety fill the social "vacuum" between the family and the community. The predisposition toward formation of age-groups is largely intensified among immigrants, especially, as has been rightly emphasized in the literature, among the second generation of immigrants. This is due, firstly, to the differences of tradition and cultural orientation between the different generations of immigrants, second, to the speed of dislocation from a familial to a nonfamilial setting and the consequent inability of the families to orient their children toward performing extra-familial roles. For this reason the peer group type of behavior seems to be more prevalent among the different ethnic groups in the United States than in European industrial countries (3).

The decreasing scope of the family does not diminish, however, its crucial importance for the understanding of our problem. The family remains, of course, the main and primary socializing agency, and its relation to the total social structure becomes perhaps even more crucial and important—from the point of view of the social development of children—than in a familial society. From the above statement, it should be clear, however, that it is not the internal structure of the family which is most important, but the relations between this structure and the total new social field (4).

In the Jewish community in Palestine these specific youth groups prevail, in different forms, in almost all sections of the social structure (5). We may distinguish between the following main types: (a) organized, legitimate "youth movements," some of them linked with different "pioneering" movements, others mostly of a recreational character; (b) relatively unorganized, or loosely organized, cliques, recreational groups of children of a given neighborhood, school, and so forth; (c) "delinquent groups," which engage in pilfering, smuggling, and other illegal practices. It has been estimated that about 30 per cent of urban and semiurban youths are organized within the first type, and many more have passing contact with them. Even more participate, of course, in the unorganized groups, of which no detailed statistical accounts exist. Although in principle the different types can be distinguished one from the other, in actual fact they overlap and intermingle to some extent. While the structural difference between, on the one hand, the legitimate, accepted youth movements, whose activities are in varying degrees oriented toward the realization of the basic values of the community, and, on the other, the delinquent, deviant youth groups in very large, their common background makes comparison between them both easier and more interesting. All this brings us to our main problem. Which family types and types of new environment give rise to socially adapted youth groups and which to delinquent groups? The common process of migration, with its dislocations, can, perhaps, account for the general emergence of "youth groups," but not for variations in type. We must therefore compare the internal structure of these two main youth groups, and then analyze the different family constellations and environmental influences under which they emerge.*

II

Our investigations showed that all these types of youth groups have some common characteristics, associated mainly with the needs they fulfill. Interviews, observation, and analysis of the internal literature of the movement indicated quite clearly a number of motivations, varying in intensity in the different groups. These were as follows: (a) acquirement of various social skills, especially in the sphere of spontaneous competitive behavior, which are not fully developed at home; (b) the possibility of achieving not-too-distant goals (play, recreation, and so on), in contrast to the more distant ones toward which most of their activities at home are oriented; (c) acquisition of a fuller, more independent status within a group, in contrast to their dependent status at home, school, and in the occupational field (if there is any status at all in the latter); (d) identification with a small primary (nuclear) group, with whose members

* This analysis is based on three different research projects conducted by us at the Sociological Research Seminar of the Hebrew University, 1948–1953. These projects are: (1) The Problems of Oriental Jews in Palestine, completed in 1947, (2) The Absorption of New Immigrants since 1948, and (3) Problems of Youth Movements—these two carried out from 1948 to 1951. As no specific, thorough, statistical investigations of this problem have been undertaken, the conclusions are necessarily tentative, but they seem to converge into some definite pattern. They are based on about 300 families and comparative analysis of several youth movements.

one shares the same experiences; (e) more direct experience of social activities and values which are outside the scope of the family and school and which give to the youngsters a feeling of fuller and more direct participation in the community.

It is interesting to note that these factors have been equally emphasized by members of the socially adapted and the delinquent groups; no significant difference could be found among them from this point of view. In each group formation these functions were fulfilled by different sets of activities, or, to put it another way, the activities of each type of youth group were organized in different ways and oriented toward goals and values.

When differences between these two types of groups were investigated it was discovered that they did not lie mainly in the nature of these activities, e.g., sports, recreations, excursions, attending the cinema, reading. The main difference seemed to lie in the structure and organization of the group. The most important factors were found to be the following:

STABILITY, ORGANIZATION, AND SOLIDARITY OF THE GROUP. In all these respects a very marked difference existed, the delinquent groups in every case ranking lowest. In fact, the stability of any delinquent group and its component members was as a rule extremely low. The youths changed their groups very often and the group had only a minimal degree of organization. There scarcely existed any permanent goal toward which its activities were directed. Groups would shift their attention from one direction to another, for example, from pilfering to going to the cinema, each shift involving a change in membership and in organization. There existed scarcely any fixed types of role and the youths' relations with one another changed frequently, following, however, a leader-follower pattern in which physical aggression played a major part. In contrast to this, the socially adapted groups showed a higher degree of stability and organization.

DEGREE OF ORGANIZATION OF THE DIFFERENT GOALS IN A DEFINITE HIERARCHY. This is, of course, closely connected with the above. Among the delinquent groups it was found that the different goals toward which their activities were directed were not to any large extent arranged in any definite hierarchy, involving some patterning of priorities and ordering in time. They were more or less unrelated to one another, and, with constant shifts among them, each of them would acquire a temporary priority, only to be forgotten when the next goal came within their field of perception. A concomitant characteristic was the great stress laid on the *immediacy of attainment* of a goal and a minimal ability to see it in a somewhat longer temporal perspective, and to be able to arrange other activities as steps toward this attainment. This characteristic gives rise in the delinquent groups to many tensions, as it does not enable them to gain any of the adult social aims toward which they aspire. By contrast, in the socially adapted groups, the aims and activities of the members are well organized in definite patterns and in a means-ends sequence. Even here the "temporal" span is always shorter than that accorded to the children within the orbit of adult society (home, school). Importance is attached to a fuller and quicker achievement of status within the peer group, but all these goals and activities are organized in more or less definite patterns and hierarchies.

COMMUNICATION AND IDENTIFICATION WITH THE GENERAL COMMUNITY AND ITS VALUES. We have seen earlier that one of the main functions of the youth group is to provide its members with a channel of communication with those aspects and values of community life toward which the family does not orient them in an effective way, and to give them the feeling of a fuller participation in the community. This function explains why in all these groups—socially adapted and delinquent alike—considerable emphasis is laid on goals and "virtues" which symbolize the adult world and status, and certain of its aspects from which children may be excluded at home and in school: competitive behavior, full physical prowess and strength, independence in a spontaneity of recreation, social and political problems, activities, and so forth. This common orientation toward the adult community, however, takes entirely different directions in the two types of youth groups. The main difference lies in the fact that in the socially adapted groups there is a gradual and more or less orderly preparation for socially sanctioned adult roles, whereas in the delinquent groups emphasis is mainly on "symbolic" goals, which do not lead to such accepted adult roles, and on a more "vicarious" type of identification with the values of the community. The marked emphasis on immediate attainment of different external symbols of full social status—clothes, spending money, frequenting various recreational (and/or vice) resorts—is a manifestation of this tendency. This difference between the two types of group is also manifest in their communication with the adult world. In the socially accepted groups, with the gradual extension of new social perspectives, attempts to establish more intensive, regular, and organized communication with the adult world are almost always made, and the tensions between the generations do not have a "rebellious" and totally negative character. In the delinquent groups these tensions are only rarely overcome and neither effective communication with the adult world nor extension of participation in regular and recognized common social situations, roles, and identifications develops to any large extent.

This difference in the attitude toward the adult world can be well illustrated by comparing the following examples quoted from interviews with members of an organized, socially accepted youth movement and of a semidelinquent gang respectively:

I think that we are all very interested to learn many of those things that adults do, and to be able to understand the adult's world. It is true that many of them are very dull and do not interest me, but it is not true of all of them. I think we can learn from grown-ups, especially from those who understand us and do not try to be very remote. I think my father is really such a man and so is also the "madrich" (leader, guide) in the movement. I like to spend my time with them although they sometimes irritate me.

. . . All the "grown-ups" do is make constant demands on one and pretend to be very important or a different race of man. They grab all the good things that are to be had, and they don't allow anyone to take these things from them. . . . Of course, I want to be like them. I want to have as much money as they, nice clothes, to play around with girls and women, but I do not think they will let me have all this when I want it— only when I am an old man and unable to enjoy it. That is why I hate them so much. . . .

INCIDENCE OF INTERNAL AND EXTERNAL AGRESSION. The instability of delinquent groups and lack of attainment of full social roles gives rise among them to a higher incidence of internal and external aggression. Internally, this aggression is usually connected with the constant changing of roles and the strong emphasis on force and physical prowess. In external relations, the feeling of insecurity of their own status quite often gives rise to verbal or physical aggression, the main aim of which is to emphasize their full "status." This feeling is, for instance, very frequently seen in their behavior toward waiters in coffeehouses or cinema attendants.

These characteristics of the socially accepted and delinquent youth groups respectively show us that the basic difference between them lies in the way they solve the psychological and sociological problems arising from the discontinuity between the family and the community —a discontinuity which exists in any modern industrial society and which is emphasized among immigrants. From the sociological point of view, the main characteristic of the delinquent group is that it does not provide its members with effective channels of communication with the adult community and its values, and that it constitutes an uneven and disorderly field of social activity and perception through which only very few stable, recognized social roles can be learned and performed (6).

III

Our next problem is to consider under what conditions the formation of these groups takes place. For reasons of space, only the briefest outline of the conclusions arrived at during our investigations can be given. From the outset it was clear that the usual "objective" socioeconomic indices could not fully account for the formation of the two different types of group. We had to look for more specific and, at the same time, dynamic factors. Those were mostly related to some dynamic relations between the family structure and the "absorbing" environments. While only about 50 per cent of the children belonging to the type of family to be described took part in the delinquent groups, about 85 to 90 per cent of the children participating in these groups belonged to such families. This emphasizes, on the one hand, the need to elaborate our formula, and, on the other, the possible inadequacy of purely sociological explanation.

The most universal condition under which delinquent youth forma-tion took place was absence of identification and presence of intensive conflict between the family (especially the head of the family) and the new country and social structure. It should be emphasized that we are not alluding here to "mere" differences in norms, values, and so forth, which are quite prevalent among the most different types of immigrants. Of much greater importance than the "objective" differ-ence and discrepancy is the attitude taken by the immigrants toward this difference, in other words, their (and the absorbing population's) social definition of this difference. Whenever immigrants establish a positive identification with the new social structure and its values, and whenever this identification is not blocked by the "absorbing" en-vironment, the cultural and social differences only rarely give rise to a high incidence of delinquent group formation among the children and adolescents. Even when the parents are apathetic toward the new social structure, the incidence of delinquent group formation is rather low, although higher than in the former case. In our example (which is not, of course, representative of the whole immigrant population, new and old) only about 5 per cent of children from the first type of family and only 15 per cent of the second (apathetic) type were involved in some delinquent groups. On the other hand, about 50 per cent of the children from families where parents did not identify themselves with the new social setting were involved in such activi-ties. The explanation of this fact seems to be the following: Those parents who identify themselves with the social system and its values tend to transfer this identification to their children and to orient the children toward the new environment and its social demands. Even if they themselves cannot effectively teach the children the new skills and roles, they do not hinder, and may even encourage, such acquisi-tions. As one of the parents put it in an interview:

I do not understand many of these things which I see around me, and sometimes they are quite strange to me, and not always can I say what is good and what is bad. But this is our country, and all this is a part of it, and I want my children to know all this better than I do. That is why I do not interfere with them very much and sometimes even help them. I want only to see that they have good comrades and instructors—that is what is important.

Of course, conflicts and disagreements do occur, but these develop only very seldom into a definite, emotional upheaval. In the case of more apathetic parents a positive orientation toward the new social structure is absent, but the relative lack of interest of the parents ensures at least that no intense conflict will be generated. In such cases it seems that the adequacy of the "absorbing" conditions is the crucial factor in the predisposition to delinquent group formation. What are the main manifestations of this negative identification? The following seem to be the most important ones:

INCONGRUITY IN CONCEPTIONS OF SOCIAL STATUS. One of the most frequent manifestations—or causes—of the negative identification is that among the parents there exists a very great rigidity in their conception of their own status, which was mainly influenced by their old social and cultural setting. Any change means loss of status, and correspondingly any emergence of new types of demands on the children —whether in schooling, leisure-time activities, etc.—is greeted with hostility. Pressure—physical, emotional, etc.—is exerted on the children not to perform the new social roles or to satisfy the new "needs."

Take, for instance, the following typical interview with a middle-aged father, an immigrant from Central Europe.

I do not want my children to be wild and to behave in a manner in which they should not. I must always remember my education and my previous position, even if I have not yet got it here, and even if some clever people make fun of it, and even my own children do not really understand it. Here, almost all children are wild—they shout, are neither polite nor obedient, are not interested in working—only in playing and excursions. They do not dress properly; boys and girls mix too freely. I have many difficulties with my children and sometimes have to beat them; otherwise they will not become real men. . . . Here, at least, in my home, I must have some authority. . . .

One of his children summed up thus:

Father still lives in the past and thinks himself very important. But really he does not understand very much here. He makes life very hard for us, and we cannot get any fun with him. He gets terribly angry if we have some fun on our own. . . . But never mind, we shall do what we like, and he will be very sorry for it.

It is among the children from these families that the highest rates of truancy from school, absenteeism from work, and so forth, are found. The result of this is, of course, that the children find it more and more difficult to establish for themselves a recognized social status according to the criteria of the new social structure, while the "old" status of their families lacks any reality in the new setting. Such a situation may develop—either in extreme cases or in thorough and prolonged undermining of the family structure—into a complete disruption of family life and of its ability to achieve any status at all. In such cases we witness the exclusive emphasis on a few basic biological needs and satisfactions and a lack of any stable roles and social relations. The relations between the parents and children become based more and more on sheer physical force which is not backed by any social participation or orientation. While among children of these "extreme" families, the various indices of delinquent group behavior are usually intensified, it may quite often be found that they are unable to form any group relations at all, as the degree of organization of their personalities is minimal and their ability to perform any stable social roles undeveloped.

CONFLICTS OF CONCEPTIONS OF AUTHORITY. This problem has been most widely emphasized in the literature on delinquency among immigrants (7). The stable and effective transmission of social and cultural orientations from the parents to the children is dependent on the acceptance of the parents' authority by the children. This is undermined whenever the conception of authority in the new social setting is different from the old and transmitted to the children through the "wider, nonfamilial" environment. In these cases the children's ability to perform new social roles and achieve full status within the new environment is jeopardized to the extent that the old authority norms are enforced on them, and the ensuing conflict predisposes the youths toward delinquent group formation. The emergence of such conflict is, of course, related to the difference of norms between familial-patriarchal and industrial-individualistic societies, but is not a necessary outcome of this difference. It is the degree of insistence on the old authority-dependence relations in the new environment which is the predominant factor. This attitude also can be illustrated from our interview material. The following excerpts are from an interview with an immigrant from North Africa:

I cannot really understand what happens here with parents and children. I do not think that what they do here is right and really it is a great sin. . . . At home we knew our place with our father, and he would not allow any disobedience. He knew what was right for us. But here children are becoming wild and unruly . . . they think that they should not obey their parents, that they are much wiser than the father and mother. They tell me openly that I do not understand what is good here. . . . It is the school, their teachers, and their "groups" that teach them all this. Whoever has heard that children should have groups of their own and not obey the elders? . . . I try, always, to assert my authority and if they will not accept it, I shall throw them out. . . .

DISCREPANCY BETWEEN THE PARENTS' LEVEL OF ASPIRATION IN THE NEW COUNTRY AND THE POSSIBILITY OF ITS REALIZATION. This applies mainly to those immigrants who were initially more predisposed to change their social roles and to orient their aspirations toward the new social setting but did not succeed in realizing them. It is in this context that cultural differences become of greater dynamic importance, since the lack of various skills and knowledge which are necessary for the performance of these new roles may seriously impede their realization. As one of them put it:

I have always thought that here I should begin a new life, become more prosperous and more influential. But these were vain hopes. The people here are hard and jealous and do not like to give me a chance. They always say that I do not know this or that and so on, as if they were the only wise people in the world. And so I am here, as you can see, in such conditions. What makes me really very angry is that now my children go out and play there with their children; they imitate them and they also think that all wisdom is there. I am very angry at them and I think we do not understand one another any longer. . . . They live in a world apart and are not interested in me. . . . I have really got no influence over them. . . .

Although no exact comparisons can be made, it seems that among children of these families a more intensive manifestation of the different delinquent symptoms can be found.

These main manifestations of a negative identification and conflict with the new social structure have been found to exist—although in different proportions—among all ethnic groups and socio-economic strata. They could not be attributed either to cultural heritage or to socio-economic positions, but mainly to other factors, such as motives for immigration to Palestine, types of Jewish life and identification, consciousness and degree of social security as Jews in the countries of origin, and so forth. These causes were analyzed by us in great detail in connection with the project of absorbing new immigrants, but are outside the scope of this paper.

In conclusion we must mention the type of conditions in the country of immigration which intensify the discontinuity and tensions between the family setting and the community. Although no full-scale analysis can be given in this short paper, some general indications should be mentioned. It has been found that generally this discontinuity is increased insofar as: (a) the new immigrants are put in undefined and unorganized settings in which no clearly defined rights and duties are assigned them and in which their own inclination to emphasize only the basic, biological needs is intensified; (b) they encounter their new social setting mainly through bureaucratic channels and institutions in which they perform merely passive and subordinate roles; (c) they cannot fully participate in informal, face-to-face groups and relations with the old inhabitants and are mainly confined to formal relations in which only minimal mutual identification can develop; and (d) they are discriminated against by the old inhabitants. This last condition is, however, rare.

In other words, the predisposition toward delinquent group formation is minimized where the new immigrants (and specially the children and adolescents) can find or are enabled to acquire new, permanent and recognized social roles and to participate in close personal relations with the old inhabitants. The existence of personal channels through which the immigrants can be introduced to the new social setting is the prerequisite of absorption. In many cases, the existence of such channels mitigates the results of unfavorable family settings, and the identification fostered through them may sometimes overcome the negative identification between the families and the community.

REFERENCES

1. Tappan, P. W., *Juvenile Delinquency*, New York: McGraw-Hill, 1949, pp. 139–140; Hentig, H. V., *The Criminal and His Victim*, New Haven: Yale University Press, 1948, pp. 259–297; Reckless, W., *The Crime Problem*, New York: Appleton-Century-Crofts, 1950, pp. 71–73; Sellin, T., *Culture Conflict and Crime*, Social Science Research Council, Bulletin 41, 1938; Eisenstadt, S. N., "The Sociological Structure of the Jewish Community in Palestine," *Jewish Social Studies*, January 1948; Eisenstadt, S. N., "Oriental Jews in Palestine," *Jewish Social Studies*, July 1950; Frankenstein, C., *Juvenile Delinquency* (in Hebrew), Jerusalem: The Henrietta Szold Foundation for Child and Youth Welfare, 1947; Poliak, A. N., *The Jewish Community at the End of the Second World War* (in Hebrew), Tel-Aviv: Sifri'at Hapo'alim, 1945.

2. Thomas, W. I., and F. Znaniecki, *The Polish Peasant in Europe and America*, New York: Alfred A. Knopf, 1927.

3. Bossard, J. H. S., *Sociology of Child Development*, New York: Harper and Brothers, 1948, pp. 493–520.

4. McKay, H. D., "The Neighbourhood and Child Conduct," *Annals of the American Academy of Political and Social Science*, January 1949, 261, pp. 32–42.

5. Eisenstadt, S. N., "Youth Culture and Social Structure in Israel," *British Journal of Sociology*, Vol. II, 1951, pp. 105–114.

6. ———, "Unstructured Social Behaviour in a Situation of Culture Contact," *Proceedings of the 14th International Congress of Psychology*, Edinburgh, 1948.

7. Child, Irving L., *Italian or American, the Second Generation in Conflict*, New Haven: Yale University Press, 1943 (See also [1] above).

Chapter 6

Changing Patterns of Youth Problems in Contemporary Societies

I

The "youth problem" or various youth problems have constituted a part of modern society and of modern social problems since the beginning of the development of modern society in Europe. The processes of development of modern societies, of what is now often called modernization, have created a great variety of conditions which have tended to intensify the perception and self-perception of youth as a distinct category, with problems of its own, within the broad contours of modern society.

As in so many other spheres, our thoughts and perception of these problems and of the ways to deal with them have been greatly influenced by the initial forms which these problems have undertaken and by the initial responses to them as they have developed in the ideological and policy-making spheres. But, in the meantime, the conditions which gave rise to these problems have been greatly changing; new constellations of these conditions have developed, producing new types and new expressions of the youth problem. It is the purpose of this discussion to explore, in a very preliminary way, some of these

The first parts of this chapter have been adapted from S. N. Eisenstadt, "Archetypal Patterns of Youth," *Daedalus*, Winter 1962, pp. 28–46. The latter parts have been especially written for this book.

new developments and their repercussion on pedological-ideological and policy approaches.

But in order to be able to analyze these problems it would be best to start with a general comparative analysis of youth problems.

II

Youth constitutes a universal phenomenon. It is first of all a biological phenomenon, but one always defined in cultural terms. In this sense it constitutes a part of a wider cultural phenomenon, the varying definitions of age and of the differences between one age and another (1). Age and age differences are among the basic aspects of life and the determinants of human destiny. Every human being passes through various ages, and at each one he attains and uses different biological and intellectual capacities. At each stage he performs different tasks and roles in relation to the other members of his society: from a child, he becomes a father; from a pupil, a teacher; from a vigorous youth, a mature adult, and then an aging and "old" man.

This gradual unfolding of power and capacity is not merely a universal, biologically conditioned, and inescapable fact. Although the basic biological processes of maturation (within the limits set by such factors as relative longevity) are probably more or less similar in all human societies, their cultural definition varies from society to society, at least in details. In all societies, age serves as a basis for defining the cultural and social characteristics of human beings, for the formation of some of their mutual relations and common activities, and for the differential allocation of social roles.

The cultural definitions of age and age differences contain several different yet complementary elements. First, these definitions often refer to the social division of labor in a society, to the criteria according to which people occupy various social positions and roles within any society. For instance, in many societies certain roles—especially those of married men, full citizens, independent earners—are barred to young people, while others—as certainly military roles—are specifically allocated to them. Second, the cultural definition of age is one important constituent of a person's self-identity, his self-perception in terms of his own psychological needs and aspirations, his place in society, and the ultimate meaning of his life.

Within any such definition, the qualities of each age are evaluated according to their relation to some basic, primordial qualities, such as vigor, physical and sexual prowess, the ability to cope with material, social, and supernatural environment, wisdom, experience, and divine inspiration. Different ages are seen in different societies as the embodiments of such qualities. These various qualities seem to unfold from one age to another, each age emphasizing some out of the whole panorama of such possible qualities. The cultural definition of an age span is always a broad definition of human potentialities and obligations at a given stage of life. In terms of these definitions, people map out the broad contours of life, their own expectations and possibilities, and place themselves and their fellow men in social and cultural positions, ascribing to each a given place within these contours.

The various qualities attributed to different ages do not constitute an unconnected series. They are usually interconnected in many ways. The subtle dialectic between the unfolding of some qualities and the wanning of others in a person is not a mere registration of his psychological or biological traits. Rather, it constitutes the broad framework of his potentialities and their limits throughout his life span. The characteristics of any one "age," therefore, cannot be fully understood except in relation to other ages. Whether seen as a gradually unfolding continuum or as a series of sharp contrasts and opposed characteristics, they are fully explicable and understandable only in terms of one another. The boy bears within himself the seeds of the adult man. Otherwise, he must as an adult acquire new patterns of behavior, sharply and intentionally opposed to those of his boyhood. The adult either develops naturally into an old man or decays into one. Only when taken together do these different ages constitute the entire map of human possibilities and limitations, and, as every individual usually must pass through them all, their complementariness and continuity (even if defined in discontinuous and contrasting terms) become strongly emphasized and articulated.

The same holds true for the age definitions of the two sexes, although perhaps with a somewhat different meaning. Each age span is defined differently for either sex, and these definitions are usually related and complementary, as "sexual image" and identity always constitute basic elements of man's image in every society. This close connection between different ages necessarily stresses the problem of transition from one point in a person's life to another as a basic constituent of any cultural definition of an "age." Hence, each definition of age must necessarily cope with the perception of time, and changes in time, of one's own progress in time, one's transition from one period of life to another.

This personal transition, or temporal progress, or change may become closely linked with what may be called cosmic and societal time (2). The attempt to find some meaning in personal temporal transition may often lead to identification with the rhythms of nature or history, with the cycles of the seasons, with the unfolding of some cosmic plan (whether cyclical, seasonal, or apocalyptic), or with the destiny and development of society. The nature of this linkage often constitutes the focus around which an individual's personal identity becomes defined in cultural terms and through which personal experience, with its anguish, may be given some meaning in terms of cultural symbols and values.

The whole problem of age definition and the linkage of personal time and transition with cosmic time has become especially accentuated in that age span usually designated as youth. However great the differences among various societies, there is one focal point within the life span of an individual which in most known societies is to some extent emphasized: the period of youth, the transition from childhood to full adult status or full membership in the society. In this period the individual is no longer a child (especially from the physical and sexual point of view) but is ready to undertake many attributes of an adult and to fulfill adult roles. But he is not fully acknowledged as an adult, as a full member of the society. Rather, he is being "prepared" or is preparing himself for such adulthood.

This image of youth—the cultural definition of youth—contains all the crucial elements of any definition of age, usually in an especially articulated way. This is the stage at which the individual's personality acquires the basic psychological mechanism of self-regulation and self-control, when his self-identity becomes crystallized. It is also the stage at which the person is confronted with some models of the major roles he is supposed to emulate in adult life and with the major symbols and values of his culture and community. Moreover, in this phase the

problem of the linkage of the personal temporal transition with cosmic or societal time becomes extremely acute. Any cultural definition
of youth describes it as a transitory phase, couched in terms of transition toward something new, something basically different from the
past—hence the acuteness of the problem of linkage.

The very emphasis on the transitory nature of this stage and of its
essentially preparatory character, however, may easily create a somewhat paradoxical situation. It may evolve an image of youth as the
purest manifestation and repository of ultimate cultural and societal
values. Such an image is rooted first in the fact that to some extent
youth is always defined as a period of "role moratorium," that is, as a
period in which one may play with various roles without definitely
choosing any. It does not yet require the various compromises inherent in the daily participation in adult life. At the same time, however,
since it is also the period when the maximum identification with the
values of the society is stressed, under certain conditions it may be
viewed as the repository of all the major human virtues and primordial qualities. It may then be regarded as the only age in which full
identification with the ultimate values and symbols of the society is
attained—facilitated by the flowering of physical vigor, a vigor which
may easily become identified with a more general flowering of the cos-
mos or the society.

The fullest, the most articulate and definitive expression of these
archetypal elements of youth is best exemplified in the ritual dramati-
zations of the transition from adolescence to adulthood, such as the
various *rites de passage* and ceremonies of initiation in primitive tribes
and in ancient civilization (3). In these rites the pre-adult youths are
transformed into full members of the tribe. This transformation is
effected through, first, a series of rites in which the adolescents are
symbolically divested of the characteristics of youth and invested with
those of adulthood, from a sexual and social point of view. This investment, which has deep emotional significance, may have various
concrete manifestations: bodily mutilation, circumcision, the taking on
of a new name, or symbolic rebirth.

Second, the transformation is made through the complete symbolic
separation of the male adolescents from the world of their youth, especially from their close attachment to their mothers—in other words,

their complete "male" independence and image are fully articulated (the opposite usually holds true of girls' initiations).

Third, the dramatization of the encounter between the several generations, a dramatization that may take the form of a fight or a competition, in which the basic complementariness of various age grades—whether of a continuous or discontinuous type—is stressed as another means of effecting transformation. Quite often the discontinuity between adolescence and adulthood is symbolically expressed, as in the symbolic death of the adolescents as children and their rebirth as adults.

A fourth means of transformation is the transmission of the tribal lore with its instructions about proper behavior, both through formalized teaching and through various ritual activities. This transmission is combined with a fifth means, a relaxation of the concrete control of the adults over the erstwhile adolescents and the substitution by the adolescents of self-control and adult responsibility.

Most of these dramatic elements can also be found, although in somewhat more diluted forms, in various traditional folk festivals in peasant communities, especially in those, such as rural carnivals, in which youth and marriage are emphasized. In an even more diluted form, these elements may be found in various spontaneous initiation ceremonies of fraternities and youth groups in modern societies (4). Here, however, the full dramatic articulation of these elements is lacking, and their configuration and organization assume different forms.

The transition from childhood and adolescence to adulthood, the development of personal identity, psychological autonomy and self-regulation, the attempt to link personal temporal transition to general cultural images and to cosmic rhythms, and to link psychological maturity to the emulation of definite role models—these constitute the basic elements of any archetypal image of youth. However, the ways in which these various elements become crystallized in concrete configurations differ greatly from society to society and within sectors of the same society. The full dramatic articulation of these elements in the *rites de passage* or primitive societies constitutes only one—perhaps the most extreme and articulate but certainly not the only—configuration of these archetypal elements of youth.

In order to understand other types of such configurations, it is necessary to analyze some conditions that influence their development. Perhaps the best starting point is the nature of the social organization of the period of adolescence: the process of transition from childhood to adulthood, the social context in which the process of growing up is shaped and structured. There are two major criteria that shape the social organization of the period of youth.

One is the extent to which age in general and youth in particular form a criterion for the allocation of roles in a society, whether in politics or in economic or cultural activity—aside from the family, of course, in which they always serve as such a criterion. The second criterion is the extent to which any society develops specific age-groups, specific corporate organizations, composed of members of the same age, such as youth movements or old-age clubs. If roles are allocated in a society according to age, this greatly influences the extent to which age constitutes a component of a person's identity. In such cases, youth becomes a definite and meaningful phase of transition in an individual's progression through life, and his budding self-identity acquires content and a relation to role models and cultural values. No less important to the concrete development of identity is the extent to which it is influenced, either by the common participation of different generations in the same group as in the family, or, conversely, by the organization of members of the same age-groups into specific, distinct groups.

The importance of age as a criterion for allocating roles in a society is closely related to several major aspects of social organization and cultural orientation. The first aspect is the relative complexity of the division of labor. In general, the simpler the organization of the society, the more influential age will be as a criterion for allocating roles. Therefore, in primitive or traditional societies (or in the more primitive and traditional sectors of developed societies) age and seniority constitute basic criteria for allocating social, economic, and political roles.

The second aspect consists of the major value orientations and symbols of a society, especially the extent to which they emphasize certain general orientations, qualities, or types of activity (such as physical vigor, the maintenance of cultural tradition, and the achievement and maintenance of supernatural prowess) which can be defined in terms of broad human qualities and which become expressed and symbolized in specific ages.

The emphasis on any particular age as a criterion for the allocation of roles is largely related to the concrete application of the major value orientations in a society. For instance, we find that those primitive societies in which military values and orientations prevail emphasize young adulthood as the most important age, while those in which sedentary activities prevail emphasize older age. Similarly, within some traditional societies, a particular period such as old age may be emphasized if it is seen as the most appropriate one for expressing major cultural values and symbols, as, for instance, the upholding of a given cultural tradition.

The social and cultural conditions that determine the extent to which specific age-groups and youth groups develop differ from the conditions that determine the extent to which age serves as a criterion for the allocation of roles. At the same time, the two kinds of conditions may be closely related, as we shall see. Age-groups in general and youth groups in particular tend to arise in those societies in which the family or kinship unit cannot ensure (they may even impede) the attainment of full social status on the part of its members. These conditions appear especially (although not uniquely) (5) in societies in which family or kinship groups do not constitute the basic unit of the social division of labor. Several features characterize such societies. First, the membership in the total society (citizenship) is not defined in terms of belonging to such family, kinship group, or estate, nor is it mediated by a certain group.

Second, in these societies the major political, economic, social, and religious functions are performed not by family or kinship units but rather by various specialized groups (political parties, occupational associations, and so on), which individuals may join irrespective of their family, kinship, or caste. In these societies, therefore, the major roles that adults are expected to perform in the wider society differ in orientation from those of the family or kinship group. The children's identification and close interaction with family members of other ages does not ensure the attainment of full self-identity and social maturity on the part of the children. In these cases, there arises a tendency for peer groups to form, especially among the youth; these can serve as a transitory phase between the world of childhood and the adult world.

This type of social division of labor is found in varying degrees in different societies—primitive, historical, or modern.

III

The fullest development of this type of division of labor can be found in modern societies. The inclusive membership in modern societies is usually based on the universal criterion of citizenship and is not conditioned by membership in any kinship group. In these societies the family does not constitute a basic unit of the division of labor, especially not in production and distribution, and even in the sphere of consumption its functions become more limited. Occupations are not usually transmitted through heredity. Similarly, the family or kinship group does not constitute a basic unit of political or ritual activity. Moreover, the general scope of activities of the family has been continuously diminishing, while various specialized agencies have tended to take over its functions in the fields of education and recreation.

To be sure, the extent to which the family is diminishing in modern societies is often exaggerated. In many social spheres (neighborhood, friendship, informal association, some class relations, community relations), family, kinship, and status are still very influential. But the scope of these relations is more limited in modern societies than in many others, even if the prevalent myth of the disappearance of the family has long since been explored. The major social developments of the nineteenth century (the establishment of national states, the progress of the industrial revolution, the great waves of intercontinental migrations) have greatly contributed to this diminution of scope, and especially in the first phase of modernization there has been a growing discontinuity between the life of children, whether in the family, the traditional school, or in the social world with its new and enlarged perspectives.

These varied developments were closely related to marked changes in the social functions and organizations of education. In premodern societies, the process of education was usually divided into several rather compartmentalized parts. The "central" educational institutions were mainly oriented to the education of elite and upper strata and to the upholding and developing of the central cultural tradition in its varied manifestations.

The local educational institutions, which were usually only loosely connected with the central ones, were mostly oriented first to the maintenance of some general and diffuse identification of the various strata with the overall symbols of society, without, however, permitting these strata any closer participation in the central political and cultural activities. Second they were oriented to the provision of the technical know-how which would "fit" their position in society. In between the two there were several educational institutions which served as either channels of restricted "sponsored" mobility into the central spheres of society or of some specific vocational preparation.

On the whole, the educational system in these societies was geared to the maintenance and perpetuation of a given, relatively nonchanging, cultural tradition and did not serve as a channel of widespread occupational and social mobility. The type of education given to different classses was greatly, although not entirely, determined by the class's social-economic position and not vice versa. This has begun to change with the onset of modernization. Educational institutions began to deal with problems of forging new national communities and their common symbols, the access to which would be more widely spread among different strata, and, at the same time, they began also more and more to serve as a channel of overall occupational selection. Moreover, the system of education tended to be more centralized and unified, thus ensuring its permeation to wider strata of the society.

Truly enough, these developments in the organization and function of education tended to develop gradually and unevenly in different sections of modern societies. But the general trend was common to most, and it greatly contributed to the development of the different types of "youth activities" and youth problems.

IV

Youth groups tend to develop in all societies in which such a division of labor exists. Youth's tendency to coalesce in such groups is rooted in the fact that participation in the family became insufficient for developing full identity or full social maturity and that the roles learned in the family did not constitute an adequate basis for developing such identity and participation. In the youth groups the adolescent seeks some framework for the development and crystallization of his identity, for the attainment of personal autonomy, and for his effective transition into the adult world.

Various types of youth organizations have a tendency to appear with the transition from traditional or feudal societies to modern societies, along with the intensified processes of change, especially in periods of rapid mobility, migration, urbanization, and industrialization. This is true of all European societies and also of non-Western societies. The impact of Western civilization on primitive and historical-traditional peoples is usually connected with the disruption of family life, but beyond this it also involves a change in the mutual evaluation of the different generations. The younger generation usually begins to seek a new self-identification, and one phase or another of this search is expressed in ideological conflict with the older generation.

Most of the nationalistic movements in the Middle East, Asia, and Africa have consisted of young people, students, or officers who rebelled against their elders and the traditional familistic setting with its stress on the elders' authority. At the same time there usually has developed a specific youth consciousness and ideology that intensifies the nationalistic movement to "rejuvenate" the country.

The emergence of the peer group among immigrant children is a well-known phenomenon that usually appears in the second generation. It occurs mainly because of the relative breakdown of immigrant family life in the new country. The more highly industrialized and urbanized the country (or the sector absorbing the immigrants) is, the sharper the breakdown. Hence, the family of the immigrant or second-generation child has often been an inadequate guide to the new society. The immigrant child's attainment of full identity in the new land is usually related to how much he has been able to detach himself from his older, family setting. Some of these children, therefore, have developed a strong predisposition to join various peer groups. Such an affiliation has sometimes facilitated their transition into the absorbing society by stressing the values and patterns of behavior in that society—or, on the contrary, it may express their rebellion against this society or against their older setting.

All these modern social developments and movements have given rise to a great variety of youth groups, peer groups, youth movements, and what has been called youth culture. The types and concrete forms of such groups vary widely: spontaneous youth groups, student movements, ideological and semipolitical movements, and youth rebellions connected with the Romantic movements in Europe and, later, with the German youth movements. The various social and national trends of the nineteenth and twentieth centuries have also given impetus to such organizations. At the same time there have appeared many adult-sponsored youth organizations and other agencies springing out of the great extension of educational institutions. In addition to providing recreational facilities, these agencies have also aimed at character molding and the instillation of civic virtues, so as to deepen social consciousness and widen the social and cultural horizon. The chief examples are the YMCA, the Youth Brigades organized in England by William Smith, the Boy Scouts, the Jousters in France, and many kinds of community organizations, hostels, summer camps, or vocational guidance centers.

Thus we see that there are many parallels between primitive and historical societies and modern societies with regard to the conditions under which the various constellations of youth groups, youth activities, and youth images have developed. But these parallels are only partial. Despite certain similarities, the specific configurations of the basic archetypal elements of the youth image in modern societies differ greatly from those of primitive and traditional societies. The most important differences are rooted in the fact that in modern society, the development of specific youth organizations is paradoxically connected with the weakening of the importance of age in general and youth in particular as definite criteria for the allocation of roles in society.

In primitive and traditional societies, youth groups are usually part of a wider organization of age-groups that covers a very long period of life, from childhood to late adulthood and even old age. To be sure, it is during youth that most of the dramatic elements of the transition from one age to another are most fully manifested, but this stage constitutes only part of a longer series of continuous, well-defined stages.

From this point of view, primitive or traditional societies do not differ greatly from those in which the transition from youth to adult-hood is not organized in specific age-groups but is largely effected within the fold of the family and kinship groups. In both primitive and traditional societies we observe a close and comprehensive linkage between personal temporal transition and societal or cosmic time, a linkage most fully expressed in the *rites de passage*. Consequently, the transition from childhood to adulthood in all such societies is given full meaning in terms of ultimate cultural values and symbols borne or symbolized by various adult role models.

In modern societies the above picture greatly changes. The youth group, whatever its composition or organization, usually stands alone. It does not constitute a part of a fully institutionalized and organized series of age-groups. It is true that in many of the sectors of modern societies the more primitive or traditional archetypes of youth still prevail. But the full articulation of these elements is lacking, and the social organization and self-expression of youth are not given full legitimation or meaning in terms of cultural values and rituals.

The close linkage between the growth of personality, psychological maturation, and definite role models derived from the adult world has become greatly weakened. Hence the coalescence of youth into special groups only tends to emphasize their uncertain standing from the point of view of cultural values and symbols. This uncertainty has created a new constellation of the basic archetypal elements of youth. This new constellation can most clearly be seen in what has been called the emergence of the problems and stresses of adolescence in modern societies. While some of these stresses are necessarily common to adolescence in all societies, they become especially acute in modern societies.

Among these stresses the most important are the following: First, the bodily development of the adolescent constitutes a constant problem to him (or her). Since social maturity usually lags behind biological maturity, the bodily changes of puberty are not usually given a full cultural, normative meaning, and their evaluation is one of the adolescent's main concerns. The difficulty inherent in attaining legitimate sexual outlets and relations at this period of growth makes these problems even more acute. Second, the adolescent's orientation toward the main values of his society is also beset with difficulties. Owing to the long period of preparation and the relative segregation of the children's world from that of the adults', the main values of the society are necessarily presented to the child and adolescent in a highly selective way, with a strong idealistic emphasis. The relative unreality of these values as presented to the children—which at the same time are not given full ritual and symbolic expression—creates among the adolescents a great potential uncertainty and ambivalence toward the adult world.

This ambivalence is manifested, on the one hand, in a striving to communicate with the adult world and receive its recognition; on the other hand, it appears in certain dispositions to accentuate the differences between adolescents and adults and to oppose the various roles allocated to adolescents by the adults. While they orient themselves to full participation in the adult world and its values, adolescents usually attempt also to communicate with this world in a distinct and special way.

Parallel developments are to be found in the ideologies of modern youth groups. Most youth groups tend to create an ideology that emphasizes the discontinuity between youth and adulthood and the uniqueness of the youth period as the purest embodiment of ultimate social and cultural values. Although the explicitness of this ideology varies in extent from one sector of modern society to another, its basic elements are prevalent in almost all modern youth groups.

These processes have been necessarily accentuated in modern societies by the specific developments in cultural orientations in general and in the conception of time that has evolved in particular. The major social developments in modern societies have weakened the importance of broad cultural qualities as criteria for the allocation of roles. Similarly, important changes in the conception of time prevailing in modern societies have occurred. Primordial conceptions of time (cosmi-mythical, cynical, or apocalyptical) have become greatly weakened, especially in their bearing on daily activities. The mechanical conception of time of modern technology has become much more prevalent. Of necessity this has greatly weakened the possibility of the direct ritual links between personal-temporal changes and cosmic or societal progression. Therefore, the exploration of the actual meaning of major cultural values in their relation to the reality of the social world has become one of the adolescent's main problems. This exploration may lead in many directions—to cynicism, idealistic youth rebellion, deviant ideology and behavior, or a gradual development of a balanced identity.

Thus we see how all these developments in modern societies have created a new constellation of the basic archetypal elements of youth and the youth image. The two main characteristics of this constellation are the weakened possibility of directly linking the development of personality and the personal-temporal transition with cosmic and societal time, on the one hand, and with the clear role models derived from the adult world, on the other.

In terms of personality development, this situation has created a great potential insecurity and the possible lack of a clear definition of personal identity. Yet it has also created the possibility of greater personal autonomy and flexibility in the choice of roles and the commitment to different values and symbols. In general, the individual has been thrown much more on his own powers in his search for the meaning of his personal transition.

These processes have provided the framework within which the various attempts to forge youth's identity and activities—both on the part of youth itself and on the part of various educational agencies—have developed. These attempts may take several directions. Youth's own activities and attempts at self-expression may, first, develop in the direction of considerable autonomy in the choice of roles and in commitment to various values. Conversely, they may develop in the direction of a more complete, fully organized, and closed ideology connected with a small extent of personal autonomy. Second, these attempts may differ greatly in their emphasis on the direct linkage of cultural values to a specific social group and their view of these groups as the main bearers of such values.

In a parallel sense, attempts have been made on the part of various educational agencies to create new types of youth organizations within which youth can forge its identity and become linked to adult society. The purpose of such attempts has been twofold: to provide youth with opportunities to develop a reasonably autonomous personality and a differentiated field of activity, and to encompass youth fully within well-organized groups set up by adult society and to provide them with full, unequivocal role models and symbols of identification. The interaction between these different tendencies of youth and the attempts of adult society to provide various frameworks for youth activities have given rise to the major types of youth organizations, movements, and ideologies manifested in modern societies.

These various trends and tendencies have created a situation in which, so far as we can ascertain, the number of casualties among youth, i.e., of delinquents of different kinds, has become very great—probably relatively much greater than in other types of societies. Youth's search for identity, for finding some place of its own in society, and its potential difficulties in coping with the attainment of such identity have given rise to the great increase of casualties observed in the numerous youth delinquents of varying types. These failures, however, are not the only major youth developments in modern societies, although their relatively greater number is endemic in modern conditions. Much more extensive are the more positive attempts of youth to forge its own identity, to find some meaningful way of defining its place in the social and cultural context and of connecting social and political values with personal development in a coherent and significant manner.

V

The central, concrete manifestations of youth problems in early modern societies were two. The first one was what may be called "social problems" of youth developing out of urbanization, early industrialization, and immigration, and the different problems of dislocation created by such problems. The main problems here were those of the loss of control by the family over its younger members, the lack of adequate employment opportunities, problems of maleducation, the lack of adequate vocational guidance, and, beyond these, problems of juvenile delinquency. Here it was mostly the occupational discontinuity, the inadequacy of older economic and societal frameworks, and the lack of adequate new opportunities, as well as the general occupational and economic dislocations, that were most clearly emphasized. The urban slum, the "street corner society," and the "gang" have become the main symbols of this type of youth problem.

The second major manifestation of youth problems in modern society which became prominent in the public eye was that of different

youth movements, student movements, and spontaneous youth organizations which have developed, especially in Central Europe, taking part in wider social movements or aiming at the reformation of
the society in terms of some distinct, specific youth values. Participation in the various movements was part of a wider phenomena of dissatisfaction, of "restlessness" of youth in its confrontation with the
cultural and political frameworks and symbols presented to it by the
new patterns of society then developing.

This restlessness was manifest in youth's general attitude toward
adult society and toward the newly developing forms of social, political, and cultural patterns and symbols.

The best example in our times of the extrme upsurge of specific
youth consciousness is seen in the various revolutionary youth movements. These range from the autonomous Free German youth movements to the less spectacular youth movements in Central Europe and
also to some extent to the specific youth cultures of other more flexible
youth groups. Here the attempt has been made to overcome the dislocation between personal transition and societal and cultural time. It
is in these movements that the social dynamics of modern youth have
found their fullest expression. It is in them that dreams of a new life,
a new society, freedom and spontaneity, a new humanity, and aspirations to social and cultural change have found utterance. It is in these
youth movements that the forging of youth's new social identity has
become closely connected with the development of new symbols of
collective identity or new social-cultural symbols and meanings.

These movements have aimed at changing many aspects of the social and cultural life of their respective societies. They have depicted
the present in a rather shabby form; they have dubbed it with adjec-
tives of materialism, restriction, exploitation, lack of opportunity for
self-fulfillment and creativity. At the same time they have held out
hope for the future—seemingly, the not too distant future—when
both self-fulfillment and collective fulfillment can be achieved and
materialistic civilization of the adult world can be shaken off. They
have tried to appeal to youth to forge its own self-identity in terms of
these new collective symbols, and this is why they have been so attrac-
tive to youth, for whom they have provided a set of symbols, hopes,
and aims to which youth can direct its activities.

Within these movements the emphasis has been on a given social group or collectivity—nation, class, or the youth group itself—as the main, almost exclusive, bearer of the "good" cultural values and symbols. Indeed, youth has at times been upheld as the sole and pure bearer of cultural values and social creativity. Through its association with these movements, youth has also been able to connect its aspiration for a different personal future, its anxiety to escape the present wishes, plans, and hopes for a different cultural or social future.

These various manifestations have played a crucial part in the emergence of social movements and parties in modern societies. Student groups have been the nuclei of the most important nationalistic and revolutionary movements in Central and Eastern Europe, in Italay, Germany, Hungary, and Russia. They have also played a significant role in Zionism and in the various waves of immigration to Israel. Their influence has become enormous in various fields, not only political and educational but also cultural in general. In a way, education istelf has tended to become a social movement. Many schools, universities, and teachers have been among the most important bearers of collective values. The very spread of education is often seen as a means by which a new epoch might be ushered in.

The search for some connection between the personal situation of youth and social-cultural values has also stimulated the looser youth groups in modern societies, especially in the United States, and to some extent in Europe as well—though here the psychological meaning of the search is somewhat different. The looser youth groups have often shared some of the characteristics of the more defined youth movements, and they too have developed an emphasis on the attainment of social and cultural change. The yearning for a different personal future has likewise become connected with aspirations for changing the cultural setting, but not necessarily through a direct political or organized expression. They are principally important as a strong link with various collective, artistic, and literary aspirations aimed at changing social and cultural life. As such they are affiliated with various cultural values and symbols and not with any exclusive social groups. Thus they have necessarily developed a much greater freedom in choice of roles and commitment to values.

VI

These major initial types of youth groups and problems have also necessarily greatly influenced the types of broad general attitudes and of social policy that have developed with regard to the problems of youth. One such attitude was manifested in the interest of all social movement politicians and political parties in their ability to absorb the potential social-political interest and wider orientations of the youth groups into their own frameworks. Thus, special youth sections or organizations were developed by most of the political and social movements and organizations that developed in modern societies.

Similarly, there have developed many agencies of what has been called "civic education," whose main aims were, first, to channel the potential civic orientations of youth into accepted and "safe" areas and to show a "peaceful" way of absorbing into the more central institutions the less developed, more peripheral groups of the society which constituted the majority of the population.

These activities have very often overlapped but certainly were not identical with the second more specific type of social policies which were developed to deal with youth problems, especially with problems related to occupational and educational guidance. One major aim of these policies was to deal with the general amelioration of external conditions of life in urban centers and to provide youth with many amenities and services which it lacked in the new urban environments. Most important there were manifold attempts to establish special services, especially recreational and semieducational services, for youth.

Third, were the various corrective systems, ranging from probation officers and juvenile judges to some types of social workers who strived to establish adequate means for the control of the more disruptive aspects or manifestations of youth.

Fourth, there also developed several educational and social policies which attempted to take care of the special problems arising out of the new needs of the economy for more differentiated types of manpower and which, it was believed, would be able to provide adequate guidance to the labor market.

These educational policies tended to develop in two different, sometimes complementary, sometimes contradictory, ways. One was intended to assure the limited selection of the more gifted or select groups into the main stream of "central" educational activities. The other was the continuation for broader groups of differential vocational guidance of education which would make them more adjustable to the change and economic problems, but at the same time, would still keep these groups within the concrete opportunities open to them in the newly developing economy.

These different social policies dealing with youth tended to develop out of different starting points, and they tended to deal with different, seemingly even disconnected, aspects of the so-called "youth problem." They necessarily developed different approaches to different groups and strata of the population, and very often they were undertaken by different groups and agencies. And yet, most of the basic ideological assumptions of these different policies were relatively similar or common to most of these agencies and tended to depict their problems in relatively uniform terms of the problem of "youth" and of "adolescence" as it was briefly depicted above. Their main aim was to close the gap between youth and adults, to bring youth back, as it were, into the fold of adult society. This tendency to a somewhat homogeneous approach was necessarily strengthened by the unification and centralization of the educational system which was commented on above.

VII

But, in the meantime, especially after the Second World War and in the 1950's, the forms of youth rebellion and youth problems have greatly changed and become diversified. Side by side with the older types of youth problems which still persist and will, presumably, continue to persist, many new ones have developed, and the older ones have undertaken new forms. Thus, politically oriented youth and students can be found in some countries, especially in Latin America in the so-called Political University—a somewhat new type or form of youth or student rebellion. Similarly, in Japan there developed among the students some intensive political activities, best exemplified by the Zengakuren which, while having many traits in common with the older type of student unrest, are much more active and "anarchist" than most. In many countries, like India, student unrest does not necessarily take on the form of explicit political activities and is very often focused more against the university than on the political system. Similarly, the problems of dislocation and of delinquency stemming out of rapid urbanization and migration have also been found both in many countries or sectors in the first stages of industrialization or of excessive urbanization.

But, side by side with these new types of youth, groups and behavior have developed which have, on the whole, changed and diversified the overall picture of youth problems and youth rebellions.

VIII

In order to be able to analyze both the common characteristics and the great varieties between these new types of contemporary youth subcultures, we have to examine the constellations and impact of the new social developments. As has already been indicated above, the basic roots of these developments can be found in some of the general characteristics of modern societies, and in the very processes of continuous modernization. However, these broad, general characteristics have, in contemporary societies, crystallized into new constellations which, while evincing some new common characteristics, have also created a greater variety of different constellations than before.

We may just as well start with the most important developments in the economic and occupational and, to some extent, educational fields. Several developments in these fields have gone, in many modern or modernizing societies, beyond the traditional forms of dislocation rooted in rapid, initial urbanization and industrialization. Needless to say, all these older forms still exist and develop in many of the Western and especially in the newly developing nations. But, it is not the only form which economic and social changes undertake.

The most important new developments in these fields have been the growth of social specialization of economic planning, the growth of bureaucratization of most types of economic markets, as well as the increase in the close interrelationship between occupational placement and educational attainments.

The growing economic specialization and demand for specialized activities had the double effect of increasing the demand for special skills and creating difficulties for those with only more "general" preparation or education—education which was not geared either to some "traditional" occupation or style of life of any group, to any continuously diminishing crafts, or to the continuously expanding industrial labor force market.

The constant expansion of educational facilities and of market economy with its growing pressures for different types of occupational systems has, in general, greatly increased the relations between educational and economic opportunities and occupational placement. This has not only created greater possibilities of vocational guidance, but also has given rise to new types of discrepancies and problems. One of the major problems was the different types of "drop-outs" mentioned above. This problem of drop-outs has not been confined to the older types of professional, "intellectual," or student unemployment, but has extended even to the lower echelons of the primary school levels, which have become especially important both in many of the newly developing societies, on the one hand, and in the many "underdeveloped pockets" of highly industrialized societies, on the other.

Moreover, the problem of drop-outs has become greatly complicated by the continuous bureaucratization and centralization of the labor markets, by the greater responsibility of the State and of communal agencies both to provide work and educational facilities and by the fact that in many countries (especially in many New States) the government has become one of the most important employers of the prestige occupations, such as civil service and the professions.

Another important series of problems arose in connection with the various systems of educational selection which have become fully or partially institutionalized in many modern societies—the most extreme examples of which can be found in England and Sweden, and in one way or another in almost all other countries. Within this range, the most important series of problems was that related to the early placements which later restricted mobility and change and which gave rise to early limitation of vision and to the feeling, found in many sectors of these societies, of an early constriction and lack of possibility of advancement within a relatively expanding society and economy. The tendency to earlier marriage, which has become very widespread in many contemporary societies, seems also to have become closely related to these developments.

IX

A somewhat different, but closely connected, complex of problems which influences the configuration of youth groups and subcultures arises from developments in the spheres of values and culture and in the forging of national and social tradition and identity. If the developments in the occupational and consumptive spheres have, in a great variety of ways, opened up to youth more direct access to adult society while at the same time making for the possibilities of growing restrictions of vision, the various developments in the field of values have created somewhat different, but at the same time parallel, possibilities.

Perhaps the most important single, overall development in this field has been the transfer of emphasis from the creation and participation in the forging of future-oriented collective values to the growing institutionalization of such values. This transfer has been manifested in the institutionalizing of the aims and values toward the realization of which these movements were oriented and in the acceptance of such youth organizations as part of the general educational and cultural structure of their societies.

In Russia, youth movements became fully institutionalized through the organization of the Komsomol. In many European countries the institutionalizing of youth groups, agencies, and ideologies came through association with political parties or through acceptance as part of the educational system—an acceptance that sometimes entailed supervision by the official authorities. In the United States, many groups (such as the Boy Scouts) have become an accepted part of community life and, to some extent, a symbol of differential social status. In many Asian and African countries, organized youth movements have become part of the nationalistic movements and, with national independence, have become part of the official educational organizations.

This institutionalizing of the values of youth movements in education and community life has been part of a wider process of institutionalizing various collective values. In some countries, this has come about through revolution, in others, as a result of a long process of political and social evolution. Perhaps only some Latin American countries, for reasons connected with their particular type of development, have not yet felt the full impact of these developments.

From the point of view of their impact on youth, these processes have had several important results. The possibility of linking personal transition both to social groups and to cultural values—so strongly emphasized in the youth movements and noticeable to some extent even in the looser youth culture—has become greatly weakened. The social and sometimes even the cultural dimension of the future may thus become flattened and emptied. The various collective values have become transformed. Instead of being remote goals resplendent with romantic dreams, they have become the mundane objectives of the present, with the concomitant emphasis on the shabby details of daily politics and administration. More often than not they have become intimately connected with the processes of bureaucratization rampant in many sectors of modern societies.

All these changes in value-orientations are associated with a notable decline in ideology and in preoccupation with ideology among many of the groups and strata in modern societies, with a general flattening of political-ideological motives and a growing apathy toward them. This decline, in turn, is connected with what has been called the spiritual or cultural shallowness of the new social and economic benefits accruing from the welfare state—an emptiness illustrated by the fact that all these benefits are in the nature of things administered not by spiritual or social leaders but, as Stephen Toulmin has wittily pointed out, by "the assistant postmaster." As a consequence, we observe the emptiness and meaninglessness of social relations so often described by critics of the age of consumption and mass society.

This meaninglessness has been closely related to the changing perception of time and the relation between individual and societal time perspective. These developments have brought about the flattening of the image of the societal future and have deprived this image of its allure. The ideological discontinuity between present and future has become smaller. The present has become more important, if not more meaningful, because the future has lost its characteristic as a dimension different from the present. Out of these conditions has grown what Riesman has called the "cult of immediacy." This cult is reinforced by the growing institutionalization of the educational system, its continuous spread, and its growing bureaucratization. These have weakened the direct relation of the educational system to cultural creativity and have created also the various attempts to go out of it in order to experience more creative possibilities.

Thus youth in many such countries, be they from the New States, Communist, or European welfare states, face not only "reactionary" parents who do not want to allow them to change society, but also successful revolutionaries—people whose revolutions have succeeded and who through this success have become part of a new "establishment," creating a new collective reality which the youth have to face. This was no longer a reactionary, "retrograde" reality, but the embodiment of revolutionary, collective, and spiritual values.

In general, these developments made it more difficult for youth to establish some meaningful identity in relation to the continuously changing historical processes which were taking place around them. They have greatly changed the nature of most of the student uprisings and unrest. Some of the older types of unrest still persist, but new ones have also developed, oriented either to direct economic problems—such as in the various students' trade unions developed recently in Western Europe—or to the search for new types of personal experience, unrelated to any organized collective goals.

Only in Japan and Latin America do we find still the persistence of some older types of student rebellions, but even there they are already undertaking new forms. In Japan they have been closely connected with and dramatized by the problems of feelings or of historical discontinuity succeeded by defeat in World War II, the occupation, and the gap created both between the generation which grew up to adulthood during the occupation and their parents, on the one hand, and their children or younger brothers, on the other.

But these new problems and orientations tend to spread beyond the student movement and spill over to the more general atmosphere of new types of confrontation between generations, and they can be found, even if in different ways, also in Western societies and in Communist countries.

All these processes and changes have greatly changed the attitudes of youth toward the common symbols of the community and youth's perception of the possibilities of its own participation in the framework of such a community and have also changed the relations between generations in a way which has not been known before.

X

Out of these trends there developed several new constellations and characteristics of the youth problem in many contemporary societies.

One of their common characteristics is that the span of areas of social life that the specific youth culture encompasses tends to expand continuously to cover many more areas than the "traditional" ones. First of all, youth culture extends over a longer period of life. Second, it includes areas of work, of leisure time activity, and of many interpersonal relations. Third, the potential and actual autonomy of these groups and their direct access to various areas of life (connected with the growth of the direct access of young people to the major spheres of society), to the spheres of work, marriage and family life, political participation, and to consumption, have greatly increased, and their dependence on adults in this field has greatly decreased.

But, paradoxically enough, this growing direct access of young people to the various areas of life gave rise to a growing insecurity of status—of occupational and economic status, of communal participation, and of their status in the family. This insecurity was also felt in the development of meaningful relations, in terms of personal identity, with the continuous processes of historical change which swept over the world and over their respective societies. These characteristics have been manifested in the marked changes that developed in the overall trends of juvenile delinquency in many countries, especially in the continuous increase in the more "violent" types of delinquent activities—as against the more "traditional" trends of petty crimes, such as crimes against property.

But, while these characteristics found their most extreme manifestations in various types of delinquency and extreme literary movements, they have also continued to appear in varying degrees in most other types of youth culture. They were very closely related to the na-

ture of social and cultural participation which began to be characterized by a growing shift to more individualistic, "hedonistic" values, to
the weakening of orientations, and to collective goals—although very
often there were also many new "positive" potential developments
which took place in the form of the development of many new possibilities and avenues for individual and group activity and creativity.

But, although these various characteristics seem to be common in
different degrees to most of the new developments in youth societies,
there has not developed any one type of such subculture. Rather, the
very nature of these characteristics has given rise to a very great variety of subcultures.

Perhaps the most widely noticed type of rebellion has been that of
the "Teddy Boys," the insecure offenders, and the "Halbstarke." It
is, in a way, these new developments that have attracted so much attention and have also given rise to most of the new pedagogical literature dealing with these problems.

But even this new type of youth rebellion, which has been very
often treated as a relatively homogeneous and unified one and was
perceived as a rather general new type, is really a much more differentiated one. Its various manifestations differ to some extent according to class and occupational origins and backgrounds, according to
age and marital status of parents, according to educational experience,
as well as according to the general cultural and political atmosphere
prevailing.

Moreover, it certainly has not been the only new type of youth
problem, but, in a way, a rather special manifestation of the more
general developments which have many more variegated, and differentiated, and concrete manifestations. Within this context, one special
category of youth problems which tended to develop in different levels of the educational and occupational structure was the different
types of "drop-outs," from the schools. These ranged over all levels
of the educational ladder, from primary school, through secondary,
high, and vocational schools, up to and including colleges and universities. Different types of youth groups and youth problems very often
merge with different social, political, and artistic groups which maintain, in different ways, a great variety of what has been called "subter-
ranean traditions" of youth. Here the various "angry young men"

and the "beatniks" are of particular interest as bearers of special values and traditions. The growing attention paid to them constitutes an important indication of the feeling of the development and existence of a new problem, or rather a new constellation of an old problem.

Thus, in contemporary societies, there develop many varied and variegated types of youth cultures—of specific, even if not always fully defined, types of subcultures focused around or borne mainly by adolescents, youths, or relatively young people. These types are much more varied than those which tended to develop in the earlier phases of modernization. They differ from one another according to a great many variables. They differ in internal cohesion, continuity, and span of membership. The nature of the symbols around which their identity develops also varies greatly and ranges from relatively mild emphasis on the activities of youth up to fully rebellious attitudes toward adult society. These groups differ in their attitudes toward some basic occupational, social, communal, and leisure activities, and in their aspiration with regard to these activities and their self-perception in terms of these values and of the more general society. They also vary in their perception of the general society, of their own place or places within it, and of the possibilities open to them to advance within it. They have different attitudes toward the older generation, both on a social and personal level, as models of their own future activities, as bearers of power in the various spheres of the society, and as, what may be called, channels of transition to the general society. Perhaps more than in any preceding period these constellations of youth problems and cultures are becoming foci both of personal and cultural disorganization and creativity.

In terms of personality, there has developed a great potential insecurity and a possible lack of a clear definition of personal identity. Yet, there developed also the possibility of greater personal autonomy and flexibility in the choice of roles and the commitment to different values and symbols. The individual, in his search for the being of his personal transition, has been thrown much more on his own powers, and the possibilities for social and cultural creativity have become greater and more varied but their realization perhaps also more difficult.

NOTES

1. A general sociological analysis of the place of age in social structure has been attempted in S. N. Eisenstadt, *From Generation to Generation*, Glencoe, Ill.: The Free Press, 1956.

2. The analysis of personal, cosmic, and societal time (or temporal progression) has constituted a fascinating but not easily dealt with focus of analysis. For some approaches to these problems, see "Man and Time" (papers from the *Eranos Yearbooks*, edited by Joseph Campbell, London: Routledge and Kegan Paul, 1958), especially the article by Gerardus van der Leeuw. See also Mircea Eliade, *The Myth of the Eternal Return*, translated by W. R. Trask, New York: Pantheon Books, 1954 (Bollingen Series). For a fuller exposition of this part of the analysis, see S. N. Eisenstadt, "Archetypal Patterns of Youth," *Daedalus*, Winter 1962, pp. 28–46.

3. For a fuller exposition of the sociological significance of initiation rites, see Mircea Eliade, *Birth and Rebirth*, New York: Harper and Brothers, 1958, and *From Generation to Generation* (1).

4. See Bruno Bettelheim, *Symbolic Wounds, Puberty Rites and the Envious Circle*, Glencoe, Ill.: The Free Press, 1954.

5. A special type of age-groups may also develop in familistic societies. See *From Generation to Generation* (1), Chapter 5.

SECTION III

Bureaucracy and Bureaucratization

THE STARTING POINT of the essays in this section is again the "structural-organizational" one—the analysis of the condition of development of one particular type of institutional organization, the so-called bureaucratic organizations. This type appears in varying degrees and forms in different societies and in different institutional spheres. Some of the broader analytical problems of approach to such heterogeneity have previously been dealt with in Chapter 1 of this book.

The first essay (Chapter 7) in this section, that on "Bureaucracy and Bureaucratization," attempts to spell out the broad contours of the problem, emphasizing from the very beginning the drawbacks of a "homogeneous" approach which assumes that a given organizational or institutional type is equally distributed within certain societies or that it undertakes the same contours within each society.

In this essay special emphasis is laid on the different implications and structural consequences of the setting up of such organizations. It is pointed out that such consequences may lead in different directions —to the establishment of controlled bureaucracy, to bureaucratization, or to debureaucratization. Hence it is necessary to specify the conditions under which different degrees and crystallizations of such organizational and institutional patterns and different structural consequences of their establishment became predominant, and an attempt at such specification is presented in the last part of the essay.

The second essay (Chapter 8) contains a more detailed analysis of these different possibilities in one specific historical-sociological setting —namely in that of the so-called centralized bureaucratic empires.* The last essay (Chapter 9) in this section, written by Professor Elihu Katz and the author, presents an analysis of the development of one major tendency—namely that of debureaucratization—in the concrete setting of the absorption of new immigrants in Israel. In this essay great attention is paid to the interrelationship between the attitudinal and behavioral aspects of the crystallization of institutional patterns and to the possible structural outcomes of such different interrelationships.

* The social and political characteristics and processes of these empires are analyzed in the author's book *The Political Systems of Empires*, New York: The Free Press of Glencoe, 1963.

Chapter 7

Bureaucracy, Bureaucratization, Markets, and Power Structure

/

Bureaucracy and Bureaucratization—The Setting and the Problem

Concern with bureaucracy is of long standing in modern sociological literature. It can be traced, on the one hand, to Ferguson's theories of Oriental Despotism, which stressed the special character of officialdom as an instrument of oppression in oriental states. On the other hand, this concern can be found in the writings of Marx and Tocqueville, both of whom discerned the trend toward "bureaucratization," toward growing regimentation of social life in the modern world and tried to interpret these trends according to their major analyses of the trends in the development of modern society. It has been rightly stressed by Lipset and Bendix (1) that the works of these authors feature a strong preoccupation with growing bureaucratization as part and parcel of their general analysis of modern society and of its political structure and development.

In all these writings, however, the discussion of bureaucracy was

This chapter is reprinted in part from "Bureaucracy and Bureaucratization, A Trend Report," *Current Sociology*, Vol. VII, No. 2, 1958, in part from "Burocratizzazione, Mercati et Struttura di Potere," *Quaderni di Sociologia*, Vol. XII, No. 2, 1963, and from "Bureaucratization, Markets, and Power Structure," *Transactions of the Westermark Society*, Vol. X, 1964, and in part is based on new materials.

embedded in, and constitutes only a part of, analyses which were focused mainly on other problems. It was only with Max Weber, R. Michels, and G. Mosca that the structure of bureaucracy and processes of bureaucratization became a focus of independent major analysis. True, both Weber and Michels built on foundations which were laid, to some extent, by others (Stein, Schmoller, and other German historians, as well as Ostrogorsky, in his analysis of modern parties). But Weber, Michels, and Mosca brought the problems of bureaucracy into the limelight and presented them as one of the major foci of modern sociology and of the analysis of modern society. In their works, analysis of bureaucracy and of bureaucratization processes became closely interwoven, on the one hand, with the examination of problems of power and its control and legitimation in modern society, and, on the other, with the analysis of processes of rationalization, in terms of growing efficiency and specialization, in society. It has been rightly said that for Max Weber, "bureaucracy plays the same part that the class struggle played for Marx and competition for Sombart" (2).

Mosca was the first to treat the bureaucratic state as a distinct type of political system and organization of the ruling class. He contrasted it with the feudal regime (and to some extent with city-states) and attempted to analyze what may be called its internal dialectics of stability and disorganization.

Bureaucracy and bureaucratization have been taken up in different directions in the works of political scientists like Friedrich and Finer and, in the last attempt at a major "total" sociological interpretation of modern society, in the work of Karl Mannheim. In their writings, these problems are thrown into sharp relief as major trends in the development of modern society. Here, bureaucracy and bureaucratization are related to and closely interwoven with problems of democracy, totalitarianism, and mass society. Aside from and contemporaneously with these major interpretations, there appeared a host of more specialized studies, representing several major trends in scientific inquiry, which touched on and expressed various viewpoints regarding different aspects of the problems of bureaucracy. Although many of these studies dealt only with special and partial aspects, they contributed much toward the systematic analysis of the bureaucratic system. The analyses of isolated aspects of this problem in the course of time converged, and the major themes that were presented in the works of the "classics" were gradually investigated by systematic researches and their interrelations were systematically explored.

Let us first summarize those aspects of the bureaucracy which constituted topics for analysis in the sociological classics and then turn to a brief survey of the major trends in specialized research in this field.

Almost all the classical works dealing with bureaucracy are preoccupied with one basic dilemma—namely, whether bureaucracy is master or servant, an independent body or a tool, and, if a tool, whose interests it can be made to serve. This dilemma is posed in different ways. Max Weber considers bureaucracy to be the epitome of rationality and efficiency—the most rational means of implementating a given goal. From his standpoint it follows that bureaucracy is directed by those who can set the goals, although he did not systematically examine the problem of the relation of bureaucracy's structure to the nature of the polity's goals. On the other hand, however, he frequently alludes to and analyzes bureaucracy as a powerful, independent body which advances and conquers new areas of life in modern society, monopolizes power, and tends to rule over and regulate the life of the individual. It is this second standpoint that underlies Weber's critique of socialism and his partial resignation to its inevitability, in some countries at least.

Concentration of power in the hands of the bureaucracy, the growing bureaucratization of different social organizations, and the diminishing voluntary participation in such organizations constitutes, as is well known, the main focus of the work of Robert Michels. Perhaps his main contribution is to pose the problem of the displacement of goals by the bureaucracy and to analyze the internal and external conditions responsible for such displacement. Although Michels is concerned chiefly with problems of internal usurpation of power by bureaucrats or oligarchs (and it is significant in itself that he rarely distinguishes between the two), in the course of his analysis he also specifies some of the external conditions under which this usurpation can take place—such as the concentration of communication with the outer world and of access to various facilities in the hands of the elite. Moreover, he poses, at least implicitly, the problems of the relation between bureaucratization as a political process and bureaucratic organization as a technical arrangement for the implementation of certain goals and provision of services. Although he does not state this in so many words, he proceeds on the important hypothesis that the two are inversely related and that growing bureaucratization or usurpation of power by the bureaucrats is accompanied, first, by a process of displacement of goals by the bureaucracy and, second, by its growing disregard of its initial purpose and *raison d'être*—implementation of some goals of the polity.

An ambivalent attitude toward bureaucracy characterizes much of the social thought of the last half of the nineteenth and the first decades of the twentieth centuries and is especially prominent in liberal-socialist polemics. It is significant that no side—liberal, conservative, or socialist—took an unequivocal and clear stand in relation to the bureaucracy. The liberals and the conservatives often strongly objected to the bureaucracy and depicted it as a colossus which would engulf the various areas of life and cancel the traditional liberties of the people and which would engender a mechanized and oppressive civilization, choking the individual and regimenting his every activity. While this view in its extreme form, as expressed for instance by L. V. Mises, is no longer taken seriously, the problem itself remains and looms large in contemporary social thought. On the other hand, however, many liberals and conservatives stressed the importance of bureaucracy as a means of implementing social reforms and upheld the ideal of a neutral civil service. Although many of the naive assumptions about the clear, unadulterated benefits that would accrue from social reforms implemented by bureaucracy are long forgotten, the main problem remains, accentuated by the growing awareness of the problem of power. As Kaufman has stressed rightly in a recent review article: "The whole analysis of public administration has shifted, . . . from seeing administration as the best way of implementation of social goals, to problems of public control of bureaucratized administration (3)."

An ambivalent attitude toward bureaucracy is also featured by the socialist and the communist camps. There is the realization of its importance as a means of implementing social goals and reforms, and yet there is the suspicion of it as a tool in the hands of the capitalist ruling classes. From a different vantage point the socialists have often depicted bureaucracy as a mere appendage of capitalist society and oppression which will become obsolete and unnecessary under socialism and its rational management of things, not of men. Paradoxically enough, the tables have recently been turned on the socialists and especially on the communists by the liberal or social-democratic camp, with the growing realization that bureaucracy may easily become a tool of oppression, especially under conditions of great concentration of power—i.e., in Socialist societies—the very fear expressed by socialists regarding capitalistic bureaucracy. The liberal camp has come to realize that the major problems facing modern regimes are the effective political and democratic control of the bureaucracy and the planning for possible debureaucratization in different spheres of life.

This ambivalent attitude toward bureaucracy is also manifest in the views regarding what may be called the professional aspect of bureaucratic behavior and attitudes, an aspect of professional detachment, of conformity with rules, and of dealing with various problems and people *sine ira et studio*, efficiently, preserving secrecy, and so on. Bureaucracy's professional, detached attitude is frequently upheld as one of its main virtues. Yet it has often been shown that such an attitude may have several, "unanticipated," negative consequences. Thus it may either give the bureaucrat almost unlimited and uncontrollable power both over his clients and his nonbureaucratic superiors, such as political lay leaders, or make him into a subservient tool of any master who may arise. These two seemingly contradictory possibilities have, in practice, at times developed side by side in one and the same organization, as shown by the example of German officialdom under the Weimar Republic.

One of the most debated set of questions concerning bureaucracy that is representative of its problematic nature was centered on the political neutrality of the civil service. The main concrete problem was whether the civil service, the highest echelons of which were usually recruited from the upper and upper-middle strata, would be willing to implement radical reforms, envisaged by a labor or socialist government. Large portions of the polemical literature, which was characterized by a Marxist or semi-Marxist bias, came to be based on the assumption that the civil service would always be class-bound in its orientation, would never be willing to implement social change, and would sabotage any large-scale political and social program. Immediately after the Second World War, with the rise of the Labor government to power in Britain, the political orientations of the bureaucracy constituted an acute problem, the Canadian aspect of which was taken up by Lipset. The British case seemed to substantiate Finer's view (against Kingsley's) of the political neutrality of the civil service and of its loyalty to democratically elected political leadership (4).

Obviously the conditions determining the effects of bureaucracy's political neutrality varied in different countries, and one of the main problems facing the comparative study of bureaucratic organization was to elucidate these situations. However, the complexity and severity of the problem of the consequences of the civil service's total political neutrality was emphasized owing to the course of events in Germany. True, it has been shown that some branches of the German Beamtentum attempted to sabotage many of the Weimar reforms and never did become fully loyal to the Weimar Republic. But at the same time their political passivity and nonparticipation made them an easy tool in the hands of the Nazis, and their very neutrality and (official or unofficial) willingness to accept political masters of any kind (even if they did not serve them with good heart) facilitated the rise of the Nazi regime.

The major issue implicit in this discussion was to what extent it would be justifiable for the civil service to use the potential power at its disposal for the support of any regime. The very complexity of this problem indicates the absence of a simple answer to the grave question regarding the desirability of passive instrumentality on the part of bureaucracy in any political situation.

Whatever the concrete problems investigated within this context, most of the various attitudes toward bureaucracy evince this basic ambivalence. The source of all these ambivalent attitudes toward bureaucracy is twofold. First, it lies in recognition of a basic paradoxical aspect of the structure and organization of bureaucracy. This paradox is rooted in the fact that in order for a bureaucracy (any bureaucracy —whether governmental, economic, military, or social) to perform efficiently its functions as an instrument of implementation of goals or provision of services, it must necessarily develop some autonomy. Its members must have some professional orientations and standards and be immune to various inside and outside pressures. It must have and uphold a set of internal rules, and there must be some spheres of activity which are left to its discretion. Moreover, by the very nature of its activities, a bureaucracy fulfills some mediating and regulating functions with respect to different groups and, as a result, is put in a certain power position in relation to these groups. Thus the tension between bureaucracy as a tool and as an independent body or master is inherent in its very genesis and nature.

Second, this ambivalence is rooted in the fact that, whatever its genesis, every bureaucracy—in virtue of the services it performs, the areas it regulates, the interests between which it mediates, and its own structure and organization—develops into a center of power which may become independent and unregulated. Consequently, there arise problems of the relations of this center of power to other centers of power in society and especially to those in which the legitimate power of a society is vested, problems concerning: (a) the relations between bureaucracy and its masters (such as political leaders, owners of industrial enterprises, and bodies of trustees) with regard to the extent to which bureaucracy will accept the general direction of its leaders or whether it will generate independent power and policy making; (b) the relation of bureaucracy to its clientele, the degree to which bureaucracy accepts their legitimate demands and attempts to provide them with the services due to them—or conversely, the extent to which it attempts to dominate and regulate its clientele and (c) (cutting across [b]) the extent of what may be called legitimate exercise of power by the bureaucracy in terms of mediation between different groups and interests in society.

The relations between any bureaucracy and the other centers of political power in a society pose a basic dilemma of how to establish effective control over the bureaucracy and at the same time not to restrict its autonomy to the point of making it impotent, formalistic, and inefficient.

Thus, in more general terms it may be said that the main problem facing the study of bureaucracy is the relation between bureaucracy and bureaucratization, between the development of organizations aiming at implementing various goals, providing services, and accordingly fulfilling various important functions, on the one hand, and the growing acquisition of unregulated power by these organizations, their increasing regimentation and domination of vast areas of social life and their own benefits and goals, on the other. In short, every bureaucracy is caught between the acquisition of power necessary for fulfillment of what are seen as the society's goals and the bureaucracy's legitimate functions, and usurpation of such power, displacement of goals, and growing bureaucratization.

Thus it can be seen that the study of bureaucracy cannot be confined to an analysis of the internal structure of various organizations. Even the earlier attempts at such an analysis referred to the relations between the organization and its wider social setting. It was only through reference to wider problems that the study of bureaucracy came to focus on the major themes discussed above and to be undertaken by systematic research.

It is the purpose of this chapter to explore, in a preliminary way, some of the social conditions which may influence both the scope of the process of bureaucratization and the different ways of controlling or "countervailing" it.

Two basic meanings of the term bureaucratization can be discerned. One, the most prevalent in the literature, emphasizes the tendency of every simple bureaucratic organization to extend the scope of its activities beyond its "legitimate" goals and to multiply the number of its organizations. The other sense in which the term bureaucratization has been used—albeit not very often, although it has been already implicit in Max Weber's work (5)—is the extension of the bureaucratic mechanisms as general, regulative, allocative, and integrative mechanisms in the society.

We may perhaps start with a brief indication of what is usually meant by a bureaucratic organization. One broadly accepted definition, based on Max Weber's famous ideal-type analysis of bureaucracy, points out that the major characteristics of a bureaucratic organization are :

1. "The regular activities required for the purposes of the organization are distributed in a fixed way as official duties.". . .

2. The organization of offices follows the principle of hierarchy; that is, each lower office is under the control and supervision of a higher one. . . .

3. Operations are governed "by a consistent system of abstract rules . . . (and) consist of the application of these rules to particular cases." . . .

4. The ideal official conducts his office . . . (in) a spirit of formalistic impersonality, "*Sine ira et studio*," without hatred or passion, and hence without affection or enthusiasm. . . .

5. Employment in the bureaucratic organization is based on technical

qualifications and is protected against arbitrary dismissal. "It constitutes a career. There is a system of 'promotions' according to seniority or to achievement, or both."(6).

This definition implies that a bureaucratic organization *can be* seen as a special subspecies of what has been often designated as (specific) goal-oriented organizations (7).

Different goal-oriented organizations share with bureaucracies not only some internal-structural characteristics but also certain types of basic interrelation with their environment, and it is in these interrelations that the tendencies to bureaucratization are rooted.

These interrelations of goal-oriented organizations in general and of bureaucratic organizations in particular can be derived from some of the basic conditions of their development.

Comparative researches show that goal-oriented, or "rationally administrated" organizations tend to develop in those societies or sectors thereof in which

1. There develops a great degree of differentiation between the many roles and institutional spheres (economic, political, religious, etc.).

2. The crucial roles in the society are allocated not according to criteria of membership in the primary, particularistic groups (kinship and territorial), but rather according to universal criteria or criteria of membership in more flexible groups.

3. There evolve many functionally specific groups (economic, cultural, religious, social-integrative) which are not embedded in territorial and kinship groups.

4. The definition of the total community is not identical with, and consequently is "wider" than, any such particularistic group.

5. There develops a growing complexity of different spheres of social life.

6. The value system of the society evolves wide group orientations and contains some universalistic elements.

7. The major groups and strata in the society develop, uphold, and attempt to implement numerous political, economic, and/or social service goals which cannot be implemented within the limited framework of given ascriptive, kinship, and territorial groups. The imple-

mentation of these goals requires the large-scale coordination of specialized and expert activities.

8. There exists a strong competition between different groups over the order of priority of different goals and for resources needed for the implementation of these goals (8).

These developments result in the development, within these societies or sectors thereof, of "free-floating" resources, that is, manpower and economic resources, as well as commitments for political support which are neither embedded in, nor ensured to, any primary ascriptive-particularistic groups. Consequently, the various groups and institutional spheres in the society have to compete for resources, manpower, and support, and the major social spheres are faced with many regulative and administrative problems.

Goal-oriented organizations in general and bureaucratic organizations in particular develop under such conditions because they are able to help in the implementation of relatively differentiated goals, in the provision of resources, and in the regulation of intergroup relations and conflicts, while the availability of such free resources facilitates the maintenance of the organizations' activities.

These two factors—the usefulness of such organizations from the point of view of the performance of various functions and the importance of "free" resources for the functioning of such organizations— do not as yet explain fully how such organizations arise. As yet these conditions do not ensure that there will arise people or groups who will be able to combine these two conditions and crystallize the appropriate organizational forms. But they do at least explain how, if such people or groups do arise, these broader conditions may facilitate the development and continuity of such organizations.

The availability of various free-floating resources and the development of several centers of power which compete over such resources are of crucial importance for the understanding of the interrelations of goal-oriented organizations and their environments. As a result of the very conditions which gave birth to it, any goal-oriented organization and any bureaucratic organization are obliged to compete for resources, manpower, general support, and clientele.

The classical theories of bureaucracy rightly recognized that any bureaucracy is always dependent on the outside world for its resources.

Unlike traditional ecological, family, or kinship groups, it is not and cannot be self-sufficient and, characteristically, the incumbents of its offices do not get direct remuneration from their clients, nor do they own their "means of production." But because many of these theories referred chiefly to governmental bureaucracies, they took the supply of the requisite resources for granted and only emphasized the fact that dependence on external resources assures the relative segregation and independence of the bureaucrat's role. In reality, however, the need to compete for legitimation and resources faces governmental departments as well.

Thus, from the very beginning, any bureaucratic organization is put in what may be called a power situation in relation to its environment and has to generate processes of power on its own behalf.

Goal-oriented organizations in general and bureaucratic ones in particular are characterized and distinguished from other social groups by the need to work out their interrelationships with their environments as autonomous organizations, based on the specialization of tasks as well as the "rational" division of labor and allocation of roles specific to their goals and conducted according to specific autonomous criteria. The exact way in which a bureaucracy works out its interrelations with its environment differs from society to society and from period to period and may involve its orientation to new goals, incorporation of such goals in its structure, as well as processes of bureaucratization (or debureaucratization).

The tendency toward bureaucratization, toward excessive domination by the bureaucracy of parts of its environment, is therefore inherent in the very position from which any bureaucracy develops, although the extent of its realization varies from case to case 'and constitutes one of the main foci of comparative research (9). This tendency is also closely related to a bureaucracy's mediatory-regulative functions. While at first glance it would appear that the main functions and *raison d' être* of any bureaucracy are to ensure implementation of its manifest goals and to provide services, these functions entail additional ones. For, through goal implementation and provision of services, the bureaucracy comes in contact with its environment of differentiated social groups competing over available resources. If any bureaucracy—and especially a governmental one—depends on its environment for external resources, various social groups come to depend on the bureaucratic organization. The rules governing goal implementation and service provision necessarily affect the distribution of power and allocation of resources to different groups. Thus a bureaucracy's role is not only technical but mediatory or regulatory as well.

These added functions enhance its potential power position and increase the competition of other groups for its services. Thus, from its very inception the bureaucratic organization is in a state of constant interaction with its environment and works out different ways of maintaining a compulsory equilibrium of relations of mutual impingement between itself and the environmental forces.

The Components of Bureaucratic Organizations

However, in order to understand more fully the ways in which the scope of the activities of bureaucratic organization is extended, we have first to analyze in greater detail the basic characteristics of such organizations and their major components.

The starting point of such analysis should, of course, be the fact that any bureaucratic organization constitutes a social system; that its internal division of labor is determined not only by its technical problems of goal implementation but also by its other needs and problems; that there exist within the bureaucratic organization special roles and activities geared to providing for these needs; that therefore there can be no purely "rational" bureaucratic organization, free from personal, primary, or power elements, and that, on the contrary, some such elements are functionally important in the organization.

Hence, each of these roles is systematically related to the outside world by virtue of its need to "manipulate" several aspects of the external environment (for example, the directors must deal with boards of members, legislative committees, the sales-managers with buyers and sellers in different markets, the manager with trade unions and labor exchanges) and by virtue of the necessary contact between the incumbents of such roles and similar (parallel) role incumbents in other organizations with which they have relations. These persons may easily establish professional, solidary, or conflict relations and various reference orientations and identifications, which might cut across their organizational affinity and at the same time greatly influence their behavior in their organizations and consequently affect the performance of these organizations as well. They also emphasize the relation between the bureaucratic role within the organization and their other roles in the family, community, and especially the type of motivation, for performance of their bureaucratic role, which they bring from their social background.

In addition, the clients with whom the incumbent of each type of bureaucratic role within any given organization comes into selective contact might put him under pressure with respect to the performance of his bureaucratic roles. Such pressure may at times be exerted by means of various professional or community roles and organizations in which both the bureaucrat and the client participate or which are specific to the clients and the public. This can become especially evident if we examine in somewhat greater detail the major types of roles which can be found in any bureaucratic organization.

These may be best classified as:

TECHNICAL, that is, concerned with the "materials" (physical, cultural, or human) which must be processed, and the kinds of cooperation of different people requisite for the organization's effective performance.

MANAGERIAL OR ADMINISTRATIVE, that is, concerned with mediating the organization's external relations and with "administering" its internal affairs. Both purposes of the managerial role involve the "decision-making" processes which have been the center of so much recent attention. The external mediation task of this role means: mediation of relations with the "clients" or "customers," that is, those utilizing the "products" of the organization's technical function, and procurement of the financial and physical resources and recruitment of personnel which are necessary in order to carry out this function.

GENERAL SUPERVISORY. Just as a technical organization, at a sufficiently high level of the division of labor, is controlled and "serviced" by a managerial organization to which it is in some sense "responsible," so a managerial organization, in turn, is controlled by the "institutional" structure and agencies of the community of which it is a part. This third level of organization may take the form of the representative community functions of the school boards in the educational field, of trustees of various types of private, nonprofit organizations, and, indeed, under the fully developed corporate form, of the Board of Directors of business corporations (10). Each type of bureaucratic role may, of course, be divided into various subtypes which differ from one type of organization to another.

The technical, managerial, and general supervisory roles have several systematic connections with the outside world which necessarily influence the attitudes and performance of their incumbents within the organization and which may add some components to the basic bureaucratic roles. In addition to the various types of external relations and connections pointed out in the preceding discussion, we should emphasize the professional and community orientations which may develop at each level of bureaucratic role and function. Thus, on the technical level there may develop various labor and professional organizations and contacts which may impinge on the performance of the bureaucratic role. On the administrative-managerial level there may develop professional and "market" orientations and connections. On the general supervisory level there may develop community, political, and value orientations and connections.

The orientations and connections developed at each level impinge on the performance of the bureaucratic roles and on the functioning of the organization as a whole. They impinge on the bureaucrat by exerting pressure on him and inclining him toward differential application of the bureaucratic rules, partial deviation from them, and by setting up of new goals for the organization.

Another consequence of bureaucracy and bureaucratic organization as a social system is the recognition of the fact that within each such organization there develop various subgroups (workmen, foremen, departmental) and subsystems, and that each organization is faced with the problem of coordinating these subgroups, of regulating their relations with each other and with the organization as a whole. Such subgroups may have entirely different conceptions of and attitudes toward the organization's goals and needs, and these must be taken into account by those who wish to study the functioning of any bureaucratic organization.

Thus, the interaction between the different subgroups in any bureaucratic organization constitutes a continuous process of communication, of allocation of rewards, of adjustment of mutual perception, a process by which some—but only some—fusion (the extent of which necessarily varies from case to case and from period to period) between the motives and goals of different individuals and subgroups and the overall organizational goals is effected (11).

It is here that the multiplicity of the organization's external relations and internal subgroups may lead to the development, either in it or on its behalf, of many different types of activity which transcend the specific bureaucratic roles and relations within the organization, thereby becoming interested in bettering its internal "human relations," providing facilities for its members and their families, and integrating its activities with those of other social groups as in community affairs, all seemingly in order to improve the performance of the bureaucratic role.

Such activities, in turn, bring the incumbents of the bureaucratic role into various personal relations which go beyond the basic premises of such a role. These relations might consequently lead to new goal orientations, to processes of bureaucratization—that is, attempts on the part of the bureaucrats to impose bureaucratic conceptions and goals on these activities and groups.

Here we are confronted once again with an aspect of the bureaucratic organization which is of major importance to our analysis, namely, the changeability and flexibility of its goals. It would appear that any bureaucratic organization is oriented, or evolves, as a means of implementing a specific goal or set of goals. But the very conditions responsible for its development, the multiplicity of its internal subgroups, and the numerous pressures to which it is subjected facilitate or perhaps even necessitate continuous change of at least some of its goals. Such flexibility is, as Thompson and McEwen have rightly stressed, almost a condition of the bureaucratic organization's survival (12).

It is largely by continuously incorporating new goals and attempting to ensure the requisite resources for their implementation that any bureaucratic organization strikes out its equilibrium with its environment. Through the processes of goal definition, of mobilization of resources for the implementation of these goals, and of recruitment of manpower, the bureaucratic organization exerts its influence on its environment, establishes various rules which influence the training of people aspiring to be enrolled into it, and may indirectly influence general educational standards and impose its own cultural orientation on parts of its environment. It is through such processes, in addition to those of competition for resources and power, that different types of equilibrium between the bureaucratic organization and its social environment develop.

Bureaucratic and Nonbureaucratic Integrative Mechanisms

But in order for these different types of relations between the bureaucratic organizations and their environments to be fully explored we have to analyze the second meaning of the term bureaucratization. This second meaning refers mostly to the ways in which bureaucratic regulation can be compared with other types of mechanisms of allocation, integration, or decision making (e.g., decisions about allocation of services and people to different roles) in a society (13).

For the purpose of our present discussion we may distinguish (in a somewhat simplified way) between two major aspects of any regulative and allocative mechanism in a society. These aspects are, first, "who" allocates or "integrates" different roles and facilities, and, second, how is the process of allocation, regulation, and consequent interpretation organized or structured (14).

As for the first, one can distinguish between ascriptive and nonascriptive "allocation" or regulation. Ascriptive allocators or regulators are those who perform certain roles by virtue of their ascriptive, usually hereditary, position in some group such as kinship, territorial, or estate groups. The nonascriptive regulators are characterized by the fact that they occupy their positions by virtue of some achieved position, either by their being chosen to represent other people or groups, or by virtue of their ownership of special capital—whether monetary capital, or offices which they have bought, or capital of some specific knowledge or expertise.

The second aspect of regulative and allocative mechanisms is the structure of the mechanism of allocation and integration. Here we may distinguish between direct and indirect allocation, according to the extent of directness of the interaction between the allocator and his "clients."

The direct type of allocation may be subdivided, first, into allocation organized in hierarchical channels through a chain of command and, second, into allocation through a process of direct bargaining between those participating and interested in a given "product."

Contrasted with direct allocation of various kinds (but often overlapping) is indirect allocation, that is, allocation of products through various indirect mechanisms according to the relative positions of people within such mechanisms or framework. Of special importance here are the various "impersonal" systems, such as the monetary and price systems, the market system, or different types of allocation through partial competition in different social spheres (15). The various types of allocative mechanisms can also be distinguished according to the extent of control which is exerted on them by other people, either by their "clients" or by various representatives of different groups.

These are only very preliminary and not fully systematic distinctions. Quite obviously, in most concrete relevant cases, there may exist a great extent of overlapping between these various types. We shall not enter into a more detailed and systematic analysis of all possible combinations of these criteria here but shall only dwell upon some problems which are most closely related to problems of bureaucracy and bureaucratization.

Bureaucratic regulation—the type of regulation which has been often assumed to be most prominent in bureaucratic organizations—is characterized by a combination of several of the previously enumerated criteria. It is one of what may be called the nonascriptive types of regulation, that is, types of allocation which are not regulated according to ascriptive criteria.

However, within this broad type, bureaucratic allocation is characterized by several specific traits which distinguish it from other nonascriptive systems of regulation and allocation. First, it is characterized as regulation by "experts" or by people whose major qualification is some specific knowledge—either general administrative or more specific professional or technical knowledge. These experts are in turn supervised to some extent by holders of political, economic, or communal power, but only to a very little extent *directly* by the clients to whom they provide their services. Any such direct supervision by the clients which goes beyond some minimal, well-defined measure is very often seen as a very serious infringement on the autonomy of the bureaucratic organization. Second, bureaucratic allocation is characterized by the prevalence of direct allocation of resources, facilities, and services according to some general (universalistic) criteria transmitted mainly through hierarchical channels. Third, the "ideal type" of bureaucratic regulation stresses the "rational," "computative" (16) allocation and decision making which is worked out "rationally" according to the exigencies of any given situation and belittles allocation by elected representatives, by organs of self-government, through processes of political or legislative decision, or by exigencies of the "impersonal" mechanisms of the market.

In this context bureaucratization means, first, the growth of the sphere of the actual competence or power of any given bureaucratic, "computative" mechanism—whether within any organization or in its relations with other social units—beyond its legitimate sphere of competence at the expense of some other types of regulative mechanisms. Such bureaucratization may manifest itself in the weakening of the control of various "nonexpert" bodies and groups over any given bureaucratic organization, in the growth of the actual power of the administrative experts at the expense of the representatives of the holders of communal or economic power. Second, such bureaucratization may manifest itself in the weakening of the scope and competence of nonbureaucratic mechanisms of regulation, of market mechanism or of public legislation in the relations between a given bureaucratic organization and the "outside" world—i.e., in the ways through which bureaucratic organizations obtain their resources and manpower and dispose of their products. It may accordingly also give rise—perhaps paradoxically—to the growth of some direct, hierarchical relations or direct bargaining in the relations between different bureaucratic organizations and between the providers of their resources and the clients of their products and services.

Bureaucratization as Extension of Computative and Bargaining Integrative Mechanisms

The various works and analyses which have stressed the increase of the trends of bureaucratization in modern societies have been based on several—implicit or explicit—assumptions.

The first such assumption is that "computative" mechanisms are predominant in bureaucratic organizations and that therefore the very extension of the number of such organizations necessarily implies the extension of this type of regulative mechanism in the society as a whole.

But a close examination will show that owing to the very basic conditions of the development of bureaucratic organizations there develop within them additional, noncomputative mechanisms both in their relations to their environment and in their internal structure. Moreover, several of the various roles which exist within any bureaucratic organization are by their very nature predisposed to various noncomputative mechanisms.

It has been very often shown that the ultimate ownership or control of any bureaucratic agency, which is never purely bureaucratic, necessarily involves allocation through legal decree representation, market mechanisms, or bargaining. Similarly, in the more informal relations between different groups within a bureaucracy and in the broad sphere of labor-management relations, there are necessarily many types of direct bargaining.

Such noncomputative mechanisms of regulation and integration develop not only within any goal-oriented or bureaucratic organization, but also in the organization's relation with the external environment from which it has to mobilize different resources and manpower and to which it renders services or sells its products. Any single bureaucratic organization may receive these resources through any type of allocative mechanism—either through legislative allocation, through market activities, through bargaining, or through a combination of all of them.

Thus, any bureaucratic organization necessarily has recourse, both in its internal and external relations, to many types of regulative mechanisms which go beyond the "ideal type" of bureaucratic or computative allocation, and it has to compete with other types of organizations and mechanisms for resources and scope of activity.

A Comparative Approach to Bureaucratic Organizations

The general conclusions about the nature of the interrelations between bureaucratic organizations and their environments can best be illustrated through a comparative analysis of different types of bureaucratic organizations. Many different approaches to a comparative analysis of bureaucratic organization can be attempted, but in this context it would perhaps be most valuable to distinguish between bureaucratic organizations according to their predominant goals.

The preceding discussion emphasized the goals which any bureaucratic organization has to implement and the services which it has to provide to various groups and strata as crucial factors in its genesis. It follows that the major goals of any bureaucratic organization, the place of these goals in the social structure of the society, and the type of dependence of the bureaucracy on external forces (whether clients, holders of political power, or other prominent groups) may be of great importance in influencing its internal structure. These factors, while they are to some extent interdependent, are at the same time not identical. Each in its own way brings into relief the interdependence of the bureaucratic organization with its social setting. The bureaucracy's goals are of strategic importance because they naturally constitute one of the most important connecting links between the given organization and the broader social structure in which it is placed. What, from the point of view of the organization, is its major goal may often be, from the point of view of the total society, the organization's specific societal function. Hence the various interrelations among the organization, other groups, and the total society are, to a very large extent, mediated by the nature of the organization's goals. This applies both to the resources needed by the organization and to the products it gives out to the society. In the following discussion we shall analyze the influence of the bureaucracy's goals on its structure, mainly by means of examining its relations with its environment. In this way we shall attempt to bring it in line with the preceding analysis (17).

*The Goals of Bureaucratic Organizations and Their
Influence on Organizational Structure*

In order to illustrate the relation between the goals and structure of bureaucratic organizations, we shall now examine the influence of several types of goals on the division of labor within a bureaucracy and on its relations with its external environment. We shall deal mainly with the structural differences between bureaucratic organizations which are oriented to economic, socio-political, and cultural goals.

Hypotheses regarding the influence of each type of goal on the bureaucracy's relations with the external world (especially with the clientele and the general supervisory authorities) and on its internal specialization and division of labor will be proposed. This list of goals is necessarily preliminary and not exhaustive, but it should be sufficient for the present purposes of illustration.

Economically oriented bureaucratic organizations have markets other than their major clientele. These markets consist of other organizations and firms and/or an amorphous consumer clientele. The availability of resources to such a bureaucracy ultimately depends on the reactions of the markets to its produce although agencies, such as various financial and credit agencies, whether private (for example, banks) or governmental, may intervene. "Ultimate" societal control over such enterprises is exercised not only by the "impersonal" forces of the market but also by various financing and governmental agencies. The degree to which these factors are important naturally differs from one regime to another.

What effects do economic goals have on the internal structure of bureaucratic organizations? First, such bureaucracies usually feature a relatively sharp demarcation between the policy-making, managerial-administrative, and technical roles. Different types of specialization and skill are required on each level, and overlapping is meagre. In older firms, this demarcation was most clearly seen in the distinction between owner and employee. With the growing separation between ownership and management, this distinction applies mostly to managerial-entrepreneurship functions on the one hand and to more routine jobs on the other. At the same time, however, the nature of the economically oriented clientele engenders a new type of specialist on the managerial level, the man dealing with "public relations," the "lobbyist," and the like.

Organizations oriented predominantly to social or political goals, such as political parties, social agencies, and, to a smaller extent, governmental bureaus, have different relations with their clientele and, consequently, somewhat different internal structures. The clientele, in most such cases, consists of the various holders of political power, and of various groups with potential influence over the political and social course of events—such as voting and pressure groups and public opinion leaders. The extent to which such organizations are oriented more to the holders of power than to the wide "electorate," or vice versa, depends greatly on the nature of the political regime, the power of the given organization, and its specific aims and locality. The existence of politically or socially oriented organizations usually depends largely on their striking some sort of balance between these two types of clientele. This has several repercussions on the control and authority structure of these organizations. On the whole, the demarcation between "policy making" and routine (except for the organization's purely technical staff) is not very sharp, whereas the extent of "interference" of external elements, such as various notables and party bosses, is much more marked. This interference influences the activities and recruitment policies of these organizations.

In cultural organizations (scientific, educational, literary, etc.), the situation is again somewhat different. The clientele of such organizations is also the wide public or some select group (for example, students) within it. However, the cultural organization is not as directly related to or as dependent on the powerholders as are the sociopolitical organizations. True, it may be greatly dependent on them for financial appropriations. However, the type of dependence is different—or, rather, its responsibility is defined in a different way. As a rule it is expected to produce a certain amount of marketable goods or to provide a certain amount of votes for a given group or party. While cultural organizations may at times be committed in both respects, such commitments are considered by these organizations, and quite often by other groups, as deviations which can perhaps be justified only in terms of exceptional circumstances. The very nature of these exceptional circumstances indicates the usual definition of the responsibilities of such organizations. In general, the function of these organizations is to educate rather than to propagandize and manipulate.

It can perhaps be said that cultural organizations deal mainly with problems of basic, rather than secondary, orientations. They are controlled by factors other than those controlling economically and politically oriented organizations, as manifest most clearly in the pure, nonmixed types of such organization, such as academies and institutes for pure research.

Cultural organizations are characterized by relatively little differentiation between the higher policy-making bodies and most (except the purely technical) of the personnel. This is true at least of most aspects of the organization's policy which is directly related to its main goals, as borne out by ritual application and religious education in the church and by education and scientific planning in the university. It is chiefly in connection with the more "technical," at times perhaps crucial, aspects of the policy problems that many (mostly external) elements of division of labor and specialization enter.

However, in the culturally, unlike the socio-politically, oriented organization, the relative absence of differentiation between various echelons of its personnel does not imply a great extent of external interference. On the contrary, most of the personnel is "internal," recruited according to the autonomous criteria of the organization. External elements may come in at some of the higher, formal levels, such as at board of trustee meetings and religious conventions. At times the external elements may even appoint the head of the cultural organization, as, for example, in the case of the appointment of university presidents. But as a rule even such external control is governed by the organization's own basic values and takes into account the opinion of its members. Moreover, these external elements do not usually exert pressure on the organization in order to influence its goal definition or direction, but, rather, they represent those sections of the general public which are oriented to the organization's basic values. Consequently, in most cultural organizations, the influence of external factors on the recruitment of personnel is relatively small, although by no means nonexistent.

We shall now examine in somewhat greater detail the effect of different goal orientations on the internal organization of bureaucracies with respect to the extent of specialization, the division of labor, and the decision-making process.

The extent of specialization and differentiation, of division of labor, is greatest in the economically oriented administrative organizations, less in the culturally, and least in the politically oriented. These differences are intimately related to the nature of the different goals and to the types of activity required for their implementation. In economic organizations, great emphasis is laid on "rationality" and on accountability in quantitative terms. This makes, within certain limits, for maximum actualization of the possibilities inherent in a complementary division of labor. While the qualifications demanded of each employee may be relatively minimal, the quantitative and qualitative differences between the main levels of employees are comparatively great.

In culturally oriented organizations, the extent of specialization required of employees is far greater than in economic organizations. But in these organizations there is relatively little complementary division of labor among members except among the purely technical personnel. The majority of full-status members of most such organizations as a rule perform similar and parallel, rather than complementary, tasks. Thus in the Catholic Church the priests, and in principle even the cardinal, fulfill at least some similar basic functions, and in a university all the full members of the faculty perform similar tasks (though differing in content). Accordingly, the existence of differences in rank and status within cultural organizations does not necessarily imply a great extent of division of labor. As we shall see, this fact has important repercussions on the authority system of these organizations.

In the organizations with socio-political goals (especially political parties), the extent of specialization and "rational" division of labor is, as stated, least. There are usually few formal qualifications for specialized training in most organizations of this kind. While in some political (or social) organizations there may officially be a relatively complicated division of labor, the extent of complementarity in them is usually relatively small. The lack of an extensive division of labor is related to the basic aim of these organizations which is to manipulate the contingent loyalties of various groups. Because of the frequent shifts in the issues upon which political parties may be focused, it is difficult to lay down any specific qualifications for recruitment, except the general ability to manipulate people in various ways. And this aim of manipulation has to be borne in mind by most of the personnel—there can exist but little complementary specialization and division of labor.

In politically (or socially) and, to some extent, culturally oriented organizations, the tendency is usually toward a territorial rather than functional division of labor. As a rule the various territorial units tend to duplicate, rather than functionally complement, each other. Consequently, the control exercised over such territorial divisions by the central organs is of a political rather than a functional nature.

How is the system of authority in bureaucratic organizations related to their goal orientations? The main criterion of comparison at this stage of our discussion will be the extent to which authorized decision making is centralized and the decisions regarding the organization's problems are routinized.

Thus as the nature of its problems and goals demands rather unitary, "quantitative" decisions, economic organizations feature the highest type of centralization. The extent of "collegiate" authority is greatest in cultural organizations, although it varies from one such organization to another. The reasons for the predominance of a collegiate type of authority system in cultural organizations are: (a) the parallel (even though differing in content) specialization of members which prevents their judging one another (this is true especially of universities), and (b) the "basic equality" of all members in relation to the ultimate values of the organization.

In the authority system and decision-making process, socio-political organizations are rather unstable. On the one hand they feature what may be called a monolithic tendency (natural in such organizations) toward unification of command in political battles. On the other hand, however, they often develop a tendency toward decentralization of the decision-making pattern, even to the point of lack of coordination resulting in contradictory policies. Centralization is brought about largely through the agency of numerous external forces which impinge on the decisions of the political organization and have direct relations with and power over many of its employees.

The preceding discussion showed that it is possible to analyze systematically the relation between the goal orientation of a given bureaucratic organization and its internal structure. It was necessarily discursive and not exhaustive (similar methods can obviously be applied, for example, to public corporations and to military and governmental bureaucracies), and its sole purpose was to bring out the general fact that various aspects of bureaucratic organizations, as well as their "deviations" from the ideal type of bureaucracy, are systematically related to their goal orientations. It has been shown that the effect of the predominant goal orientation on the internal structure of the bureaucracy's organization can be explained by the type of internal criteria of role allocation which these goals involve and by the type of relation the organization establishes with the external world by pursuing and implementing such goals.

Bureaucratic Roles

The major variables enumerated above also necessarily influence
the structure of the main bureaucratic roles and determine the relative predominance of their components. In other words, it can be
postulated that each of these variables, or their different constellations, can influence the relative importance of the internal elements in
the definition of the bureaucratic role (for example, detachment, professional specialization) as well as of the external elements which constitute part of the bureaucrat's "role set." Here also there is an abun-
dance of material which has not yet been fully and systematically
explored. We shall first briefly illustrate the influence of the bureaucracy's goals on the nature of the bureaucratic role.

The economically-oriented organization usually develops the most
specialized role conception, especially among the nonentrepreneurial
staff. To some extent, a specialized approach (though obviously
differing in content) can also be found among the managerial echelons. However, the role conception of the highest echelons might feature some diffuse, community-oriented elements.

The role conception of culturally oriented organizations features
both professional and some very explicitly diffuse elements. These latter elements derive from the diffuse nature and orientation of most
cultural symbols. The socio-political organizations are characterized
by the least developed, professional role image, as the pressures for
socio-political activity tend to be very diffuse and weaken professional
orientations.

Unfortunately, systematic studies of the relation of different bureaucratic role conceptions to the above-listed variables are few. However, numerous additional illustrations are scattered throughout the
literature in this field, and they certainly are amenable to further
analysis. But even the available materials show that the assumption
about the necessary predominance of the computative mechanisms in
bureaucratic organization is not always true and that the extent of
such predominance varies among different organizations.

*Tendencies to Bureaucratization and the Access of
Bureaucratic Organizations to Resources and Clients*

Such variations may be greatly influenced by the predominant goals of bureaucratic organizations. Such variations may differ according to the nature of the resources on which the bureaucracy depends for the implementation of its goals.

This dependence or relation may be defined in terms of:

1. The chief function of the organization; that is, whether it is a service, market, or membership recruitment agency. (This distinction is closely related to, but not necessarily identical with, the nature of its goals.)

2. The extent to which its clientele is entirely dependent upon its products, or, conversely, the type and extent of competition offered by other (parallel) agencies.

3. The nature of the internal (ownership) and extent of the external control and supervision to which it is subjected.

4. The criteria according to which the success is measured, and especially the extent to which it is measured by changes in the behavior of the bureaucracy's clients.

5. The spheres of activity of both its personnel and its clientele that the function of the bureaucracy encompasses.

While here also most of the research is still before us, some general indications are not out of place. It seems that influence of the bureaucracy's external dependence on its structural characteristics is as follows:

1. The greater bureaucracy's dependence on its clientele in terms of their being able to go to a competing agency, the more it will have to develop many communication techniques and other additional services in order to monopolize its clientele.

2. Insofar as bureaucracy's great external dependence is due to the fact that criteria of successful organizational performance are based on the number and behavior pattern of the organization's members, it will have to take an interest in numerous spheres of its clients' activi-

ties and either establish its control over them or be subjected to their influence and direction.

3. Insofar as the extent of the bureaucracy's external dependence is relatively small and its power basis assured (as is the case in governmental service agencies), it tends toward formalization of its organization and activities and toward growing detachment from its clientele.

Many overlappings may, of course, develop between these possibilities, some of which will be taken into account in the subsequent discussion. These are necessarily very cursory and partial illustrations. Neither the list of variables nor the series of hypotheses concerning their influence is exhaustive or final. At this point our purpose is only to illustrate the importance of the type and extent of the bureaucratic organization's dependence on other centers of power and on its clientele for the understanding of its activities.

Conditions of Bureaucratization in Modern Societies

The preceding comparative analysis has shown that the assumption that in every bureaucratic organization the computative mechanism is necessarily the predominant one and always leads to bureaucratization is not borne out.

A similar critical analysis can be applied to other assumptions about the social conditions which facilitate, especially in modern societies, the intensification of the trends toward bureaucratization. Among such conditions most often mentioned in the literature is, first, the growing scope of the activities of governments in general and of various public and semipublic agencies in particular.

Second are the growing absorption of greater parts of the population within the scope of activities of these agencies and the growing ability of these organizations to deal with the problems of these groups. This growing ability is due mainly to the growth of importance of detailed concrete problems (e.g., problems of distribution of services, of allocation of subsidies) as distinct from wider political or ideological issues which are susceptible to being dealt with through representative legislative types of activities.

Third are the growing specialization and "complexity" within different spheres of life and the growing dependence on expert, specialized knowledge, which may minimize the effectiveness of control over the bureaucratic organization by the "nonexpert" holders of economic, political, and communal power.

Fourth is the growth of the number of people employed by various bureaucratic organizations which necessarily increases the general potential influence of these organizations on the style of life of the population (18).

And fifth is the increasing importance of formal educational qualifications demanded by such organizations which may, although it need not, also increase the general social and cultural influence of the bureaucratic organization (19).

There can, of course, be no doubt that the development of multiple bureaucratic organizations has certainly facilitated the extension of "computative" mechanisms and of mechanisms of direct bargaining between different organizations. Such development could easily minimize the possibility of the organizations' supervision and control by more public or legal bodies. The growth of the scope of such mechanisms can be seen in what has recently been called the "new feudalism"—a term which refers to the extension of the scope of direct relations between various interest groups and the public bureaucracy at the expense of allocation through representative institutions (20). However, a close examination of these assumptions will fail to bear them out.

The broad conditions are in a way only specifications in terms of modern societies of the more general conditions of the development of goal-oriented and bureaucratic organizations that were examined earlier in the chapter. But these general conditions of the development of bureaucratic organization—such as the development of social differentiation, specialization, and market economy—also give rise to the development of other types of organizations and regulative mechanisms, especially various types of nonascriptive mechanisms and organizations, such as craft organizations, voluntary associations, and legislative bodies (21).

These developments may, paradoxically, create some potential for the development of various nonbureaucratic mechanisms. Such possibilities may have arisen both in the internal structure of the bureaucratic organization, through the diversification of different types of roles, and in the ways in which such organizations relate to their external environment.

Thus, first, this growing specialization necessarily gives rise to the development of new roles, to a more complex division of labor within different bureaucratic organizations, and to a growing similarity in the nature of the qualifications demanded by different organizations. Technical, manpower, and professional roles tend to develop which are to a large extent similar or parallel in different organizations and which enhance both the competition between different organizations for such manpower and the similarity of many of their organizational and professional problems. These various roles may create some new professional or semiprofessional identifications which cut across different bureaucratic organizations.

While such professional groups first developed in the more "traditional" areas, such as medicine and law, lately they have also begun to extend to fields, such as labor relations, which are seemingly more susceptible to direct bargaining.

Second, the growing proliferation of bureaucratic organizations necessarily gives rise to many problems of coordination and thus raises the possibility of new nonbureaucratic types of regulative and integrative mechanisms.

Third, these developments also sharpen in many ways the problem of the relation between the bureaucratic organizations and their clientele. There develop various possibilities of exerting legitimate pressure on bureaucratic organizations through various clients (consumers) and public and community organizations and associations. These associations are by the very nature of their orientations more intermittent and discontinuous, not easily susceptible to becoming bureaucratized. Hence they also have recourse not only to direct pressure and bargaining but also to more open legislative and public control mechanisms.

Bureaucratization and Structure of Markets

The preceding analysis shows that the general social conditions—the development of social differentiation and of wider markets for economic and noneconomic goods—which facilitate the extension of the number and scope of bureaucratic organizations can be seen as necessary but not as sufficient conditions of bureaucratization. The development of such conditions also creates "countervailing" forces which may impede or control the progress of bureaucratic organizations and mechanisms. The extent of bureaucratization is dependent not on the development of such markets, but on their structure.

The available material—which is as yet sporadic—indicates that purely computative-bureaucratic and direct-bargaining mechanisms tend to develop under conditions of relatively closed and/or monopolistic markets and reinforce such monopolistic structures. The nonbureaucratic mechanisms tend to develop more in situations of relatively free entry into these markets, of wider distribution of power, and of successful attempts to restrict monopolization within them (22).

The maintenance of such free entry or access to these markets may be maintained through two different types of mechanisms. One is the type which *limits* the scope of activities of bureaucratic organizations through the upholding, within various social spheres, of either more traditional types of organization (e.g., guilds, social clubs) and/or nonbureaucratic types of goal-oriented organizations (voluntary associations, craft organizations, etc.), in this way removing the operation of bureaucratic organizations from various spheres of social life.

Such mechanisms are mostly operative within those periods and areas of social life where the scope of social differentiation and complexity and the very scope of any bureaucratic organization is relatively small. (This need not necessarily limit the possibility that any single bureaucratic organization will develop strong tendencies to bureaucratization within the area of its activities.) They are also operative under conditions of wide distribution of power and values within such sectors. These market conditions are closely related to the intermittancy and interchangeability of goals toward which the activities of these groups are oriented (23).

The second type of mechanism for the maintenance of free entry or access to markets operates not only through the isolation and limitation of the scope of the activities of bureaucratic organizations and mechanisms but also and mainly through the development of various "controlling" and countervailing mechanisms which operate *across* well-developed bureaucratic organizations. They do not usually limit the scope of these markets but mainly influence the basic conditions of entry into them and their internal organization and regulate and supervise the activities of the participants within them.

These types of mechanisms usually develop in a later stage of modernization under conditions of growing complexity of the social structure. They are closely related to the extension of the number and scope of bureaucratic organizations, which have been discussed above, and to the development of wider, potentially centralized and unified markets. Needless to say, very often these two types of nonbureaucratic mechanisms exist side by side and reinforce one another. There are for instance cases in which nonbureaucratic voluntary community organizations tend to control, through their participation in community and political affairs, the activities of various countrywide bureaucratic services operating in a community.

Bureaucratization and Distribution of Power in Society

This necessarily brings us to the problem of the social conditions under which such different types of markets develop and to the problems of the conditions of entry into these markets and of the possibilities of control over them. Although the state of the research in this field is as yet too "underdeveloped" to be able to offer any generalization, we would like to present the following evidence as tentative leads for further investigations.

Among such aspects of social structure, we would like to single out at the present stage of our analysis, first, the extent of development of differentiated forms of organizations and activity within any social group or strata. Of special importance within this context is the extent to which there develop within such groups or strata: (a) a great extent of social and economic differentiation, free-floating resources, and social mobility; (b) relative predominance of universalistic elements in its orientations and goals.

Second is the extent of internal cohesion of different groups and wider social strata, as measured especially by the extent of social interaction between different occupations and ecological groups and by their ability and willingness to become socially and politically articulate and active on the community and country levels. Third is the extent of cooperation and interchange between such different groups or, conversely, the extent of cleavage between them (24).

Of special importance here is the extent to which there exists a relatively wide distribution of power and values in the economic, cultural, and political spheres among many groups. Also of importance is the maintenance of continuous struggle and the extent to which there exist politically oriented and strongly articulated groups and goals, which can maintain control over the implementation of these goals by the holders of political and communal power.

It may be suggested, first, that the greater the ability of such various groups to develop a great variety of activities and organizations in the pursuance of various specific goals, the smaller their dependence on any one type of regulative mechanism or organization. On the contrary, the smaller the extent to which different groups evince any ability to implement specific goals, the smaller also their ability—if they are put into a relatively differentiated structure—to counteract the activities of centralized, bureaucratic activities and organizations.

Second, the smaller, in general, the internal cohesion of major social groups, the greater the extent of such cleavages; the greater their recourse to various computative bureaucratic and bargaining mechanisms, the smaller their ability to control the operation of such mechanisms and organizations. Similarly, the greater the extent of the cleavage between different groups and strata, the smaller usually their ability to evolve autonomous mechanisms, to cooperate between themselves, and to maintain some common ways of political articulation whether on the community or on a wider societal level.

Insofar as there exists a great extent of interaction between different groups and a great extent of social and political articulation, the greater will be the ability of many groups to control, to some extent at least, the conditions of entry into the markets and the attempts to monopolize within them (25).

These broad social conditions tend also to influence the interrelations between various subgroups within bureaucratic organizations and the wider environment. The extent to which the cohesion of social groups is great and cleavages between such different groups are small determines the extent to which the various subgroups within bureaucratic organizations are not closed or limited to any one such organization but tend to have wider linkages, connections, and reference orientations. In cases of a great extent of cohesion these subgroups (e.g., workers' groups, professional groups) could cut across several organizations— both bureaucratic and nonbureaucratic—minimizing the monopoly of any one organization over its members and enhancing the possibility of the development of some mechanisms of control over the bureaucratic organization.

Bureaucratization in Different Types of Modern Societies

The broad social conditions which influence, according to the preceding analysis, the scope of the process of bureaucratization are not evenly distributed in all modern societies, polities, or sectors thereof. Accordingly, also, the ways in which the problems of bureaucratization are dealt with in different systems vary greatly. In autocratic and especially in totalitarian regimes, or in sectors of other regimes which have an autocratic structure, most of the efforts of the political elite are oriented to the maintenance of the rulers' control over bureaucratic organizations. Their efforts leave, however, the upper echelons of the bureaucracy as a part of the ruling elite and usually enhance the scope and importance of the bureaucratic regulative mechanisms. They enhance the scope of the representative or market mechanisms, as these political systems are necessarily inimical to the development of those types of regulative mechanisms which can develop into autonomous centers of power (except for purely traditional centers of power also enhance the scope of the representative or market mechanisms, as in the more autocratic regimes).

Thus we find that in such societies or sectors thereof, where any given group establishes a power monopoly over parts of its environment, this group may use the bureaucracy as an instrument of pure power and manipulation, may distort its autonomous roles and professional orientation, and may subvert some of its echelons through various inducements and professional gratifications.

Hence within these regimes we find that the spread of bureaucratic organization gives rise mostly to "illicit" or semi-illegal practices of bargaining between different organizations, of the type which has been amply illustrated in studies of Soviet industry. These tend to increase the scope of bargaining and more informal arrangements but not of legislative or public control (26). This tendency is related to relatively small internal cohesion and political articulation of different groups in the society and to a great extent of cleavage between the groups, both tendencies being fostered by the regime.

A somewhat different pattern emerges in the political regimes which develop in the so-called Developing Areas or New States. Here the tendency to bureaucratization is due to the prevalence of the more traditional groups and to the relative weakness of any but the new elite groups to deal with many of the problems of modernization and to implement various, differentiated goals. The outcome of such conditions is very often the development of bureaucratic organizations and mechanisms as the main or only ones able to deal with such "modern" problems and to perform various specialized functions. Sometimes it may lead to the partial or total abdication of the political elite from effective political control or to the bureaucratization of the elite itself. In these cases the tendency toward excessive bureaucratization can be checked, on the one hand, through the development of a relatively strong and cohesive political elite and, on the other hand, through development of a higher extent of political articulation of both traditional and modern groups. Insofar as such cohesive elites and political articulation of broader groups do not develop, the various bureaucracies and especially the central political bureaucracy tend to develop, as the only "nonascriptive" regulative mechanisms that combine a great extent of more traditional elements within them (27).

It is mostly with democratic regimes that there exist the necessary conditions for the checking of excessive tendencies toward bureaucratization. It is within them that there exists a wide enough spread of centers of power and of different types of social organizations to facilitate the development of some of the conditions propitious for the articulation of nonbureaucratic mechanisms of regulation and allocation. However, these general conditions existing in democratic societies are only necessary or facilitating. They are certainly not sufficient conditions for the development of the antidotes to bureaucratization. The exact and concrete ways in which these mechanisms develop in these societies depend greatly on the constellation of the aforementioned variables within any democratic regime or sector thereof.

The preceding discussion indicated some possible approaches to the analysis of bureaucratization as a type of regulative mechanism in modern societies and to the analysis of the conditions under which this type of mechanism may predominate. These necessarily preliminary approaches and suggestions attempted to indicate some of the possibilities and lacunae of research in this field and some ways of bringing different theoretical approaches, such as some aspects of organization theory, economic theory, and socio-political analysis, to bear on these problems.

NOTES

1. R. Bendix and S. M. Lipset, "Political Sociology," *Current Sociology*, Vol. VI, No. 2, 1957, pp. 91 ff.

2. T. Parsons, *The Structure of Social Action*, Glencoe, Ill.: The Free Press, 1949, p. 509.

3. H. Kaufman, "Emerging Conflicts in the Doctrines of Public Administration," *American Political Science Review*, Vol. 50, 1956, pp. 1057–1074.

4. H. Finer, "Critics of Bureaucracy," *Political Science Quarterly*, Vol. 60, 1945, pp. 100–112. S. M. Lipset, *Agrarian Socialism*, Berkeley: University of California Press, 1950. J. D. Kingsley, *Representative Bureaucracy*, Yellow Springs, Ohio: Antioch Press, 1944.

5. See M. Weber, *Wirtschaft und Gesellschaft*, Tubingen: J. C. B. Mohr, 1922, especially pp. 126 ff., 158–165, 758–778.

6. Adapted from Peter M. Blau, *Bureaucracy in Modern Society*, New York: Random House, 1956, pp. 28–34. See also Peter M. Blau and W. Richard Scott, *Formal Organizations*, San Francisco: Chandler Publishing, 1962.

7. For the relations between bureaucracy and other goal-oriented organizations see A. L. Stinchcombe, "Bureaucratic and Craft Administration of Production: A Comparative Study," *Administrative Science Quarterly*, Vol. V, No. 4, 1959, pp. 168–187; and Stanley H. Udy, Jr., " 'Bureaucracy' and 'Rationality' in Weber's Organization Theory: An Empirical Study," *American Sociological Review*, Vol. 24, No. 6, December 1959, pp. 791–796.

8. For the analysis of conditions of development of bureaucratic or-

ganizations in a specific historical setting see S. N. Eisenstadt, *The Political Systems of Empires*, New York: The Free Press of Glencoe, 1963.

9. In the existing literature there has been little distinction between conditions which make for the growth of bureaucracy and those conducive to increasing bureaucratization. Gouldner's polemics against those who foresee the inevitability of bureaucratization are to some extent due to the lack of this distinction. See A. Gouldner, "Metaphysical Pathos and the Theory of Bureaucracy," *American Political Science Review*, Vol. 49, No. 2, June 1955, pp. 496–507.

10. This follows largely T. Parsons, "A Sociological Approach to the Theory of Organizations," in *Structure and Process in Modern Societies*, New York: The Free Press, 1960, pp. 16–59.

11. Conrad M. Arensberg and Geoffrey Tootell, "Plant Sociology: Real Discoveries and New Problems," in Mirra Momarovsky (editor), *Common Frontiers of the Social Sciences*, Glencoe, Ill.: The Free Press, 1957, pp. 310–337.

12. J. D. Thompson and W. J. McEwen, "Organizational Goals and Environment," *American Sociological Review*, Vol. 23, No. 1, February 1958, pp. 23–31.

13. The analysis of the bureaucratic organization in terms of types of decision making and allocation can be found first in Max Weber's discussion of authority structures; Weber, *Wirtschaft und Gesellschaft*, *loc. cit.* More recent developments of some aspects of this problem can be found in R. A. Dahl and C. E. Lindblom, "Politics, Economics and Bargaining in Political Economics," in *Research Frontiers in Politics and Government*, Washington: Brookings Lectures, 1955, pp. 45–70, and in J. D. Thompson and A. Thuden, "Strategies, Structures and Processes of Organizational Decision," in J. D. Thompson et al. (editors), *Comparative Studies in Administration*, Pittsburgh: University of Pittsburgh Press, 1959, pp. 195–217. See also J. March and H. Simon, *Organizations*, New York: John Wiley and Sons, 1958.

14. Dahl, *loc. cit.*, Thompson and Thuden, *loc. cit.*

15. This distinction is especially dealt with by Dahl, *loc. cit.*

16. The term "computative" is used here as in Thompson and Thuden, *loc. cit.* See also Dahl, *loc. cit.*

17. For a parallel analysis see also T. Parsons, "A Sociological Approach to the Theory of Organizations," *loc. cit.* See also J. D. Thompson, "Or-

ganizational Management of Conflict," *Administrative Science Quarterly*, Vol. 4, 1959–1960, pp. 389–409.

18. The best known exposition of this point can be found in W. Whyte's *Organization Man*, New York: Simon and Schuster, 1956.

19. This point has been stressed by J. Gusfield, "Equalitarianism and Bureaucratic Recruitment," *Administrative Science Quarterly*, Vol. 2, 1957–1958, pp. 518–521.

20. H. W. Ehrman, *Interest Groups and the Bureaucracy in Western Democracies* (mimeographed), prepared for Conference on the Comparative Role of Groups in Political Systems, Social Science Research Council, 1960. H. W. Ehrman (editor), *Interest Groups in Four Continents*, Pittsburgh: University of Pittsburgh Press, 1958.

21. P. M. Blau, *Bureaucracy in Modern Society*, New York: Random House, 1956. The possibility that these broad conditions may give rise also to other types of specialized organizations has recently been developed by A. L. Stinchcombe, "Bureaucratic and Craft Administration of Production —A Comparative Study," *Administrative Science Quarterly*, Vol. 4, No. 2, September 1959, pp. 168–187, and from a somewhat different point of view in Stanley H. Udy, Jr., " 'Bureaucracy' and 'Rationality' in Weber's Organization Theory: An Empirical Study," *American Sociological Review*, Vol. 24, No. 6, December 1959, pp. 791–796.

22. Although the general relation between development of market economy and bureaucratic organization has been recognized for a long time, the investigation of the specific relation between types of markets and types of bureaucratic organization is still very much in the beginning stage. For some such first approaches, see H. Leibenstein, *Economic Theory and Organizational Analysis*, New York: Harpers, 1960, especially Chapters I and IV: J. S. Bain, *Industrial Organization*, New York: John Wiley and Sons, 1959, especially Chapter VII; A. L. Stinchcombe, "The Sociology of Organization and the Theory of the Firm," *The Pacific Sociological Review*, Vol. 3, No. 2, Fall 1960, pp. 75–83. For classification of markets which has some affinity to ours, see also A. S. Feldman and W. E. Moore (editors), *Labor Commitment and Social Change in Developing Areas*, New York: Social Science Research Council, 1960, pp. 41–62, and B. F. Hoselitz, "The Market Matrix," in Bert F. Hoselitz and Wilbert E. Moore (editors), *Industrialization and Society*, Paris: Unesco-Mouton, 1963, pp. 217–238.

23. See A. L. Stinchcombe, "Bureaucratic and Craft Organization of Production," *loc. cit.*

24. For an analysis of the general conditions of development of bureaucratic organization, see pp. 185–186 and also S. N. Eisenstadt, *Political Systems of Empires, loc. cit.* Some of the variables proposed here, especially those dealing with social cohesion and cleavages, are closely related to those proposed by W. Kornhauser, *The Politics of Mass Society,* Glencoe, Ill.: The Free Press, 1959, and indicate the possibility of bringing together some aspects of analysis of bureaucracy and of political sociology. See also S. M. Lipset, *Political Man,* New York: Doubleday, 1960, Chapter I, and S. N. Eisenstadt, *Modernization, Growth, and Diversity,* Carnegie Seminar, Department of Government, Indiana University, Bloomington, Ind., 1963.

25. J. S. Bain, *Industrial Organization, loc. cit.*

26. J. S. Berliner, *Factory and Manager in the USSR,* Cambridge, Mass.: Harvard University Press, 1957, especially Chapter XI.

27. These problems have been dealt with in greater detail in S. N. Eisenstadt, "Problems of Emerging Bureaucracies in Developing Areas in New States," in Hoselitz and Moore (editors), *op. cit.,* pp. 159–175. See also S. N. Eisenstadt, *Essays on Sociological Aspects of Political and Economic Development,* The Hague: Mouton, 1961, especially pp. 42–50, and S. N. Eisenstadt, "Bureaucracy and Political Development," in J. LaPolambara (editor), *Bureaucracy and Political Development,* Princeton, N.J.: Princeton University Press, 1963, pp. 96–120.

Chapter 8

Political Orientations of Bureaucracies in Centralized Empires

I

The purpose of this essay is to analyze the main types of social and political orientations of bureaucratic administrations (especially of their upper echelons) and their participation in the political struggle in historical centralized empires. The major characteristics of these polities were analyzed in several former papers, and the analysis presented here will be supported by the main conclusions of these papers and on the wider work on which these papers are based (1).

The analysis here, as in the former essays, is rooted in a number of pre-modern historical examples: the Ancient Egyptian Empires, the Sassanid Empire of Persia, the Chinese Empires from the period of Han onward, the Byzantine Empire, the Abbasid and Ottoman Empires, certain European countries in the 11-18th centuries, and the Spanish-American Empire. For reasons of space we shall not be able to present in full analysis a case study of any single society, and most of the materials presented here will be mainly descriptive, although we shall attempt, as far as possible, to present these illustrations in a systematic way, related to the major problem of the analysis.

As already pointed out in former papers, in most of these societies the bureaucratic administrations were either created or reorganized by the rulers—the Emperors or Kings—as one of the most important instruments in their attempts to create a relatively centralized, uni-

216

fied polity and to develop ways for the implementation of autonomous political goals (2).

The success of the rulers in the establishment of these polities and in the development and maintenance of the bureaucratic administrations was usually dependent either on the existence or development of specific conditions in the structure of their societies. The most important of these conditions were a relatively differentiated social structure, emergence to some extent of a market economy, a relatively flexible status system, and the growth of some universalistic cultural orientations. All these were connected with the development of various free-floating resources and with relative predominance of various non-ascriptive rural and urban groups in the social structure of these societies (3).

The rise of bureaucratic organizations and their very activities have played an important part in the establishment and continuation of the basic conditions and premises of these polities. Their rise has also helped in the development of those relatively differentiated and non-traditional strata that provided the backbone of these polities and of the "free" resources needed by the rulers, and in the maintenance of continuous interrelations between the rulers and these strata.

But these conditions were not always given or assured for an indefinite period of time. Various social groups, such as the aristocracies, some more traditional ascriptive urban groups, and religious elites, often waged a struggle against the rulers and the institutional structure of these polities and attempted to undermine those conditions which enabled the maintenance of these premises. The rulers attempted with varying degrees of success to counteract these tendencies through the implementation of policies which could ensure the continuous maintenance of basic conditions, especially the existence of some free-floating resources, on the one hand, and the ruler's control over these resources, on the other (4).

In the implementation of these aims the bureaucratic administrations have played, as indicated above, a very important part (5). But in this way the bureaucratic administrations were necessarily caught in the political struggle that developed in these societies between different social groups and between the administrations and the rulers.

Thus the bureaucratic administrations in these societies were posed between the rulers, who very often wanted to use them almost exclusively for their own needs and purposes, and some of the major groups and strata, from whom the rulers and the administrations wanted to mobilize various resources and who usually developed on their part some expectations of services from the bureaucracy (6).

In conjunction with these different pressures the bureaucratic administrations (and especially their higher echelons) developed several rather diversified types of activities and some specific organizational characteristics of their own. The most important of these was the tendency to emphasize, to some extent, their internal organizational and professional autonomy and self-perpetuation.

This tendency was manifest in two major aspects of their activities. First, the bureaucratic administrations tended, insofar as they did take into account the demands and interests of both the rulers (the monarch) and the various strata, to develop some autonomy vis-à-vis both of them. They usually developed and maintained certain general usages or rules and standards of service, executed them with regard to the strata and groups to which they applied, took into consideration some general interests of the population, and withstood the pressure of those interested in changing these usages continuously or intermittently for their own benefit. Second, most of these bureaucracies developed some conception of themselves as servants of the "state" or of the community (even if the state was symbolized mainly by a dynasty) and not only as *personal* servants of the rulers (7). Even though in none of these cases were all these manifestations of the autonomy of the bureaucracy as developed as in modern "civil service," they did exist in an embryonic form.

Such autonomy of the bureaucracy was, however, very often suspected by the rulers, who therefore tried to restrict it, to maintain some measure of political control over it, so as to minimize the possibility of its developing relatively independent political goals and activities. Thus, throughout the implementation of their different tasks, the bureaucratic administrations were faced with the problem of striking some equilibrium between these different pressures and tendencies, namely between organizational and social autonomy, and controls and pressures from the rulers and some of the major strata.

But the attainment of balance between all these tendencies and pressures was not always easy, as there could easily develop a strong preponderance of one of the tendencies, undermining or weakening the others, and influencing accordingly the scope and direction of the activities of the bureaucracy. This development occurred for several reasons, all of them connected with the basic conditions of development of the bureaucratic administrations in these polities and with the fact that the bureaucracy was caught in the political struggle that developed therein.

First, the very power position which these bureaucracies acquired, in societies in which there usually existed but few "constitutional" limits on power and in which the access to power was relatively limited, placed the members of the bureaucracy in an especially privileged position (8). Second, the great emphasis, in these societies, on some sort of ascriptive symbols of status necessarily "tempted" the members of the bureaucracy to use their position for acquisition of symbols or to make these positions into bases of such symbols. Third, the relatively low level of economic development and social differentiation enabled only a little development of special professional roles and of adequate remuneration for such roles. The fact that in most of these societies the sale of offices was very common attests to this (9).

As a result of all these conditions, the different echelons of bureaucracies may have often distorted many of their customary or explicit rules and diverted many of their services for the benefit of some social group with whom they might become identified and/or for their own benefit, in order to become both alienated from other strata and groups in the society and oppressive toward such groups. In other words, the bureaucratic echelons may have displaced their service goals to the rulers and/or to the various social strata and emphasized goals of self-interest and aggrandizement instead.

On the other hand, the relative weakness of many political groups and the great dependence of the bureaucracy on the kings could often cause the undermining of the relative autonomy of the bureaucracy. This could happen through the bureaucracies' total subjugation to the rulers by the ruler diverting all the activities of the bureaucracy for his own exclusive use without allowing it to perform any continuous services to different strata in the society and to uphold any general rules of provision of services.

For all these reasons the bureaucratic administration in these societies could develop political orientations which were to some extent opposed to the basic premises of their polities, undermine the polities' foundations, and generate processes of change which could not be contained within the framework of these polities.

It is the main purpose of this paper to analyze the major types of such political orientations of the main echelons of the bureaucratic administrations in the historical-bureaucratic empires, and to investigate the conditions under which each of these orientations and patterns of activities tends to develop.

II

The preceding discussion indicates that the major types of political orientations developed by the bureaucracies in the historical-bureaucratic societies were the following: (a) maintenance of service orientations to both the rulers and the major strata (with, in the societies studied here, usually greater emphasis on services to the rulers); (b) development into a merely passive tool of the ruler with but little internal autonomy or performance of services to the different strata of the population; (c) displacement of bureaucracies' service goals to various strata and to the rulers in favor of goals of self-aggrandizement and usurpation of power exclusively in its own favor and/or in favor of a group with which it becomes closely identified; (d) displacement of bureaucracies' service goals to the major strata in favor of goals of self-aggrandizement and attainment of political power—but together with maintenance of service goals to the rulers.

Needless to say all the bureaucratic administrations in the historical-bureaucratic polities usually evinced some mixture or overlapping of all these four tendencies or orientations, although a particular tendency was usually predominant, for at least part, if not the whole, of the history of a particular bureaucratic-historic polity. It is with this relative predominance and its influence on the continuity of the political systems of these societies that we are mainly concerned here.

The discussion of the political orientations of the bureaucracies would be incomplete without considering how these were related to the scope of their activities. Various studies reported in earlier papers have shown that in general the scope of the activities of a bureaucracy, as measured by the institutional spheres in which it was active and by the extent of specialization of departments, was closely related to the extent of development of the basic conditions of these societies—i.e., the extent of differentiation of the institutional structure of these societies and the scope of the autonomy of political spheres within them (10).

However, in all these discussions we have not differentiated between several types of activities in which the bureaucracy may be engaged and especially between technical or regulatory activities, i.e., between activities oriented mainly to the performance of technical services and between activities oriented to social and political regulation of different groups. While it is obvious that every bureaucratic administration in any of the historical-bureaucratic societies is engaged in both types of activities, the predominant activity may vary greatly from one case to another.

Moreover, there necessarily existed also great variations as to the criteria of such regulation and especially for whose benefit the regulation was done. All these variables were, as we shall see in greater detail, influenced by the political orientations and activities of the bureaucracy.

III

We shall begin with a description of the major types of political orientations and activities of the bureaucracies that can be found in the historical-bureaucratic societies.

We start with analysis of those cases in which the bureaucracy maintained its service orientation to both the rulers and some of the major strata, even if, in the societies with which we are concerned, there was always a greater emphasis on service to the ruler. Such political orientations and tendencies of the bureaucracy were developed and maintained in the Sassanid Empire, especially during the first period of its history and during the reign of Khawad (11), in the Byzantine Empire through most of the period between the 7th and 10th centuries (12), in the Spanish-American Empire in the first century and a half of its existence (13), in France, especially in the period from the Fronde to the last decades of Louis XIVe reign (14), in England in the 17th and 18th centuries (15), in the Chinese Empire throughout the first and middle periods of most of its dynasties (16), and in the Abbasid Empire until the 11th century (17).

In most of these cases, the bureaucracy maintained some of its internal organizational autonomy while at the same time the ultimate control of the rulers was not weakened—even if there always developed many tensions and quarrels within the bureaucracy and between it and the rulers. In most of these cases continuous and general usages or even explicit rules of service, appointment, and promotion were maintained within the bureaucracy. There also developed some relatively strong professional and even departmental *esprit de corps*, some extent of internal collegiality and responsibility, and various internal supervisory and disciplinary bodies which attempted to maintain the standards of discipline and service (18).

At the same time the rulers successfully held their control over the bureaucracy through special officials (private officials of the inner courts, special *intendants* or visitors), through a relatively strong control over allocation of budget and over private traffic in offices (19), and through the monarch's direct participation in the process of decision making within the upper echelons of the bureaucracy (20).

IV

The second main type of political orientation of bureaucracy that can be found in the historical-bureaucratic societies is characterized by the bureaucracy's total subservience to the king, to the exclusion of almost any subservience, except for some minimal technical services, to the major strata of the population. The best examples of this development can be found in Prussia in the 17th and 18th centuries (21), and in the Ottoman Empire especially during the first century and a half of its existence (22), while more embryonic developments can be discerned also in other conquest empires like the Spanish-American Empire (23) in the first stages of its development, in periods of rapid change and of reorganization of royal power in Sassanid Persia under Khusro (24), and in Byzantium, in periods of great external dangers, especially under Heraclius (25).

In all these cases the strong hand of the rulers over the bureaucracy could be discerned first in the internal organization of the bureaucracy. The bureaucracy's most crucial characteristic, in such cases, was the very small extent of internal autonomy. This was manifested in the continuous shifting of officials from place to place and office to office without any fixed general rules, in the destruction by the rulers of any distinct career patterns, in the maintenance by them of strong and often arbitrary discipline not based on any general rules or criteria, in their destruction of any departmental or professional *esprit de corps* and cooperation (26), and in their insistence on the bureaucrats being "personal" servants of the ruler and of the "State" as personified by the ruler. This strong and often ruthless direction of the bureaucracy by the rulers made it for sometime—especially during the first stages of the establishment of new polities—a relatively efficient instrument for the implementation of the rulers' main goals, such as mobilization of resources, unification of the country, and suppression of opposition. From a long-term point of view, however, this "strong hand" of the rulers often diminished the efficiency of the bureaucracy, quashed the initiative of officials, and gave rise to overformalistic attitudes and activities and to many subterfuges and tricks through which officials tried to avoid the rulers' control (27). Moreover this often led, as we shall see, to the growing rapacity and self-assertion of the bureaucracy.

V

The third main type of political orientation of a bureaucracy was that which stressed the bureaucracy's own autonomy and self-interest to an extent that may have involved evasion of all political supervision from above and/or the displacement of its service goals to different strata. In these cases the upper echelons of the bureaucracy attempted to act almost exclusively in their own self-interest or in the interest of groups or strata with which they became allied or identified and, insofar as possible, they attempted to minimize their service orientation and professional and political responsibility.

The most extreme manifestations of this tendency, in our case studies, can be found during the various periods of aristocratic predominance in Sassanid Persia (28), the decadent stages of the Chinese dynasties when the bureaucracy became rapacious and almost fully identified with some specific gentry groups (29), the final period of the Byzantine empire (30), the period of aristocratic reaction in France in the 18th century (31), and, to some extent, at the close of the Hapsburg era, during the decline of the Spanish-American Empire (32), and in the later stages of the Abbasid Empire (33).

This type of socio-political orientation of the bureaucracy was usually connected also with several developments in its internal structure. All these developments were rooted in the partial or total transformation of the administration into a relatively inefficient, self-seeking group, concerned mostly with the maximization of its own benefits with but minimal regard to public duties or efficiency.

The most important manifestations of these developments were: (a) recruitment of bureaucratic personnel, mainly through various nepotistic channels within the bureaucracy itself; (b) conception of bureaucratic posts by their holders, as mainly sinecures, private, even hereditary property, and the consequent development of an intensive unrestricted and unregulated traffic in office; (c) a consequent proliferation of bureaucratic personnel beyond the necessities of bureaucratic tasks, and a tendency toward the implementation of "Parkinson's Law" (34); (d) a growing proliferation of departments with consequent difficulties in coordination; (e) a weakening of the effectiveness of the activities of the bureaucracy (35); (f) a growing "formalization" and "ritualism" in bureaucratic practice, both in the internal relations within the bureaucracy and in the bureaucracy's relations with its clients.

VI

The fourth type of political orientation of bureaucracy which tended to develop in the historical-bureaucratic societies was characterized by the combination of strong self-orientation of the bureaucracy (i.e., orientation of self-aggrandizement in the social, economic, and political spheres), together with service orientation to the policy and the rulers with an almost total lack of any service orientation to other strata or social groups. Two main types of such semiusurpatory bureaucracies which maintained some political responsibility and service can be found in our material.

First, we find such a type in the less developed, more "traditional" societies, such as Ancient Egypt and Sassanid Persia (in its patrimonial stages, e.g., in the first two periods of its history (36) where a relatively autonomous bureaucracy was often closely allied with a traditional, semipatrimonial ruler). Second are the cases, best exemplified by Prussia and Austria in the late 18th and early 19th centuries (37), when the bureaucracy, together with some of the aristocratic groups, developed some *modus vivendi* with the kings within the framework of a relatively differentiated bureaucratic polity.

In both these cases the organizational pattern and the patterns of activities of the bureaucracy differed in some important respects from both a totally subservient and a totally aristocratized bureaucracy. Although, in most of these cases, the bureaucracy evinced many of the characteristics of a relatively "closed" group, with membership restricted mainly to members of upper social groups, at the same time it maintained a relatively efficient administrative structure and some type of departmental division of labor and internal system of supervision which enabled it to implement, in a relatively efficient way, various policies and political goals. Moreover, in most of these cases the various echelons of the bureaucracy tended to maintain some professional or "service" ideology and status image, in which service to the polity was to some extent at least emphasized (38).

VII

What were the conditions under which each of these major types of political orientation in the bureaucracy developed? Our preceding analysis indicates that the development of different political orientations of the bureaucratic administrations was very closely related to its standing within the society and especially to its relations to the rulers and to various strata in the society. Therefore, in order to understand the variations of the bureaucracy's political orientation, it is necessary first to examine its position in the social structure.

This position may be analyzed according to the following criteria:

(a) the position of the main echelons of the bureaucracy in the hierarchy of status and power; (b) the extent to which the bureaucracy, or its upper and middle echelons, constituted an independent status group, or, conversely, the extent to which its different echelons were considered parts of other social strata; (c) the criteria according to which the bureaucracy (or its different echelons) was differentiated from other strata or substrata, and especially the extent to which the proximity to the ruler and exercise of power served as such criteria; (d) the extent to which the bureaucracy was alienated from other social groups.

VIII

The analysis of material bearing on the societies referred to above indicates that there existed a very close relation between the social position of the bureaucracy (and especially of its upper echelons) and its major political orientations, and that one of the main mechanisms through which these two were connected was the patterns and avenues of recruitment into the bureaucracy.

Thus the material shows, first, that the maintenance of service orientation to both the rulers and the major strata by the bureaucracy was very closely related to either its partial incorporation in various flexible and "free" strata or at least nonalienation from such strata, and, second, that the greater the extent of the bureaucracy's incorporation within such strata, the greater was the emphasis, by the bureaucracy, of service orientation to both the rulers and the main strata.

The greatest extent of such incorporation of the bureaucracy within "flexible," nontraditional, upper and middle, urban and peasant (or gentry) groups developed in England and China. In these cases the bureaucracy was largely viewed as a part of these strata, using the same major symbols of status and participating largely in similar styles of life, although it developed and emphasized its distinctive occupational roles and career patterns. These specific bureaucratic careers usually ranked, in such cases, as one possibility within the range of occupational and status roles open to members of these (respective) strata.

Thus in England we find that the administrative careers were, to a very large extent, one of the possibilities within the accepted way of life of the upper rural classes and to a smaller extent of the upper urban classes (39). In China the bureaucracy, although greatly subordinated in every instance to the ruler and deriving part of its prestige from him, emphasized, through the system of examination, classical (Confucian) education as the main criterion of status. This bureaucracy was generally considered to be a part of the wider literati group and was greatly, although not entirely, rooted in the gentry. Its official prestige was derived from the examination degrees and from its devotion to the Confucian ideals which it shared with the literati. Although the extent to which the Chinese bureaucracy constituted an entirely autonomous group, differentiated from the gentry is yet subject to debate, there can be little doubt that there existed very strong interrelations between these two terms of a common cultural tradition (40).

Less fully developed incorporation of the bureaucracy in various middle and social strata can also be found in France during the reign of Henri IV and immediately afterward. There such incorporation could be seen especially with respect to the middle echelons of the bureaucracy, in the very strong relation between the developing *noblesse de robe* and the rising urban groups (41).

In these cases the members of the higher and middle echelons of the bureaucracy were recruited from various higher and middle flexible strata, i.e., mostly from upper and middle urban groups, from professional circles, and from the gentry and upper peasant groups, and these members continued, to a very great extent, to maintain close relations with their groups of origin. They often constituted an important channel of linkage with the more traditional groups and the provinces, and with the differentiated types of political activity that had developed at the centers of these polities.

A somewhat different social pattern among a service-oriented bureaucracy (with special emphasis on service to the rulers) could be found in Sassanid Persia under the reigns of Khawad and Khusro, during early and middle Byzantium, in the Spanish-American Empire, and in the Abbasid Caliphate. Here the upper echelons of the bureaucracy developed into relatively autonomous status groups emphasizing either their services and political position and/or power as the main criterion of their distinct status. However, in these cases, the bureaucracy, even while constituting a nearly separate group emphasizing its own criteria of status, continued to maintain some relation with different upper and middle urban, professional gentry and upper peasant groups, from whom many of its members were recruited. In most of these societies the members of the bureaucracy were not alienated from these strata and constituted an important link between these groups and the central political institutions—even if the bureaucracy and these strata were not entirely identical, and even when there existed between them great differences of style of life and of social and political participation.

Thus, in early and middle Byzantium we find that the bureaucracy constituted a comparatively independent status group, oriented mostly to the implementation of the Emperor's goals and policies, given to his strict supervision, and tending to emphasize service both to the Emperor and to the polity. In conjunction with all these characteristics, its members usually stressed the occupation of a bureaucratic office as basic status criteria. In the social sphere the bureaucracy was relatively autonomous and distinct from other groups but closely associated with some major social strata, especially with the upper peasant merchant and urban professional and cultural groups. This applies to most periods of the 7th through 10th century Byzantium (with the partial exception, perhaps, of the reign of Heraclius) which was then at its prime (42). It was only during its decline, when the State was weakened and the aristocracy became powerful, that the bureaucracy became very closely associated with the aristocracy and to some extent (although never entirely) incorporated into it, becoming alienated from the more differentiated middle groups (43) and oppressive toward them and toward lower groups.

A similar situation can be found in the Spanish-American Empire. Here the bureaucracy initially constituted a separate group, differentiated from both the Spanish settlers and the natives and emphasizing (with the full approval of the Crown) its autonomous status. But it was also closely associated with the upper classes of the local settlers and the groups of local aristocracy. As in Byzantium, the bureaucracy tended toward aristocratization and assimilation into the upper strata when the power of the rulers and their ability to implement their goals weakened (44). Similarly, such tendencies toward social autonomy, based on the bureaucracy's service to the rulers and its power positions but linked with a relatively close and positive relation to various (especially middle urban and rural) groups, can be found in the Abbasid Empire up to the end of the 9th and middle of the 10th centuries (45).

In these societies the upper and middle echelons of the bureaucracy were usually also recruited from various middle urban and rural groups, but the process of recruitment was a rather selective one, tending to emphasize the distinctiveness of the bureaucratic career pattern, to remove the recruits from their groups of origin, and to weaken their relations with groups—even if no special attitudes or alienation were developed or stressed.

IX

The bureaucracy's subservience to the rulers was usually closely connected with its being a separate status group, with strong emphasis on power and service to the rulers as the main distinctive social characteristic. Although socially autonomous, with a status based on its special position, such bureaucracies were subject politically to the rulers' supervision. In the first stages of the Ottoman Empire, both the political subservience and social autonomy of the bureaucracy were assured by the "slave" system wherein most of the bureaucracy's members were the Sultan's personal slaves, recruited from alien elements (46). In Prussia in the 17th century the Hohenzollerns established a widespread bureaucratic organization entirely subordinate to the ruler, deriving its status and power from its relation to the rule, and markedly hostile, in the first stages of its development, to the aristocracy, older town autonomies and the various "Stande" organizations (47).

In these cases the upper and middle echelons of the bureaucracy were usually recruited from the lower or from the very weak, middle strata and sometimes from alien groups. They were removed from their groups of origin, and the process of recruitment stressed their alienation and total distinctiveness from any established social status.

The bureaucracy was usually, at least for the period during which the rulers were able to control it, alienated from the strata from which many of its members were recruited, and its members developed a marked "punishment" orientation toward this strata. It tended very often to develop monolithic status aspirations and often, with the encouragement of the rulers, it strove to establish itself as the sole apex of a status hierarchy based largely on the criterion of power.

However, the bureaucracy's great dependence on the king made difficult the full realization of its aspirations to autonomous power and status. As long as the rulers maintained their strong control, the bureaucracy could not usually develop into a separate and cohesive status group; its members and their families were very often subject to the vicissitudes and arbitrariness of the monarch's will. Therefore it often happened that, as the bureaucracy developed and became more stabilized and diversified, it tried to find various ways to assert its own status and sought allies among some especially aristocratic groups which could provide it with symbols of status and social standing against the rulers (48).

X

The development by the bureaucracy, or rather by its upper echelons, of tendencies toward displacement of service goals to the various strata and/or the rulers was closely connected with the development of the bureaucracy into some sort of strongly ascriptive stratum, either an independent semiaristocratic or "gentry" stratum (emphasizing power as a status criterion) or a part of an existing aristocratic stratum. These bureaucracies were alienated, to some extent at least, from the rulers. Such development took place in the periods of decline (from the 13th century onward) in Byzantium (49) and in the Abbasid Empire, during the aristocratic reaction in 18th century France (50), and to a smaller extent in the period of decline of several Chinese dynasties.

In such cases the bureaucracy tended usually to weaken and deemphasize the distinctiveness of its occupational and career patterns and its professional ideology and self-image as servants of the country. It tried to lend the basic attributes of aristocratic status to its position, to make the offices into some sort of private hereditary possessions or fiefs, to limit recruitment into the bureaucracy to members of bureaucratic families, and to minimize its accountability to various strata and, in extreme cases, to the rulers as well (51).

It was only insofar as an aristocratized bureaucracy was not alienated from the rulers and was not strongly opposed to one of the other strata, as was the case in Ancient Egypt and to some extent in Prussia and Russia in the 17th and 18th centuries, that it maintained some orientation toward the maintenance of public service.

XI

Thus we see that each of the main political orientations of the bureaucracy was connected with the occupation by its members of specific types of positions in the social structure. What were the specific conditions that influenced the nature of the social standing of the bureaucracy and, through this standing, its political orientations and patterns of activities?

The main variables influencing the political orientations and activities of the bureaucracy were, first, the extent of differentiation and the goals of the rulers. Second, however, because of the special position of the bureaucracy in the political and social structure of these societies, the very constellation of the political forces and process in the society and especially the extent of compatibility between the goals of the rulers and the political orientations of the major groups were of crucial importance in influencing the development of the social status and political orientations of the bureaucracy.

We may start with a brief analysis of the influence of the major goals of the rulers on the social standing and political orientation of the bureaucracy. In cases where the rulers emphasized political, collective goals (i.e., military and expansionist goals, or goals of internal political consolidation), the bureaucracy emphasized its own autonomous status position. Such goals stressed the autonomy and the special position of the rulers who were in a way the main bearers of these goals and therefore of the bureaucracy (52). In cases where the rulers emphasized mainly cultural or economic goals (as in China, Abbasid Empire, or England), the bureaucracy usually became incorporated into some wider, relatively flexible groups and strata (53).

However, the predominant goals of the rulers provided only the framework within which the social and political orientations of the bureaucracy (and its patterns of activities) could develop. The concrete

developments of these orientations depend to a large extent on the
other conditions specified above, namely the extent of compatibility
between the goals of the rulers and those of the major groups and the
extent of differentiation of the social structure.

When the goals and interests of the major strata were basically incompatible with those of the rulers, the bureaucracy, aided by the
rulers, developed power as its main autonomous criterion of status. It
either became entirely autonomous and alienated from other strata
and greatly dependent on and subservient to the rulers, or it tried to
find some *modus vivendi* with some of these strata—the choice de-
pending on the relative strength of the rulers and these "opposing"
strata. Where these strata were not very powerful or politically active
or where the rulers had sufficient power to repress them and make
them politically passive, the bureaucracy (and especially its higher
echelons) established power as a main criterion of status and attained
autonomous status on the basis of this criterion. The two best examples of such development, from our cases, are Prussia and the Ottoman Empire (54). In both these countries the bureaucracy originally
constituted an independent group or stratum, differentiated from all
other strata and oriented against the aristocracy, the town, and estates.
This bureaucracy was initially considered the monarch's means of implementing his goals, and it derived its status entirely from him and
from its service to him.

In these two cases, however, both the social autonomy and political
subservience of the bureaucracy diminished with time—as a result of
the financial and social stability attained by its members and in close
connection with a realignment of the relations between the rulers and
some of the aristocratic groups and forces.

When the opposing strata were stronger, and when the rulers were
weak and unable to control them, as was the case in many periods of
decline of the historical polities, then the bureaucracy tended to ally
itself with these (mostly aristocratic) groups at the expense of both
the rulers and other strata and to develop a tendency to displacement
of its service goals.

On the other hand, the greater the compatibility between the major
goals of the rulers and the political orientations of the major strata,
the more the bureaucracy tended to become incorporated into some
free stratum or at least to be nonalienated from the rulers and major

strata and to maintain its service orientation to the rulers and these strata. In such cases the bureaucracy's potential aspirations for social and political autonomy were curbed by the strength of both the rulers and the various flexible strata. At the same time, however, the very interaction between different strata and between the rulers exerted pressures on the bureaucracy and enabled it to develop some organization, occupational autonomy, and some autonomous professional image. Yet, the bureaucratic occupational patterns were easily incorporated into the general style of life of these strata. Such maintenance of service orientation was most developed in those cases in which the flexible "middle" strata were strong and relatively predominant in the social structure—i.e., when the extent of the differentiation of the social structure was relatively great, as in Byzantium between the 7th and 12th centuries, in China throughout most of its history, or in Western Europe in the 17th century (55).

Some such orientations could also develop when the scope of differentiation of the social structure was small and when the aristocracy or an aristocratized bureaucracy constituted the predominant social strata and when there existed a basic compatibility between the political goals of the rulers and those of the politically active aristocracy and the more passively oriented weak middle strata. In such cases the aristocracy, although relatively predominant in the social and economic hierarchy, was to some extent "domesticated" within the framework of the bureaucratic polity. Its own power and economic positions were to a great extent dependent on the existence of these frameworks and hence tended to develop some *modus vivendi* with the rulers.

Two such main types of aristocratized service bureaucracy can be found. One developed in the traditional, relatively nondifferentiated societies, such as Ancient Egypt or Sassanid Persia (56). In these cases the bureaucracy developed in two major directions. When the autonomous aristocratic-patrimonial hierarchy was relatively strong (as was the case through the greater part of Sassanid Persia's history), the upper echelons of the bureaucracy were usually incorporated into and absorbed by these elements (57). If the aristocracy was weak, however, as in Ancient Egypt (58), or oppressed by the rulers, as during several periods in Sassanid history (to some extent in the beginning of its history and especially in the reign of Khawad and Khusro), the upper echelons of the bureaucracy usually developed into a more autonomous stratum with some emphasis of the power criterion as an autonomous designate of status. But even in such cases the tendency to adopt an aristocratic style of life prevailed, although the new aristocracy was mainly one of service (*Amteraristokratie*) (59).

The lower and middle echelons of the bureaucracy were, in such cases, usually recruited from the society's marginal groups or from outside, and, whatever their personal prestige and power, they rarely developed into an independent stratum. These echelons were either, to the extent that they aimed at economic position and security, in the same category as the lower strata (e.g., the peasantry) or outside the main status hierarchy of the society (60).

The second type of aristocratized service bureaucracy can be found especially in Prussia, from the time of Frederick the Great, and to a lesser extent in Austria and Russia in the 18th and 19th centuries. After an initial period when the bureaucracy constituted an avenue for social advancement for the middle classes and was antiaristocratic in its orientation, there was in Prussia, under Frederick the Great, an aristocratic reaction on the part of the rulers and a growing infusion of the bureaucracy with aristocratic elements. Similar developments can also be seen in Austria and Russia (61). In these cases the ruler's control over the bureaucracy and the bureaucracy's service orientation were not entirely weakened as a result of the bureaucracy's partial aristocratization. They were greatly increased by the ruler's dependence on the bureaucracy and the political power of both the bureaucracy and the aristocratic group.

This development followed a period during which various aristocratic groups and, to a smaller degree, the (traditional) towns became adjusted to the demands of the rulers. They benefited economically from the political framework, and, when the rulers themselves, after some "flirting" with various middle groups, tended to emphasize their conservative orientations and distrust of some of the more flexible groups, these groups continued to be of some importance in the social structure (62).

A total displacement of service goals by an aristocratized bureaucracy developed mainly in those cases when the policies of the ruler depleted or alienated the various origins of free-floating resources and political support. This displacement also occurred when the ruler became less able to uphold his distinct political orientations and goals and more dependent on various conservative-aristocratic forces. These forces attempted to monopolize the most important economic and political positions in the society, thus furthering the dwindling of the "flexible" strata or their alienation from the framework and symbols of the existing political institutions. Usually in such cases the bureaucracy attempted either to incorporate some of these strata with its own status hierarchy, based on the criterion of power, or to develop as an independent aristocratic stratum and acquire for itself many of the symbols of aristocratic status.

Such conditions could develop both in societies, like the Ottoman Empire and (to a smaller extent) the Spanish-American Empire, in which the bureaucracy was initially subservient to the rulers, and in those societies, like Byzantium, the Abbasid Empire, and France, in which for relatively long periods of time there existed a service-oriented bureaucracy.

XII

The various conditions connected with the development of the different types of political orientations of the bureaucracy were not fixed. In any society these conditions could change throughout its history, and these changes would bring about alterations in the social standing and political orientation of the bureaucracy.

Thus in many of the societies studied here an initially strong subservience of the developing bureaucracy to the ruler very often gave way to a more differentiated service orientation of the bureaucracy to both the ruler and the major strata. This was the case, for instance, in Byzantium after the 7th and 8th centuries and in the Spanish-American Empire in the first two centuries of its development. In some circumstances, especially in periods of external danger, such service orientation again became weakened, and subordination to the rulers developed or was re-established.

In many other cases the ruler attempted to check the tendencies of the aristocracy to self-aggrandizement. The various periodic attempts by the ruler (or his active ministers) to effect reforms of the bureaucracy are very instructive from this point of view. Many reforms, such as those of Frederick Wilhelm in Prussia (63), Wang An-shih in

China (64), and Heraclius and Leo in Byzantium (65), aimed at the re-establishment of the control of the ruler over the bureaucracy and aimed against the growing usurpation of power and displacement of service goals by the upper echelons of the bureaucracy. They were very often directed against those structural characteristics of the bureaucracy which were seen as the most important manifestations of its total independence, and especially against: (a) the narrowing of the base of recruitment to the bureaucracy; (b) the conception of the bureaucratic position as a sort of sinecure; (c) overformalization and ritualization; (d) proliferation of uncoordinated activities and departments and lack of control.

In all of these cases, and especially where reforms were successful, the rulers were aided by different social groups in their attempts at reform of the bureaucracy, especially by the rising middle classes (or in some instances, like that of Byzantium, by the rural middle classes).

The most frequent and prevalent change to be found in the political orientations of the bureaucracy, in periods of decline of the political systems studied here, was the development of a ruler-centered or a service-oriented bureaucracy into a self-centered aristocratic or semi-aristocratic body.

XIII

The preceding analysis has illustrated and substantiated the thesis that the political orientations of the bureaucracy in centralized, bureaucratic, political systems can be fully understood only in connection with the bureaucracies' status position in the social structure and its relation to the constellation of political forces within this social structure. We have seen that the nature of the political orientation and the patterns of activities of the bureaucracy were greatly influenced by the bureaucracy's social position within the society, and that this position was influenced by, first, the extent of differentiation of the social structure, second, the major goals of the rulers, and, third and most important, by the relative strength of the major social strata vis-à-vis the ruler and vis-à-vis one another and by the extent of compatibility between the goals of the ruler and the political orientation of these strata.

We have seen also that these social and political conditions which influenced the development of the political orientations of the bureaucracy were not fixed in any society, but tended to change according to the relative strength of social forces and the outcome of the political struggle.

Because of the crucial position of the bureaucracy in the political struggle, these different political orientations and activities may have had many repercussions on the changes in the constellation of political forces in the bureaucratic societies. In order to fully understand such repercussions it is worthwhile to analyze the patterns of activities developed by the different types of bureaucracies in the historical-bureaucratic societies.

As indicated above, the scope of the activities of the bureaucracy was mainly influenced by the extent of structural differentiation and by the major goals of the rulers of these societies. However, as also indicated, the political orientations of the bureaucracy greatly influenced several aspects of its activities, especially the relative importance of technical or regulative activities.

The emphasis on technical and regulative activities was mainly developed by those bureaucracies that maintained service orientations to both the rulers and the major strata. The extent to which these bureaucracies emphasized more technical or regulative activities and the criteria according to which such regulation was effected depended on the relative predominance of the rulers or the major strata in the political field and on the scope of the autonomous regulative mechanisms developed by the different strata.

Thus, in Byzantium or in the Spanish-American Empire, where the rulers were predominant, the bureaucracies provided many technical services to the population. At the same time, they also implemented many regulative policies in the major institutional spheres—economic, political, and cultural—policies that were mainly guided by the interests of the rulers. On the other hand, as in England and to a more limited extent in China, where several of the social groups and strata were very strong, the bureaucracies emphasized the provision of technical services more, and only the indirect control of major social strata and institutional spheres and their regulative activities were greatly influenced by the interests of the politically strong strata.

In most cases in which there existed a dominant emphasis on the regulative activities of the bureaucracy, the extent of the political participation of the major groups in the organs of political struggle was small. We find the same situation where there was an emphasis on regulative and technical activities, and where the extension of the scope of the bureaucratic activities was usually evident in the growing participation of the major strata in the organs of political struggle.

The second factor which influenced the relative importance of regulative or technical activities of the bureaucracy was the scope of the autonomous mechanisms developed by the major social strata in the main institutional fields. The greater the scope of the activities of these autonomous mechanisms, the smaller the extent of regulative activities of the bureaucracy (66).

XIV

The predominance of regulative activities, with small emphasis on technical service, developed usually in those types of bureaucracies that minimized the service orientations to various groups and strata and strongly emphasized service to the rulers and/or self-aggrandizement.

Where the bureaucracy was entirely subservient to the ruler (as in Prussia and the Ottoman Empire), it tended to develop, under his direction, various regulative activities which aimed to assure the power position of the ruler and the bureaucracy—and the resources needed by them—in opposition to the potentially active social strata.

The most important among these activities were: (a) attempts to regulate *in toto* most of the social spheres, aiming not only at providing different groups and strata with technical services but also at establishing the general principles governing the regulation of social, economic, political, and cultural activities and/or at creating many new types of such organizations and activities; (b) attempts to penetrate into many social spheres and groups, even if they did not seem to be in need of these specific services of the bureaucracy; (c) attempts to develop various legal activities aiming at regimentation and prescription of many aspects of social life, and (d) attempts to develop various party-political and propagandist activities, the main purpose of which was to control and even monopolize the free-floating political potential in the society and to minimize the possibility of development of independent centers of power (67).

A similar pattern of activities was developed by bureaucracies that displaced goals of service in favor of goals of self-interest and self-aggrandizement. In those cases the bureaucracy usually developed various usurpatory regulative-prescriptive activities, serving mostly the interests of the upper echelons of the bureaucracy and allied groups instead of the rulers and other groups and strata.

Activities of these bureaucracies were not, in these cases, geared to the implementation of any predominant political goals or of any consistent set of policies. They served the diverse and often inconsistent interests of different bureaucratic and aristocratic groups. Hence such bureaucracies usually evinced a much smaller degree of efficiency and unity of policy than were found in the initial stages of "oppressive" bureaucracies, totally subservient to the rulers.

Those bureaucracies which combined a tendency to *partial* usurpation of power and strong autonomy together with orientations to performance of public services emphasized strong regulation of most aspects of social life in the society. However, they were usually not as oppressive and self-oriented as those of the totally aristocratized bureaucracies. The various echelons of the bureaucracies tended to maintain some professional ideology and image, in which service to the polity was strongly emphasized; hence their regulative activities were often guided by some consistent policies and goals.

XV

The preceding analysis demonstrates the ways in which activities of the bureaucracy influenced the basic social conditions of the political systems of the historical-bureaucratic societies, the constellations of political power, and the political process.

Insofar as the bureaucracy maintained its basic service orientations to both rulers and major strata, it usually contributed to the continuity and stability of the regime, and especially to the maintenance of the basic conditions of the centralized bureaucratic regimes. In those societies or periods in which such service orientations were maintained by bureaucracies, the rulers were able, with the help of the bureaucracies, to maintain their own positions and the positions of those strata supporting them, and to keep in check those strata opposed to the basic prerequisites of the centralized political systems. Insofar as the bureaucracy was able to monopolize the highest social, political, and economic positions and to minimize its political responsibility and responsiveness to the ruler and/or the major flexible strata, it tended very often to contribute to the weakening of the institutional frameworks of these Empires.

Because of the strong (actual or potential) involvement of the bureaucracy in the political struggle in these societies, the development of different political orientations of the bureaucracy has necessarily many repercussions on this political struggle.

Thus the total subservience of the bureaucracy to the ruler, as in Prussia and the Ottoman Empire, was usually connected with the utilization of a very high degree of force in the implementation of the ruler's goals, against strong opposition, and with relatively little direct support from those groups (such as urban classes, free peasantry) which could provide the requisite resources needed for the implementation of the ruler's goals and the development of centralized, bureaucratic polities. Such political orientation of the bureaucracy was usually connected with the establishment of rigid political systems. Because of the paucity of requisite free resources and the strongly prescriptive orientations of the rulers, these systems ultimately had to turn to the more traditional and ascriptive (aristocratic) groups, to use their social prestige, and ultimately to reach some sort of *modus vivendi*. These systems very often contributed to the weakening or alienation of the more flexible groups and strata.

The displacement of the bureaucracy's service goals by goals of illegitimate, self-aggrandizement, usually connected with at least partial aristocratization and with development of usurpatory policies, tended to contribute to the grave weakening of those flexible, nontraditional strata, which were the mainstay of usurpatory policies, as well as to the dwindling of both economic resources and political support requisite for the continuous functioning of these policies. This in turn, as shown in a former paper (68), was a contributory cause in the gradual disintegration of these political systems, either by the strengthening of the aristocratic, ascriptive elements and the development of a prebureaucratic (patrimonial or feudal) system, by outright disintegration and dismemberment of the polity under external pressure, or by the development, usually through some revolutionary movement, of a more differentiated, "modern" type of political structure.

XVI

The preceding analysis indicates the rather paradoxical relationship of the bureaucracy to the basic prerequisites of the functioning of the political systems of historical-bureaucratic societies.

The bureaucracy, by virtue of its central regulative functions in the society, performed very important tasks in the internal regulation of free-floating power in the historical-bureaucratic societies, and in the ensurance of a continuous and regulated flow of such power and resources. Insofar as the bureaucracy became a semi-independent stratum, or was not effectively controlled in the political field, it may become itself an omniverous consumer of such free resources, and it may greatly impede the functioning of the basic institutional frameworks of these societies, constituting a stumbling block on the continuous flow of regulated, generalized power. This relation of the bureaucracy to these prerequisites of the functioning of political systems in historical-bureaucratic societies can be seen in the differences in the conditions which make for growth of the scope of bureaucratic activities, as compared with those which increase the possibilities of bureaucracy's usurpation of political power and social position.

The general scope of activities (especially technical) of the bureaucracy was closely related to increased differentiation, growing development of free resources, and the rise of various mobile strata. But the scope of *regulative* activities of the bureaucracy was inversely related to the social and political strength of these strata. Although the range of technical activities of the bureaucracy usually increased with growing social differentiation, the extent to which the bureaucracy was able to become a socially and politically independent group was severely limited insofar as this differentiation was connected with growing social, economic, and political self-regulation of the major social groups and with the existence of politically powerful ruler and groups.

This incompatibility, between the conditions which gave rise to the extension of the technical and service activities of the bureaucracy and between those which enabled its usurpation of political control and displacement of service goals, was inherent in the structural position of the bureaucracy and in the bases for its growth. It was inherent in the fact that the bureaucracy was, on the one hand, a functional group performing relatively specific tasks and, on the other, a group so closely related to the bases of power as to be able to monopolize power positions and develop into an independent social stratum, which could impede the continuity of the political systems.

It is this potential contradiction in the structure and orientation of the bureaucracy that accounts for the fact which has been, in a way, the focus of our analysis here; although bureaucracy's political orientations always and necessarily presuppose the basic premises of the bureaucratic polity, some of them may undermine the bases of these premises. In other words, the bureaucracy's tendency toward displacing its goals and activities, a tendency which may develop under certain conditions inherent in bureaucracy's growth, might nullify the possibility of its performing its basic tasks in the social structure, thus contributing to the weakening of the fundamental premises of centralized polities.

NOTES

1. S. N. Eisenstadt, "Political Struggle in Bureaucratic Empires," *World Politics,* Vol. IX, 1956, pp. 15–36; "Internal Contradictions in Bureaucratic Politics," *Comparative Studies in Society and History,* Vol. I, No. 1, October 1958, pp. 58–75; "Sociological and Historical Analyses of the Downfall of Empires," *Diogene,* No. 34, 1961; "Religious Organisation and Political Process in the Centralized Empires," *Journal of Asian Studies,* Vol. XXI, No. 3, May 1962, pp. 271–295. For a full analysis of the social and political structure and processes of these empires, see S. N.

Eisenstadt, *The Political Systems of Empires*, New York: The Free Press of Glencoe, 1963.

2. Eisenstadt, "Internal Contradictions," *loc. cit.*, and Eisenstadt, "Political Struggle," *loc. cit.*

3. A more detailed analysis of the social conditions under which these polities develop is given in Chapters I–VI of *Political Systems of Empires*.

4. Eisenstadt, "Internal Contradictions," *loc. cit.*; Eisenstadt, "Political Struggle," *loc. cit.*

5. For some examples of the conditions of the development of these bureaucracies see on Byzantium, L. Brehier, *Les institutions de l'empire byzantin*, Paris: Albin Michel, 1949, pp. 89–165, 166–186; C. Diehl, "The Government and Administration of the Byzantine Empire," *Cambridge Medieval History*, Vol. V, No. IV, Cambridge: Cambridge University Press, 1923, pp. 726–744; on China, O. Lattimore, *Inner Asian Frontiers of China*, New York: Capitol, 1951, pp. 39–53; W. Eberhard, *A History of China*, London: Routledge and Kegan Paul, 1950, especially pp. 71–74, 178–204; on Sassanid Persia, F. Altheim and R. Stiehl, *Ein Asiatischer Staat*, Wiesbaden: Limes Verlag, 1956, II. Teil, especially pp. 131–175; F. Altheim and R. Stiehl, *Finanzgeschichte der Spätantike*, Frankfurt am Main: V. Klostermann, 1957, pp. 70 ff.; A. E. Christensen, *L'Iran sous les sassanides*, Copenhagen: Munskgaard, 1936, pp. 92–136; on different European countries, H. Rosenberg, *Bureaucracy, Aristocracy and Autocracy, The Prussian Experience, 1660–1815*, Cambridge, Mass.: Harvard University Press, 1958, pp. 46–88; R. A. Dorwart, *The Administrative Reforms of Frederick William I of Prussia*, Cambridge, Mass.: Harvard University Press, 1953; O. Hintze, "Der Oesterreichische und der preussische Beamtenstaat im 17ten Jhd., 18ten Jhd.," *Historische Zeitschrift*, Vol. 86, 1901, pp. 401–449; G. Schmoller, "Der deutsche Beamtenstaat vom 16ten bis 18ten Jhd.," *Umrisse und Untersuchungen zur Verfassungs-, Verwaltungs-, und Wirtschaftsgeschichte*, Leipzig: Duncker, 1896, pp. 289–313; H. Finer, *The Theory and Practice of Modern Government*, New York: Holt, Rinehart and Winston, 1949, pp. 784–794.

6. On the development of some of these rules see C. J. Friedrich, *Constitutional Government in Democracy*, New York: Ginn and Co., 1950, pp. 37–58; H. Finer, *The Theory and Practice of Modern Government*, *loc. cit.*; on China, W. Eberhard, *Conquerors and Rulers*, Leyden: Brill, 1952, Chapters 1 and 3; C. Chang, *The Chinese Gentry*, Seattle: Univer-

Bureaucracy and Bureaucratization

sity of Washington Press, 1955; on Byzantium, L. Brehier, *Les institutions,* *loc. cit.;* on Sassanid Iran, Altheim and Stiehl, *Ein asiatischer Staat, op. cit.,* pp. 227–251.

7. Rosenberg, *Bureaucracy, Aristocracy and Autocracy, op. cit.,* pp. 1– 46; Friedrich, *Constitutional Government and Democracy, loc. cit.;* Finer, *The Theory and Practice of Modern Government, loc. cit.;* R. des Rotours, *Le traité des examens,* Paris: Ernst Leroux, 1932.

8. The lack of constitutional limits on power in most of these societies (with the partial exception of some of the European countries, especially England) has been very often stressed in the literature. M. Weber, *Wirtschaft und Gesellschaft,* München: C. B. Mohr, 1920, pp. 122–166; K. Wittfogel, *Oriental Despotism,* New Haven: Yale University Press, 1957; W. Eberhard, "The Political Function of Astronomers and Astronomy in China," in J. K. Fairbanks (editor), *Chinese Thought and Institutions,* Chicago: University of Chicago Press, 1957, pp. 33–40. On the rather different situation in Europe, see in general, M. Beloff, *The Age of Absolutism,* London: Hutchinson, 1954, pp. 11–28, 170–181.

9. On sale of offices in general see K. W. Swart, *Sale of Offices in the 17th Century,* The Hague: Nijhoff, 1949; G. Kolias, *Ämterung Würdenkauf im früh- und mittelbyzantinischen Reich,* Athens: Verlag der byzantinisch-neugriechischen Jahrbücher, 1939; C. Chang, *The Chinese Gentry, op. cit.,* pp. 8–32, 188–197; J. H. Parry, *The Sale of Public Offices in the Spanish Indies under the Hapsburgs,* Berkeley, Calif.: University of California Press, 1955; G. Pages, "La venalite des offices dans l'ancienne France," *Revue Historique,* Vol. 169, 1932, pp. 476–495.

10. Eisenstadt, "Internal Contradictions," *Comparative Studies in Society and History, loc. cit.;* "Political Struggle," *World Politics, loc. cit.; Political Systems of Empires,* New York: The Free Press of Glencoe, 1963.

11. See Christensen, *L'Iran sous les sassanides, op. cit.,* pp. 201–253; on the institutions see Christensen, "Sassanid Persia," *Cambridge Ancient History XII,* Cambridge: Cambridge University Press, 1939, pp. 114– 118; Altheim and Stiehl, *Finanzgeschichte, op. cit.,* pp. 55–75; and F. Altheim, *Reich gegen Mitternacht,* Hamburg: Fischer Verlag, 1955, pp. 73– 126.

12. On the general social and political situation of Byzantium in this period see G. Ostrogorsky, *History of the Byzantine State,* Oxford: Blackwell, 1956, pp. 79–128; on administration see Brehier, *Les institutions de l'empire byzantin, loc. cit.;* Diehl, "The Government and Administration of

the Byzantine Empire," *loc. cit.;* E. Stein, "Introduction a l'histoire et aux institutions byzantines," *Traditio,* VII, 1949–1951, especially pp. 113–138.

13. See C. H. Haring, *The Spanish Empire in America,* New York: Oxford University Press, 1947, Chapters 7 and 12; J. M. Ots Capdequi, *El Estado Espanol en las Indias,* Mexico: Fondo de Culture Economica, 1946, pp. 1–25, Chapters 3 and 4; Capdequi, "Institutiones economicas de la America espanola durante el periode colonial," *Anuario de historia del derecho espanol,* 1932; S. Zavala, *New Viewpoints on the Spanish Colonization of America,* Philadelphia: University of Pennsylvania Press, 1943, Chapters 7 and 8; M. Gongora, *El Estado en el derecho indiano,* Santiago: Universidad de Chile, 1951; R. Konetzke, "Die Entstehung des Adels in Hispano-America während der Kolonialzeit," *Vierteljahrschrift für Sozial- und Wirtschaftsgeschichte,* XXXIX, 1952, pp. 215–250.

14. G. Pagés, *La monarchie d'ancien régime en France,* Paris: Armand Colin, 1946; G. Zeller, *Les institutions de la France au XVIᵉ siècle,* Paris: Presses Universitaires, 1948; P. Sagnac, *La formation de la société française moderne,* Paris: Presses Universitaires de France, 1945, I, pp. 50–147; F. L. Ford, *Robe and Sword: The Regrouping of the French Aristocracy after Louis XIV,* Cambridge, Mass.: Harvard University Press, 1953, especially p. 2, Chapter 5; Beloff, *The Age of Absolutism, op. cit., passim.*

15. On England see, for instance, M. Ashley, *England in the 17th Century,* London: Penguin Books, 1952; J. H. Plumb, *England in the 18th Century,* London: Penguin Books, 1950; L. B. Namier, *The Structure of Politics at the Accession of George II,* 2 Volumes, London: Macmillan, 1929; D. Matthew, *The Social Structure in Caroline England,* London: Oxford University Press, 1948; G. E. Aylmer, *The King's Servants, The Civil Service of Charles I,* London: Routledge and Kegan Paul, 1961.

16. On the Chinese Empire in general see W. Eberhard, *A History of China,* London: Routledge and Kegan Paul, 1950; Eberhard, *Conquerors and Rulers, loc. cit.;* H. Stange, "Geschichte Chinas, vom Urbeginn bis auf die Gegenwart," in *Der Geschichte Asiens,* München: F. Bruckmann, 1950, pp. 431–496; E. Balazs, "Les aspects significatifs de la societé chinoise," *Asiatische Studien,* VI, 1952, pp. 80 ff. On the administration and its relations with different social groups see des Rotours, *Le traité des examens, loc. cit.;* des Rotours, *Traite des fonctionnaires et traité de l'armée,* Leyden: Brill, 1947, 2 Volumes; Chang, *The Chinese Gentry, op. cit.,* pp. 163–

204; C. O. Hucker, "The Tung-Lin Movement of the Late Ming Period," in Fairbanks, *op. cit.*, pp. 132–167; E. A. Kracke, *Civil Service in Early Sung China*, Cambridge, Mass.: Harvard University Press, 1955.

17. See B. Lewis, *The Arabs in History*, London: Hutchinson, 1950, pp. 64–115; W. Muir, *The Caliphate, Its Rise, Decline and Fall*, London: Religious Tract Society, 1924; C. Cahen, *Leçons d'histoire musulmane*, Paris: Centre de Documentation Universitaire, 1957, Volumes I–III, especially Volume II; Cahen, "Les facteurs économiques et sociaux dans l'ankylose culturelle de l'Islam," in R. Brunschvig and G. E. von Grunebaum (editors), *Classicisme et declin culturel dans l'histoire de l'Islam*, Paris: Besson and Chante Merle, 1957, pp. 195–217; A. Mez, *The Renaissance of Islam*, London: Luzac, 1937.

18. For some examples of such developments in the bureaucracy see Friedrich, *Constitutional Government and Democracy*, *loc. cit.*; Finer, *The Theory and Practice of Modern Government*, *loc. cit.*; A. Rosenberg, *Bureaucracy, Aristocracy and Autocracy*, *op. cit.*, pp. 88–109; G. Zeller, *Les institutions*, *op. cit.*, *passim*; G. Schmoller, "Der preussische Beamtenstaat," *loc. cit.*; O. Hintze, "Der oesterreichische und preussische Beamtenstaat," *loc. cit.*; L. Brehier, *Les institutions*, *loc. cit.*; E. Stein, "Introduction à l'histoire et aux institutions byzantins," *op. cit.*, pp. 188–254; A. H. M. Jones, "The Roman Civil Service," *Journal of Roman Studies*, Vol. 39, 1949, pp. 38–53; des Rotours, *Le traité des examens*, *loc. cit.*, C. K. Yang, "Some Characteristics of Chinese Bureaucratic Behaviour," in D. S. Nivison and A. F. Wright (editors), *Confucianism in Action*, Stanford: Stanford University Press, 1959, pp. 134–165; Cahen, *Leçons d'histoire musulmane*, *op. cit.*, Volume II; Cahen, "Les facteurs économiques," *loc. cit.*

19. Swart, *loc. cit.*

20. Diehl, *The Government and Administration of the Byzantine Empire*, *loc. cit.*; Brehier, *Les institutions*, *op. cit.*, pp. V–XVIII, 1–89; des Rotours, *Traité des examens*, *loc. cit.*; Beloff, *The Age of Absolutism*, *op. cit.*, especially Chapters III, IV, and V.

21. F. L. Carsten, *The Origins of Modern Prussia*, London: Oxford University Press, 1954; Rosenberg, *Bureaucracy, Aristocracy and Autocracy*, *loc. cit.*; O. Hintze, "Die Hohenzollern und der Adel," *Historische Zeitschrift*, Vol. 112, 1914, pp. 494–524.

22. A. Lybyer, *The Government of the Ottoman Empire*, Cambridge, Mass.: Harvard University Press, 1913; W. L. Wright (editor and trans-

lator), *Ottoman Statecraft*, Princeton, N.J.: Princeton University Press, 1935, especially pp. 21–60.

23. Haring, *loc. cit.*

24. Christensen, *L'Iran sous les sassanides*, *op. cit.*, pp. 358–436; Altheim and Stiehl, *Ein asiatischer Staat*, *op. cit.*, II Teil, 3 Kapitel.

25. Ostrogorsky, *History*, *op. cit.*, pp. 83–110.

26. W. Dorn, "The Prussian Bureaucracy in the 18th Century," *Political Science Quarterly*, Vol. XLVI, 1931, pp. 405–423, and Vol. XLVII, 1932, pp. 75–94, 259–273; Schmoller, "Der preussische Beamtenstaat," *loc. cit.*; Lybyer, *The Government of the Ottoman Empire*, *loc. cit.*

27. Dorn, *loc. cit.*; Rosenberg, *loc. cit.*; Schmoller, *loc. cit.*; Lybyer, *loc. cit.*

28. Christensen, *L'Iran sous les sassenides*, *op. cit.*, *passim*; Altheim and Stiehl, *Ein asiatischer Staat*, *loc. cit.*

29. O. Berkelbach van der Sprenkel, "High Officials of the Ming," *Bulletin of the School of Oriental and African Studies*, Vol. 14, 1952, p. 113; E. Pulleyblank, *The Background of the Rebellion of An Lu-shan*, London: Oxford University Press, 1955, Chapters 3 and 5; Ch'ang Tu-hu, "The Yellow River Administration in the Ching Dynasty," *The Far Eastern Quarterly*, Vol. XIV, 1955, pp. 505–515.

30. P. Charanis, "On the Social Structure and Economic Organization of the Byzantine Empire in the Thirteenth Century," *Byzantinoslavica*, Vol. XII, 1951; G. Ostrogorsky, "Die Perioden der byzantinischen Geschichte," *Historische Zeitschrift*, Vol. 163, 1941, pp. 238–254.

31. Ford, *Robe and Sword, loc. cit.*

32. Haring, *The Spanish Empire in America*, *op. cit.*, Chapter XVII; J. H. Parry, "Latin America," *New Modern Cambridge History*, Vol. VII, Cambridge: Cambridge University Press, 1957, pp. 487–500.

33. Cahen, "Les facteurs economiques," *loc. cit.*

34. It is also usually connected with the growing corruption of the bureaucracy and its use of its position for personal and family interests.

35. Ch'ang Tu-hu, "The Yellow River Administration," *loc. cit.*; E. Balazs, "Les aspects significatifs," *loc. cit.*; Rosenberg, *Bureaucracy, Aristocracy and Autocracy*, *op. cit.*, pp. 88–109; Dorn, *loc. cit.*

36. On Egypt see H. Kees, *Agypten, Kulturgeschichte des Alten Orients*, München: C. H. Back, 1933, pp. 201 ff.; H. Stock, *Die erste*

Zwischenzeit Agyptens, Rome: Pontificium Institutum Biblicum, 1949; Kees, *op. cit.,* pp. 282 ff.; E. Drioton and J. Vaudier, *L'Egypte,* Paris: Presses Universitaires, 1938, Chapter 6; W. F. Edgerton, "The Government and the Governed in the Egyptian Empire," *Journal of Near Eastern Studies,* Vol. VI, 1947, pp. 152–160; on Sassanid Persia in these stages see especially Altheim and Stiehl, *Ein asiatischer Staat, op. cit.,* pp. 35 ff.

37. See Rosenberg, *Bureaucracy, Aristocracy and Autocracy, op. cit., passim;* Beloff, *The Age of Absolutism, op. cit.,* pp. 104–135; and the papers of A. Goodwin on Prussia and H. S. Schenk on Austria in A. Goodwin (editor), *The European Nobility in the Eighteenth Century,* London: A. C. Black, 1953.

38. See Kees, *loc. cit.;* Rosenberg, *op. cit., passim;* Beloff, *loc. cit.;* and the papers in Goodwin, *loc. cit.*

39. M. Ashley, *England in the 17th Century, op. cit.,* Chapters XI and XVI; J. H. Plumb, *England in the 18th Century, op. cit.,* Chapters 1 and 5; W. R. Brock, "England," *New Cambridge Modern History,* Vol. VII, Cambridge: Cambridge University Press, 1957, pp. 241–268; Aylmer, *The King's Servants, loc. cit.*

40. For the different views see D. Bodde, "Feudalism in China," in *Feudalism in History,* R. Coulborn (editor), Princeton, N.J.: Princeton University Press, 1956, pp. 49–92; E. Pulleyblank, *The Background of the Rebellion in An Lu-shan,* London: Oxford University Press, 1955, Chapters 3 and 5; Wittfogel, *Oriental Despotism, loc. cit.;* Eberhard, *Conquerors and Rulers,* Leyden: Brill, 1952, Chapters 1 and 3; E. Balazs, "Les aspects significatifs," *loc. cit.;* Eisenstadt, "The Study of Oriental Despotism and Systems of Total Power," *The Journal of Asian Studies,* Vol. XVII, 1958, pp. 435–447.

41. See Pagés, *La monarchie de l'ancien régime, loc. cit.;* P. Sagnac, *Le formation de la société française moderne, loc. cit.;* on Byzantium in this respect see, in addition to the studies quoted above, Diehl, *Figures Byzantines,* Paris: Armand Colin, 1956; Diehl, *Le Société byzantine a l'époque des Commenes,* Paris: J. Gamber, 1929; S. Runciman, *Byzantine Civilization,* London: Arnold, 1933, Chapters VIII and XIX; L. Brehier, "Les populations rurales au IXᵉ siècle d'après l'hagiographie byzantine," *Byzantion,* I, 1924, pp. 201–213.

42. L. Brehier, *Vie et mort de Byzance,* Paris: Albin Michel, 1947, especially pp. 368–830; P. Charanis, "On the Social Structure of the Later

Roman Empire," *Byzantion*, Vol. XVII, 1944–1945, pp. 39–58; C. Diehl, *Les grands problèmes de l'histoire byzantine*, Paris: Armand Colin, 1943; Ostrogorsky, "Die Perioden," *loc. cit.*; Ostrogorsky, "Die wirtschaftlichen und sozialen Entwicklungsgrundlagen des byzantinischen Reiches," *Vierteljahrschrift für Social- und Wirtschaftsgeschichte*, Vol. XXII, 1929, pp. 12–143.

43. P. Charanis, "On the Social Structure and Economic Organization of the Byzantine Empire in the 13th Century, *op. cit.*, pp. 94–154; G. Ostrogorsky, "Die Perioden," *loc. cit.*; G. Ostrogorsky, *History of the Byzantine State*, Oxford: Blackwell, 1956, pp. 271–491.

44. Haring, *op. cit.*, Chapters II, VII, VIII, and XI.

45. Cahen, "Les facteurs économiques," *loc. cit.*

46. Lybyer, *loc. cit.*; B. Miller, *The Palace School of Muhammed the Conqueror*, Cambridge, Mass.: Harvard University Press, 1941.

47. Rosenberg, *op. cit.*, pp. 137–175; Schmoller, *loc. cit.*

48. *Ibid.*

49. Charanis, "The Social Structure and Economic Organization," *loc. cit.*; Ostrogorsky, *History*, *op. cit.*, pp. 371–415.

50. Ford, *Robe and Sword*, *loc. cit.*; Sagnac, *La formation de la société française moderne*, *loc. cit.* II; Pagés, *La monarchie*, *op. cit.*, pp. 182–216.

51. Dorn, *loc. cit.*; Rosenberg, *loc. cit.*; Schmoller, *loc. cit.*; Lybyer, *loc. cit.*

52. Pagés, *loc. cit.*; Sagnac, *loc. cit.*; Haring, *loc. cit.*

53. Pagés, *loc. cit.*; Segnac, *loc. cit.*

54. See Carsten, "Prussian Despotism at Its Height," *History*, Vol. XL, 1955, pp. 42–68; Rosenberg, *loc. cit.*; Lybyer, *op. cit.*, *passim*; Wright, *loc. cit.*

55. See the general literature quoted in Note 5 and especially Ostrogorsky, "Die wirtschaftlichen und sozialen Grundlagen," *loc. cit.*; Haring, *loc. cit.*; Pagés, *La monarchie d'ancien régime en France*, *loc. cit.*; Sagnac, *La formation de la société française moderne*, *loc. cit.*, I; Eberhard, *Conquerors and Rulers*, *loc. cit.*; Chang, *The Chinese Gentry*, *loc. cit.*; on England see Brock, "England," *loc. cit.*

56. On Egypt see Kees, *Ägypten, Kulturgeschichte des Alten Orients*, *op. cit.*, pp. 201 ff.; Stock, *Die erste Zwischenzeit Ägyptens*, *loc. cit.*; Kees, *op. cit.*, pp. 282 ff.; Drioton and Vandier, *L'Egypte*, *op. cit.*, Chapter 6; W. F. Edgerton, "The Government and the Governed in the Egyptian

250 Bureaucracy and Bureaucratization

Empire," *Journal of Near Eastern Studies*, Vol. VI, 1947, pp. 152–160; on Sassanid Persia in these stages see especially Altheim and Stiehl, *Ein asiatischer Staat, op. cit.*, p. 355 ff.

57. Altheim and Stiehl, *Ein asiatischer Staat, loc. cit.*

58. See W. Edgerton, "Government and the Governed," *loc. cit.*; W. Edgerton, "The Question of Feudal Institutions in Ancient Egypt," in *Feudalism in History*, R. Coulborn (editor), Princeton, N.J.: Princeton University Press, 1956, pp. 120–132.

59. Altheim and Stiehl, *Ein asiatischer Staat, loc. cit.*

60. J. A. Wilson, *The Burden of Egypt*, Chicago: Chicago University Press, 1951, pp. 104–125, 154–206.

61. Rosenberg, *op. cit.*, pp. 137–175; Beloff, *op. cit.*, especially pp. 104–133, 170–181; Schmoller, *loc. cit.*

62. Rosenberg, *loc. cit.*; Schmoller, *loc. cit.*

63. See Schmoller, *loc. cit.*; Rosenberg, *op. cit.*, pp. 46–75; R. A. Dorwart, *The Administrative Reforms, loc. cit.*

64. H. R. Williamson, *Wang An-shih: A Chinese Statesman and Educationalist of the Sung Dynasty*, London: A. Probsthaim, 1937, *passim*; F. H. Michael, "From the Fall of T'ang to the Fall of Ch'ing," in H. F. McNair (editor), *China*, Berkeley: University of California Press, 1946, pp. 89–110. See also O. Franke, "Der Bericht Wang An-shih's von 1058 über Reform des Beamtentums," *Sitzungsberichte der Preussischen Akademie der Wissenschaften*, Berlin, 1931–1933, pp. 264–312.

65. Ostrogorsky, *History, op. cit.*, pp. 83–110; Stein, "Introduction," *op. cit.*, pp. 102 ff.

66. For reasons of space we shall not go into a further documental analysis of this hypothesis. Such analysis and documentation are provided in Eisenstadt, *The Political Systems of Empires*, New York: The Free Press of Glencoe, 1963.

67. Carsten, *The Origins of Modern Prussia, op. cit.*, especially pp. 253–270; Carsten, "Prussian Despotism at Its Height," *loc. cit.*; O. Hintze, *Die Hohenzollern und ihr Werk*, Berlin: Verlag von Paul Parey, 1910, pp. 255–272; H. A. Gibb and H. Bowen, *Islamic Society and the West*, London: Oxford University Press, 1950, pp. 26–200.

68. Eisenstadt, "Internal Contradictions," *op. cit.*, pp. 71–75.

Chapter 9

Some Sociological Observations on the Response of Israeli Organizations to New Immigrants

ELIHU KATZ AND S. N. EISENSTADT

This chapter has its origin in preliminary observations on the patterns of contact between Israeli organizations and recent immigrants from non-Western countries. The pilot study resulting from these observations is concerned first with "the socialization of the client," that is, with the adaptation of newcomers from traditional familistic backgrounds to new role expectations such as those implicit in becoming a factory worker, a hospital patient, a client of a social welfare worker, or even a bus passenger. Secondly, the study is equally concerned with the changes that occur in the organizations themselves in response to the large influx of clients new to Western ways. It is to preliminary reflection on this second problem that the present paper is devoted.

Reprinted from *Administrative Science Quarterly*, Vol. 5, No. 1, June 1960. This paper is a by-product of a collaborative effort to design research on the developing bureaucratic framework of immigrant absorption in Israel. In 1957–1958 a research seminar on this topic was conducted by the authors at the Hebrew University in Jerusalem. Participating in the seminar, and in the pilot study that emerged from it, were the following faculty members and students: Rivka Bar-Yossef, Batsheva Bonné, Esther Carmeli, Nina Toren, Arie Eliav, Uri Horowitz, Rivka Kaplansky, Yael Lissak, Penina Morag, Dorit Pedan, Ozer Schild, Dov Weintraub, and Rina Zabelevsky. Mr. Schild and Mrs. Bar-Yossef are currently directing the pilot study, which is being supported, in part, by the Ford Foundation. We are indebted to Professors Peter M. Blau and David Riesman for a critical reading of an earlier draft.

Rather than consider the organization as a whole, we are restricting our focus to those officials having direct dealings with new immigrants. We are concerned, in other words, with the official-client relationship where the official is usually of European birth or parentage and where the client is a recent immigrant from a non-Western country.

According to sociological theory, there was good reason to expect that the rapid influx of large numbers of new immigrants would increase the bureaucratization of the organizations to which they came.[1] This meant that one could expect, first, an increasing impersonality of relations between bureaucrats and clients.[2] One could also expect an increase in the degree of universalism—equality before the law—in the orientation of bureaucrat toward client. Similarly, the pressure of work resulting from the large influx ought to make the official more stringent in his enforcement of the rules. And, of course, one could expect official-client relations to become more businesslike and specific, becoming more narrowly limited to officially relevant concerns. Finally, one could expect the official to rely more heavily on the ascribed authority of his office and on the symbols and the power accompanying it to get his job done.[3]

These are some of the dimensions in which we expected to find changes in the official-client relationship as a result both of the large and rapid increase of clients and of the tensions arising from the radical cultural differences between officials and clients. We found such examples, of course, but we also found many examples of change in exactly the opposite direction. Rather than a marked increase in the degree of bureaucratization in official-client relations, we found evidence of debureaucratization. We often found officials relating to clients personally, taking sympathetic account of the status "new immigrant," and not confining themselves to their officially relevant roles. And frequently we found officials trying to get their job done, not so much by means of the power and symbols of office, but on the basis of exchange of services, or persuasion, or personal charisma.

In the pages that follow, we shall try to explain how such relationships appear to arise. But it is important to bear in mind that these are, so far, only impressionistic observations. The pilot study and, ultimately, the full-scale research, we hope, will be better founded.

Theory and Research on Bureaucratization

In the broadest sense, the theoretical problem here deals with the conditions affecting the degree of bureaucratization of an organization, specifically of the bureaucrat-client relationship. We are interested in the factors that make for varying degrees of bureaucratization as well as the factors (presumably the same ones) that influence the direction of organizational change. Indeed, in the writings of Max Weber and Robert Michels the problem of organizational change is essentially identical with the theme of bureaucratization.[4] If the classical sociological writings were concerned with bureaucratization, the later writings have devoted themselves to the problems of overbureaucratization. Thus, discussions of deviations from the ideal-type bureaucracy outlined by Weber focused on overbureaucratization as a threat to the attainment of the very goals for which the organizations were established. The leading character in these discussions, the official who converts means into ends, has been frequently described both in literary and scientific publications. The same is true for the accompanying manifestations of exaggerated hierarchy and red tape.[5]

Recently, however, with the beginning of empirical research on organizational behavior, these assumptions about the unidirectional evolution of organizations have been put into broader perspective. Thus, recent empirical research seems to suggest that (1) the trend toward total bureaucratization of organizations may sometimes be averted;[6] (2) actual bureaucracies are compounded of nonbureaucratic elements also;[7] (3) bureaucracies, once established, are by no means unchanging;[8] and (4) when changes do take place, they are not always in the direction of greater bureaucratization and formalism.[9]

Factors Affecting Bureaucratization in the Official-Client Relationship

The literature provides a number of suggestions concerning the factors affecting bureaucratization in general. Weber's emphasis has al-

ready been noted.[10] Succession is another familiar example. When a
new director takes over from a predecessor, he has little choice but to
insist on relatively greater formal relations, to demand adherence to
the appointed channels of communication, and the like.[11] Another
factor is monopolization. When an organization has a monopoly on
certain goods or services (as most public bureaucracies have, of
course), there is little chance of effective protest on the part of the
client and no possibility of recourse to a competitor; under such conditions, bureaucrats may permit themselves an attitude of detachment
and ritualistic formalism vis-à-vis their clients.[12]

The reverse of each of these influences should be associated with a
lesser degree of bureaucratization. Thus, a smaller organization or
one which suffers a reduction in size ought to be less bureaucratic. So
should an organization that is aware that its clients have a choice between it and a competitor.

Each of these factors, of course, has its impact on the official-client
or the superior-subordinate relationships.[13] But there are other factors worth singling out for their specific impact on these relationships.
It is well known, for example, that soldiers in combat relate to others
and to their officers in a much less bureaucratic way than they do behind the front lines or in peacetime.[14] Closely related findings
emerge from a study of the informal social organization that super-
seded the formal organization of a naval unit on a tiny, unpopulated
Pacific island.[15] Similarly, workers on the night shift were treated
differently by their supervisors than were day-shift employees,[16] just
as, in Gouldner's study, workers in the mine successfully resisted
greater bureaucratization while office workers in the same company
did not.[17] The common elements in these situations would seem to be
the relative danger or unusualness of the task, the relative isolation
from social contacts outside the organization, and relative independence from the immediate presence of upper echelons in the hierarchy.
One suspects that certain of these factors would also be appropriate to
cases such as Diamond's study of the debureaucratization of a quasi-
military group by early American settlers organized as the Virginia
Company.[18]

As a final example of debureaucratization, Turner's study of the
navy disbursing officer during wartime will serve particularly well.[19]
Turner indicated several factors that influenced these officers to de-

part from the orientation prescribed by the rule book to establish more diffuse relations with some of their clients and to show favoritism. First, many clients of the disbursing officer were his superiors in rank and, consequently, his superiors in other role relationships. Secondly, he found it advantageous to help others who could reciprocate, such as the mess officer. This dependence, in part a function of his isolation from other social contacts, was embedded in a more general interdependence created by the war.[20] Finally, client and bureaucrat were dependent on each other because, especially during the war, the higher authorities who were to be consulted in case of doubt were both physically and psychologically distant.

This dependence of clients and officials on each other appears as a key factor in the other cases as well, and for much the same reasons.[21] The danger, the isolation, the aborted hierarchy of combat, the night shift, the mine, the Virginia Company, and the naval unit on the Pacific island made men dependent upon each other over and above the specific relations defined for them by their formal organizations. The attempt to enforce ordinary peacetime or daytime relations under such circumstances—that is, the attempt to behave in the accepted bureaucratic manner, or even more, to be overbureaucratic—is what apparently leads to desertion (where one is able to leave) or to mutiny (where one cannot).

Role Impingement as a Characterization of Bureaucratization and Debureaucratization

The notion of dependence may be viewed sociologically as a special case of the impingement of other role relationships on a given bureaucratic relationship. In Turner's study, for example, the observed debureaucratization could be considered a product of the regularized contacts in other roles that existed between the disbursing officer and his clients. Moreover, if debureaucratization may be characterized in terms of the impingement of nonbureaucratic roles on bureaucratic ones, then overbureaucratization may be characterized as either the formalistic segregation of a bureaucratic relationship from all other role relations (even relevant ones) or, in its totalitarian form, as the imposition of the bureaucratic relationship on relations outside the

scope of the bureaucracy. The bureaucratic ritualist would be an example of one who arbitrarily views all extrabureaucratic roles as irrelevant to the conduct of his office, while the totalitarian bureaucrat
"takes his authority home," as, for example, the sergeant bullying his
men off duty.

In effect, overbureaucratization and debureaucratization represent a
disturbance in the relationship between an organization and its environment that is not envisioned by the classical model of bureaucracy. This model envisages the roles of both bureaucrat and client as
segregated to some extent from their other roles; their roles are "specific" to the interaction setting and in this bureaucratic setting it is irrelevant, for example, that both bureaucrat and client belong to the
same political club. However, even in the ideal-type bureaucracy a
role is not completely independent of other roles; some outside roles
clearly may be, or must be, considered. If an old man, obviously unable to wait his turn in a long queue, is given special attention by a
clerk, this is not a case of an irrelevant role relationship being allowed
incorrectly to impinge on the bureaucrat-client relationship. In general, the classic model of bureaucracy requires only that the bureaucratic organization not be directly dependent on external factors for
its manpower, its resources, or its motivation for carrying out its organizational task. If an organization relies directly upon any one segment of the population for financing, or for political protection, these
sources of support will clearly receive particularistic attention in the
dispensation of the organization's services. It is such direct dependence that mechanisms such as boards of trustees, budget bureaus, and
the like try to avert by insulating bureaucratic organizations from
their sources of support. What is true for the organization as a whole
is true for its members as well. If a bureaucrat receives direct rewards
from outside the organization in addition to, or instead of, his rewards
from within, obviously his independence of action as a bureaucrat is
thereby reduced.[22]

Clearly, then, there is a very delicate balance—varying from organization to organization—between the specific roles defined as relevant
to relations within the bureaucracy and those outside roles defined as
irrelevant. Note the parallel to our notion of role impingement in
Gouldner's concept of "latent identity." [23]

Israeli Officials and New Immigrants

Increasingly, in recent years, the contact between immigrants and
the new societies to which they have come is mediated by profession-
als and bureaucrats. The customs agent, the social worker, the police-
man, the public health nurse, the housing administrator, and the like
constitute the immigrants' main connections with the community to
which they come, and it is these officials who provide aid and advice,
which in earlier migrations were obtained more informally or not at
all. This change is characteristic not only of the reception of immigrants in present-day Israel but also of the reception of Puerto Ricans
and Southern Negroes in New York and Chicago, and of other immigrant groups in the areas receiving them.[24] This change is in part a
consequence of the greater bureaucratization of these areas in the last
generation and in part a consequence of the theory and practice of the
welfare state which, adapting itself to the immigrant, proffers many
social services unknown to the immigrant of an earlier generation. In
Israel, this change is also a consequence of the different pattern of
motivation and different demographic composition of present-day immigrants compared with the "pioneer" immigrants of the turn of the
century.[25]

The remainder of this chapter is devoted to a preliminary discussion of some of the problems arising out of the contact between immigrants to Israel and the officials with whom they deal, viewed against
the theoretical considerations set forth in the first part of this chapter.
The kind of immigrant with whom we are particularly concerned
comes from non-Western countries (such as Yemen, Morocco, Iraq,
and so on), where he is likely to have had little or no contact with
formal organizations.

The question to which we now turn is why so many of the official-
client relations observed seemed to be moving in the direction of lesser
bureaucratization. We do not mean to imply that Israeli organizations
prior to the influx of the non-Western immigrants were close approxi-
mations of the Weberian ideal-type, for the small size of the country
and the common struggle made for wide networks of interpersonal
relations embracing officials and clients alike. The pioneering and

egalitarian ideologies frowned on status differentiation, differential distribution of rewards, as well as on formalities of all sorts. Not least important, political parties exerted considerable influence on appointments to and conduct of the public bureaucracies.

As we have already said, the mere increase in organizational size and responsibility might have been expected to result in increased bureaucratization of relations between official and client, between supervisor and worker, and so forth. To this rapid increase in numbers add the divergence of cultural background between the majority of recent immigrants coming from non-Western countries and the European bureaucrats dealing with them, and one would certainly expect an increase in bureaucratic formalism.[26]

Yet our preliminary observations indicate that this is not the case. We have, of course, found some evidence of increasing bureaucratization as a response to the influx of new immigrants. Thus, in one cooperative organization, for example, the hierarchy became sharply elongated. Previously any member was able to reach the highest official of the organization rather directly and informally, nor was it particularly important whether he brought his problem to one or another of the top officials. Now, the same organization has developed a strict chain of command and a new immigrant with a problem must proceed strictly through the established channels and talk only to the relevant official. Yet, even in this organization, as far as the actual interaction between official and client is concerned, there is evidence of considerable debureaucratization.

Repeatedly, however, we have found in institutions as diverse as health clinics and bus companies widespread evidence of debureaucratization in the relationship between officials and new immigrants. We have found cases where the official has assigned himself a greater number of tasks vis-à-vis his clients than those assigned him by his organization. We find considerable evidence of the growth of personal relationships between officials and new immigrants. We have even found cases where the official becomes the leader of a kind of "social movement" composed of new immigrants, thus completely reversing the expected trend which is supposed to lead from movements to bureaucracy. A major key to this unanticipated phenomenon is the notion of dependence we have developed, which takes quite a different form at this point. We shall try to describe what we think we have found, and, in part, we shall do this in terms of case studies. In one case, officials assumed a teaching role vis-à-vis their clients. In another, officials departed from their prescribed role as agents of socialization in certain patterned ways. In the third case, officials became the leaders of an incipient social movement.

Bureaucrats as Teachers: Dependence on the Client's Performance of His Role

The most characteristic form of debureaucratization in the relationship between bureaucrats and new immigrants in Israel is the assumption by the bureaucrat of the role of teacher along with (or at the expense of) his other functions. Consider, for example, the bus driver who gets out of the bus to teach the idea of a queue—"first come, first served"—an idea which is new to many of his new immigrant passengers. Similarly, the nurse at the well-baby clinic may be seen teaching women, informally, which of their needs are appropriate to the health services and which should be taken to other organizations. Or, the manager of the government-subsidized grocery in the new immigrant settlement may take the initiative and go into homes to teach housewives how to prepare certain foods with which they have had no previous experience.

In all these examples, the bureaucrat takes the time and effort to teach a client something about his (the bureaucrat's) expectations concerning how the client role is to be played. In other words, the bureaucrat teaches the client how to be a client so that he (the bureaucrat) can go on being a bureaucrat. This, it seems to us, is a form of dependence, but one which we have not considered so far; it is dependence on the client to act in a way which makes it possible for the bureaucrat to do his job.

In other words, it is expected by the bureaucrat and the bureaucracy that the client will bring with him to the bureaucratic context certain knowledge of expected roles from "outside," even though he may have had no previous contact with this particular bureaucracy. In Western society, for example, one is prepared for one's first encounter with a customs inspector by virtue of one's single-purpose relationships with other officials, tradesmen, and the like. When this preparation is lacking, the bureaucrat himself, in the examples cited, added a dimension—teaching—to his relationship with the client. And this change is an example of debureaucratization both because it adds another role to the specifically prescribed one and because the quality of interaction in the teacher-student relationship necessarily impinges on the more formal bureaucrat-client relationship. Yet these are the very elements which are officially alien to the ideal-type bureaucracy.[27] What is more, as we shall presently see, the teaching relationship may bring further debureaucratization, although conceivably it may simply permit the bureaucrat to perform his role as originally prescribed.

Consider the case of the bus driver. Introductory texts in sociology like to cite the driver-passenger relationship as an example of a purely instrumental, secondary relationship. Neither party matters to the other as an individual. One would not expect the bus driver to modify his behavior vis-à-vis new immigrants or anybody else, yet our preliminary observations seem to indicate that he does. Like other bureaucrats who come into contact with new immigrants, the bus driver tends to assume a teaching role, too. Besides trying to teach the idea of queuing, bus drivers were observed trying to persuade immigrant passengers that the cost of a ride on one bus was the same as the cost on the bus that had just gone by, or that the driver did not personally profit from each fare he collected, or that the decision for the bus to leave the terminal was not his. The consequences of the formal organization of a bus company that are understood by client and bureaucrat in modern society are simply not "obvious" to the non-Western immigrant.

Moreover, we have the impression—and the research now in progress will permit confirmation—that a kind of joking relationship grows up between drivers and new-immigrant passengers. This seems to be the case particularly where the passengers in the bus know one another—as in buses serving suburban settlements and city neighborhoods populated largely by new immigrants. Indeed, drivers on routes with concentrations of new immigrants have told us explicitly that they consider it desirable to get to know their passengers personally, because a new driver is likely to encounter "trouble" with non-Western immigrants, who may become unruly or begin to ask the usual questions anew: "How much is the fare?" "May I get off here?" and so on. In fact, we have had some indication that the bus companies recognize the desirability of less frequent changes of drivers on lines serving new immigrants. This "personalization" of the bureaucratic relationship represents a deviation from the impersonal, universalistic, specific relationship between driver and passenger which, in principle, ought to be unaffected by the substitution of one driver for another. It is an example of debureaucratization, which is the product of the dependence of the bureaucrat on the client's ability and motivation to perform his role as client.

It is important to note, however, that an official's dependence on the client to perform his role is probably of a different order from the kinds of dependence we discussed in the other examples reviewed in the first part of this chapter. In the earlier examples, the client actually had power over the bureaucrat—he could affect his well-being both as a member of the bureaucratic organization and as an individual. Thus, the clients of the disbursing officer were his superiors in other relationships, or the men in combat or in the mine could withdraw their reciprocal protection of their superior. In the present instance, however, the passenger has power over the driver in very much the same sense that a baby has power to disrupt the family schedule, and clearly this creates dependence of quite a different order.[28]

Bureaucrats as Socializing Agents

The process of a bureaucrat stepping outside his role to teach a new immigrant how to act his role as client is highly reminiscent of the processes of socialization and social control as analyzed by Parsons.[29] In the socialization of the child, or in the process of psychotherapy, the socializing agent steps out of his place in the larger social system and assumes a role in the "deviant" subsystem. Thus, the mother is a member of the inclusive family system consisting of father, mother, and children. To bring a new child into this more inclusive system, she must use her role in the earlier mother-child subsystem and selectively reward the child for obedience and disobedience to the new expectations of the inclusive system while at the same time providing a basis of support for the child in his effort to learn the new role. At times, however, the mother may fail as socializing agent, because she herself prefers to remain in the "deviant" subsystem and, ignoring the father and the rest of the family, acts to "keep the child for herself."

The parallel seems striking to us. The assumption of a teaching role by the bureaucrat and the "personalizing" of the bureaucrat-client relationship seems to function for the process of immigrant socialization as does the behavior of the socializing agent vis-à-vis the child. One of the objects of our empirical study will be to determine whether this kind of bureaucratic behavior (whatever its dysfunctions for the organizational routine) contributes more to the adaptation of the new immigrant than the unbending bureaucrat-client relationship.

Even more striking, perhaps, is the parallel to the kind of mother who "keeps the child for herself." Thus, a bureaucrat who has assumed a teaching role may fail to bring the new immigrant client to play the role expected of him by the bureaucracy and may, instead, remain a member of the "deviant" subsystem. This possibility is most conspicuous perhaps in the case of the village instructors who are assigned to each new settlement of immigrants. These instructors are part of a regional Settlement Authority which, in turn, is part of a nationwide Settlement Department. Sometimes, instead of mediating between the new immigrants and the authorities, the instructor becomes so much a part of his village community that his major effort is devoted to "representing" the interests of his clients vis-à-vis the authorities.

The village instructor typically lives among his clients and is potentially available all day long. His job, as compared with the bus driver's, is a highly diffuse one and includes teaching the settlers, who were semiskilled craftsmen or peddlers, to be farmers, co-operators (as this is understood in the *moshav*),[30] and Israelis. In this case debureaucratization is manifested not merely in the establishment of informal relations, but rather in the surrendering of part of the bureaucrat's commitment to his bureaucracy in favor of acceptance of a role in the system which he is expected to change.

Of course, this is only one of the ways that the instructor—given his highly diffuse and flexible role—can shape his relations with his clients. Some instructors, obviously, take quite the opposite position. The control of the resources necessary for the very existence of their clients permits them to move in the direction of overbureaucratization. They may interfere in matters—religious observance, for example—which ought properly to be outside their (very broad) spheres of influence.

An even more complicating factor is that the instructor, apart from his bureaucratic role, is often eager to make his clients full-fledged members of the nationwide small-holders co-operative movement or even of his political party, and to have them identify with its ideology, participate in its activities, and so on. Among the instructors who play this double role—which is by no means always considered illegitimate by the upper echelon of the Settlement Authority—many tend to view the various aspects of their bureaucratic role of training immigrants in agriculture and administration as a means to the end of full citizenship. This goal, for the ideologically oriented Israeli, implies the assumption of political and ideological commitments. Such instructors aim at making their clients members of a solidary movement of which they themselves are a part. This subsidiary aim makes the instructor even more dependent on the settlers. They may easily threaten not to participate in the movement unless the instructor provides them with various benefits and allocations for which he is the intermediary, though these may not be their due. In response the instructor may either move in the direction of debureaucratization and succumb to these demands, or he may attempt to use his bureaucratic position to force the clients to assume the political and ideological roles he envisages for them.

Bureaucrats as Leaders

A bureaucrat serving as "representative" or as "organizer" of his clients is by no means the extreme example of the kind of debureaucratization which may result from the bureaucrat's assumption of the role of socializing agent. Sometimes bureaucrats become charismatic leaders of groups of their clients.

Consider, for example, the case of several nurses employed at a well-baby clinic in a relatively segregated immigrants' "transitional community" within one of the major cities. In this setting the nurse —like the village instructor—is expected to be a teacher and to establish the kind of relationship required for successful teaching. Thus, along with the curative and preventive medicine practiced in such clinics, she must teach the women how to care for themselves and for their children in the particular manner prescribed by the modern scientific and philosophical orientation of the well-baby clinic. The authority of the nurses observed, however, extended beyond these rather broadly defined functions. They became generalized counselors and the clinic soon took on the air of a kind of social center where women gathered to greet each other, to gossip, and to move within the orbit of the nurses.

Some of the nurses had become preoccupied with the position of women in non-Western families. Apparently, this particular problem had first attracted attention as a result of the frequently negative reactions of their clients' husbands to one or another of the practices recommended by the clinic. Having thus become sensitized to the subordinate role of their clients within their families, the nurses added the reconciliation of family conflict to their counseling efforts, and, in fact, some of the nurses considered it part of their job to teach women their "rights" vis-à-vis their husbands. In several instances we have even heard nurses recommending divorce to their clients! Step by step, then, these nurses seem to have moved out from their broad but relatively well-defined functions (which include teaching) to assume an even broader teaching and counseling role and, in some instances, to leadership of a kind of "suffragette" movement among their clients. In such cases, the leader does not appear averse to illustrating her message with reference to her own private life or that of her friends. And to the extent that they follow, the clients look to their leaders for active support and guidance, and for a share in the consequences of their behavior.

The leadership role, as played by the bureaucrat, represents a considerable degree of debureaucratization. It represents, in part, exchange of the authority vested in the bureaucratic office for the "voluntary" loyalty of clients; that is, such leadership exists not only by virtue of an "appointment" but by virtue of being "chosen" by followers as well. To that extent, the bureaucrat must submit himself to the authority, and to some of the norms, of his followers. Moreover, he has considerably extended the sphere of his influence from the specific tasks assigned to him to the wider, more diffuse, tasks inherent in the leadership role.

Direction of Future Research

The variety of official relations with new immigrants in Israel provides us with a unique opportunity to locate the conditions under
which debureaucratization, overbureaucratization, or both these organizational changes take place. Thus, we would expect debureaucratization to occur more often in relatively isolated settlements of
new immigrants than in immigrant communities within the larger
cities. In the isolated settlement the bureaucrat is far more dependent
on the voluntary co-operation of his clients, both for the performance
of his task and for his social and emotional (i.e., nonbureaucratic)
well-being. One would also expect a greater dilution of the bureaucratic
role with the teaching role in situations where a community of immigrants is transplanted more or less at the same time, compared with
situations where migration was stretched over a long period of time.
Under the former conditions, the immigrant community will have
had less opportunity to educate itself and to develop the leaders, in-
termediaries, and interpreters who permit the bureaucrat to play his
role uninterruptedly. In both the isolated immigrant community and
in the transplanted immigrant community, the "segregated" equilibrium between the organization and its environment is likely to be
more upset, and hence more marked organizational change may be
anticipated. In both these cases, one might argue that the direction of
change might well be toward greater, rather than lesser, bureaucratization in the sense that the organization has a unique opportunity to
impose itself on more aspects of its clients' lives than is usual. Our
hypothesis holds otherwise, as we have tried to argue above, but the
plausibility of the competing hypothesis illustrates how the two osten-
sibly opposite directions or organizational change stem from closely
similar conditions.

Our study will enable us to make other comparisons, too. For example, we can compare bureaucrats who come into contact with clients of
their own ethnic origin with bureaucrats whose clients are not of their
own group. We can compare bureaucrats who are relatively isolated
from contacts with their colleagues—instructors who live in the
villages—with those who live among their colleagues in the newly

built Rural Centers and commute daily to the nearby villages. In the same way, we can compare the pattern of official-client relations characteristic of the bus companies whose drivers have only sporadic and brief contact with their new immigrant clients to the behavior of bureaucrats in organizations which require more extended contacts.

Again, it is easier to choose the situations in which deviation from the ideal bureaucratic norm is more likely to occur than it is to predict the direction of the deviation. Thus, when the bureaucrat is confronted primarily by clients of his own group he is likely to move either in the direction of bureaucratic formalism, studiously seeking to demonstrate his rootedness in Israeli life and to resist the particularistic expectations of the relative newcomers to Israel, or he may move in the direction of debureaucratization in the sense of reaccepting portions of the pattern of traditional authority and behavior of which he was once a part. Compared to the bureaucrat dealing with members of his own ethnic group (who may, because of his better understanding of the group, be more successful in his task), the bureaucrat without an ethnic affiliation with his clients will display more affective neutrality, though this may still lead to overbureaucratization. Again, we expect to find that bureaucrats in close touch with their colleagues can maintain a more detached, objective, service-oriented attitude to their clients than bureaucrats dependent on their clients for social and emotional acceptance and interaction. And, for the same reason, we expect bureaucrats with more extended contacts with a given group of clients to depart from the norms of bureaucratic behavior to a greater extent than bureaucrats with relatively brief and less regular contact.

In this report of preliminary observations on the contact between Israeli organizations and the mass immigration from non-Western countries into Israel in recent years, we have tried to formulate an approach to the study of organizational change, particularly to change in the official-client relationship in response to this new kind of clientele.

Contrary to the expectations of classical sociological thinking, we have considerable impressionistic evidence pointing to a process of decreasing bureaucratization, at least in the relations between immigrant-clients and those parts of the bureaucracy which come into contact with them. We have tried to explain this finding by reference to the constraints operating on the bureaucrat who comes into contact with the public to train the immigrant client to perform the client role in order that he (the bureaucrat) may perform his own role adequately.

It seems to us that this process implies a certain kind of dependence on the client as far as the bureaucrat is concerned. Specifically, the bureaucrat is dependent on the client's proper performance of the client role, although in a different sense than the client is dependent on the bureaucrat's performance of his. Beyond this, the kinds of situations we are exploring include those where the bureaucrat may look at his client for sociability, or may recognize him as a member of the same ethnic group, or may seek to enlist his client in other organizations of which he is a member. All these exemplify situations of heightened dependence and, presumably, greater deviations from bureaucratic norms.

We have tried to suggest that the various forms of dependence which we found to be related to the process of debureaucratization may be subsumed under the more general heading of the articulation of role relations in modern society. The bureaucrat-client relationship is presumed to be segmented in certain ways from other kinds of social relations. Variations in the degree to which a given role relationship is insulated from other role relationships affects the degree of its bureaucratization. Thus, the process of debureaucratization may be characterized as an impinging of nonbureaucratic roles, or of other bureaucratic roles, on the specific bureaucratic role in question, while overbureaucratization may be expressed either in terms of the artificial insulation of the bureaucratic relationship from all other roles (however relevant) or, in its more totalitarian form, in the impinging of the bureaucratic relationship on relations not relevant to the bureaucratic role.

We have tried to set down some theoretical guidelines for a discussion of the problems of organizational change, with specific reference to the official-client relationship in a situation where there has been a rapid influx of immigrants having little previous contact with formal organization. We have tried to show that, in Israel, the process of decreasing bureaucratization is not an uncommon response in this situation, although we wish to emphasize that both increasing and decreasing bureaucratization may find simultaneous expression in different parts of the organization and, sometimes, in the very same relationship between official and client.

NOTES

1. An elaboration of the well-known Simmel hypothesis on the effects of the size of a group for the specific case of migration can be found in Frank E. Jones, "A Sociological Perspective on Immigrant Adjustment," *Social Forces*, 35, 1956, pp. 39–47.

2. In general, our use of the terms official (or bureaucrat) and client is meant to refer also to superior-subordinate relationships within an organization.

3. Here and elsewhere we made use of Parsons' terminology. Although we make an effort to communicate the meaning of the several concepts we employ, for a full discussion see Talcott Parsons, *The Social System*, Glencoe, Ill.: The Free Press, 1951, Chapter II.

4. Max Weber, "The Presuppositions and Causes of Bureaucracy," in Robert K. Merton, Ailsa P. Gray, Barbara Hockey, and Hanan Selvin (editors), *Reader in Bureaucracy*, Glencoe, Ill.: The Free Press, 1952, pp. 60–68. Of course, Weber was also concerned with the role of internal factors making for a greater degree of bureaucratization in the organization, a notable example being his discussion of "The Routinization of Charisma," which tends to develop when a group faces the problem of leadership succession, *ibid.*, pp. 92–100. This also gives a brief statement of Robert Michels' argument (*ibid.*, pp. 88–92), as does his *Political Parties*, Glencoe, Ill.: The Free Press, 1949.

5. The best known of these essays is probably Robert K. Merton, "Bureaucratic Structure and Personality," in Merton et al., *op. cit.*, pp. 361–371.

6. Seymour M. Lipset, Martin A. Trow, and James S. Coleman, *Union Democracy*, Glencoe, Ill.: The Free Press, 1956, try to specify the conditions that contribute, in at least one case, to the maintenance of trade-union democracy rather than oligarchic bureaucracy.

7. This, of course, refers to the dominant trend of present-day research, which has been concerned with the existence and the functions of informal social relations in the context of formal organization. But more important for our present purpose is the incipient concern for informal aspects of relationships between bureaucrats and the public. See, for example, Morris Janowitz, Deil Wright, and William Delaney, *Public Administration and*

the Public, Ann Arbor, Mich.: Institute of Public Administration, University of Michigan Press, 1958; Edwin J. Thomas, "Role Conceptions and Organizational Size," *American Sociological Review,* 24, 1959, pp. 30–37; George F. Lombard, *Behavior in a Selling Group,* Cambridge, Mass.: Harvard University Press, 1955. For a recent critique of the assumption that the several elements of Weber's ideal-type bureaucracy are necessarily intercorrelated, see Stanley H. Udy, Jr., " 'Bureaucracy' and 'Rationality' in Weber's Organization Theory," *American Sociological Review,* 24, 1959, pp. 792–795.

8. See Peter M. Blau, *The Dynamics of Bureaucracy,* Chicago: Chicago University Press, especially Chapter III.

9. See Ralph H. Turner, "The Navy Disbursing Officer as a Bureaucrat," in Merton et al., *op. cit.,* pp. 372–379. Also compare Blau, *loc. cit.,* for an example of the way in which variations in supervisory practice affected the extent to which employment agency officials used racial bias vis-à-vis their clients.

10. Max Weber, "The Presuppositions and Causes of Bureaucracy," in Merton et al., *op. cit.,* pp. 60–68.

11. Alvin W. Gouldner, *Patterns of Industrial Bureaucracy,* Glencoe, Ill.: The Free Press, 1954, pp. 59–101.

12. Merton et al., *op. cit.,* p. 369.

13. For a discussion of the effect of size, see Thomas, *loc. cit.*

14. Samuel A. Stouffer et al., *The American Soldier: Combat and Its Aftermath,* Princeton, N.J.: Social Science Research Council, Special Committee, 1949–1950, p. 100.

15. Charles H. Page, "Bureaucracy's Other Face," *Social Forces,* 25, 1946, pp. 89–91.

16. Lipset et al., *op. cit.,* p. 139.

17. Gouldner, *op. cit.,* pp. 105–154.

18. Sigmund Diamond, "From Organization to Society: Virginia in the 17th Century," *American Journal of Sociology,* 63, 1958, pp. 588–594.

19. Turner, *loc. cit.*

20. For example, Turner omits the interdependence based on the common danger.

21. Note again that we are using "bureaucrat-client" in a generic sense, implying superordinate-subordinate relations (such as in combat, the mine, the Virginia Company) as well.

22. To cite a familiar example, a civil servant looking to a political party for rewards for his performance in his role as civil servant may do so because he is a political appointee, because he is ideologically committed to his party, or for other reasons.

23. After developing this analysis of role impingement, we encountered Gouldner's concept and noted its close similarity. "It is necessary to distinguish," says Gouldner, "between those social identities of group members which are consensually regarded as relevant to them in a given setting and those which group members define as being irrelevant, inappropriate to consider, or illegitimate to take into account. The former can be called the manifest social identities, the latter, the latent social identities. . . . When group members orient themselves to the latent identities of others in their group, they are involved in a relationship with them which is not culturally prescribed by the group norms governing their manifest roles. . . . It would seem clear that latent identities and roles are important because they exert pressure upon the manifest roles, often impairing conformity with their requirements and endemically threatening the equilibrium of the manifest role system." Gouldner goes on to give an example concerning deference to elders in a universalistic setting which is very similar to the one we have presented. See Alvin W. Gouldner, "Cosmopolitans and Locals: Toward an Analysis of Latent Social Roles, I and II," *Administrative Science Quarterly*, 2, 1957–1958, pp. 281–306, 444–480, especially pp. 282–287. It should be noted also that the problem of role impingement or latent social identity differs from the problem of role conflict. Role impingement refers to the multiple role relations played by official and client vis-à-vis one another. Role conflict generally implies the multiple (and conflicting) roles of a given actor vis-à-vis several different others—e.g., the official's relationships to his wife and to his boss. Still a further distinction, recently introduced by Merton, is that of the role set, which has to do with the multiple role relations implicit in any given role—e.g., the official's relationship to his boss, his secretary, his colleagues. Others who have employed analytic concepts similar to the concept of role impingement are Lloyd Fallers, *Bantu Bureaucracy*, Cambridge: Heffer and Heffer, 1957; Frank Jones, *The Infantry Recruit: A Sociological Analysis of Socialization in the Canadian Army*, unpublished doctoral dissertation, Harvard, 1956; Thomas, *loc. cit.*

24. A review, by Nathan Glazer, of several recent books treating Puerto Rican migration makes this point; see "New York's Puerto Ricans," *Commentary*, 26, 1958, pp. 469–478.

25. See S. N. Eisenstadt, *The Absorption of Immigrants,* Glencoe, Ill.: The Free Press, 1955, pp. 64–68, 172 ff., "The Framework of Bureaucratic Absorption."

26. In 1948, at the time of the establishment of the state of Israel, persons born in Africa and Asia constituted 15 per cent of the population; five years later, in 1953, they constituted 38 per cent of the population. See Moshe Sicron, *Immigration to Israel: 1948–1953,* Jerusalem: Central Bureau of Statistics, 1957, pp. 43–50.

27. This would be particularly true when a bureaucrat's aim is to bring his client to want the bureaucrat's services; thus, this might be more true of a storekeeper than a nurse, and more true of a nurse than a bus driver.

28. Replying to a query whether the "dependency" of the child does not sometimes confer power equal to or superior to that of the person on whom dependency exists, Parsons distinguishes between power defined as "relative importance in carrying out the functional performance of the system" and as the "ability to cause trouble by threatening to disrupt the system." In this latter sense, "the child, and other persons or groups in dependent positions have considerable 'power.'" See Talcott Parsons and Robert F. Bales, *Family, Socialization and Interaction Process,* Glencoe, Ill.: The Free Press, 1955, p. 46, n. 18. It is this second type of power which concerns us at this point.

29. *Ibid.,* Chapter II.

30. See S. N. Eisenstadt, "Sociological Aspects of the Economic Adaptation of Oriental Immigrants in Israel: A Case Study of Modernization," *Economic Development and Cultural Change,* 4, 1958, pp. 269–278; Alex Weingrod, *From the Millah to the Moshav: Culture Contact and Change in a New-Immigrant Village in Israel,* unpublished doctoral dissertation, University of Chicago, 1959.

SECTION IV

Social Mobility

IN THIS SECTION we pass from a "structural" starting point to a greater emphasis on behavioral aspects of institution-building in the process of social mobility. The two essays included here are devoted to the analysis of one of the basic processes which bridges, as it were, the behavioral and attitudinal aspects of institutions with the structural aspects.

In the first essay (Chapter 10), "Social Mobility and Institutional Structure," an attempt is made to indicate the possibility of relating this process to various aspects of institutional structure. This attempt is based on an evaluation of some of the existing general orientations in this field and proceeds to a more detailed analysis on the basis of the critical evaluation of two recent books—on the processes of mobility in one major historical society, namely the Chinese Empire. It ends up by pointing out some possibilities of further research in this field.

The second essay (Chapter 11) reports on the interrelationships between personal (behavioral) and structural aspects of mobility in one emerging institutional setting—Israel.

The two essays together attempt to show some possible ways of, on the one hand, combining the behavioral and the structural aspects of mobility and on the other, of relating the processes of mobility to broader aspects of institutional structures and especially to the problems of the continuity and changes of such structures.

Chapter 10

Social Mobility and Institutional Structure

I

Studies of mobility have been in the forefront of sociological inquiry for a long time. Many studies in different countries—the United States, England, Scandinavia, Germany, France, Japan, and others —have analyzed the scope of social mobility, e.g., the extent to which sons follow the occupations of their fathers or do better or worse than their fathers, and conversely the extent to which fathers' occupational positions are filled by sons.

Some of these studies have tested hypotheses about differences in the rate of mobility in various modern societies; others have provided very broad statistical-demographical studies and descriptions of changes in the patterns of organization of different occupations. Still others are concerned primarily with methodology. Most of these works have been very succinctly summed up and critically evaluated by S. M. Miller's trend report (1). This very able survey sharply points out that the great proliferation of different studies has not yet been matched by a concomitant development in the posing of questions or problems which the study of mobility has to answer. Some of the

This chapter is based on a previously unpublished paper presented at a meeting of the Committee on Stratification and Mobility of the International Sociological Association, and on parts of a review article published in the July, 1964, issue of *Comparative Studies in Society and History* (Vol. VI, No. 4).

more specific studies, such as those analyzing conditions of the supply of talent to different occupations or the blocking opportunities through educational selection and the relation of such selection to class structure, have a very definite focus. Such a focus may also be found in other—less numerous—studies which deal with the effect of mobility on "class consciousness" or on the professional and occupational orientations of different groups.

The implicit assumptions about the nature of mobility as a social mechanism and about its influence on the operation of the social structures have not been made explicit or operationalized. It has been, of course, generally recognized that the process of mobility is an important mechanism for the placement of available human personnel in different social positions, for the differential redistribution of population to each position, and sometimes for the creation of new social groups and positions. Similarly, it has been generally recognized that there exists some close relationship between the processes of placement and redistribution and the continuity of a given structure or system, or between the different changes which take place within this structure.

Which aspects of this process are most important for the understanding of the functioning of a given social system? Which contribute to its stability, and which generate changes, and what kind of changes? To what extent are these different aspects of mobility and their effects common to all societies, or do they differ between societies? Do we have systematic knowledge about the influence of different patterns of mobility on the availability of talent for different social and cultural positions? Often some general assumptions that a certain circulation of elites is good for the maintenance of fresh blood in the central organs and positions of a society, or that mobility is good, at least for a democratic society, can be found in the literature. But there have been, as Miller's survey clearly shows, relatively few systematic analyses of existing materials to test or operationalize these assumptions.

It is our contention that it would be difficult to evaluate the causes and consequences of mobility without recourse to the full and systematic analysis of the relationship of processes of mobility to the social structure in which mobility takes place. Although some very general characteristics, common to all processes of mobility, can be discerned, the full articulation of these characteristics can be understood only in relation to the social structures in which the processes take place.

From this point of view, a question of special importance is the extent of the connection between processes of mobility and structural and institutional change in various modern societies. It seems that quite often, in many studies measuring intergenerational mobility, not enough attention is given to the fact that these processes are very closely related to institutional change and expansion, and that many of the specific problems and consequences of mobility are very closely related to the interconnection between mobility and institutional change.

In this chapter we shall present some queries about these problems of mobility, in historical and modern societies. What will be said is in no way definitive, exhaustive, or fully systematic—it aims only to serve as a starting point of discussion, to present a possible plan for codification of the field, and to point out some gaps in our knowledge about mobility.

II

Some mobility seems to take place in almost every social system—with the possible exception of the simplest primitive societies. The process of mobility, i.e., of (generational or intergenerational) transition from one status position to another, can be seen as a part of the more general process or mechanism of placement of (biologically) new members in the social structure. In other words, mobility is part of the allocation of personnel to some basic roles in the occupational, political, or religious spheres. In most societies there are always some members who attain roles and status that differ from their fathers, or who manage to change their status, in addition to the usual changes while passing through different age grades. This may be entirely accidental, or there may exist special roles and status in the societies which in a way cannot be entirely inherited, or which are open to everybody. (Priesthood is an obvious example, but there exist many other marginal and yet highly necessary roles of this kind.) It is important to notice that such roles and status exist not only in dynamic, universalistic societies but also in more static and traditional ones.

Although the basic facts about mobility in many primitive and historical societies have been known very well, there have been, until lately, few systematic studies of the process of mobility—whether of the incidence of mobility or of its cause.

But several recent works—especially two on classical Chinese society by Ho and Marsh (2)—have greatly advanced our knowledge of the operation of mobility in at least one historical society and have enabled us to explore these problems more systematically.

III

The books by Ho and Marsh—a historian and a sociologist—deal with the problems of mobility in classical Chinese society, and both authors address themselves to the analysis of social processes in historical societies, focusing on central problems in sociological inquiry, namely, the problem of social mobility and also—in Marsh's case—the structure of the bureaucracy.

Let us start with a brief survey of the contents and problems of the two books. A common aim is to analyze the system of stratification of Imperial China (especially of Ming and Ch'ing China—although the books do not necessarily cover former periods) through the analysis of the determinants of bureaucratic advancement. Both Ho and Marsh's first steps are analyses of the general system of stratification of China. This system is defined in the usual sociological terms derived from Max Weber—i.e., as dealing with the differential distribution of wealth, prestige, and power, and with the criteria of such distribution. While there is certainly nothing novel in these appraisals or in the general description of the Chinese system of stratification—building heavily and justly on the works of Eberhard, Wittfogel, Kracke, and others—the very juxtaposition of the usual sociological categories and of the historical material brings some clarification of certain simplifications that may be very often found in the literature of China. Thus the fact that the distribution of wealth was not always identical with the distribution of prestige is not presented as an aberration of the classical Confucian-bureaucratic pattern or as a reason for bewailing the fate of the merchants. What this fact does indicate is that the Chinese system of stratification, like that of any large-scale, centralized, bureaucratic society was to some extent flexible; that certain degrees of free floating resources (i.e., not committed to ascriptive units of various kinds)—whether power, wealth, or prestige—existed in it, and that, although the official elite attempted to regulate and channelize these resources according to the criteria of Confucian bureaucracy, they never fully succeeded, and many secondary systems or "subcultures" of stratification continuously existed in China. Morover, the importance of merchants and the military—factors often looked upon as exogenous, whereas in fact they constitute a continuous part of social organization, are very important channels of mobility into the literati group and the bureaucracy, and permit the existence of a special bureaucratic-military sector (3)—is brought out by Marsh's and, even more, by Ho's systematic description.

Their analyses also make useful distinctions between the gentry, the literati, and the bureaucracy, in order to describe the position of these groups in the local structure with great vivideness.

Ho's analysis of the Chinese status system is much more elaborate than Marsh's. Ho goes into great detail in analyzing the different social strata in Chinese society and the major grades within the upper echelons of the literati and the bureaucracy, and in showing the origin of the official social ideology in the analyses of the reasons for Confucian legalism upholding the fluidity of the status system—despite some obvious ascriptive tendencies. He gives in even greater detail a historical and sociological analysis of the different avenues of advancement into the bureaucracy and sets the bureaucracy—which constitutes Marsh's main focus of analysis—within the wider context of the upper stratum of Chinese society, i.e., the gentry and literati. Moreover, he attempts to analyze the process of downward mobility and shows how, within a relatively static society with a fluid, open system of mobility, such downward movement was almost a historical or sociological necessity. Ho also gives a detailed description of some of the intrafamily mechanisms (such as conspicuous consumption) which could contribute to downward mobility.

IV

This general, background material is the basis for Marsh's analysis of the determinants of bureaucratic advancement. He aims at testing several major hypotheses, all dealing with the extent to which internal-bureaucratic seniority examinations, as against external (mainly familial) criteria, determine the extent of bureaucratic advancement. In order to test these hypotheses he analyzes by carefully statistical methods—using most of the techniques of modern mobility studies—a sample of 572 officials from "*Eminent Chinese of the Ch'ing Period.*"

His main conclusions are that, among Chinese officials, seniority tended to equalize the chances of advancement for men from official and from commoner families—once they were in the bureaucracy. Furthermore, he shows that, if the seniority rule enhanced the opportunities of some commoners' sons, it did not retard the advancement of other, more exceptional commoners. The latter commoners' sons did not have to adhere to the seniority principle but instead had rapid ascent as a result of military successes and the like.

If within the confines of the bureaucracy proper the various mechanisms of bureaucratic advancement countervailed various familial pressures, the situation was different in the overall social structure, for the broad familial and status orientation was predominant. Thus the bureaucratic elite were recruited disproportionately from the 2 per cent of the population in the elite stratum, rather than from the 98 per cent in the below-elite, or commoner, stratum.

Ho's main analyses are more concerned with the processes of mobility in the wider context of the overall Chinese societal system and the influence of these processes on its working. He is interested as well in the broader social and political determinants of such processes of mobility in different periods of the Ming and Ch'ing dynasties.

His main conclusions are that, although the Ming-Ch'ing society, like the Chinese society of earlier periods, was a regulated society, the discrepancy between the social ideals embodied in legal texts and the social realities was very great. The complex social and economic forces, together with the lack of strong will necessary on the part of the imperial government to strictly enforce the stringent law, made the maintenance of special hereditary statuses impossible. In the Ming-Ch'ing period as a whole, the status system was fluid and flexible, and there were no effective legal and social barriers to prevent the movement of individuals and families from one status to another (Ho, 1963: pp. 256–257).

Ho shows how the trend of increasing mobility continued after the founding of the Ming dynasty, when the examination and academic degree system became more elaborate and the school system truly nationwide. All this, together with the most unusual political and social circumstances in which the Ming dynasty was inaugurated, created a chapter of social mobility probably unparralleled in Chinese history. He indicates that, other things being equal, members of successful families naturally had various competitive advantages and in the long run prevailed over the humble and poor in the competitive examination. He shows that the chances of successful mobility for ordinary commoners would have begun earlier to decline drastically had it not been for the combined effect of the early stage of large-scale reproduction of basic classics and reference tools, the teachings of Wang Yang-ming, and the subsequent mushrooming growth of private academies. The rise of a large number of private academies, with their usual scholarship provisions, occurred just about the time that community schools had begun to decline (Ho, 1963: p. 261).

Ho attempts also to correlate this great upsurge of mobility with broader social conditions. He shows that the early Ming period up to 1500 was one of peace, prosperity, government retrenchment, reduced fiscal burden, and steady agricultural and commercial expansion, which, together with the government's usually sympathetic attitude toward the upward mobility of the humble and the vast expansion of educational facilities, cannot have failed to have a beneficent effect on both general social and the more specific, socio-economic mobility. He then briefly analyzes the impact of declining conditions on restriction of mobility (Ho, 1963: pp. 264–265).

V

It is difficult for a nonsinologist to evaluate the studies through the use of sources and to compare them with other studies on mobility in China, such as those of Ho or Kracke. It appears that the major problem in Marsh's book is that of his sources. He himself fully recognized that first. The *Eminent Chinese* does not contribute a statistical sample from which generalizations can be made to a larger, determinate population (Marsh, 1961: p. 191). This source is, by its very nature, biased in favor of the more "officially" (i.e., organizationally and ideologically) approved people. Other sources, such as various local chronicles or a fuller roster of materials about all central elite positions, could have modified his results, and it might have been useful and interesting, perhaps, if Marsh had traced the different career patterns—in terms of type of jobs and departments—of different "bureaucrats." As far as a nonsinologist can judge, Ho is more aware of the unreliability of many of the sources and is more cautious in using them, at the same time showing himself to be their master.

But whatever the limitations or modifications of the conclusions, these two studies indicate the possibility of the beginning of a meeting of sociological and historical methods for the analysis of social processes and institutional structure in historical societies. While Marsh shows a greater predilection for formal hypotheses and for the use of some of the modern research techniques developed by the social scientists, his analysis is weaker on the level of the overall institutional structure. This level is picked up much more masterfully by Ho.

A continuous combination of these two approaches could greatly advance the contributions of sociological analysis to the understanding of historical societies and facilitate the testing of sociological hypotheses in historical contexts.

The very materials presented by Ho and Marsh about the broad contours of Chinese society underline the necessity and importance of studying some of these larger problems and the process of mobility within their context. To mention a few of the problems emerging from these studies of Chinese society: How did the mobility from different strata and/or regions influence the identification of the mobilized groups with the broad political and cultural structure? When did different rates of mobility from different groups, strata, and regions, or concentration of mobility in special channels—i.e., of the "usual" examination system—influence this identification? How did these different patterns of mobility influence the availability of sufficient manpower to the main positions in the society, in the bureaucracy, and did the patterns affect the functioning of the different echelons and departments of the bureaucracy? What institutional changes were generated by such changes in the processes of mobility? To what extent was the famous "dynastic cycle" connected with changes in the rates and channels of mobility—as some historians have assumed? Which social and political conditions generated favorable rates of mobility, and under what conditions were the less favorable rates and channels developed?

It is important to emphasize that in posing all these questions we have to deal not only with differential *rates* of mobility but also with different institutional channels of mobility—i.e., whether mobilization occurred through the examination system, through wealth, or through the army. This consideration is especially important in the study of the Chinese case where mobility was set within the relatively stable society and where perhaps the clearest type of "sponsored" mobility could be found (4)—i.e., sponsored and regulated by an elite, oriented toward recruitment of relatively limited and clear elite patterns.

Similar questions can be asked with regard to other historical societies and systems—centralized societies, like the Roman or Byzantine Empires—or with regard to other types of historical societies, like the feudal society. Marc Bloch's classic analysis of the two feudal ages and of the changes in the composition, background, and influence of the aristocratic groups in each of these ages is a good example of a possible approach to such materials (5).

Studies of mobility in various institutional settings can also perhaps be designed to throw light on one of the most crucial and interesting problems of comparative analysis; namely, under what conditions were the various processes of mobility "contained" within the framework of a given institutional system, and when were they starting points of institutional changes.

VI

This problem of the relation between processes of mobility and institutional change becomes even more important, although perhaps more difficult to analyze, in the studies of modern societies, and yet, in these studies, it has been touched to an even smaller extent.

In order to understand some of these problems, and their relationship to problems of institutional and structural change, in general, and to modern societies, in particular, it would be worthwhile to mention first some of the more general causes of mobility which operate in all societies but probably with special strength in modern ones:

(a) Population increase and pressure; (b) economic changes, growth, and expansion; (c) structural-institutional changes, i.e., changes in the structure of different social institutions rather than economic ones; changes in the political structure, growing political participation of various groups, changes in distribution of income effected by social and political legislation, development of special educational facilities and agencies—all may greatly contribute to processes of mobility; (d) ideological changes and developments.

While these various factors of mobility are obviously interrelated in concrete situations, each of them is to some extent independent. The concrete interrelations between them may therefore vary greatly and may influence in different ways the incidence, direction, and consequences of mobility. In most of the available literature, great emphasis has been put on demographic and economic factors, whereas the other institutional and ideological elements have been neglected or dealt with as derivatives of demographic and economic changes. It is our contention, however, that these various institutional factors may be, in many cases, independent of mobility and may influence developments in ways different from the economic or demographic ones.

The various factors enumerated above are necessarily very general. In their overall operation they create some of the major consequences of mobility. These consequences are, first, the aspirations to mobility on the part of various individuals and groups, and, second, various changes in the structure of some groups in society, in their place in the institutional structure, and in this structure itself.

Third, these general factors create, as it were, both the various, new, institutional possibilities and opportunities to which the mobility may be directed, as well as the institutional obstacles to such mobility. Changes such as new openings for opportunities can be effected, on the one hand, by the creation of new positions for individual advancement in economic, occupational, cultural, and political spheres. On the other hand, such changes can be effected through the creation of new evaluations of different tasks, occupational roles, and/or new social and political privileges connected with these roles and tasks. Instances of such changes can be found in the relative status of independent farmers and agricultural laborers in the Netherlands, analyzed by Hofstee [6] or in the general "decline" of middle classes in many welfare states. Similarly, such institutional changes may come about through the creation of new patterns of participation in different spheres, especially in the cultural and political spheres.

These various factors do not operate in an undifferentiated way within the structure of any society. Quite obviously they impinge in different measures on different groups and strata of the society. A systematic analysis of the process of mobility should fully investigate these variations in the impact of the many factors on different groups in the society. Such variations probably apply not only to diverse social "classes" and occupational groups but also to regional, religious, and political groups.

Mobility, whether individual or group, does not usually take place at the same rate in all social spheres and with regard to all relevant criteria of social status. Occupational mobility need not always accompany changes in political status or in participation in cultural and social affairs.

Similarly, although the major factors or causes of mobility create both the pressures and aspirations for mobility and the various kinds of new opportunities, there need not necessarily be a close harmony or correspondence between these pressures and opportunities. This is true both in the case of relations between different factors, e.g., the economic and the political, and in the case of the pressures and opportunities created within only one sphere.

There may therefore arise many discrepancies between the different rates, channels, and criteria of mobility, discrepancies which may give rise to different degrees of dislocation of various groups and categories of people. It is these various "discrepancies" between the rates of mobility in different institutional spheres that constitute the most important focus of individual-psychological stresses, on the one hand, and of institutional change and innovation, on the other.

A full analysis of the process of mobility within any given society cannot be attained if these various aspects are not carefully studied. Hence, before we can compare processes of mobility and their outcomes in different societies, we must first analyze these structural-dynamic variables. This means that the measurement of occupational mobility is only the first step in such study, and its full significance cannot be appraised if other aspects of mobility, indicated in preceding chapters, are not also taken into account.

The systematic analysis of mobility should deal with the relation between different causes of mobility, the problems and discrepancies that arise in relation to different types of social structure, and the effects of mobility on the behavior of mobile persons and on the institutional structure of the society. These problems appear both in historical and in modern societies, and it is only through their explication that studies of mobility can be put in the context of comparative institutional analysis.

NOTES

1. See S. M. Miller, "Comparative Social Mobility," *Current Sociology*, Vol. IX, No. 1, 1960, pp. 1–89.

2. R. M. Marsh, *The Mandarins, The Circulation of Elites in China, 1600–1900*, New York: The Free Press of Glencoe, 1961, Chapter XII, 300 pp.; Ping-ti-Ho, *The Ladder of Success in Imperial China, Aspects of Social Mobility 1368–1911*, New York: Columbia University Press, 1963.

3. Already the work of des Rotours on the military government under the Tang—taken up later by Pulleyblank—has indicated this important fact. See R. des Rotours, "Les grands fonctionnaires des provinces en Chine sous la dynastie des Tang," *Toung Pao*, XXIV, 1926, pp. 219–315; E. G. Pulleyblank, *The Background of the Rebellion on An Lu-shan*, London: Oxford University Press, 1955.

4. See R. H. Turner, "Sponsored and Contest Mobility and the School System," *American Sociological Review*, Vol. XXV, No. 5, 1960.

5. M. Bloch, *La Société Féodale*, Paris: Albin Michel, 1939, p. 40.

6. E. W. Hofstee, "Agriculture and Rural Life in an Industrializing Society," *Transactions of the Fourth World Congress of Sociology, Milan and Stresa, 1959*, London: International Sociological Association, Vol. II, 1959, pp. 13–28.

Chapter *II*

Social Mobility and Intergroup Leadership

The Problem

The purpose of this paper is to discuss several repercussions of processes of mobility on the social structure in which these processes take
place and especially the integrative or disintegrative effects which they
have on this structure. It was thought that an important starting point
for such a discussion might be the analysis of the relationship between
mobility of individuals or groups and their meeting with other groups
within that society, and the place that various leaders hold within that
process. In other words, we shall focus the analysis on the problem of
the extent that mobility creates intergroup solidarity or tensions and
on the main bearers of the values and transmitters of the attitudes
which arise through these processes.

The discussion presented in this paper is based mostly on several
researches of the Research Seminar in Sociology of the Hebrew University on the absorption of new immigrants in Israel, and especially
on problems of leadership and communication among these new immigrants (1). Thus the discussion may prove to be of somewhat limited application owing to this special setting. It should be remem-
bered, however, that most of the new immigrant population in Israel

Reprinted from *Transactions of the Second World Congress of Sociology*, Vol.
II, 1953.

may be viewed as constituting, during the first period of absorption, a lower stratum within Israeli society.

We shall not reproduce here in any great detail the various findings of these researches—which have been and are being published in detailed reports—but shall dwell only on the main problems arising from them and their general theoretical indications. We shall discuss first the general theoretical framework of the inquiry, and then briefly present theoretical indications. It should be emphasized that some of these findings are necessarily tentative, and will have to be retested in different settings and under more "normal" conditions than exist among immigrants in Israel.

The existence of some special conditions in Israel has greatly influenced the nature of our report, which differs in some significant characteristics from other reports on mobility. We have not dealt with general statistics of occupational mobility—for the simple reason that, for many, perhaps most, of the new immigrants, there existed rather scarce opportunities of such mobility, and the whole economic situation was not stabilized. Only a few select groups of immigrants could be mobile. But at the same time it was found that this unique situation of a total social structure in constant flux provided an opportunity for a study of a somewhat different type. Instead of analyzing only mobility within a given, more or less fixed, institutional setting, it is possible to investigate here more general components of the process of mobility, on a higher level of abstraction. This investigation has, of course, its dangers of oversimplification and lack of concreteness, and all the findings should then be tested in more concrete and specific settings—in Israel and in other countries—according to the problems set out at the end of this chapter. But it seemed worthwhile to combine a concrete study with the more abstract approach, because of the unique opportunities afforded by our situation.

Mobility is the transition of an individual (or group) from one position within the social system to another, and usually from one group or stratum to another. This transition usually entails the attainment of new goals which are beyond the source of the group(s) of origin of the mobile individual. The aspiration to these goals implies the setting-up of new reference standards and groups. These standards both define the new goals, etc., and necessitate a revaluation of the attitude toward the group of origin (membership group). This revaluation is made both in terms of the instrumentality of the groups to the attainment of the new goals and in terms of the possibility of continued basic identification with these groups.

The transition from one position to another and the revaluation incident on this transition necessarily affect the individual's normative expectations and identification with society as a whole. It has become a commonplace of recent sociological research that membership in a group and identification with it constitute an important determinant of social behavior and sources of personal stability. Any change of such membership and identification poses to an individual important problems of social and personal adjustment and of placement within the social structure. Moreover, it has been shown that an individual's identification with the total society to which he belongs is to a very great extent mediated by his various membership and reference groups. Therefore any change in this membership and its evaluation affects not only his "objective" position within society but also his identification with it, his feeling of belongingness, and so on.

Thus the process of mobility is of great importance both from the point of view of the individual's personality integration (as already clearly shown in Durkheim's analysis of anomic suicide) and from the point of view of the integration of the social system as such. The direct relevance of the process of mobility to the latter problem can easily be understood from the fact that mobility usually entails the redistribution of power within the society and thus may also have wide repercussions on the upholding of the norms which regulate this distribution within a society and which may give rise to various types of deviant behavior through sharpening of the competition for power (2).

The intensification of the problem of adherence to institutional norms can best be understood from one point of view of the intensification of intergroup contacts through the process of mobility. Mobility necessarily entails the intensification of contacts between various kinds of groups which were previously to some extent separated from each other. These "meetings" may take place in several ways. First, it may occur through the total merging of one group with another. Second, it may take place through some individuals' performing roles in the different (formerly separated) groups, thus becoming a "bridge" between them. Third, it may take place through competition between different groups over various values and facilities within the social system. Obviously these three ways need not necessarily be concretely distinct from one another, and they may only constitute different analytical aspects of the same actual process. Whatever the actual form of contacts between the groups, these meetings obviously necessitate the establishment of some sort of communication between groups in the main spheres of social interaction—in the distribution of instrumental goals, in the field of solidary relations, and in the mutual communication and understanding of the various patterns of life, or "cultures," of the groups. From all these points of view the necessity arises to uphold the norms regulating the distribution of various facilities and rewards and to transmit and maintain the main value orientations of these groups and of the society as a whole.

Thus it may be stated that the process of mobility involves some "disturbance" of the existing social equilibrium; that it makes necessary various mechanisms of adjustment, of re-equilibrization in the various fields of social interaction; that this re-equilibrization takes place mainly through the upholding of norms and the transmission of the value orientations of the society. However, the problem is, who are these transmitters and upholders?

It is here that the problem of intergroup leadership within the process of mobility becomes important. As is well known from many researches, within almost every group there exist special channels of communication in the form of various leaders who hold key positions within the group, organize its activities, and symbolize its values. Even more important than these "internal" and perhaps rather informal leaders are those leaders whose positions of leadership in regard to certain groups are institutionalized within the social structure —the so-called "elites" of various kinds and types and of different levels of importance. It seems that such persons perform mainly two kinds of functions in regard to the various groups led by them: first they help their groups resolve various role conflicts which may occur through the necessity of acting within relatively unknown spheres and/or through conflicts of orientations and interests, and, second, they may also (although sometimes these two functions may be performed by different sets of individuals) transmit the main values and symbols of identification of the society. In a general way it may be stated that it is through the activities of these elite persons that the various levels of consensus are upheld within a society. Their importance necessarily increases during a period of mobility. But there is a more intimate relation between these activities and the processes of mobility. These processes may—both through their general transplantation of persons from position to position and through their intensification of interpersonal and intergroup contacts within a society—give rise to new leaders and elites, who would then, in their turn, affect intergroup relations. We therefore have the problems of the extent that the process of mobility gives rise to the emergence of new leaders and elites, and the functions they perform in regard to integration and stability of the society—especially from the point of view of intergroup relations incident on the process of mobility.

On the basis of these general considerations we may now state in greater detail the specific problems which we shall attempt to discuss. First is the problem of the effects of mobility on the integration of the society, i.e., on the upholding of the main institutional norms of the society and of identification with its main values. Under what conditions does mobility have integrative or disintegrative effects, especially from the point of view of intergroup relations? Second, we must ask to what extent the process of mobility gives rise to the emergence of new elites and leaders, or to what extent mobile individuals tend to perform various leadership functions in relation to their groups of origin. Third, what is the effect of these leaders and the various patterns of their leadership activities on the integration of the social system? Here the same questions that have been asked in regard to mobility are repeated, but are focused on problems of leadership emergence.

As has already been indicated, our discussion will be based mainly on the analysis of mobility and leadership processes among new immigrants in Israel; for this reason it suffers from some limitations. Our conclusions will necessarily have to be reinterpreted when applied to other "stabler" and more fully integrated societies. Moreover, we shall deal here only with one general type of mobility—namely, upward mobility—and shall not touch on downward mobility, which has received some attention in other literature (3).

General Mobility Processes

Our previous discussion has already implicitly distinguished between two types of mobility, from the point of view of the relation between the mobile individuals (or subgroup) and the group of origin. There are individuals who think that their new positions do not directly affect their old groups, i.e., that these positions do not entail the performance of any roles which constitute parts of the role clusters of these groups and which therefore do not necessitate any specific orientation. The mobile individual as such may continue to have various relations with his group, but his roles in the new position and group are, as it were, on different levels of social activity and existence. There are, on the other hand, individuals who think that there is such a relation, even a very specific one, between their new positions and their old groups. These are mostly people with aspirations toward some sort of elite position, to whom the new position seems to be related to the new group and to entail the exercise of roles within it—normally (because we are dealing here with upward mobility only) some roles of authority and leadership.

There may also be a somewhat intermediate type—found mostly among professional and semiprofessional people—that the process of mobility, although not involving the group directly, may bring into a position where the individual members would exercise some universal functions within the society (e.g., professional practice) that would bring their groups of origin within the orbit of their activities. From the point of view of the distribution of power incident on any process of mobility, in the first type the groups of origin are not directly involved in the redistribution, whereas in the second, as well as, to some extent, in the intermediary type, they are. We shall deal here with the first type of mobility and its repercussions on the integration of society. In all these discussions we shall, of course, have to distinguish clearly between the effects of mobility on (a) mobile individuals; (b) their groups of origin; (c) other groups within the social system.

What, then, are the repercussions of mobility on the conformist behavior of mobile individuals in their groups of origin? Our various investigations have until now disclosed that among the most important variables which determine this effect of mobility are the following: (a) the extent of compatibility between the mobile individual's evaluation of his powers of mobility and the evaluation of his membership group (of origin); (b) the extent to which the individual continues to maintain some solidary relations with his group of origin; (c) the extent of realizability of mobility aspirations from the point of view of acceptance and legitimization by the new groups; (d) the type of mutual evaluation existing between the groups of origin and the groups of destination of the mobile individual.

Our investigations have not rendered all the possible combinations of these variables, and therefore we shall dwell on only some of them. First, it has been shown of mobilization that the maximization of the positive effects of mobility is very largely dependent on the first variable—compatibility between the mobile individual's evaluation of his mobility aspirations and the evaluation of his group of origin. If such compatibility does not exist, i.e., if the individual does not want to implicate his group in his mobility, or the group does want to be implicated, or vice versa, or if the group evaluates the mobility of the individual negatively or the individual sees his group as an important impediment to his mobility—there seem to arise various types of deviant tendencies with disintegrative effects on the society. They may take several forms, such as development of aggressive tendencies and patterns of behavior on the part of both the individual and the group in relation to each other and to other groups of the society, or a general tendency toward regression in social participation and apathy toward the central values of the society on the part of the group. Although it is obvious that this variable will have to be broken up into several components before these various effects can be studied systematically, it seems even at this stage that, insofar as the mobile individual does not involve his group in his mobility, the effects of such lack of compatibility are mostly in the direction of aggressive tendencies on the part of the mobile individual and of regression and apathy on the part of the group, connected with free-floating, diffuse aggressiveness. However, there are almost no cases of organized, uninstitutional activity on the part of the groups.

Insofar as there exists such a basic compatibility between the evaluations of the group and the individual, other conditions being equal, the general effect of mobility on the group is positive, intensifying the group's general positive identification within the social system and, *in special cases*, strengthening or maintaining "conformist" tendencies in regard to various norms.

One thing that has become clear through the researches is that it is not the purely "intellectual" compatibility (or incompatibility) of evaluation that is so important in determining the effects of mobility, but mostly the extent to which this (in-) compatibility makes possible the maintenance of some solidary relations with the group of origin. Insofar as this is possible, despite differences of opinion and evaluation, the effects of deviant tendencies are not strongly discernible. When the maintenance of such solidary relations becomes impossible, these effects are maximized. In these cases discontinuity arises within the various solidary fields of the individual, enhancing his emotional-personal insecurity, giving rise to various phenomena of personality maladjustment, and at the same time usually having negative effects on the groups of origin. The groups are deprived of channels through which they may extend their solidarity orientation toward the wider social system and toward other groups. This enhances both regressive tendencies and diffuse deviant orientation, especially in relation to other groups which seem to have monopolized various facilities, such as the activities of their members.

But even in the case of maintenance of solidary relations between mobile individuals and their groups of origin, the picture is rather complicated, and the potential positive results not always fully realized. As we have already indicated, there is usually a general intensification of positive identification with the total society, mainly through vicarious sharing of the "glory" of the mobile persons and of the society which makes possible such success. Within the field of social participation, orientation on central values of the society, and so forth, the results, however, depend on the extent of the mobile individual's participation in his old group. Insofar as the mobile individual continues to participate in some way in his group of origin, the general effect is positive from the point of view of identification and of acceptance of the main norms of the society. The very existence of such individuals, with their visible proof of success, tends to emphasize the possibilities of the absorbing society and the value of accepting its main norms—especially, perhaps, within the instrumental field.

The effect from the point of view of the extensive social participation of the group of origin is different, however, and depends mainly on the *extent* of the mobile individual's participation within this group. If this participation continues to be more or less integrated in the structure of the group, in its solidary and expressive structure, the mobile individuals can well serve both as transmitters of the social values of the absorbing society and as channels for the extension of the solidarity and expressive integration of the group to the whole absorbing society. However, if their attachment to their groups of origin is of only a very superficial nature—visits, vague friendly relations, etc., without the performance of any definite roles in relation to these groups (such as professional advice, opinion leadership in some sphere)—it seems that they may have a somewhat negative effect on their groups' extent of participation. The groups seem to lose in this way some of their channels of communication to the wider society and its values, and very important gaps in the communicative hierarchy of these groups may occur. Such a possibility is inherent in general in the process of mobility and disattachment of certain individuals from their groups of origin. The groups may, because of this, lack adequate means for dealing with various tasks, problems, and role conflicts, which otherwise might have helped them. Here the problem of extension of solidarity and expressive pattern of these groups and their integration within the total society becomes more articulated and acute.

This possibility of creation of communicative gaps between the groups of origin of the mobile individuals and the total society is not, however, confined only to the scope of social participation and orientation to the central values of the society. It may also give rise to various potential deviant patterns of behavior—owing to the unavailability of models and guides for the solution of various role conflicts—which may arise when some relations with the distant sectors of the society (e.g., in political behavior) have to be maintained. It is from this point of view that the importance of the intermediate type of mobile persons is crucial. As we have seen, these are individuals who, although their new position is not necessarily interwoven in the structure of their old groups, nevertheless perform some universal functions which their groups of origin may enter. The best examples in this direction are professional or semiprofessional people—lawyers, teachers, doctors, and others. Some of them may just be simple mobile individuals. Some, however, may prefer to, or happen to, perform their professional functions (also or mainly) among their groups of origin. Whatever researches exist on this point indicate that in such cases the communicative gap between these groups and the total society is minimized, and that the mobile individuals perform, in addition to their professional activities, some functions of diffuse leadership and orientation, although only in a very general, nonformalized way. As has already been mentioned, such a pattern of activity is not necessarily confined to professional people, but it seems to be more prevalent among them. Although in none of these cases does any specific inter-group leadership or organization exist, the general effect of this type of activity is to mitigate potential intergroup tensions and to mediate more or less successfully in cases of conflict.

The discussion has hitherto been focused on relations between the mobile individual and his group of origin. Of equal importance, of course, is the extent of success of mobility aspirations. Their success may be mitigated in a variety of interconnected ways, among which two seem to be most prevalent. The first is a sharpening of competi-tion for power and facilities, because of aspiration to monopolization on the part of other groups and/or because of general scarcity of given facilities within a society. The second is the limitation of suc-cessful mobility to the purely instrumental, economic phase, with a lack of parallel acceptance in solidary spheres of interaction (e.g., non-acceptance within new primary groups). Obviously, the effect of these conditions tends to be negative from the point of view of either the mobile individual or the society. It seems that in most of these cases some sort of disintegrative pattern of behavior emerges, but the exact type of such behavior differs according to other conditions. Insofar as the mobile individual does not maintain any solidary relations with his group of origin and is also barred from such relations in his group of aspiration, it seems that the effect is usually expressed in some form of personality disorganization, such as apathy, drunkenness, or disor-ganized aggression. The effect is different when some sort of solidary relations are maintained with the groups of origin. Then the general outcome usually may be in two interconnected directions. First, vari-ous types of particularistic, separatist symbols of group identification may emerge among mobile individuals and then be transferred to their groups of origin. The mobile individuals may endeavor to or-ganize their groups on such a basis, meanwhile strengthening aggres-sive tendencies toward other groups. Whatever their degree of success in such endeavors—and this depends largely on the extent of their participation in the groups of origin—they obviously tend in this way to break down effective communication between their groups and others in the society, and to block the transmission of solidary orientations and identifications. Side by side with this they may also foster various deviant tendencies and patterns of behavior. This is the second possible outcome of the locking of mobility aspirations. It refers mainly to the upholding of various institutional norms regulating the allocation of facilities, and so on. Insofar as mobility gives rise to sharpened competition over scarce goods and intensification of power orientations, it necessarily undermines legitimate norms and tends to create wider fields of sheer power competition. Such power orientation may then be transferred from the mobile individuals to their groups of origin. The two—particularistic group organization and identification and sharpened power orientation—may, of course, be strongly connected in reality.

These analyses—tentative and somewhat limited in their application as they are—already provide us with some clues as to the components of the process of mobility which are of greatest importance from the point of view of our general discussion. The process of mobility and the attainment of new positions necessarily changed the position of an individual or a group in relation to other individuals and groups of the society. This change may take place both from the point of view of the intensity of relations and contacts between them and from the point of view of the sphere of social relations in which these relations are found. Thus two groups which were, before the process of mobility, in purely adaptive relations to each other may become connected in the sphere of instrumental goals, in solidary relations, and so forth. Thus not only is there a necessity for upholding the general norms regulating all kinds or relations within the society, but certain types of relations may become more problematic than others and necessities may arise for readjustments on several levels. Our analysis has indicated one very important condition of such a successful readjustment—namely the maintenance of some sort of solidarity between (a) the groups of origin, (b) the mobile individuals (or groups), and (c) the "absorbing" groups, or positions. Only if there exists or develops some such continuity can the various adjustments be attempted. From the point of view of the individual, the maintenance of such continuity ensures him some emotional stability and possibility of stable reorientation within the social system. From the point of view of the integration of the social structure, such continuity (a) ensures the minimization of normless competition for

power and positions, (b) makes possible the maintenance of solidarity within the total society, and thus (c) makes possible readjustment of the relations between different groups within various spheres
of the society.

It is not as yet possible for us to indicate the precise *systematic* conditions under which such overflow of solidarity occurs. This would
necessitate a very detailed comparative analysis of different types of
historical and contemporary societies and developments. We have
only attempted to indicate some of the directions in which such an
analysis may be attempted.

Leadership Mobility

Emphasis on the maintenance of continuity of solidarity throughout
the process of transition necessarily brings us back to the second problem under discussion, namely that of mobility which involves group
leadership and attainment of elite positions. The close relationship between the two can easily be understood from the functions of elites
and leaders in regard to the solution of conflicts of roles and in the
transmission of main social values. We have seen that the process of
mobility may give rise to a communicative gap between different
spheres of society and thus disrupt the continuity of solidarity. It is in
this context that the importance of leaders becomes specially articulated, as only they can close such a gap. We may now turn to the analysis of the different types of leaders which arise in the process of mobility and their effect on the integration of the society.

The distinct characteristic of the mobile leader is that he aspires to a
position of prestige and authority within the total society, which
would, however, be largely exercised (also) in his group of origin.
Mostly it is an aspiration to some sort of elite or subelite position in
the political, cultural, or economic field which would (a) be legiti-
mized in terms of the values of the whole society, and (b) place him
in some definite role in relation to his group of origin. Thus he tends
to fulfill active functions of transmission of values and of direction of
activities of his group of origin, and not only—as in the case of purely
mobile persons—to have an indirect effect on it. It is through this
mediation that his group of origin comes into active contact with other

groups, and it is through his activities and direction that the readjustment of intergroup relations takes place.

What, then, are the main types of such leadership, and what are their effects on society? In general it may be said that the same main variables which were found to be important in the general process of mobility are also decisive here, although obviously their effect is much more intensive because of the direct relations between mobile leaders and the various social groups in which they are active. In addition, however, there are some specific variables which are extremely important in this situation. The first of these variables is the exact nature of the power relations between the leader and the group. Unlike the former cases, it is not only general compatibility of evaluations, and so on, that are important here, but also the fact that the group is directly interested in the power redistribution incident on the mobility of its leader. The problem here is the extent to which the group shares in the new attainments of the leader, and the extent to which the leader, through his elite position, directs some new rewards toward the group. From this point of view we may distinguish, in a general way, between two main "ideal" types: the democratic and the authoritarian mobile leader.

The democratic type may be defined by the following characteristics: (a) strong positive identification with the group of origin; (b) wants to serve the group in the new situation and sees himself as a representative to help the group in its relations with the "outside"; (c) wants to be accepted by the group and does not want to force himself on it; (d) aspires to transmit new values—but only in a peaceful way; (e) does not want to exploit or to use it directly as a means of personal aggrandizement (although in reality he may of course be helped by it).

The authoritarian type is characterized by the following (a) has a negative attitude toward the values and members of the group of origin (although is usually connected to it with a very strong emotional attachment); (b) wants to force the values of the new society on it and demands obedience and power in terms of his holding of these values; (c) aspires to a strong authority position within the group and sees the group as a channel of self-aggrandizement (e.g., by procuring votes).

It can be seen that the distinction between these two types of leaders includes, in addition to the pure authoritarian or democratic attitude, different evaluations of the relation between groups of origin and various reference groups and thus touches directly on their functions of mediation, solution of role conflicts, and transmission of values.

The effects of these two types of leaders on their groups of origin are, of course, quite distinct. Authoritarian leaders usually give rise to a negative attitude toward the values of the society, and to passive or active opposition. Their authority is not usually willingly accepted, and, whenever it is forced upon the groups, evasions and rebellions ensue. The group usually feels that these leaders adversely affect its economic, political, etc., positions, and that they use the group for their own ends. The ramifications of this are, however, wider than mere opposition between the individual and the group. As a result there develops, at first, a very sharp power orientation on the part of the people themselves. They, in turn, also try to exploit the leaders in purely utilitarian and power terms, without much regard to various norms regulating such relations. Thus the strong power emphasis of the mobile individuals gives rise to a cumulative series of deviant activities and to the development of anomic fields.

Second, this alienation of the leaders from the groups also gives rise to a very widespread apathy within these groups toward the central values of the society. Sometimes this leads to outright negative identification with the new country, but more often it leads to sheer apathy and lack of interest in these central values and relations. Thus the groups' social field becomes, on the one hand, disorganized, while, on the other hand, it shrinks to a very large extent. Consequently their activities and roles do not become fully institutionalized within the new social structure. In some cases there also arise personal apathy and disorganization, particularly in cases of direct clashes with officials.

The situation among groups of democratic leaders is entirely different. These leaders are usually willingly accepted by the groups, and their authority is more or less fully legitimated. Their success in attaining new goals is approved by the groups, which hope to share in it. Consequently they also become good mediators of the central values of the social system and enhance both the positive identification of the group with these values and the group's participation within the

various social spheres (political, cultural, etc.). In these cases the redistribution of rewards, power, and authority is more or less fully
accepted by the group, which participates in the process.

But, in addition to these more or less direct effects on the groups of
origin, the two types of leaders also have very important effects on
the extent of intergroup tensions in the society. Both types of leaders
assume some roles in their groups of origin as well as in some new
groups. Insofar as these different roles are compatible with one another (a problem which we shall discuss presently), the democratic
leader tends, through cooperation with similar leaders of other
groups, to mitigate various tensions and to help solve potential conflicts. The authoritarian leader usually tends to sharpen such tensions,
mainly through emphasis on the inferiority of the group of origin
and through accentuation of any potential power orientation in the superior group. However, if he is accepted within the "superior" group,
these tensions do not become organized into any formal patterns.

The second additional variable which is specific to the mobile leader
involves his potential power relations with other elite groups within
the society. The problem of his acceptability within the aspired group
is, on the whole, not different from that of any mobile person, although it is accentuated in these cases. But, in addition, his elite aspirations and the performance of new types of leadership functions in
relation to his group of origin necessarily bring him into direct power
relations with other elite groups of the society. In connection with this
there may arise two different, although clearly interconnected, problems. First, there may arise an overall nonacceptance, discrimination,
and monopolization of power positions against the new aspirants.
Second, there may arise incompatibilities in patterns and orientations
of leadership activities, e.g., lack of understanding of the different
norms regulating solidary and instrumental relations, attempts to
substitute one for another and to exercise the leadership function in a
clearly noninstitutional way. This second possibility becomes more
acute when mobility is connected with processes of culture contact
(e.g., among immigrants), but it may also arise in "normal" societies,
for instance, in cases of rural-urban migrations. In all these cases the
effects of mobility are clearly disintegrative and maximize intergroup
tensions and conflicts. Instead of being enabled to perform functions
of intergroup mediation, the potential leaders are barred from full

participation in some groups and necessarily evolve negative attitudes toward them. Their effect on their groups of origin may be in several directions: first, regression and apathy, second and, it seems, more frequently, active organization of more or less militant groups and activities oriented against the general society, its norms and values. In this case intergroup tensions become much more organized and even tend to acquire distinct symbols and ideologies of their own. We are not as yet in the position to indicate clearly the differences, in such cases, between the activities of the "authoritarian" and the "democratic" types of leadership, although there are some indications that the authoritarian leader tends to organize more aggressive and less cohesive groups and activities.

In comparison with the general process of mobility, we find in the case of elite mobility both an intensification of the possibilities inherent in mobility as such and a growth in the scope of organization of activities, in the development of group symbols, and in the incipient development not only of intergroup tensions but also of interelite competition and struggle for power.

It should be obvious that our tentative discussion has only indicated, on the basis of material taken from a particular setting, *some* of the problems connected with social mobility. It is hoped that this discussion has indicated some ways in which mobility is connected with processes of social change, and that the testing of these indications in wider settings will provide us with more systematic knowledge about the different levels of integration of societies.

In addition, the main variables which have been discussed here should be broken up and analyzed in a more systematic way than that attempted here. Finally, it should also be worthwhile to indicate some additional, unexplored problems which are raised by our analysis: first, the various institutional conditions and developments—economic, political, etc.—which give rise to the various types of mobility should be systematically investigated. Second, the same holds true for the dynamic psychological processes which give rise to various types of mobility aspirations. Third, a field almost entirely neglected by our analysis is that of various types of ideologies emerging in connection with these processes. Fourth, the problem of elite formation and cohesion in relation to mobility should also be analyzed.

NOTES

1. See the general report on "Sociology in Israel, 1949–1952," *Transactions of The Second World Congress of Sociology, Liège, 1953,* London: International Sociological Association, Vol. I, 1954.

2. Even in societies in which the same type of limited mobility upholds the existing distribution of power, the mere *process* of mobility entails some changes from the point of view of individual and family power positions and may be a potential focus of anomie.

3. The best example of this is B. Bettelheim and M. Janowitz, *Dynamics of Prejudice,* New York: Harpers, 1950.

SECTION V

Communication and
Reference-Group Behavior

IN THIS, the last section of these essays, we deal almost exclusively with the analysis of some of the processes in which personal behavior and attitudes become interwoven with and affect the process of institutionalization and the crystallization of formal institutional settings.

All the essays in this section are based on the analysis of various aspects of immigrant behavior in Israel—but they serve as starting points for more general and comparative analysis. They deal with the processes of communication and reference-group behavior as they have been encountered in different situations among immigrants in Israel—that is, in a situation in which it was possible, even if in a partial way, to relate various aspects of these processes to the undertaking by individuals of different institutional roles and to their participation in various institutional settings, and to analyze the impact of these processes on institutional change.

The essay (Chapter 13) on "Communication Systems and Social Structure: an Exploratory Comparative Study," reports on a research which attempted to elucidate the place of reference orientations and the processes of communication to individuals' behavior in their social setting and in the broader institutional frameworks of the society. It was found that these processes and orientations serve as important mechanisms of social control which, however "informal" and "random" they may appear, often are fully structured or, at least, closely related to specific structural positions and situations within the institutional spheres of the society. The various processes of communication constitute one of the ways through which various norms of exchange, precontractual symbols, and contractual orientations are transmitted in the society.

At the same time it was found that the success of these communicative activities is not derived from the mere establishment of their structural characteristics but is dependent on some aspects of the interrelationship between the individuals placed in them. The self- and status image of the individuals may play a crucial role in influencing the effective institutionalization of communicative activities.

The possibility of failure or of the lack of success in institutionalization of communicative activities and the lack of development of communicative receptivity have been stressed throughout this essay. In this way the general theoretical point made in the first essay in this book—namely that the mere development of the "needs" of individuals and of society—does not in itself ensure the crystallization of new viable institutional settings.

Some institutional outcomes of different types of reference-group orientations of individuals in various institutional settings are analyzed in the essay (Chapter 14) on "Reference Group Behavior and Social Integration." This essay brings together materials from different researches in Israel.

The last essay also brings together these analytical orientations in a comparative study based on different types of immigrant communities in Israel—"traditional," "semitraditional," and "modern." It analyzes the different ways in which the processes of communication and reference-group behavior are structured in different societal settings, and it shows that even the extent of formalization of communicative situations, roles, and behavior is closely related to these "structural" characteristics. This analysis relates these different patterns of communication and reference-group behavior to processes of change as they have been taking place among the previously mentioned communities. It attempts to specify the conditions which facilitate or impede the successful adaptation of various groups and communities to new patterns of communication and especially to specify the extent to which such success—or lack of it—is due to "structural" similarities between the "preceding" and the new societies or to some more "behavioral" or attitudinal dimensions which may cut across such varying structural characteristics.

The general conclusions of the analyses presented in these essays may serve as starting points for the systematic exploration of the relation of processes of communication and reference-group behavior to processes of institutionalization and to comparative analysis of institutions. They point out the crucial importance of processes of communication and reference-group behavior in the crystallization and transmission of different types of symbols and norms—symbols of basic desiderata of human existence, of collective and personal identity, of the basic precontractual norms, and of different norms of exchange—which are crucial in processes of institutionalization.

They indicate also that these norms are transmitted in definite social situations and by people in definite structural positions—but that the concrete organization of these positions and of the interrelation of these various norms varies greatly in different societies, according to some systematic criteria which are explored in these essays.

Last, they also emphasize that such situations and positions in which various symbols and norms are transmitted are not always given or fixed, that they themselves are subject to processes of institutionalization, and that under some conditions they may fail to become fully or adequately institutionalized.

Chapter 12

Communications and Reference-Group Behavior

The Problem and the Research

The purpose of this chapter is to analyze certain problems related to the fields of reference group behavior and of communication, whose importance has grown and been recognized in the recent past in both sociological and psychological research. It is hoped that the analysis presented will advance the coordination of work on reference-group behavior with studies of communication and with systematic sociological theory in general. This analysis is a preliminary step in a wider work, the purpose of which is to present a systematic theory of this field.

The Problem

Before presenting our data it would be useful to state, in a very general way, what kinds of problems related to reference-group behavior struck us as requiring a more specific and systematic investigation.

This chapter is based partly on an article "Studies in Reference Group Behavior, I. Reference Norms and Social Structure," published in *Human Relations*, Vol. VII, No. 2, 1954, and partly on new materials.

In most of the available literature, the importance of reference groups as determinants of an individual's behavior, attitudes, opinions, and beliefs has been emphasized. It has been shown that an individual may identify himself with various groups to which he may not belong, and with a variety of group norms, and that he may strive to enter into these groups (1). Such identifications and aspirations influence his behavior, his attitudes toward other people, his evaluations of himself, and his own role and position as well as those of others. The analysis of the data on the *American Soldier* by Merton and Kitt, has shown the importance of such reference orientations and groups in a great variety of situations, in influencing, for instance, an individual's level of aspiration and satisfaction and his standards of comparison (2). Out of this analysis some very pertinent questions for further research have arisen. What are the individual's determinants of choice of a given reference group? What are the various types of relationship between membership and reference groups, among others?

It seems to us, however, that a somewhat different approach to the whole problem of reference groups might be attempted. While our approach probably denotes only a change of emphasis in the posing of certain problems, we felt that it might lead to their greater elucidation.

Instead of asking at the beginning what are the ways in which reference groups influence an individual's behavior, we could ask why such an orientation is necessary at all from the point of view both of a given social system and of the individual's personality. What are the functions which such orientation fulfills in the social life space of an individual and in his participation in the society of which he is a member?

Our main interest, then, is in finding out to what extent and in what ways orientations to reference groups constitute a part of the social structure, and what functions they fulfill in it. The analysis presented will attempt to specify the social situations in which such orientations are evoked and the social roles through which they are maintained. This analysis will relate this problem to the processes of communication in society. It will be shown that the maintenance of such orientations to reference groups and group norms is one of the important mechanisms of social control, and that it is closely connected with the exercise of leadership and authority, and with the processes of communication in a society. On the basis of such systematic analysis of this problem, it is easier, we hope, to understand the numerous concrete ways in which orientation to reference groups can influence an individual's behavior (3).

The Research

We shall now introduce our main research data and findings. We shall present them in a rather summary way, dealing only with those aspects and problems which seem to be of greatest interest at the present stage of discussion.

The general importance of the problems of reference groups was recognized in the first studies on absorption of immigrants in Israel, undertaken by the Research Seminar in Sociology of the Hebrew University (4). It was shown there that only insofar as various groups of immigrants develop orientations and references to various norms, institutions, and groups of the absorbing society—beyond the various actual roles that they have to perform in their various membership groups—can we speak of absorption and institutionalization of immigrant behavior. These were, however, rather general orientations, and it is only through a series of later studies and researches that the problem was systematically tackled. Some preliminary aspects of these studies have already been reported (5), but only now can we present a full report on those first systematic investigations.

These investigations were undertaken in a number of different immigrant settlements of various types (agricultural cooperatives, urban, and semiurban quarters, and so forth) in which both the institutional structure and a sample of the inhabitants were studied, and in selected samples of special "types" of immigrants—leaders of different types (communal, political, educational) and generally "mobile" persons, i.e., persons with a strong mobility orientation. The studies were made by a combination of participant observation, open-ended, and "focused" interviews, and closed questionnaires, which were used interchangeably according to the specific situation. These investigations served as a first step in a more broadly based research project which is now under way (6). At the same time it was possible to use several other research projects of the Research Seminar, such as those on youth movements, immigrant youth, and social participation (7), for elucidation of several problems connected with this.

The research presented here is based on analysis of 400 cases, of which 250 were random samples of five different settlements and urban quarters, and 150 samples of leaders and mobile persons from these settlements and from various special courses for community leaders and such.

The Nature and Different Types of Reference Orientations

The first step toward ascertaining the place of reference groups in the social structure was to see what are the main types of orientation to reference groups. An answer to this could be found in the responses to questions included in the interview and observation schedules such as "Are you satisfied or otherwise with your present job, social relations, etc., and why?" "What is good, or bad, about them?" "Why is it good or bad?" "How would you like to have it?" "Why would you like it that way?" "What do you consider to be proper standards for it?" (8)

The first important finding was that when talking of reference groups, as our basic analytical concept, we might be guilty of reifications. This has already been alluded to in the literature, when it was emphasized that a reference group is a group with whose norms we identify ourselves (9). In all our interviews it became apparent that it is this norm (or, perhaps, in a broader sense, "value") that serves most as the frame of reference toward which an individual seeks to orient himself, and that only in some specific situations is such a norm tied to a concrete group.

In order to be able to understand this process of reference orientation, it is necessary to analyze some of the more important common characteristics of such norms and frames of reference. These, on the basis of the material available, seem to be the following:

1. All such norms contain a general evaluative element, i.e., they are general standards according to which various patterns of behavior are evaluated. They may be said to transcend any given concrete act of behavior.

2. Despite their generality, these norms are, at the same time, re-

lated to and specifically focused on various clusters of roles. Hence they may be said to bring these roles into a wider context of reference.

3. This wider context does very often, although not always (in fact, in about 70 per cent of our cases), contain some elements of collectivity orientation, i.e., some evaluation in terms of behavior and participation in a given collectivity, not necessarily a concrete group, but more often—at least in our cases—a "total society" or some major subdivision of it.

The following two excerpts from interviews can well illustrate these points:

I think it is not proper to behave in such a way in this settlement. One should participate in its affairs and behave like a good worker. Otherwise, you are not really a member of this settlement, or even of the *Yishuv* at all; you are outside it . . .

It is not Jewish not to help one's neighbour, even if you do not know him. We Jews always helped each other, but here it is sometimes different, and I do not know what we are becoming.

4. These norms were usually (in about 90 per cent of the cases) perceived as prescribing the proper types of behavior in the roles and situations to which they were referring.

5. These norms usually served also as principles of perceptual organization of the social field for the individual, i.e., with their aid various social objects could be perceived in some organized way, for instance, as conforming with given norms or deviating from them, as exemplifying certain values. A good example of this may be found in the following excerpts from an interview.

When I know how one should behave, what is the accepted way here, I begin also to understand people, to know who is doing what . . . everything becomes clearer. But otherwise I am very confused; everything is rather blurred.

It seems to us that these general characteristics of reference norms are not limited only to our research, or necessarily influenced by the types of questions asked in it. Perusal of the "raw materials" of other studies of this subject, especially Newcomb's fully documented Bennington study and several studies on communication (10), indicates that most of these characteristics exist elsewhere as well, and may therefore be assumed, at least in a hypothetical way, as more or less universal attributes of reference norms.

Beyond these common characteristics, the various reference norms may be differentiated according to the kind of roles and situations to which they refer and according to the kind of normative imperatives which they prescribe to these roles. The analysis of our material showed the following main types of such norms. [Although they seem to cover the main types of institutional roles (11), it is not claimed, however, that they are the only possible norms, and it is hoped that additional work will enable a wider differentiation to be made.]

1. General norms which seem to apply to almost any kind of roles and situations and which indicate only a very general prescription of behavior, such as "good-bad" behavior, "honest-dishonest." They are not specifically related to any particular role and can be seen as applicable throughout a great variety of concrete forms of behavior.

2. General norms which indicate the type of behavior or attitude appropriate to all members of a collectivity, and which indicate also a general type of identification with such a collectivity. A good example can be seen in the excerpts from the interview quoted earlier about the "mutual help" obligations of Jews. These norms are also of a rather broad application. They do not prescribe any definite single role, but they are already clearly oriented toward a definite, even if rather wide, social setting. They may be said to prescribe the universal conditions of membership in a community.

3. Norms and values prescribing the types of behavior appropriate to certain broad categories of social roles (e.g., age, sex) or some of the major institutional frameworks and subgroups of the society (e.g., family life, economic or religious behavior). It is obvious that here there exist many possibilities according to the different institutional spheres and subgroups within a society.

4. Norms which prescribe behavior in what may be called ambiguous, potentially undefined (at least from the point of view of a given individual) situations. These norms usually define the solution to some conflict between various demands and expectations, and also some sort of hierarchy of values and preferences.

5. Norms which prescribe the possibilities of choice between various

roles in a given situation, and which prescribe the behavior appropriate in the process of choice and in the chosen role.

These were the most important types of reference norms that we encountered in our researches. While no claim is being made that this list is exhaustive, it is already sufficient to show us that there may exist at least two different types of orientations toward such wider norms, or two types of such norms and frames of reference. First, there are those norms which emphasize or delineate the proper way of behavior in a given concrete role or situation. They are, as it were, explicit formulations of the ultimate values which are implicit in any given social interaction. In other words, these norms give a wider, and not merely technical, meaning to the various roles, putting the roles in this way in the framework of wider value orientations and some sort of collectivity identification. They do not, however, relate these roles to any other specific roles, and they are firmly bound to a given concrete situation, which does not seem to be in any way problematic.

The second type of reference norms (4 and 5) seem to be of a somewhat different type, or to have at least an entirely different emphasis. They define solutions to problems, to potential conflicts (for the individual and within the society), and delineate the points and possibilities of choice. They usually deal not with a simple, unproblematic situation (or set of situations) but with several situations or roles which have to be arranged in some relation to one another. Thus the reference to wider norms, systems of values, and so forth is in this case not only a general indicator of proper behavior and attitude but also a regulator of potentially conflicting and complex modes of behavior. This difference between these two types of reference norms may be most clearly discerned in some of their internal characteristics. In the second type of norms there always exist, as already indicated, some sort of hierarchical arrangement of different roles, values, and attitudes. There is always an emphasis on the relative importance of some of these spheres of relations and roles, whereas in the first type there is usually a more simple, unequivocal emphasis on one norm of value which is given a somewhat absolute validity. The following excerpt from an interview is a good illustration of this point.

I was told that it is usually more important to perform the various civic duties than to help friends. Helping friends is also important, but not of

such great importance. Only if we shall all perform our duties to the settlement and the State, shall we and all our friends live in order and in peace.

These two different types of norms were mentioned and referred to
by most of the people interviewed. The first, simple type, was mentioned by about 90 per cent, and the second, the hierarchically complex one, by about 75 per cent.

Reference Orientations as Mechanisms of Social Control

This analysis, cursory as it may be, already shows us that these various frames of reference seem to fulfill an important function in the
individual's orientation to society. The reference to these norms relate
the various concrete roles which an individual performs to the
wider values and symbols of society. Since it is well known that the
maintenance of common ultimate values is an important prerequisite
of any society, it can be postulated that the reference to wider norms
constitutes a mechanism of social control, through which proper ways
of behavior and attitudes are maintained, whether in simple, unam-
biguous situations, or, in the second case, in potentially conflict-ridden
situations.

However, this only raises another problem—perhaps the most crucial one of our whole discussion. Namely, why and in what situations
does such reference-norm behavior develop? In what kinds of social
situations are these orientations evoked and maintained? Do there
exist any specific types of such situations, or are they fortuitously, randomly distributed throughout the social system?

The answers to these questions are not very simple for a variety of
reasons. Frist, it is necessary to remember that many of our data (as
well as those in many researches dealing with these questions) have
been collected through some type of questioning, which usually creates a new social situation. Hence it is necessary to be able to discount
this factor in the analysis of our data and rely sometimes more on systematic observations and open questions rather than on direct, structured questioning. Second—and this applies mainly to our data—we
have to distinguish between those situations which are the result of a
specific situation of immigration, culture change, and those situations

which may be assumed to exist in any stable society. We shall see that this distinction will also enable us to throw some very important light on the problem.

With these cautions in mind, we shall attempt to give an answer to these problems. The analysis of this material shows that these references to wider norms are evoked in special social and psychological situations, which can be defined from two different points of view. First, we may ask, how are they experienced and perceived by those who participate in them? Second, we may also ask whether there exist any specific characteristics which define the place of such situations in the social structure. A content analysis of interviews and observations reveals that the following seem to be the most important feelings and attitudes experienced by people in these situations.

There is the mere lack of knowledge about proper behavior and of understanding of the situation. This deficiency is not usually felt simply as a technical deficiency in perception or organization, but more often as a difficulty of ordering aims and goals into a meaningful pattern. The different goals become discrete, and to some extent disorganized. Thus it is that the possibility of conflict is often perceived by people in such situations.

Along with this we usually find a great deal of uncertainty and anxiety about establishing relations with other people. The individual feels that he faces undefined, unknown behavior on the part of other people and is not certain of being able to establish stable relations with them.

I do not know how to behave here . . . what is good or bad . . . I am always afraid what other people will think of me . . . whether they will think I am all right . . . whether I do what should be done . . . by them.

In other words, there may exist an anxiety about denial of reciprocity on the part of those with whom one may, or may have to, participate in these new, unstructured situations.

This anxiety is closely related to the fear of not attaining, or of losing, one's place in the collectivity or wider society of which one is a member, and which makes these demands. The collectivity may be an important subgroup of a society (ethnic group, social movement, and so forth), but usually there is some orientation toward the total society.

I do not feel that I am yet a member of the *Yishuv*, of the State, even of this town. It is so baffling; I do not know what to do; whether this is the way in which one becomes a part of the country here, or even a part of this factory I am working in.

In summarizing these various attitudes, it might be said that an individual feels in such situations some anxiety about his place and status within the community. Our material was not clinically oriented, and sometimes there is only rather indirect evidence, but there is usually some anxiety about the potential failure of the ego to intergrate and guide the personality. This is, of course, closely related to the problem of perceptual and moral organization which was mentioned earlier.

These various attitudes were usually quite closely interconnected. In about 60 per cent they always went together, while in 80–85 per cent of the cases at least three out of the four were linked.

The Place of Situations in Which Reference Orientations Are Evoked in the Social Structure

The foregoing discussion has shown us the psycho-sociological meaning of certain situations for those who participate in them. It has shown that we deal here not with accidental or extreme individual psychological states, but with states of uncertainty and anxiety which have clear social reference points. These various situations could probably be multiplied, and an overlap between them also exists (both analytically and concretely). But even so their main characteristics can be discerned. The following are the main situations in which those reference norms which deal with potentially conflicting roles are evoked.

1. Situations in which an individual, whose roles are usually performed in a given institutional setting (especially family, home, and place of work), is called upon to perform new roles in another setting (e.g., political, ritual, educational). Some typical instances of this

from our material are the following: (a) Whenever people in a settlement or an urban neighborhood are called upon to perform some civic duties (local or national), to join some sort of organization or association, or to participate in an election, drive, and so on; (b) when members of a settlement or of an urban area are called upon to participate in some collective ritual, such as a parade; (c) when such people are faced with educational problems brought by their children from the school and youth movement; (d) whenever such individuals become oriented to a wider setting through reading newspapers, listening to the radio, and trying to understand and cope with problems presented there.

2. Whenever for an individual a real or potential conflict exists between the participation in different social settings and groups. Typical examples here are: (a) When the demands made by the political authorities or parties seem to be in conflict with the claims of work (for instance, either in allocation of time, in the necessity to choose fellow workers, or in the demand to allocate work only to members of a given party); (b) when such demands run counter to family solidarity, once more either in terms of time allocation or of necessity to give preference to members of party or trade union and not to relatives, friends, or neighbors. Instances of this can be multiplied, and do, of course, exist in any society. However, they become more pronounced in situations of culture contact; (c) whenever people are faced with some new demands on their time, and more especially when such a demand is made in terms of participation in the total society (e.g., various types of national service, taxes, inauguration of new economic or agricultural policies); (d) the necessity to have some reference orientation becomes especially important when, in the above situations, there exists also a necessity to make an explicit choice between various roles and courses of action and/or to enter actively into a new group. Examples of this can be seen when parents have to choose for their children different types of schools (religious or secular), when there exist some possibilities of choosing between different occupational channels, such as during times of political elections. These cases may also frequently involve the joining of a new group. The outstanding example of this is, of course, joining the military service or a youth movement. As we shall see later, however, in such situations some additional elements come in.

In our investigations about 87.5 per cent of all the orientations to the more complex norms were related to the types of situations outlined above. About 5 per cent did not seem to be related to any special situation, and in 7.5 per cent of the cases no clear analysis could be made.

The common characteristics of all these situations is that in all of them the individual has to transfer his behavior from one institutional sphere to another, or he has to act concurrently in several institutional spheres and to relate them to one another. Analysis shows that most such situations may create some uncertainty and anxiety among participating individuals. It is proposed here that this is due to the following conditions which are inherent in the institutional structure of any society and in the basic aspect of social division of labor.

1. It seems that in most, or all, societies different institutional frameworks or spheres are regulated according to different principles and norms, and hence the transition from one sphere to another may involve both unfamiliarity and conflict.

2. This possibility is especially acute because people participate to different degrees in the various institutional spheres and hence may be more strongly involved in one than in another.

3. Such division of labor and degree of social participation exist not only in relation to different institutional spheres but also in the relationship between what may be called "local" and "central" activities. Most people in any society participate actively in some subgroups or subsystems of the society which have only an indirect relation to the central sphere of activity and the values of a society, but whose activity must necessarily be oriented to these values and to some extent guided by them (12).

In other words, it may be tentatively summed up that these situations of uncertainty exist in any society because of the fact that any individual's behavior, attitudes, and identification must necessarily extend beyond the actual roles which he performs at any given time and throughout his life. On the basis of the former analysis it may be proposed that the various "reference" orientations toward wider norms, groups, or values are evoked in situations of strain to counteract the anxieties or uncertainties referred to above. These orientations fulfill the functions of a mechanism of social control, because, if successfully transmitted, they can provide the necessary perceptual and moral knowledge through which the social field can be organized, behavior regulated, relations with other people stabilized, and a feeling of status security and collective identification established.

Before proceeding with our discussion, we have still one question to answer. Our preceding analysis was mostly concerned with those types of orientations which referred to undefined situations, situations of potential conflict. What about the first (perhaps in a way more common) types of reference orientations, those which simply reaffirm the main values implicit in any concrete situation or group? In what situations are orientations to such norms evoked? These questions are both easier and more difficult to answer than those questions regarding the former types of norms. They are easier because in a situation of rapid social change, such as the one we have been investigating, the evocation of these "simple" orientations and norms is frequent—perhaps even more frequent than the evocation of the more complicated norms. On the other hand, however, it is more difficult to discern and analyze exactly the situations in a stable setting in which these norms are evoked. Our data in this respect are rather impressionistic, and much more systematic research will be needed before full answers will be given.

The most general conclusion that can be reached on this matter is that these norms are evoked in situations where, for one reason or another, the routine of a given group, situation of work, or family behavior is disturbed. These disturbances seem to be due not to the systematic impingement of other institutional spheres on the group or situation, but mostly to some sort of internal disturbances due to individual tensions and differences, to lack of adequate motivation to perform some routine work, and so forth (13).

It may thus be suggested that these "simple" unequivocal norms are evoked when the stability of a fully structured and usually accepted situation is threatened, because those participating in it seem either apathetic in performing their roles or appear to view them in purely technical meaning, without seeing in them any full social and moral meaning. This interpretation—tentative and cursory as it is—finds support in the analysis of the data specific to the situation of social change and culture contact. In this situation it was found that the immigrants very often faced a gradual undermining of the most simple roles, in work, in family life, in neighborhood relations. These roles would lose some of the meaningfulness in relation to values and status images and would become purely technical and adaptive (14). This undermining would entail not only a conflict between relatively ordered and stable situations and norms; it would also be a disorganization of these elementary, simple situations, of their internally meaningful organization. It is in such situations that the references to the more simple, unequivocal norms were very often evoked, looked for, and asked for. Quite often these references would be intermingled with the reference to the more complex, hierarchically arranged norms. But even more often it was found that, in such a situation of change and disorganization, people could be disinterested and apathetic toward these more complex reference norms unless and until the meaningfulness and stability of the simpler situations and norms became reestablished. In these situations there was usually also a very strong emphasis on some sort of collective identity and participation, and it was the lack of meaning of various roles in relation to such identity that was quite often especially remarked.

It may thus be proposed that the reference orientation toward the simpler, and in a way more basic, norms also serves as a mechanism of social control, but not so much in situations of potential conflict between different subsystems of a society as in the event of potential disorganization of a stable subsystem itself. This is evident in the relatively small emphasis on any "hierarchial" organization of norms and roles in these references. However, several situations were found in which both types of reference orientations and norms were used, and the need for both of them was expressed by the participants. These situations were mainly of two types. First, the situations of choice, already mentioned. It was quite often found that, although during the process of choice between different alternatives or possibilities the more complex norms were used and referred to, once a choice was made and the individual had entered a given group in which he had to perform some concrete role, the more simple norms were also referred to. It was found quite often that during the initial process of "socialization" within a group (military, new place of work, etc.), the individual would refer to both types of norms. After he became more stabilized in the new place, however, the reference to the more complex norms would be diminished. Second, both types of norms would sometimes be referred to when new demands were made by the total society—demands that would necessitate the undertaking of some very routine and discipline-demanding activities, such as civic defense, or rounds of watches.

These examples seem to substantiate our previous analysis. They show that, in both these types of situation, there existed at the same time some conflict between various demands and attitudes—a conflict that had to be resolved by means of wide community participation and by the necessity to give wider meaning to various new concrete roles and performances.

From this analysis it is clear that there exists a multiplicity of reference norms and groups to which an individual may direct himself and that his choice between them is very largely determined by the kind of social situation he is in. These different reference norms are evoked when the impact of the institutional structure on the individual puts him in a somewhat problematic situation from the point of view of his status and collectivity aspirations. Thus it may be suggested that the kinds of reference orientations and norms that will be evoked in a given situation—whether these be simple, universal norms, or those related to specific clusters of roles (e.g., occupation, family), or the more complex, hierarchically arranged norms—will depend on the interplay between the particular social situation in which an individual finds himself and his perception of this situation in terms of his status image or levels of aspiration.

The Communication of Reference Orientations and Their Place in the System of Communication in a Society

The preceding analysis has shown us that different reference orientations are evoked and communicated in specific "places" or locations in the social system. Needless to say these orientations do not, as it were, float in a vacuum but are usually communicated to people, and these people expect to receive such communications.

Moreover it has been found that these communications are transmitted by persons in special social positions—usually positions of leadership—or by persons striving to attain such special positions, among whose functions is the transmission of such communications. Thus it was found that the transmission and articulation of reference standards in situations of potential conflict (and/or rapid social change) were usually found to be the functions of the special people who are broadly said to hold positions of leadership, or aspire to such positions, whether formal or informal (15).

Perhaps even more interesting is the fact that most of the new immigrants sought such people and expected the communication of norms from people in these positions. The absence of such people in certain instances was very often experienced as one of the main frustrations of the new situation. About 65 per cent of those investigated here either emphasized such a frustration or a deep satisfaction at the existence of such people. As one of the interviewees put it,

I felt awful when I could not find any important people who could explain to me all this and tell me how to behave . . . it was really terrible, but now it is much better, much easier when these officials explain this to me . . . (16)

These people, the communicators, were looked upon as interpreters of the new social reality, as people who could both explain and evaluate the various situations of potential conflict. It was the absence of such people in certain situations that gave rise to a predisposition among the immigrants to go after "quack" leaders (17). At the same time the absorbing structure and its representatives were always looking among the immigrants for people who could act as transmitters for the absorbing society, to communicate to the various immigrant groups. They were ready to give these transmitters positions of power and authority, in the hope that in this way their communications would be received and accepted by the various groups of immigrants. It was also found that a great part of both the formal and semiformal communciations directed toward the immigrants from the absorbing society, as well as communication coming from their leaders (ethnic, religious, or professional), consisted of such reference norms, prescriptions of behavior, and identification. Most propaganda communication covered the main characteristics of the reference norms given above. Only purely technical communication differed in this respect (18).

Thus our analysis shows that reference-group orientations, their maintenance and transmission, are an important part of the institutional structure of a society, in general, and of the processes of communication in a society, in particular.*

Characteristics of Communicative Situations

The preceding analysis indicates that special social situations exist in which communication of reference norms and groups takes place. What are the basic characteristics of such situations, and of the interaction taking place in them? Such situations were analyzed mostly through observation, but to some extent through interviewing. These situations included political party meetings, ritual occasions and ceremonies, various situations in which directions were given, various situations of professional and semiprofessional advice, as well as many

* Systematic researches on these problems, undertaken elsewhere, have also shown the same general conclusions (19). Most of the more recent communication research which is not confined merely to opinion surveys is already going in such a systematic and dynamic direction. Instead of just listing the reading or movie-attending habits of various groups of the population, this research has analyzed more and more the process of communication in a functional setting, in its relation to community life and to the individual's general orientation and participation in a social system. Foremost among these researches are those of Lazarsfeld and Associates on *The People's Choice* (20), Merton's analysis of the Smith broadcast (21) and of patterns of influentials in a community (22), Herzog and Warner's analysis of the audiences of "soap operas" and similar performances (23), Berelson's analysis of newspaper writings (24), and Janowitz's analysis of community press (25). In all these researches, one way or another, it was shown that receptiveness to different kinds of communication is conditioned to a very great extent by one's status image and aspirations, by one's aspirations to various types of community participation, and quite often by seeking solutions to some dilemmas and problems of status and participation. Moreover, in these researches is also implied—mainly through the concept of "opinion leaders" and influentials, on the one hand, and through the analysis of the structure of mass media on the other—that the process of communication constitutes part of the institutional structure of the society (26). But with the exceptions of Merton's analysis of types of influentials and Janowitz's analysis of the community press, there has been until now little systematic analysis in this direction. Such an analysis could be furthered and developed through the convergence of communication research and of reference-group research.

informal meetings. On the basis of this material it seems that the basic characteristics of such situations are the following:

A communicative situation is, almost by definition, an asymmetrical and hierarchical situation. This asymmetry is most clearly seen in the relative positions of the leader and the led, of the communicator and the recipient of the communication. The communicator has more knowledge and more authority than the recipient. He is accepted only insofar as he has these advantages. Hence, he is also expected to be the originator of more activities than the recipient. His rate of activity, at least in the communicative situation, is higher than that of the recipient, and the recipient is very much dependent on him for the execution of such activities.

This asymmetry is not, however, confined merely to differences in authority, knowledge, and rate of activity. It is also manifest in the type of activity, in the way of execution of activities, in the norms regulating activity. The leader acts not only in terms of one set of institutional norms but of several, and he attempts to resolve some of the inconsistencies which may exist between norms by arranging them in a definite hierarchy. Thus he may attempt to interpret the meaning of the various laws, which touch on family life or employment, in terms of political loyalties or in terms of an overall way of life. The recipients of communication act to a much greater degree within one set of institutional norms. This difference between the communicators and the recipients may be seen in two different, although interconnected, ways. First, because of the greater variety and complexity of spheres in which the communicator acts, he is, in a way, more instrumentally oriented than the recipients, whose instrumental orientations are more or less stabilized within the solidarity of some subgroup (family, neighborhood, and so on). Second, he somehow has to organize these broader and more complex instrumental activities into a new solidarity and expressive pattern, a broader and more inclusive one. Hence, in a way, he has to extend the solidarity of any given subgroup or subgroups with which he interacts beyond their own limits toward some broader collectivity, and to give the solidarity some meaning in terms of wider moral values and standards. The asymmetry of orientations and criteria of action and identification is here added to the asymmetry of power and knowledge. These different orientations and asymmetrical relations are, however, complementary, and it is in terms of this complementary character that the situation itself is perceived by both sides. The analysis of the various interviews and observations shows that there usually exists some understanding of this factor and a demand on the part of recipients for such asymmetry. The following excerpt from an interview well illustrates this point:

I do not think it is good for the "leaders" to be entirely like us. I have more confidence in them if they are different, better. They know more and understand more problems. Therefore, they have to act differently, perhaps in a more complicated way, with greater power than we . . . only so can they help us . . .

One of the leaders has stated this problem in the following way:

We must always do things differently . . . we have to take into account many things, problems; they see only one side, the simple way; we have therefore to be more strict, more exact . . . otherwise we shall not be accepted. . . .

A third basic component of a communicative situation is the existence, despite the differences in authority, asymmetry, and so forth, of some basic solidarity between communicants and recipients. There must be some sort of mutual identification, a sharing of common symbols and identities. Without this the communication is doomed to failure. This problem was among the most clearly articulated in the interviews. About 85 per cent stated that the "good thing" about some leader was that he maintained such solidarity. It was felt that, despite everything, he was "one of us or with us." It seems that it is this solidarity that serves as the common ground on which such various differences as power and orientations can be acted (27).

The importance of all these characteristics for the maintenance and stability of a communicative situation has been demonstrated in most (about 80 per cent) of the situations and interviews investigated. It is only insofar as these characteristics existed that the interaction between leaders and wider groups of people was effective or, in other words, that the reference orientations evoked by these leaders were accepted and acted upon by the various groups of immigrants. The leaders thus performed their functions as mechanisms of social control.

The above analysis of the major characteristics of the communicative situations shows us that these situations are, in a way, social systems of their own and that they constitute discrete subsystems within the social structure. They may greatly vary in the extent of their organization, formalization, continuity, and so forth, but they have distinct features and boundaries of their own, as related to other subsystems in the societies. These boundaries and specific structural characteristics (especially the basic asymmetry of orientations) are closely related to their placement in the "transitory" areas between the major institutional spheres and groups, which have a much more symmetrical organization.

All these characteristics of communicative situations are very closely related to the function of these situations as mechanisms of social control. By virtue of these asymmetrical relations, the communicators are able to guide the recipients in their concrete problem at the given situation by providing them with the:

1. Principles of perceptual and cognitive organization and orientation within the society or some of its major subdivisions.

2. Principles which aid in the recipient's cognitive and moral conceptualization of the society in which he participates, of his place within that society, and of his whole life and time perspective.

3. Access to mechanisms through which the individual's motivation for the performance of various roles incumbent on him and for the choice of various alternative roles are developed and maintained.

4. Access to mechanisms through which various kinds of rewards may be received (especially rewards of solidarity and esteem, full participation and acceptance within the society), and which organize the expectations and flow of these rewards.

An analysis of the interviews and talks in our own researches as well as of many published reports shows that the following aspects of the communicative situations and of the orientations and norms communicated in them have been very often stressed as significant.

The orientations communicated in these situations seem to assure the individual of appreciation and acceptance in terms of the total society. In other words, they assure him of the rewards of solidarity and esteem, from the point of view of the total value system of the society for its major subdivisions, e.g., class, ethnic group, to which he may belong or with which he may want to identify.

In addition to the assurance and rewards of solidarity and esteem, and of the concomitant acceptance and participation in the total society (or its major subsections), the acceptance of these communications and of their implications for behavior makes the individuals assured, directly or indirectly, of many instrumental rewards. Thus, while each subsystem of a society may seem to its members to be much more autonomous from the point of view of allocation of instrumental rewards (e.g., wages or other forms of remuneration in the economic subsystem, facilities for leisure time activity) than in the allocation of rewards of solidarity and esteem, there seems to be often absent a feeling that even these instrumental rewards cannot be assured without some relations to other subsystems and perhaps to some central allocative agencies of the society.

The so-called transcendental communications have a special place in this whole process of allocation of rewards. Transcendental communications are those which purport to give a "total" explanation of man's life and destiny, his ultimate relations to other people and collectivities. These communications purport to give full meaning to an individual's existence and environment. An important aspect of these communications is that they organize in a meaningful and symbolic way the time perspective of the individual and of the group—arrange their expectations, frustrations, and gratifications, and their quest for a deeper meaning in their activities, in terms of an overall time perspective. Such a perspective may include religious, otherworldly, mythological, or historical collective elements, but it is always one of the basic problems and aspects of an individual's self—and collectivity image—and the quest for it has been found by us to constitute one of the basic elements of communicative predisposition, whether in traditional or modern societies.

The analysis presented above elaborates the basic point of departure of this whole study—namely, that the communication of main types of reference orientations and the organization of the process of communication in the society are not fortuitous or random, determined only by purely accidental, individual differences and predispositions. It shows that the organization of the process of communication is very closely related to some basic problems of the social system, its organization and integration, and that this process is so organized as to be potentially able to fulfill, under certain conditions, some integrative functions in the social system.

Communicative Situations as Interlinking Spheres in the Social Structure

It is these facts that bring us to the last, perhaps the most basic, characteristic of communicative situations. They are what may be called "interlinking spheres" within the social structure. What is meant by an interlinking sphere?

As various institutional sectors within a society are usually regulated according to different integrative principles, the role expectations raised in one of them cannot always be fully gratified within the other. In such cases a lack of motivation for the performance of certain of these roles and frustrations over the impossibility of realizing others may result, and the stability of the social system may be endangered. In order to combat such dangers, various adjustive mechanisms or mechanisms of social control develop in every social system, and an interlinking sphere is one of them. An interlinking sphere is organized in such a way that, on the one hand, it enables the gratification of at least some of the role expectations roused in one institutional sector, while, on the other hand, it links these gratifications to the realization of aspirations which are oriented toward the other institutional sectors (28).

Thus it may be said that an interlinking sphere brings out the latent orientations toward a certain sector of the society which are latent in other sectors. The effectiveness of such an interlinking sphere depends on the extent to which it is permanently interwoven within the institutional structure of the society, so that the gratifications it provides and the aspirations it arouses have the full, normative backing of the society and ensure full gratification within it. Certain religious institutions (such as the Catholic confessions or some Jewish traditional holidays, particularly the Day of Atonement) or central collective rituals bear this characteristic. Thus, for instance, the analysis of many primitive ceremonies has shown that, in them, the economic, political, and ritual spheres of the society are closely interwoven. In these ceremonies, the importance of economic activities, of production, is very strongly emphasized. At the same time, however, the purely individualistic or familial aspect of economic activities and achievement, an aspect strongly stressed in everyday life, is subordinated to the collective values and political hierarchy of the society. Thus the attainment of economic prosperity is here conditioned on effective participation in the political sphere and identification with its values (29).

Most formalized communicative situations are either embedded within such different interlinking spheres or constitute such spheres in their own right. The various normative communications and references in these situations help to organize the interlinking sphere by rearranging the orientations and values of each of the "basic" (30) spheres (e.g., family and political life) in a unitary, hierarchical scheme of values, and relating its orientations to the value system of the total society.

This is made possible by the development of subsystems in which some of the orientations of each of the basic spheres are arranged in a certain definite order. Thus, for instance, in many informal associations which interlink the economic, political, and ritual spheres, we find a universalistic orientation toward general values, with particularistic criteria of membership and internal relations and an emphasis on rather diffuse relations within a somewhat specialized type of activity. In several types of informal meeting groups of neighbors and families which interlink the family and the general political and cultural spheres, we find a strong evaluation in terms of various achievement values, such as wealth and learning, coupled with rather ascriptive criteria of membership and relations or an orientation toward some universalistic activities (e.g., political participation), coupled with a strongly particularistic evaluation of individuals. Within most such interlinking spheres, there is a strong emphasis on solidary, and to some extent cultural, values that arrange other types of activities in some order of priority. The asymmetrical structure of relations, which is characteristic of these situations, is strongly related to their interlinking functions.

Conditions of Successful and Unsuccessful Communications

Implicit in the preceding analysis of communication situations, as systems of interaction between communicators and recipients, is the possibility that this process may be unsuccessful. The communication may fall on "deaf ears," the appropriate reference norms may not be evoked, and the attempts at social control may fail.

In our researches—as in many other—it was found out that endeavours to communicate were not always successful, and the would-be communicators were not always accepted by the groups of immigrants. Not all communications in all situations were received or accepted by the recipients. Only some communicators were really successful in transmitting the various reference norms and orientations they tried to communicate. Although most of the communicators did transmit wider norms and did attempt to prescribe proper norms of behavior and solutions for potential conflict, their proposals were not always successful. Only under special conditions did they attain success. In this way it was demonstrated that the mechanism of social control did not always function and that control could easily break down under certain conditions. In the language of current communication research, it may be found that the predisposition to receive communications did not always exist, and sometimes there developed what may be called communicative gaps.

Under what conditions did such failures of transmission of communication take place?

Several such conditions were found to be especially important in our researches. All these various conditions, briefly enumerated, give rise to a lack of reciprocal and complementary interaction between communicators and recipients, and we shall analyze them mostly from this point of view. First, there exists the possibility, already alluded to above, that the recipients themselves are apathetic toward the reception of any communication which implies any role performance and wider social identification and participation. This is usually due to the fact that their status image is completely shattered and that they live mostly at an adaptive level, without being able to maintain any wider orientations and identifications. In such cases normal interaction between them and different kinds of leaders who evoke wider implications is almost impossible. It is only through a gradual rebuilding, at a most elementary level, of their status image, of solidary participation, in various small groups, and by a general extension of these solidary orientations, that some such wider orientations can once more be part of their behavior and perception. Such a process, it was found, is usually dependent not on formal or semiformal leaders and communicators but on various persons in therapeutic relationships (social worker or instructor) and/or on some persons in closer, more intimate and frequent, relations with them. In such cases it is necessary first to rebuild the orientation to some very general reference norms before being able to influence behavior and attitudes in more complex situations (31).

A second major condition of disintegration of communicative situations takes place whenever there exists a basic rift in the social orientations of the leaders and their groups. The meaning of such a rift is usually that the asymmetry in their relations loses its complementary nature. This may occur in several instances. First, it occurs whenever the broader and more complicated orientations of the leaders do not correspond with the real situations faced by their groups. A good example of this is seen in a time of economic stress and unemployment, when many real and potential conflicts arise as to the principles of allocation of labor, relief, and so forth. An official may appeal to general sentiments of patriotism or political loyalty and yet seem unaware that these do not necessarily resolve conflicts between families and the labor bureau. Another typical example is that of an official or a community leader who lays down arbitrary rules in a cultural field (e.g., education) without paying attention to the possible conflict between traditional values of some group of immigrants and purely secular education. Such instances could easily be multiplied, but these will suffice to exemplify the lack of a complementary character.

Second, such a rift may arise when the authority of a leader is not effective in the wider institutional spheres in which he has to represent the group. In such cases various advantages obtainable in these spheres are not accorded to the group; members cannot obtain facilities through the action of their leader, and they feel that they cannot extend their solidarity and participation through him.

Third, such a rift may occur when a leader does not, or cannot, maintain solidarity relations with his constituents, and either lays claims to authority or position which is not accepted by the group on grounds either of personality or performance, or because of clearly authoritarian tendencies.

The third major condition of disintegration of the communication situation usually takes place when there exists a direct conflict between leaders that cannot be isolated or mediated. Our researches have demonstrated that in every community several communicative situations and several institutional and "opinion" leaders exist. We shall not go here into a detailed analysis of the social characteristics and nature of such leaders, but only assume, at this stage of our discussion, that in each major institutional sphere (economics, politics, law, religion, etc.) there are some leaders whose function is to mediate that and other spheres; the same applies to major subgroups of a society or community. In some cases and in some societies these various functions may be, of course, performed by the same persons. Each of these leaders has to resolve different potential conflicts according to somewhat different principles and hierarchies of values, but in a stable society they ultimately represent common value orientations and a common solidarity and identification. Hence, there must be some sort of compatibility between leaders. Insofar as their orientations are totally opposed to one another—for instance, either in terms of political values or religious orientations—and their basic interests, value orientations, and collective identifications are unaccepted by each other, they cannot fully perform their communicative functions. In such cases the groups in which these leaders act cannot develop or extend a common solidarity; they are faced with conflicting interpretations of reality and behavior, and their potential conflicts are not wholly resolved.

A similar outcome may result if there does not exist some complementarity between different levels or "echelons," of communicators and leaders and especially between the more "formal" and the informal ones. We have seen earlier that even in some small groups there exist people with positions of informal influence, opinion, leadership, and so on. While a great flexibility in the relation of the group to the leaders usually exists, they may quite often block or counteract communication from higher or more formal leadership. In this way leaders may minimize the effectiveness of their explanations and prescriptions of behavior, and of the development and extension of attitudes of solidarity. Although this is not the place to examine this process in detail, it is worth mentioning that it may occur frequently in situations of culture contact.

On the basis of the preceding discussion, the following hypotheses regarding the general conditions of effectiveness of communications and regarding differential receptivity to such communications may be put forward:

1. The effectiveness of any communication, especially of a communication directed to the performance of particular roles, is dependent on: (a) its positive function in conferring and maintaining status aspirations and identifications of the receivers (i.e., its being compatible with their status images and aspirations); (b) its being originated, or mediated, by prestige-bearing elites; (c) its being compatible with the cultural orientations and social interests of the elites; (d) its being transmitted by the elites in personal "primary" relations which are interwoven in already existent relations between the elites and nonelites; (e) its being assimilated through personal interaction in primary groups and relations.

2. The effectiveness of any communication or communication system is minimized whenever there does not exist a high degree of compatibility between the various conditions mentioned under 1.

3. The security of the elites' position as transmitters of effective communication is dependent on their ability to perform, through the process of communication, the following functions for the nonelite members: (a) to help them achieve and maintain their various statuses and status images within the social structure; (b) to serve successfully as mediators on their behalf with regard to the broader problems and ultimate values of the social system; (c) to enhance their prestige aspirations through identification with prestige-bearing persons and symbols; (d) to enhance their sense of participation in and belonging to the social system and their understanding of its working.

4. Whenever the elites cannot perform these functions, the effectiveness of their communication is minimized and the nonelite members become predisposed to receive communication from other persons or groups aspiring to elite status.

5. Whenever the contact between elite and nonelite members is severed without any personal relation with new elites being estab-

lished, the nonelite members become predisposed to accept various types of communication which may give them vicarious identification with and anonymous participation in the social system.

Thus we note that two central intervening variables—the extent to which communications can be envisaged by their recipients as corresponding to their status images and aspirations and the transmission of such communication by leaders of one type or another—can be seen as influencing the receptivity to communication. They constitute, as it were, the conditions of successful learning and maintenance of receptivity of different communications.

The importance of these variables was evident in our research among those who evinced, in the situation of change in which they found themselves, a breakdown of their communicative behavior and have become what may be called "low communicants."

The most important characteristic of these low communicants was that they felt that some of their very important needs were not satisfied, that the "social field" in which they lived was, to some extent, meaningless for them, and that they could not find a meaningful place for themselves in it. This meaninglessness showed itself first in the fact that they did not find, in the new situation, adequate advice or understanding with respect to the problems in which they were interested. This was true both for some of their pressing personal and family problems, mainly brought about by the exigencies of immigration, and also for their wider cultural or social interests. They felt that these problems were of little importance either to their old leaders or to the new ones. The old leaders were usually seen as interested in holding their own positions, without regard to the problems ensuing from immigration, whereas the new ones were seen as incapable of understanding, or of interesting themselves in, the immigrants' specific problems. Somehow the immigrants also felt that neither the old types of participation (in a synagogue or in coffeehouse societies) nor the new ones were adequate from the point of view of their status images and aspirations.

This meaninglessness had important repercussions on immigrants' evaluations of the social roles they continued to perform throughout the process of immigration and the roles which they had to learn in order to survive in the new environment. They saw most of their actual roles as unrelated to any of their social and cultural values. They saw those roles which were related to some of these values as entirely disconnected from the others.

This was usually very closely related to their detachment from various elites and resulted in greatly lowered receptivity to almost all but purely technical communications. The very low degree of predisposition to receive communications can, therefore, be related to the incoherence of the immigrants' status images and aspirations, the inability to build up coherent status pictures, and consequent feelings of being lost in the social structure, of not belonging and not really participating within it. It is this shattering of both the structure of an individual's social field and the coherence of his status image that minimizes his receptivity to communication.

Some interesting differences were found between those whose relatively low predisposition to receive communications was due to a narrow but stable field of participation and those whose status images, whatever their scope, were shattered. An analysis of the data showed that those immigrants with stable fields were among those who had some contacts with leaders, who received some advice from them, and who were less ambivalent in their attitudes toward their jobs.

The immigrants with unstable fields of participation were unable to "digest" properly many of the communications which were directed toward them, and very often they became panicky and disorganized without apparent cause. Those with stable fields of participation were usually better able to deal with these problems, to react in an orderly way, and to listen to some, even if few, communications.

Thus it seems that the main difference between these two types of low communicants seems to lie in the extent to which they maintain a coherent hierarchy of different levels of communication. Low communicants with stable fields of social participation maintained several communicative contacts beyond the scope of their families. Even when these contacts were relatively weak and not fully articulated, they had an element of stability and assurance about them and gave the immigrants some feeling of participation. These people maintained a relatively stable hierarchy of communicative levels, even though active communication at some of these levels rarely took place. Among the immigrants with unstable status images, no such hierarchy existed, and there was a rupture between the various levels of communication. This rupture entailed the lack of gratification of their aspirations to some sort of community identification and made them susceptible to the influence of various pseudoleaders. This finding shows that there are very close relations between the organization of the status images of the individual and of the field of his social participation, on the one hand, and the organization of his receptivity to communication, on the other.

The finding is reinforced by the fact that those immigrants who succeeded in attaining new coherent status images also experienced a gradual growth of receptiveness and attachment to new types of communication. They became interested in various educational, cultural, and political communications which were extended to them, and to which they had not previously paid attention. They tried to establish contacts with various new leaders and officials and became more interested in the public affairs of their localities. The various roles they learned and performed became meaningful to them in terms of the new values they acquired. It was in these terms that some of them explained their new communicative interests.

Conclusion

We shall now attempt to summarize briefly the main conclusions of our analysis and to indicate some further problems which can be derived from them. We attempted to analyze the place of so-called reference-group behavior within the institutional structure of society and to some extent within the personality systems of its members. We showed that orientations to reference groups are but a part of a wider process of orientation, referral to the basic norms and values of a society—norms and values which both transcend various concrete roles and are implicit in them. It was shown that this process is an important mechanism of social control. It was shown that these mechanisms operate in certain special social situations. These are (a) situations of transition from one institutional sphere to another or of contemporaneous activity in several institutional spheres, and/or in several subsystems of a society; (b) situations in which such various subsystems have to be directly connected with the central values and activities of a society; (c) situations in which the choice between various roles, possibilities, is necessary; (d) situations in which the routine of a given role or group is endangered because of apathy of members, and so forth.

In all such situations the individual is placed in a potentially ambiguous, undefined, and conflicting situation, in which his whole status image and continuity of perception and action are endangered. The orientation to various reference norms counteracts these descriptive possibilities by (a) defining, both morally and perceptually, the situation; (b) by presenting the proper ways of behavior; (c) by relating the individual to collectivity identification, generally by reassuring him in his status and in his place in a given collectivity.

It was further shown that the maintenance of these mechanisms of social control through reference norms is performed by certain special, more or less institutionalized roles within the social structure. It constitutes a basic part of the process of communication within a society. These orientations to wider reference norms are maintained mostly through the interaction of leaders, elites, and communicators of various kinds with individuals and groups in the special "communicative" situations. It was also shown that the smooth functioning of such situations depends on the extent to which this complementary interaction assumes the maintenance of common solidarity, collective identification, and the realization of the status images and aspirations of the members of the group. This interaction may thus be unsuccessful for a variety of reasons, all of which are related to the complementarity between the status and collectivity aspirations of the people and the activities of the leaders, the communicators.

Some types of such unsuccessful interaction and communication are strongly connected with anomic situations and deviant behavior of some kind.

These conclusions indicate that the integration of a social system cannot be understood only through the relations between various groups, their mutual agreement, or compatibility of interests, but that, in addition to these, there are some wider regulative mechanisms that determine a broader range of behavior and attitudes. These mechanisms are to some extent institutionalized and become fully articulated in special situations which may cut across various groups or subgroups (32).

On the basis of these conclusions, certain further problems for research can be formulated, the investigation of which will enable us to systematize further the research on reference groups. Among these problems the following seem to be of immediate importance:

1. The problem of the "universe" of reference norms and orientations of an individual. How many, and what kinds of such orientations does an individual have or develop? How are they organized; what are their mutual relations and hierarchy? What are the determinants, both social and psychological, of this choice of reference norms? How are reference norms related to his status, his status image, and social participation? When, and in what ways, do they influence his behavior?

2. The strong connection between the maintenance of orientation to reference norms and the activities of various leaders and communicants necessarily brings within the orbit of our interest the problem of selection of leaders within a society or parts thereof, their relations to the various social groups, the internal structure and cohesion of the various groups of leaders, the internal relations between different groups of leaders, and their place within the institutional structure of society.

3. Of special interest in this context is the analysis of several special subgroups in the society, e.g., the professions, some of the institutions of social control, such as law, and the attempt to see to what extent professional activities are connected with the communication of reference norms. In this way it would be possible to analyze the exact ways in which the process of communication is a part of the institutional structure of a society.

4. To be able to analyze the problem fully, it is also important to identify the various communicative situations which exist in a society, in its various subgroups and subsystems, and the special organizations devoted to the promulgation of communication (i.e., mass media).

NOTES

1. T. Newcomb, *Social Psychology*, New York: Dryden, 1950, pp. 194 ff.; M. Sherif, *An Outline of Social Psychology*, New York: Harpers, 1948, pp. 122 ff.; E. and R. Hartley, *Fundamentals of Social Psychology*, New York: A. Knopf, 1952, pp. 456–483; M. and C. W. Sherif, *Groups in Harmony and Tension*, New York: Harpers, 1953, pp. 157–182.

2. R. Merton and A. Kitt, "Contributions to the Theory of Reference

Group Behaviour," in R. Merton and P. Lazarsfeld (editors), *Continuities in Social Research*, Glencoe, Ill.: The Free Press, 1950, pp. 40–106.

3. Some indication of a similar approach can be found in E. Hartley "Process of Opinion Formation, A Symposium," *Public Opinion Quarterly*, Vol. XIV, 1950–1951, pp. 668 ff., and in C. Hovland, *Communication and Persuasion*, New Haven: Yale University Press, 1953, pp. 165–166, footnote 1.

4. See S. N. Eisenstadt, "The Process of Absorption of New Immigrants in Israel," *Human Relations*, Vol. V, No. 3, 1952, pp. 223–246, and "Institutionalization of Immigrant Behaviour," *Human Relations*, Vol. V, No. 4, 1952, pp. 373–395.

5. S. N. Eisenstadt, "The Place of Elites and Primary Groups in the Process of Absorption of New Immigrants," *American Journal of Sociology*, Vol. LVII, No. 3, November 1951, pp. 222–231; "Processes of Communication among New Immigrants," *Public Opinion Quarterly*, Vol. XVI, No. 2, Spring 1952, pp. 42–58; "Conditions of Communicative Receptivity," *Public Opinion Quarterly*, Vol. XVII, No. 3, Fall, 1953, pp. 363–375; "Reference Group Behavior and Social Integration," *American Sociological Review*, Vol. XIX, No. 2, April 1954, pp. 175–185, reprinted in Chapter 14 of this book.

6. On the general outline of this project see S. N. Eisenstadt, "The Research Project on Leadership, Mobility and Communication," *Transactions of the Second World Congress of Sociology*, held in Liège in 1953, London: International Sociological Association, 1954, pp. 106–110.

7. See "Sociology in Israel, 1948–53," *Transactions of the Second World Congress of Sociology, op. cit.*, pp. 26–32.

8. Obviously, it was mainly in the open-ended and focused interviews that clear answers to such questions could be elicited, although some general indications were also found in the closed questionnaires.

9. An interesting comment on this view can also be found in a recent paper by E. Stern and S. Keller, "Spontaneous Group References in France," *Public Opinion Quarterly*, Vol. XVII, No. 2, Summer 1953, pp. 208–218, in which some of the usual assumptions of reference-group theory are pertinently criticized.

10. See, for instance, the material given in M. Sherif, *loc. cit.*, and in T. Newcomb, *loc. cit.*; see R. Merton, *Mass Persuasion*, New York: Harpers, 1946; see M. Janowitz, *The Community Press in an Urban Setting*, Glencoe, Ill.: The Free Press, 1952.

11. The classification found here is similar to but not identical with the

one used by R. Linton in *Study of Man,* New York: D. Appleton Century, 1936, pp. 272 ff.

12. These general theoretical considerations are very closely related to those outlined by Talcott Parsons in *The Social System,* Glencoe, Ill.: The Free Press, 1957, and by T. Parsons, E. Shils, and R. Bales in *Working Papers towards a Theory of Action,* Glencoe, Ill.: The Free Press, 1953.

13. Further research may perhaps show that there exists some systemic conditions within a small group which also give rise to conditions of some uncertainty. The work of R. Bales points in such a direction.

14. Eisenstadt, "Conditions of Communicative Receptivity," *loc. cit.*

15. Eisenstadt, "The Process of Communication," *loc. cit.,* and the "Place of Elites and Primary Groups," *loc. cit.*

16. See for more material Eisenstadt, "The Place of Elites," *loc. cit.*

17. Eisenstadt, "Conditions of Communicative Receptivity," *loc. cit.*

18. Eisenstadt, "The Process of Communication," *loc. cit.*

19. Evidence for this can be found in numerous studies of small groups, especially those of R. Bales at the Harvard Laboratory of Social Relations. The analysis presented here, especially that part which deals with the relationship between social division of labor, is, to some extent, parallel to the analysis of "phase movements" in the small groups. In additional work we hope to analyze the relationship between those movements and the structure of communication with society. Evidence on the existence of such centers of communication in everyday organization and groups can be found in E. Jacobson, *A Method for Studying the Relationship between Communication Structure and Attitudes in Complex Organization,* mimeographed, Survey Research Center, University of Michigan, 1952, and L. Reissman, "Levels of Aspiration and Social Class," *American Sociological Review,* Vol. XVIII, No. 3, June 1953, pp. 233–242.

20. P. Lazarsfeld, B. Berelson, and H. Gaudet, *The People's Choice,* New York: Columbia University Press, 1948.

21. R. Merton, *Mass Persuasion, loc. cit.*

22. R. Merton, "Patterns of Influence," in P. Lazarsfeld and F. Stanton (editors), *Communication Research, 1948–9,* New York: Harpers, 1949, pp. 180 ff.

23. L. Warner and W. Henry, "Radio Daytime Serial," *Genetic Psychology Monograph,* 1948, pp. 3–71.

24. B. Berelson, "What Missing the Newspaper 'Means,'" in Lazarsfeld and Stanton (editors), *op. cit.,* pp. 111 ff.

25. Janowitz, *loc. cit.*

26. See also, for a further statement of this problem, E. Katz and P. Lazarsfeld, *Personal Influence,* Glencoe, Ill.: The Free Press, 1955.

27. This analysis closely follows Talcott Parsons' analysis of socialization in the nuclear family, for which the author acknowledges his debt.

28. The concept of "interlinking sphere" has been developed by the author in a comparative study of age-groups and youth movements, *From Generation to Generation,* Glencoe, Ill.: The Free Press, 1956. In this study it was shown that age- and youth groups arise in universalistic societies, i.e., in societies where the major institutional orientations differ from those of the family and serve as interlinking spheres. For a summary analysis see the author's paper on "African Age-Groups," in *Africa,* April 1954, reprinted as Chapter 4 in this book.

29. See, for instance, M. Gluckman, *Rituals of Rebellion in S.E. Africa,* Manchester: Manchester University Press, 1954.

30. It should be clear that the terms "basic" and "interlinking" sphere are, to some extent, relative, although some spheres (e.g., family or economic groups) seem to be only "basic." Although we do not want to enter here into a full discussion of this problem, it may perhaps be proposed that the main characteristic which distinguishes a "basic" sphere from an "interlinking" one is the essential symmetry of the mutual orientations of its members.

31. Eisenstadt, "Conditions of Communicative Receptivity," *loc. cit.*

32. A similar indication can be found from the anthropological point of view in M. Fortes, "The Structure of Unilineal Descent Group," *American Anthropologist,* Vol. 55, 1953, pp. 17–42.

Chapter 13

Communication Systems and Social Structure: An Exploratory Comparative Study

Israel is a particularly suitable site for a comparative study of processes of communication, because there many types of immigrant communities live in close proximity and are under the influence and impact of similar conditions of absorption. Several previous studies have already shown some general, common characteristics of this process, for example, the importance of leaders of various kinds as transmitters of communication (1). In these studies it became evident that there are several differences between various groups of immigrants, but these differences have not been systematically explored. It is the purpose of this chapter to attempt such a systematic exploration.

This analysis is based on the study of four different communities, three of which are rural or semirural, one of Yemenites, one of Algerians, Tunisians, and Moroccans, and the third of Yugoslavs. In addition, an urban quarter settled mostly by Yugoslavs and Bulgarians was systematically studied. Moreover, many data not yet fully analyzed were also gathered on both rural and urban inhabitants from all these ethnic groups and are used as a general background for this study. This choice of communities was made in order that the most traditional type (Yemenites), a transitional type (North Africans), and more modern types of social structure should be represented.

Reprinted from *Public Opinion Quarterly*, Vol. 19, No. 2, Summer 1955.

Communications and Communicative Systems

A content analysis of various communications which were "flowing," as it were, within these communities showed three main types. First, there are what may be called "technical" communications, the main aim of which is to transmit to the new immigrants various technical information which would enable them to orient themselves in the new set-up. Such communications deal with such problems as explanations of the Hebrew language, of new localities, of travel on buses, and of the use of various new implements (2). The second main type of communication may be called general "cognitive" orientations, which are seemingly without direct reference to any concrete social situation. Gossiping about the great people of the world, listening to foreign broadcasts of various types, and, to some extent, general, inarticulated, diffuse interest in political events are included in this category. The third category includes what may be called "normative" communications. By this we mean communications oriented to the transmittal and upholding of various social norms and to the definition of proper behavior in various roles and social situations. This category, which will be the central theme of our discussion, may be further subdivided according to the types of norms communicated.

The first type of normative communication includes those which apply to almost any kind of roles and situations and which indicate only a very general prescription of behavior, such as "good-bad," "honest-dishonest" behavior. This type is not specifically related to any particular role or concrete situation and is applicable throughout a great variety of concrete forms of behavior.

The second group is composed of communications which indicate the type of behavior or attitudes appropriate to all members of a given collectivity, as well as a general type of identification with such a collectivity. These norms are of a rather broad application. They do not prescribe any definite single role but are already clearly oriented toward a definite social setting, even if a rather wide one. They may be said to prescribe the universal conditions of membership in a community.

The third group would include norms and values prescribing the types of behavior appropriate to certain broad categories of social roles (age, sex, etc.) or some of the major institutional frameworks and subgroups of the society (family life, economic behavior, etc.). It is obvious that many possibilities exist here, according to the different institutional spheres and subgroups within a society.

The fourth group of normative communications prescribes behavior in what may be called ambiguous, potentially undefined (at least from the point of view of a given individual or unit) situations. These norms usually define the solution to some conflict between various demands and expectations, such as demands of the family and the political organization. In this way they may also establish some sort of hierarchy of values and preferences.

The last type of normative communications prescribes the possibilities of choice between various roles in a given situation, as well as the behavior appropriate in the process of choice and in the chosen role, for instance, in the selection of different schools for children.

The first three types of norms define simple roles and situations, while the last two have to arrange various situations in some hierarchical order. We shall therefore call the communications of the first broad category "simple-normative" communications (e.g., norms which usually indicate the proper way of performing routine tasks or some basic common moral prescriptions). We shall call the second category "hierarchical-normative" communications (e.g., norms which establish some hierarchy between different value orientations) (3).

These various types of communications were found in all the groups investigated and constitute the main pattern of communication within them. But several important differences were found among the various communities. These were found in the concrete contents of the communications—e.g., obviously much more religious communication is to be found among the Yemenite than among the Yugoslav groups. In addition, several important differences in what may be called the pattern of communication, the interrelations between various types of communications, the extent to which they go together or are segregated in their transmission and reception, could be found in the different communities. The same applies to the structure of the process of communication.

We may now turn to the analysis of the types and patterns of communications within the different communities. Each group investigated shows a pattern of its own. The description of the pattern of communication in each community will be given here in general terms, without full quantitative documentation. It should, of course, be understood that there may exist within each group many more individual deviations from the pattern. These various deviations, however, were either not found or were considered of no great consequence.

Communication in a Traditional Yemenite Community

Among the Yemenites there is a great extent of differentiation and separation between the various types of normative communication. In this group normative communications of the "simple" norms are confined mostly to daily situations, whereas the "hierarchical" and communal norms are usually pronounced only on special social and ritual occasions. However, most technical communications are interwoven with simple normative orientations—for instance, most technical arrangements of work, handicraft, and house building have definite moral connotations (4). To some extent the same is true of the cognitive-gossip type, which is also usually interwoven with various "legendary" tales or folkloristic morals. Sometimes, of course, the gossip type may be found separately, flourishing in informal tales of neighbors, in the synagogues, or coffeehouses.

There is a rather strong differentiation between various hierarchical-normative communications. Thus, there are special communications which deal with the relations between economic and religious-communal problems and with problems of communal and political participation, of family life and education, and so forth. These communications are usually transmitted on separate occasions, sometimes by different people. The separation is also very strongly emphasized by the recipients. Because of this the recipients have quite often proved to be a despair to the various instructors who have been sent to guide them and who usually cannot understand the almost complete apathy of the people to communications in which this separation does not exist. In this community there is almost no specific "communal" or collectivity-oriented propaganda or communication. The allocative aspect or orientation is usually fully embedded within the other communications. "Patriotic-Zionist" propaganda usually falls on deaf ears, although the groups show a fierce loyalty to the State of Israel.

This differentiation between the various types of communication, and the reluctance to mix them, does not mean that these immigrants do not see any connection between these types or between the various norms and values expressed in them. The opposite is true. But only on very special occasions, such as the Day of Atonement, are they prepared to receive communications (in the form of special preachings or interpretations of the Scripture) in which the various types of communication are brought together. One of the Yemenites expressed the attitude this way: "He—the agricultural instructor—speaks everyday as if it were Yom Kippur (the Day of Atonement) and wants to be taken seriously."

Perhaps the most significant feature of this process of communication is the relatively great differentiation between transmitters of the various types of communication. The various hierarchical-normative communications are usually transmitted by people with definite elite and leadership positions—rabbis, Khakhams, heads of the biggest family groups—who are also the more or less acknowledged leaders of the community. They and they alone (with the exception of some very old "wise" people of a more charismatic character) are expected to make various normative demands on the people.

It is also felt that such communications should usually be expressed on what may be called "formal" occasions—in the synagogue, on the Sabbath, or at various festivals. Only when someone is guilty of gross misbehavior or has a very urgent personal problem are such communications made less formally. Even then the strong hierarchical difference in prestige and authority is always emphasized.

There is rather less differentiation between the various elites with regard to different kinds of hierarchical communications. The more important religious and moral communications are usually transmitted by the religious officers, whereas the more instrumental communications are usually transmitted by the elite of wealth. The latter also deal with "external" relations and with such problems as the relations with the central political authorities. There is no rigid specialization between these elites with regard to these communications (5).

The picture is different with regard to technical and simple normative communications. These are usually transmitted by elder members of a family or neighborhood, or elder women or people with some special knowledge in a particular sphere. They are also transmitted on many informal occasions, as the need arises, either as answers to definite problems (e.g., technical problems connected with work) or in performing various "educational" tasks with regard to relatively younger people. Some emphasis is laid as well on differences in authority and respect, but these differences are not very pronounced and are sometimes, though rarely, nonexistent. Although various "opinion-leaders" exercise their influence on many neighborhoods, their position is neither stable nor formalized. They do not usually encroach on the sphere of the elites; most such attempts are frowned upon and rejected.

General cognitive information is often coupled with both types of normative communications and communicators, although it has a more "legendary" and "moralistic" aspect with the elite and a more "gossipy" aspect in daily relations and encounters. In addition, there are certain people who hold a semimonopoly of outside news. They are the readers of modern newspapers, the owners of broadcasting sets, or simply those who, for various reasons, have some accidental outside contact (6). The elite who are transmitters of such communications are usually the younger, less experienced members—quite often those already aspiring to more modern positions, such as teaching. There are also many indications that in former times—and to a smaller extent now—women performed such functions and were composers of special "songs."

Most communications (with the partial exception of the cognitive communication) are transmitted in close connection with real situations, as answers to problems arising in these situations and as prescriptions of definite patterns of behavior and definitions of mutual duties to be performed.

Communication in a North African Settlement

The pattern of communication in the North African settlement differs to a very great extent from that of the Yemenites. The first, most marked difference is that normative communications are more dissociated from "cognitive" ones. This is true of both simple-and hierarchical-normative communications, although somewhat more so of the first. Various types of news or gossip have an importance of their own, without necessarily being connected with any moral norms and connotations, but there is a much closer connection between cognitive and various collectivity-oriented communications. Much of the newspaper and radio news and political gossip is strongly connected with various patriotic speeches and political occasions and is evaluated in terms of its importance from this point of view. As one respondent put it: "I always like to listen to the news and the radio. It is very important because only in this way can I feel that I know what happens in the State, that I am a real citizen." Neither this news nor daily gossip is, however, strongly connected with those "simple-normative" communications which make explicit demands on behavior and performance of roles.

The differentiation between simple- and hierarchical-normative communications exists in this community to a great extent, but not so much as in the Yemenite community. In many situations, especially those relating to various collective orientations and duties, the two are quite often intermingled.

In the North African community there is a very interesting distinction which is almost nonexistent in the Yemenite community, namely that between what may be called purely "local" and "society-wide" communications in the North African community. Little differentiation was made between these in the Yemenite settlement. There, society-wide collectivity-oriented communications were usually strongly interwoven with local communal affairs, and from the point of view of the individual member of the settlement there was little differentiation between the two (7).

A second interesting differentiation is that between what may be called "moral-" hierarchical communications and more "professional" ones. By moral communication we mean those types which point out the general value system of a society and its application to a given situation, or sets of situations, and therefore emphasize the excessive values and integration of the society. By professional communication we mean communications oriented toward the solution of individual conflicts or problems, through the application of various rules and values. In the professional communication the instrumental aspect is emphasized to a greater degree.

We may now turn to the social organization of communication in this community, showing some parallels to the pattern of contents of communication. In the North African settlement the elites do not have unequivocal positions of prestige and monopoly with regard to the hierarchical communications, and a greater differentiation already exists among the elites. The two phenomena are, of course, strongly interconnected.

The difference between communications bearing on local and country-wide matters is paralleled by a distinction between different types of elites. The newspaper and radio are much more prominent as transmitters of normative communications and orientations, and not only of general, semimythologically interpreted news and stories. Hence, radio ownership, the reading of newspapers, and the effective transmission of their contents are not necessarily monopolized by the elite, although many elite members, particularly teachers and some of the younger instructors, are very active in this respect. It is significant, from this point of view, that many would-be leaders, hoping to receive positions of prestige in the new conditions, seize upon the transmission of communications as one way of influencing people and winning prestige. Similarly, there is also a greater differentiation among the elites. Certain people are seen as better guides in religious, political, or economic affairs. There are also, as we have already seen, some elites with a more professional standing, such as the person versed in law and some of the instructors.

Quite often various hierarchical communications are transmitted by and received from people with high "personal" esteem but with no prescribed roles. Such fluidity seems to be especially great in the transmission of technical and simple-normative communications.

A parallel picture can be found in the structure of communicative processes and situations. Fully formalized and structured situations with a strong emphasis on asymmetrical relations with regard to authority and prestige are as frequent here as in Yemenite settlements. There already exist, however, many, less formalized situations in which hierarchical communications are transmitted. This usually happens when universalistic norms are transmitted, either in the political and cultural field through newspapers and the like or in more professional arbitrations. Even if the differences in knowledge and power are emphasized in these situations, this way of communicating is seen in a much more impersonal and specialized way.

A much smaller proportion of cognitive and even normative communications is closely connected with concrete situations and with the prescription of proper behavior in such situations. Many communications in this community give more *general* moral and social orientations and information about other groups of the society. Among the Yemenites most normative communications refer to norms, symbols, and sometimes persons, but here they also refer to various *groups* within the community (e.g., other local groups, families, economic groups) as bearers of these norms. Only here do we find *reference groups* as an important part of the system of communication of a society.

Communication in Modern Communities

The patterns of communication found in the Yugoslavian settlement and in the preliminary investigation of an urban quarter with a population of mixed European origin were very similar and very close to the patterns mentioned in different communication studies in modern communities (8).

In this group a new type of relationship between simple- and hierarchical-normative communications appeared. Here a simple-normative communication, proclaiming some universal norms or prescribing a pattern of behavior in a routine situation, tends to be communicated together with a hierarchical norm and is related to general, broad value and community orientations.

Such simple-normative communications may also be connected with some cognitive communications which provide a general orientation within the social system. They may, for instance, be related to some news read in a newspaper or heard on the radio. Within the agricultural settlement most simple-normative communications are connected with a strong emphasis on *local* community problems. Most simple-normative communications which are not connected with hierarchical or cognitive communications become simple technical adjunctions.

Most cognitive orientations—with the partial exception of daily neighborhood gossip, and so forth—are strongly connected with normative, especially collective, orientations. They are derived mostly from various mass media.

There is a great actual, although not fully formalized or prescribed, differentiation between several kinds of hierarchical-normative communications. On the one hand, the scope of purely professional communications is increased. On the other hand, various collectivity-oriented communications (both local and society-wide, the differentiation between the two being relatively small in the agricultural settlement and greater in the urban neighborhood) are very often transmitted without relation to any other communications—by various mass media and in political meetings.

The values and norms communicated here (especially in hierarchical-normative communications) are very often symbolized by various (*reference*) *groups*, and not only by individuals, mythological figures, and the like.

Generally, the differentiation between various communications is less great here than in other communities, although it exists to some extent, especially since communications dealing with different institutional spheres are usually separate. The extent of this differentiation is, however, less in the agricultural settlement than in the urban neighborhood.

In modern communities we also find a much weaker connection between transmission of communication and prescription of concrete roles and patterns of behavior. Although such connections exist in many simple-normative, and of course in professional, communications, they are lacking in most cognitive and hierarchical communications not connected with simple ones. (This is much more evident in the city than in the agricultural settlement.) Many of these communications give general orientations in the social structure, as well as some "expressive," sometimes vicarious, satisfaction (9).

There seems to be the least formalization of the process of communication in the modern community. Communication is transmitted by people in special positions of authority and leadership, but informal "opinion" leadership usually prevails. Shifts and changes are much less frequent—but more pronounced—in the agricultural settlement than in the urban neighborhood. In the settlement leadership is somewhat more formalized, especially in the economic and political fields.

The informal differentiation between the various opinion leaders generally corresponds to the main institutional spheres in which they are most prominent. This differentiation is, however, not fixed, and some overlapping often occurs. In addition a differentiation may also be found between local and "cosmopolitan" leaders, as described by Merton (10).

A large part of these communications are transmitted in various impersonal ways—by mass media or through meetings. Through these media the people come into contact with the formal country-wide leaders.

Much of the communication is transmitted through semiformal and informal groups, in which sectors of the population participate and through which large parts of informal opinion leadership are exercised.

Within these communities there is a much greater differentiation between the various groups and their communicative activity and receptivity. There are strata of the community which are receptive to none of the hierarchical or professional communications. Usually this lack of receptivity is closely connected with a small extent of participation in the various groups and associations. Here the pattern is very similar to that found in any modern communities depicted in studies of communication.

Within these communities, and especially in agricultural settlements, the immigrants have difficulty in adjusting to the pattern of communication of the absorbing country. The main difficulty, however, lies not as much in the different *pattern* of communication as in the different contents of communications (e.g., stronger emphasis on collective values, national and social service) and in the strong competition among different groups of leaders for positions of authority.

Comparative Analysis

On the basis of the analyses of the patterns of communication in the countries described above we shall attempt now to draw some conclusions—or rather to present some hypotheses—about the conditions explaining the differences in the patterns of communication in various societies. Can we find any systematic way to account for at least some, if not all, of the differences among types of communication systems and the ways such systems are related to structural characteristics of various societies in which they develop and function?

The structure and contents of processes of communication are apparently most closely connected with certain aspects of the societal division of labor, and especially with (a) the extent of internal differentiation of roles and specialization within each major institutional sphere; (b) the extent of openness or restrictedness of major institutional areas of social activity; (c) the extent to which the various areas of social activity are governed by different value orientations.

In what way do these variables influence the structure of communication? We shall present here a series of hypotheses about such relationships—based on the preceding analyses—starting with hypotheses about the relationship between the extent of differentiation and structure of communication.

1. The greater the internal differentiation of roles in a society, the smaller will be the differentiation between simple- and hierarchical-normative communications, and the more will each such type of communication be somewhat dissociated from the ultimate values of the society.

2. The greater the internal differentiation of roles, the greater usually will be the differentiation between the bearers of various types of information and their scope of activity, and greater will be the number of informal "opinion leaders" and of shifts among them.

3. The greater the differentiation of roles in a society, the smaller will be the formalization and structuralization of communicative situations, and the greater will be the development of impersonal mass media.

The extent to which participation, especially in the political and ritual spheres, is restricted to particular persons or groups (elites and stratified groups), who transmit those values to other members of the society, will influence the structure of communication in the following ways:

4. The greater the restriction of social participation, the greater also will be parallel monopolization of hierarchical communications by the elites.

5. The greater the restriction of social participation, the greater will be formalization of the communicative situation, with a very strong symbolic emphasis on the asymmetry of authority and on knowledge between communicators and the recipients of communica-

tion. In such cases transmission of communication is often closely connected with prescription and performance of definite roles in the communal and religious fields.

Finally, we propose some hypotheses about the relationship between the structure of processes of communication and the extent to which institutional spheres are regulated according to different criteria and orientations, and especially between particularistic and universalistic, and diffuse and specific orientations. Traditional communities, even when there are some differences among the value orientations of various spheres, are usually marked by a more common emphasis on particularistic orientation. In the more modern communities, universalism and specificity are the basic orientations in wider social spheres.

6. The greater the scope of such differences, the more important and crystallized become the various hierarchical communications which attempt both to resolve potential conflicts between these various spheres and to maintain the overall solidarity of the society. Consequently:

7. The greater these differences between the value orientations of the major social spheres, the greater will be also (a) the differentiation between various types of hierarchies, especially professional or semiprofessional types; (b) the development of communications which are specifically oriented toward emphasis on collective values and symbols of identification; (c) the normative, and especially collective-solidary, significance attached in these cases to wider cognitive orientation; (d) the development of mass media and impersonal communication; (e) the difference between local and country-wide leaders of opinion and communication.

The last two items (d) and (e) seem also to be connected with the first variable—the extent of internal differentiation within the social system—but they probably become even more intensified when such growing differentiation is accompanied by a growing difference between the value orientations of the major institutional spheres.

8. Similarly, the greater the differences in value orientations of different social spheres, the greater also will be the differences, within any given group or society, in the communicative behavior of its members according to their respective position in the group and to their different personalities. Whereas such differences exist in all groups, their

extent increases greatly and becomes a major characteristic of the communicative pattern of a group in the more differentiated societies.

All these hypotheses are substantiated by the material at hand. Additional and to some extent crucial evidence for them can be found in the various processes of change which have taken place in patterns of communication of the various groups of immigrants. The general impact of the absorbing society has been in the direction of greater specialization and differentiation, greater direct participation in various spheres of social life, and stronger emphasis on universalistic value orientation within these spheres. Under the impact of these conditions there is a continuous change in the pattern of communication in the direction of greater differentiation between various elites and between different types of communications and communicative situations and greater internal differentiation of communicative dispositions and activities between various strata of the community. All these changes are directly related to the changing social organization, growing complexity and differentiation, and the growth in number and complexity of situations where people look to the social structure for guidance and orientation.

The processes of change in the pattern of communication of these communities also show that structural changes alone are not sufficient to establish new, stable patterns of communication. These changes quite often give rise to various manifestations of apathy, aggressive receptiveness to rumors, development of various aggressive symbols of identification, and so on. The various structural changes give rise to new psychological problems and anxieties. Only if new personal status images and expectations develop side by side with these changes does a new stable pattern of communication arise. Otherwise a discrepancy develops between the communicative expectations and demands of the people and the communications transmitted to them. But the analysis of these processes is beyond the scope of this essay.

NOTES

1. See, for instance, Charles Y. Glock, "The Comparative Study of Communications and Opinion Formation," *Public Opinion Quarterly*, Vol.

16, No. 4, Winter 1952–1953, pp. 512–523; S. N. Eisenstadt, "Processes of Communication among Immigrants in Israel," *Public Opinion Quarterly*, Vol. XVI, No. 2, Spring 1952, pp. 42–58; "Conditions of Communicative Receptivity," *Public Opinion Quarterly*, Vol. XVII, No. 3, Fall 1953, pp. 363–375; "Studies in Reference Group Behavior," *Human Relations*, Vol. VII, No. 2, 1954, pp. 191–216.

2. See: "Processes of Communication among New Immigrants," *loc. cit.*

3. A more detailed analysis of this problem can be found in Chapter 12 of this book.

4. A good example of this can be found in the following excerpt: "When you work on your handicraft everything is important. The way you weave, the way you use your needle is important. It is the right way for this work."

5. This pattern of receptivity applies to most of the Yemenites (70–75 per cent), but not to all. There have been some who were prepared to listen to the instructors beyond purely technical matters; some show total apathy. They do not seem to significantly affect the pattern. See Eisenstadt, "Conditions of Communicative Receptivity," *loc. cit.*

6. This is similar to the pattern described by J. M. Stycos, "Pattern of Communication in a Rural Greek Village," *Public Opinion Quarterly*, Vol. 16, No. 1, 1952, pp. 59–70.

7. See, on this distinction, R. K. Merton: "Patterns of Influence," in P. Lazarsfeld and F. Stanton (editors), *Communication Research, 1948–49*, New York: Harper and Bros., 1949.

8. See for instance: R. K. Merton, *loc. cit.*, P. Lazarsfeld, B. Berelson, and H. Gaudet, *The People's Choice*, New York: Columbia University Press, 1948; M. Janowitz: *The Community Press in an Urban Setting*, Glencoe, Ill.: The Free Press, 1953.

9. See for some researches dealing with this problem, R. Arnheim: "The World of Daytime Serial," in P. Lazarsfeld and F. Stanton (editors), *Radio Research, 1942–43*, New York: Duell, Sloan and Pearce, 1944; L. Warner and W. Henry, "Radio Daytime Serial," *Genetic Psychology Monographs*, 1940.

10. R. K. Merton, *loc. cit.*

Chapter 14

Reference-Group Behavior and Social Integration: An Exploratory Study

Recently, sociologists have shown a renewed interest in the problems of reference groups. This is as it should be since reference groups are important determinants of an individual's behavior and social orientation and of the behavior of people in multiple-group contexts. Much attention has been focused on the question of why an individual will choose a particular group, and how this choice is related to his status aspiration (1). Both Shils' and Merton and Kitt's commentaries on the American Soldier contributed a great deal to our understanding of the relationship between membership and primary groups, on the one hand, and of reference groups, on the other (2).

However, most of the research on reference groups tends to deal with them as determinants of some segments of individual behavior rather than the individual's behavior as related to the functioning and integration of the society. This essay will report on some tentative explorations in this latter direction. We will try to show how an investigation of reference groups can be interpolated into a systematic analysis of the functioning of a society. Among the questions concerning

Based on *American Sociological Review*, Vol. 19, No. 2, April 1954. The research reported here has been done under a grant for sociological research from Dr. G. Wise, President of the American Friends of the Hebrew University and Chairman of the Board of Governors of the University. The author is indebted to Dr. S. Klausner for help in the drafting and revision of this essay and for many suggestive comments and criticism.

reference groups, we will emphasize three which seem important.

First, there is the problem of the relation of the reference groups, chosen by an individual, to the institutional structure of the society. Are reference groups chosen fortuitously from a welter of existing groups, or does there exist a tendency to choose them in terms of some of the values of the society and according to some of the institutional premises and arrangements of that society? Most of the researches on reference groups have clearly indicated that it is through this "referring" that an individual orients himself beyond his immediate roles toward some wider roles and parts of the society. We are still not clear, however, about the relationship between such orientations and the values and organizations of the social system in which the individual participates, and its influence upon his identification with society.

Second, in order to study the influence of reference groups on an individual's participation within his society, we should investigate the relationship between the various reference groups and the actual membership-group roles which an individual performs. It can be postulated that orientation toward reference groups reflects the aspirations of an individual in regard to his various social roles. The realizability of levels of aspiration influences the individual's satisfaction with his social role and position and, consequently, his identification with the society in which he lives. Thus, it seems that it would be theoretically important for us to evaluate the individual's membership groups in terms of his reference groups and standards. It is not enough to indicate—as has often been done—the relative influence of reference or membership groups on a given segment of an individual's behavior or attitudes. We need to know the extent to which an individual finds his reference standards realizable within his actual roles. It is proposed here that the extent of this realizability is an important determinant of his identification with the social system, its values, and his conformity with its norms. Then we could investigate the way in which evaluation of membership groups in terms of reference groups influences an individual's identification with the society in which he participates and his conformity with its norms. The hypothesis that such a relation may exist at all is based on the assumption that (a) the various reference groups chosen by an individual are closely related to the institutional setting of the society in which he participates and   (b) the choice of reference groups by an individual is not fortuitous but is definitely related to some of the most important aspects of his personality.

It is here that we touch on the third basic problem of reference groups, namely the investigation of the determinants of an individual's reference groups in terms of his personality needs and the relation of these needs to the individual's place within the society.

The Research

The analysis presented here is based on several research projects of the Research Seminar in Sociology at the Hebrew University. The importance of the relationship between membership groups, reference groups, and identification with the social system was first discerned in a *general* way in the first stages of the research project on the Absorption of Immigrants in Israel (3). Some of the insights and the systematic conclusions attained at that stage led us to attempt a special small-scale investigation to elucidate the problems in this field. This investigation served as a starting point for much wider research.

At the same time it was found that some aspects of other research projects, mainly those on youth movements, deal with these problems. The following analysis is specifically based on our small-scale, special investigation, which we will immediately describe, and on more general conclusions from other investigations.

The special research focused on problems of communication, leadership, and mobility (4). The sample consisted of 187 new immigrants, who were participating in special courses for community leaders and professional people. We used an open-ended, focused interview, which concentrated on the following points: (a) satisfaction with present situation (economic, social, etc.); (b) aspirations to change and action to achieve these changes; (c) relations within the immigrants' main social groups (family, neighborhood, work, etc.); (d) extent of social participation and relations with old inhabitants; (e) identification with the country; (f) attitudes toward the main social norms, values, and groups.

These interviews served as a basis for a much wider investigation of the total population of participants in various training courses in

Israel and of the population of certain selected local areas and ethnic groups.

The Choice of Reference Groups

What did the choice of different reference groups mean to the individual? The people investigated not only identified their reference groups, but they were also asked why they attached importance to them and why they chose these particular groups. There was no uniformity in the choice of particular concrete groups, although quite often several individuals would choose the same concrete groups. There was, however, a marked parallel between the explanations for the particular choices. A content analysis of the answers revealed that the most important single reason for choice, reflected by about 90 per cent of the respondents, was the importance of their groups in terms of status conferral within the social structure (5). Whatever the choice, it was usually made because it was thought that this particular group could confer some prestige in terms of the institutional structure of the society. The following two excerpts from an interview well illustrate this point:

I want to be like the old settlers in X . . . (a cooperative settlement); they know how to live . . . and they are very much respected and honored. They have much influence; they can arrange matters, and everybody listens to them. If we were like them, we would be important people.

I try always to go to town, to see the young people there, those who are in the clubs. I do not always understand them, and sometimes they seem to me to behave badly, but they are important. They can get what they want; everybody seems to obey them. They behave as if they were important people . . . maybe they are . . . therefore we want to be like them.

Along with this rather general orientation toward status conferral in the choice of reference groups, most of the interviewed differentiated between aspects of their status aspirations. Roughly speaking, the following differentiation was found among most of them (about 85 per cent): (a) those aspects which are related to economic goals in the widest meaning—generally to the attainment of various instrumental goals (money, earnings, dwelling, job, various facilities); (b) these aspects related to social participation and solidarity (the kind of people one lives with and generally associates with, the extent of sharing values with them, etc.); (c) those aspects related to a cultural evaluation of a general pattern of life. The interview material showed that the relationship between (b) and (c) was a very close one. The extent to which this differentiation was clearly articulated varied. The following is an excerpt from a relatively nonarticulated interview:

> There are so many things I should like to have, like so many people over here. Some people are rich; they may also be nice, but not always. Sometimes, I want to be like them, but sometimes they do not seem good pals to me; they do not like to help people. But it is good to know them, to have money and power like them. But their customs are also very strange. I think that our customs, the old customs, are best, but we do not get along very much with them.

Our exploration has so far indicated, in a general way, that the choice of given groups as reference groups is very much determined by the status aspirations of an individual. Analysis of the interviews has also shown that aspirations are evaluated in terms of the institutional structure of the society in which the aspiring individual participates. Whatever the concrete variety of groups chosen, they tend to have a common denominator in terms of the way the individual evaluates them as status conferrers. The choice of reference groups does not seem, therefore, to be purely fortuitous—either from the point of view of the individual or from that of the social structure. It is the status evaluation and aspiration that seem to be the focus of this choice, from both points of view. Different individuals may, of course, have different status evaluations and hence choose different groups for reference.

Status aspiration is not, however, a unitary dimension, and we have seen that, among most of those investigated, three different dimensions of such aspiration existed. It is in terms of this differentiation that the fact that many individuals may choose several reference groups can be easily explained. These findings are in line with those of Hyman's pioneer study on the psychology of status but tend to emphasize more the institutional aspect of status aspirations and choices (6).

Broader Societal Implications of Reference-Group Behavior

On the basis of these explorations we can now proceed to our next problem, namely, to the evaluation of membership groups in terms of reference groups and its influence on identification with the society and conformity with its norms.

The following four types of evaluation were distinguished: (a) a totally positive one (i.e., the membership groups are seen as repositories, or representative bodies, of the main reference standards and norms); (b) a totally negative one (total opposition); (c) and (d) partial opposition or congruity—only some membership groups succeed or fail to meet reference standards. Types (c) and (d) may be seen as two subtypes of partial evaluation with different overall emphases. It was found that there were 55 people with complete positive evaluation, 26 with complete negative evaluation, 62 with partially positive and 44 with partially negative evaluations.

We had, then, to discover how the different types of evaluation related to the extent of identification with the society and conformity with its norms. For this purpose, some of the more significant variables of identification and conformity found in the first research on immigrants (7) were explored and more systematically elaborated.

On the basis of this elaboration, the following variables were systematically investigated in the interviews: (a) identification with the society—positive or negative; (b) conformity with the main norms of the society, especially in intergroup relations, or deviancy from such relations, particularly intergroup aggression.

Table I shows us some interesting data that make it clear that the evaluation of membership groups in terms of reference groups is not a very simple one. Thus the simple, common-sense hypothesis that those satisfied with their membership groups tend to be conformist members of the society and to be strongly identified with it, and those who are dissatisfied the opposite, has to be rejected. We see that there exists some such consistency among those who have a wholly negative evaluation, but this consistency does not hold for those with a partially negative or partially positive evaluation or for those with a wholly positive one. Those with a partially negative or negative evaluation usually have a positive identification with the society and are divided on the conformist-deviant variable, whereas those with a positive evaluation are more or less equally divided on both variables.

TABLE I. RELATION BETWEEN EVALUATION OF MEMBERSHIP GROUP, IDENTIFICATION WITH THE SOCIETY, AND CONFORMITY WITH ITS NORMS

Type of evaluation of membership group	Identification		Conformist or Deviant Tendency		
	Positive	Negative	Conformist tendency	Deviant tendency	Total
Positive	25	20	24	21	45
Negative	3	23	2	24	26
Partially positive	57	5	34	28	62
Partially negative	40	4	20	24	44
Total					177

Single and Multiple Reference Groups

The explanation of this great complexity of the data and of the general difference between those individuals with consistent and non-consistent evaluations and attitudes can be made only with the help of an intervening variable. We found and explored one which proved to be of crucial importance in this respect. This variable was the extent to which the individual's various reference groups were unitary or differentiated.

Within any complex society many groups and standards exist to which the individual may refer himself. Different individuals choose different reference groups in terms of their purposes and goals. But individuals may differ as to whether they *define* and evaluate these groups as different from one another or whether they tend to define them as constituting one, rather undifferentiated cluster, or whether they even identify them entirely with one another. Both of these types were found in our research. It became obvious that the definition of the total reference-group complex determined very much the extent of the actual choice of different groups. Those with a single-group referent tended to limit their possibility of choice, focusing on a very limited number of actual groups that could be brought within the framework of their unitary, rigid standards. Those with a multiple group referent evince a possibility of broader choice within the society.

The limitation of the choice of the first type was evident in the fact that individuals usually applied almost the same concrete standards to every type of group chosen. They looked for the identity between groups, so that actually their perception of the possibilities of choice was limited. Of special interest is the fact that they usually applied the three main criteria—the instrumental, cultural, and social—to the same cluster of groups, with almost no differentiation whatsoever.

It was found that those with totally positive evaluation were almost equally divided (24 and 21) into multiple- and single-reference groups, and that among those with totally negative evaluation, 23 (out of 26) were single reference-group centered. Among all the other types there were 102 (out of 107) who had multiple-group references.

This extent of single- or multiple-group reference was shown to be crucial in determining the individual's identification with society and his conformist or deviant tendencies. Thus, within the totally positive group there was almost a complete correlation (only 4 exceptions) between those who had a multiple-group referent and positive identification and conformist tendencies, and between those with a single-group referent and deviant tendencies (with negative identification).

It may thus be provisionally postulated that a single-group referent is very closely correlated with negative identification and deviant tendencies, whereas a multiple-group referent is closely connected with positive identification (but not necessarily with conformist tendencies).

The mere correlation does not, however, provide the reasons for the choice of a single- or multiple-group referent.

Ritual and Open Status Images

We have seen that the choice of reference group is closely related to the individual's status aspirations. Thus, it is within the individual's status image that we should look for some determinants of this choice. Which aspects of the organization of a status image are relevant? Obviously, it is not the *content* of the status aspirations (and the parallel reference groups) that is crucial here, because there existed a great variety of contents both among the single- and the multiple-referent group.

We found that a formal, organizing principle was the crucial one—a principle which we had already encountered in our first research on immigrants (8). This principle concerned the extent of openness or ritual closeness of the status image. Let us explain the way in which we have been using these terms.

The status image of an individual is that hierarchy of values according to which he judges himself and his place within the society. Although values may be of different concrete contents, they always relate to some basic orientations of the individual. We have seen that there seem to be three such basic orientations: (a) the attainment of various goals; (b) the attainment of solidary primary-group relations of mutual affection and response; (c) the attainment of certain cultural goals, patterns of values, of a way of life. These are the main axes about which every status image of an individual revolves. One of the most important problems in the organization of the status image is the extent of interdependence among these three different orientations. Although some such interdependence may be necessary for the integration of the personality, these orientations are also to some degree autonomous. The second and third orientations in particular may be interdependent of the first, that is, an individual may feel that he is acceptable socially and a "good man," even if he does not attain certain goals. On the other hand, an individual may perceive himself in such a way that his social acceptability and his goodness depend on the attainment of certain goals and facilities—such as money, dwelling, and type of job. These facilities become his symbols of status. It is this type of status image that we call ritual, whereas the former type is an "open" one (9).

It was found that most (about 90 per cent) of the individuals with a ritual status image tended to focus their aspirations on one cluster of reference groups and to evaluate these groups as a unitary, undifferentiated field. This tendency is closely and manifestly related to the individuals' lack of differentiation, as exemplified in their focusing on one undifferentiated field. It should be possible to find such people among those with positive and those with negative overall evaluation of their membership groups. However, within our sample, such individuals tended to concentrate among the negative cases. Only half of the positive ones focused on a single group. Those with the open status images, on the other hand, were found among half of the positive consistent and most of the inconsistent cases. Thus, it seems that there is a very strong correspondence between an individual's status image and his choice and organization of reference group. This could explain some of the seeming contradictions encountered above. It is the organization of the status image which mediates between consistency of evaluation, according to different reference standards, and the focusing of evaluation on single or multiple groups.

It seems now that the relationship between the determinants of single- or multiple-group referents, positive or negative identification with the society, and conformist or deviant tendencies also becomes clear.

Those persons with ritual status images could not distinguish very much between the attainment of the various types of goals and social relations. The attainment of social solidarity is, for them, conditioned by the attainment of a specific type of instrumental goal and pattern of life. Hence, they cannot differentiate to any large extent between various reference groups, finding within each one the satisfaction of a particular type of goal, but focus all their aspirations on one undifferentiated field with which they identify their overall status aspirations.

For those with a ritual status image it was found that the whole society is symbolized in this field and constitutes an almost unitary reference group. Their identification with the society is conditioned by the maintenance of this status image. This would help to explain their totally negative attitude in case of nonrealizability, as well as the strong aggressive and deviant element in case of realizability of their status aspirations. Even when these individuals are satisfied with their position, the implications of this satisfaction run counter to some of the normative aspects of a multiple-group society, and they develop strong aggressive tendencies toward some subgroups of the society.

The dichotomy between open and ritual status images and single- and multiple-group referents provides us with important organizing principles of reference-group behavior and its relation to the integration of a social system. On the basis of this analysis, it can be postulated that those with ritual status image tend to choose their reference groups and standards to maximize overall disintegrative tendencies —whether manifest or latent—whereas those with open status image tend to choose their reference group to spread out the risks between different types of disintegrative behavior and to maximize the possibilities of adjustment within the social system.

Our explorations show us, then, that merely positive or negative evaluation of membership groups in terms of reference groups, mere satisfaction or dissatisfaction with given roles, is not, in itself, sufficient to determine the individual's basic attitudes toward his society. It is only insofar as this satisfaction or dissatisfaction is related to his basic status aspiration that it becomes an important determinant. But even here it was found that different individuals tend to be more or less flexible in their status aspirations and that, insofar as they are more flexible, the possibilities of maximization of satisfaction and adjustment are greater.

However, our analysis is not yet complete. Although it has explained the very marked correlation between ritual status aspirations and negative identification with the society and deviant tendencies, it has not yet explained all the variations among those persons with open status images. Truly enough most of them evince positive identification with the society, but there does not exist such a consistency in relation to the conformity-deviance dichotomy. There are about 52 cases with deviant tendencies. These are more or less proportionally distributed among those with a partial negative or positive evaluation of the membership groups. How can these facts be explained? Some general indications are borne out by our material.

The existence of some deviant tendencies among those with open status images could mean that dissatisfaction with even one sphere may sometimes be of such importance as to undermine, if not the individual's basic identification with his society, at least his conformity with its basic norms. Can any kind of dissatisfaction be strong enough

to influence an individual in a deviant way, or is it confined to dissatisfaction in a specific sphere? Our material suggests that negative evaluation of membership groups in the *solidary* sphere seems to be of
special importance to an individual. Thus, among the deviant open
individuals there were 40 who insisted on a negative evaluation of
their solidary sphere, whereas among the conformist open ones there
were only 12 out of 54. In the interviews the importance of the solidary sphere has also been often emphasized by the individuals in several ways. The exact importance of this sphere in relation to others is
not, however, yet fully clear, and all that has been said above is
merely an indication for further researches. It seems that it would be
worthwhile to differentiate in a more systematic way between various
types of conformity and deviancy and their relation to the various
spheres of social activities.

Some Indications from Research on Youth Movements (10)

Let us turn to the research on youth movements. What light can
the aforementioned results throw upon the variables investigated
here?

Two of the problems investigated dealt with the motives for joining the movements and the types of identification with the social system which the different movements engendered (11). Broadly speaking, we could have distinguished between those movements which
more or less accepted the main values of the society (though perhaps
giving relatively more emphasis to their source, as with the pioneering values) and those which had a more deviant, rebellious character.
Although such a distinction could be relatively easily made, it was
found that, to some extent, this distinction cut across the different
movements, because in most of them there were members who tended
to put one interpretation or another on the values of their movements. It was found that a rebellious attitude was usually directed toward members of out-groups and toward the general "renegade"
adult society. We attempted to correlate these attitudes and types of
identification with the movements with the main types of motivation
for joining the youth movements. The common motivation was the
feeling of some inadequacy in family and school roles. The individu-

als often felt that they could obtain as full social acceptance as equals, express satisfaction, personal independence, and the like, through the movements since these personal desires were not fully gratified in the family and school life. In a way this and the motivation for joining peer groups are similar in most modern societies. In addition, however, there is a special element in the Israeli scene. Most of the youth movements claim not only to satisfy various social needs of their members, but also, and perhaps mainly, to represent the main collective values of the community. Thus, joining them is usually connected with some sort of desire to attain full social status and participation in respect to these common values and symbols of identification of the society. Consequently many members of these movements evaluate the several roles which they perform in their various membership groups, school, family, and others, not only in terms of the satisfaction of immediate personal needs, but also in terms of their relation to the ultimate values of the society. In other words, these values and the status aspirations connected with them serve as one of the main reference standards of the adolescents.

From this point of view, it was found that only a few of the members of the youth movements saw their basic membership groups as fully representative of the standards and values of the society. They differed greatly as to whether they thought these groups were relevant to some of the main values of the society and represented them or were basically incompatible with them. Thus, one member would say that good education and moral atmosphere are found at home; the school gives proper schooling, whereas the youth movement in its form gives him "social" education. Another member would stress the total opposition of the family and school life to the values represented by the movements, which were seen as the only repositories of the central values of the society.

As could be expected a very high correlation was found between negative evaluation of the membership group and aggressive attitudes to nonmembers of the youth movements. But even more important, these negative evaluations and aggressive attitudes were very clearly correlated with focusing on certain values and reference standards as the sole manifestations of collective values and the only proper channels for status attainment (or, in the terms of our former discussion, a ritual status image). Coupled with this was a tendency not to participate in many diverse membership groups but to concentrate on one primary group (the nuclear primary group of the youth movements) as the sole or main group, whose roles carry full cultural and status evaluation for their members. All the other roles did not provide a basis for the evaluation and were of purely technical and instrumental importance. These instrumental roles were segregated from those which bore a full, solidary, expressive value. Among those members of the youth movements who evaluated the various role clusters as complementary, such a complete segregation did not exist, although there were difficulties in emphasis on the different roles and role clusters.

These conclusions tend to corroborate those of the previous section about the relations between status-image and reference-group orientation. In addition, they provide a dynamic analysis of the interaction between the type of status aspiration and images an individual develops in his behavior in respect to some of the basic institutional possibilities of participation open to him in the social system and their repercussions on his identification with the social system.

The researches on which this essay is based also shed some light on the internal structure of the membership groups which are evaluated by their members. Hitherto we have concentrated on the evaluation and have not yet analyzed how this evaluation is related to the actual structure of these membership groups, the interaction of their members, and their actual roles within these groups. We will indicate here some of the more general conclusions. A high correlation was found between the negative evaluation of membership groups in terms of ritual status aspirations and a nonsolidary structure of the membership group (a very small extent of mutual primary identification between the members and with the group as such). It is as yet difficult to say whether it is this nonacceptance in the group that motivates the member to seek reference goals beyond it, or vice versa, but there clearly exists some relationship between the two factors. This conclusion corresponds very closely to that arrived at in the initial research on absorption of immigrants, in which the concept of ritual status image was developed. There it was found that there was a functional relationship between nonsolidary families and ritual status aspirations and that it was because of the lack of emotional security within the family that an individual clung to the ritual status image.

Discussion and Conclusions

What conclusions may be drawn from this material? What further possibilities and problems for research are indicated? It seems that there are at least two possible ways in which reference groups, chosen by individuals, and the institutional structure of the society are related. First, most of the choices of reference groups seem to be made in terms of status aspirations of the individual and his evaluation of the status-conferral possibilities of different groups within the institutional structure of the society. We have also seen that there may well exist several, but determinate, status dimensions of an individual—the instrumental, solidary, and cultural—in terms of which his choice of reference groups may be made.

Second, the data on youth movements seem to show that within the society there are special institutional organizations and arrangements through which reference to the basic values of the society is developed and maintained. Within complex societies there are many such frameworks. The problem here concerns the relation between these institutional possibilities open to an individual and his actual choice of reference groups, the extent to which there is some congruence between the two, and the limits of variability of choice in this respect. There is a problem which still awaits further elaboration both in comparative and intensive small-scale investigations. We have only been able to begin to work on these problems.

We have distinguished an individual's two main types of choice and organization of different reference groups. These are the single-group reference, where all the different reference groups and standards are focused on one undifferentiated cluster of groups, and the multiple-group reference, involving a greater differentiation and flexibility. We have seen that these types of choice and organization are closely related to ritual or open status images of an individual. It is through this organization that the individual refers himself to the total society in which he participates, minimizing or maximizing the possibilities of adjustment within it and evaluating his participation in his identification with that society.

This last problem has been explored by analyzing the relationship between the individual's evaluation of his membership groups in terms of his reference groups and his identification with the society and its norms. It has been shown that mere satisfaction or dissatisfaction with actual roles is not enough to determine identification and conformity. In general those individuals who, because of their ritual status image, focus their choices on one cluster of groups tend to maximize deviant possibilities (even when satisfied, but, of course, much more when dissatisfied), whereas those with open status image and multiple-group references may spread out their dissatisfaction and hence minimize its influence on deviant behavior.

This distinction between single- and multiple-group referents and the influence of these referents on the interpretation of the social system are both closely related to some suppositions developed by R. Williams and K. Lewin. In his work on intergroup tensions, Williams has submitted the proposition that a society ridden by many minor cleavages is in less danger of open, mass conflict than a society with only one or a few major cleavages (12). This supposition is closely related to Lewin's comparative analyses of American and German societies. Our analysis corroborates these suppositions, but it also shows the necessity of distinguishing more closely various types of groups between which the choice can be made. It is from this point of view that the distinction between different types of integrative behavior becomes pertinent.

Indications for Further Research

Further research might attack the cluster of problems relating to the determinants of the choice of reference groups by an individual. The importance of different types of status images for this choice has been demonstrated, but this leaves open the question of the conditions which determine the development of these various types of status images and aspirations. In this respect it might be interesting to look into (a) the structure of the various membership groups, their interrelation, and the individual's position within them and (b) the individual and group's position in the main institutional spheres of the social structure.

In addition these determinants of choice should be explored from the point of view of the personality structure of the individual. By combining these two approaches, we could study the relative importance, for the individual, of different reference groups and their influence on his participation in and identification with society.

We have discussed the ordering of the various reference groups in uniform or diverse clusters mainly from the point of view of the individual. A parallel analysis should be attempted from the point of view of the social structure. Are there within different social structures various ways of ordering the framework of reference group choice and of the social structure's main integrative mechanisms? Here once more Lewin's analysis is indicated, but many more systematic researches are needed. What is the mechanism existing within a society whose function it is to develop and maintain reference orientations among society's members? Although there has been little systematic exploration in this direction, it seems that promising results are to be expected from connecting problems of reference groups with those of communication and leadership (13). Through such an analysis, we could explore the institutional implications of reference-group behavior.

We have only stated the problem of deviance and deviant behavior in a preliminary way. There are at least two directions in which it can be explored. First, the main components and types of deviance and deviant behavior, as analyzed by Parsons in *The Social System,* should be systematically studied in their relation to various types of reference-group behavior. Second, looking into the development of deviant referent-group orientations and identification with them should prove fruitful. It seems that here, once more, an analysis in terms of communication, and similar terms, may be very profitable.

NOTES

1. For most up-to-date presentation of the data see T. Newcomb, *Social Psychology,* New York: Dryden, 1951, Chapters 6 and 7; E. and R. Hartley, *Fundamentals of Social Psychology,* New York: A. Knopf, 1952, pp. 465–477.

2. See their papers in R. Merton and P. Lazarsfeld (editors), *Continuities in Social Research,* Glencoe, Ill.: The Free Press, 1951.

3. See on this the author's papers on "The Process of Absorption of New Immigrants in Israel," and "Institutionalization of Immigrant Behavior," in *Human Relations*, Vol. V, No. 3 and 4, August and November 1953.

4. See the author's memorandum on this Research submitted to the Second International Congress of Sociology, Liège, 1953, mimeographed by the Research Seminar in Sociology, The Hebrew University, Jerusalem.

5. *Ibid.*

6. It should be emphasized that in our study there were only 16 (about 9 per cent) cases in which the choice of reference groups was not explained in terms of one of these status dimensions, and, of these, 5 were cases of inadequate answers, misunderstanding, and the like.

7. Eisenstadt, "Institutionalization of Immigrant Behavior," *loc. cit.*

8. Eisenstadt, "The Process of Absorption of New Immigrants in Israel," *loc. cit.*

9. Within the situation of immigration and adaptation, the distinction between these two types could become clear because of the scarcity of many goals and the needs of changing goal aspirations. These were empirically established by such questions as: "What is the most important thing you want to attain here?" "From what do you suffer most here?" "What were your main difficulties?" "How could they be helped?" "Who could help you?" "Would they like to help you?"; and similar open-ended questions.

10. This research has been directed jointly by the author and Dr. J. Ben-David of the Department of Sociology of The Hebrew University to whom the author is indebted for discussion and help in regard to the problems analyzed here. We shall not present here the full data from this research (the results of which will be separately published) but will only touch on some of those problems related to the main problems discussed in this paper.

11. As we shall see, the various youth movements constitute, within Israeli society, one of the main institutional frameworks through which adolescents are referred to some of the goals and ultimate values of the society.

12. R. Williams, Jr., "The Reduction of Intergroup Tensions," *Social Science Research Council, Bulletin 57*, 1947, pp. 56–57 ff.

13. See the author's paper "Elites and Primary Groups in the Process of Absorption of New Immigrants," *American Journal of Sociology*, 57, November 1951, pp. 222–231, and the report on this research submitted to the Second International Congress of Sociology, *loc. cit.*